Congress

Congress

The First Branch

SEAN M. THERIAULT
Professor, The University of Texas, Austin

MICKEY EDWARDS
Former Member, US House of Representatives

New York | Oxford
OXFORD UNIVERSITY PRESS

Oxford University Press is a department of the University of Oxford.
It furthers the University's objective of excellence in research, scholarship,
and education by publishing worldwide. Oxford is a registered trade mark of
Oxford University Press.

Published in the United States of America by Oxford University Press
198 Madison Avenue, New York, NY 10016
http://www.oup.com

For titles covered by Section 112 of the US Higher Education
Opportunity Act, please visit www.oup.com/us/he for the latest
information about pricing and alternate formats.

Library of Congress Cataloging-in-Publication Data

Names: Theriault, Sean M., 1972- author.
Title: Congress : the first branch / Sean Theriault and Mickey Edwards.
Description: First edition. | New York : Oxford University Press, [2019] |
    Includes bibliographical references.
Identifiers: LCCN 2018035232| ISBN 9780199811304 (Paperback : acid-free
    paper) | ISBN 9780190940270 (Ebook)
Subjects: LCSH: United States. Congress. | Political parties—United States.
Classification: LCC JK1021 .T315 2019 | DDC 328.73—dc23
LC record available at https://lccn.loc.gov/2018035232

9 8 7 6 5 4 3 2 1
Printed by Sheridan Books, Inc., United States of America

CONTENTS

PREFACE

Ask almost any American citizen—for that matter, almost any journalist, teacher, politician, or political activist—to name the head of government in the United States and the odds are great that a good number of them will point to whichever president happens to be occupying the White House. Even many members of Congress would probably give the same answer—and the White House's own website (www.whitehouse.gov) makes such a declaration.

The omniscient Google even suggests the primacy of the president in our system. During the last six months of 2017 and the first six months of 2018 (so as not to bias the number from the inauguration or the 2016 or 2018 elections), "Donald Trump" had more than 18 times the number of "hits" than his vice president ("Mike Pence"), 26 times the Speaker of the House ("Paul Ryan"), and 71 times the Senate majority leader ("Mitch McConnell"). And these results that are heavily skewed toward the president are closer to parity than the numbers the parallel time of Barack Obama's second term: his name had 15 times the number of results of the vice president ("Joe Biden"), 93 times the Speaker of the House ("John Boehner") and 103 times the Senate majority leader ("Harry Reid").

The framers of the US Constitution, meeting in Philadelphia in 1787, would be dismayed by this imbalance. What they established was a system of government where the three branches jointly exercised the power of the head of government. Almost every major power of the federal government—setting tax policies and tax rates, deciding how much to spend and on what, determining whether to go to war and with what restrictions, establishing the rules and regulations governing the armed forces, appointing the nation's generals and admirals, approving or rejecting international treaties, deciding who sits on the federal bench (including justices of the Supreme Court), and even deciding who may sit in the president's cabinet and who may run federal agencies—is an unchallenged responsibility of the US Congress. In a representative government it is the members of Congress—in the House and in the Senate—who are the citizens' appointed representatives to act as their agents and their voice and, even if acting contrary to a citizen's wishes, to do so in the citizens' best interests as their representative sees it. It is indirectly government by the people, but always, when it works correctly, government for the people.

You may have noticed that we described these congressional roles as a *responsibility* rather than the usual formulation as *powers*. That is because while it is the Congress, and only the Congress, that is constitutionally authorized to make such decisions, the framers' purpose was not to honor or reward members of Congress, but to place on them the great burden of making wise decisions on behalf of the ultimate sovereign of the US government, the American people themselves. If the Congress fails to act when action is called for, if it adopts practices that preclude thoughtful consideration of important national questions, if it acts in excessively partisan ways, if its members are chosen by undemocratic means, if it fails to insist on its constitutional prerogatives and defers instead to the executive branch of government, it is not surrendering *its* power, but the power of the citizens whose voice the members represent.

This realization led to our decision to write this book. It is a unique collaboration: One of us is a former long-time member of Congress who followed that career with nearly two decades of teaching about the political system. The other is a scholar and teacher whose entire career has been spent carefully analyzing how the government works, as well as why, sometimes, it does not. By bringing together these two very different but complementary perspectives, it is our goal to not only put our unique Congress-centered American system of government before students in ways that are easy to understand, but also delve deeply into the important issues of how we govern ourselves.

While much may divide us, we are united in our commitment that Congress lives up to its constitutional duty. The framers of the Constitution thought it so important that they created it *first*, in Article I; indeed, before the Constitution was adopted, Congress was the only branch of the federal government, where all power resided, making it truly the "First Branch." And yet, it is easy to imagine how today's casual observer would think that it is secondary to the president. We offer two examples where that perception could originate. First, every January, the president gives his State of the Union address. It is perceived as a message to the entire nation and, to a considerable extent, that is precisely what it is. The president's speech is delivered in the chamber of the US House of Representatives, with representatives, senators, cabinet members, Supreme Court justices, and ambassadors from most of the world's countries sitting attentively in the audience. It is easily imagined, therefore, that our system calls on the head of government to tell the Congress what it is expected to do, to give the nation's legislators their marching orders (with failure to follow through seen as an abdication of responsibility). In fact, the opposite is true: the Constitution in Article II, Section 2, Clause 1, requires the president to "give to Congress Information of the State of Union" and for more than one hundred years of the nation's history, presidents did so by simply sending a written statement of where things stood in regard to the executive's responsibility to properly execute the laws the Congress had enacted, along with the president's personal suggestions as to what other legislation he thought would be in the public interest.

Similarly, the president annually submits to the Congress a national budget. Again, it is assumed that the president, as the head of government, is detailing what the Congress is to do and how much it is to spend on each item. Again, the facts are different: presidents submit budgets because Congress has ordered the executive to do so, not because such a budget would necessarily be followed, but to give the members of Congress the information they need to make decisions about spending or tax policies. The president's budget is just the starting point for members of Congress. They retain the right to amend, reject, and even ignore his recommendations. In fact, President Obama's 2011 and 2012 budgets did not receive a single senator's vote; his 2016 budget did secure the vote of senator Tom Carper (D-DE), thus failing 1–98.

As the authors of a nonpartisan textbook, we do not take a position as to which proposed policies should be followed (in fact, we do not share a common political philosophy). We are both aware, however, that whether it is the electoral systems or governing systems that are in question, a sound understanding of the role of Congress in national policymaking is essential to all kinds of decisions that must be made by the overseers of Congress (the people themselves). It is our goal in this book to ensure that America's college students, no matter what political outcomes they desire, understand the way the government is intended to work, the ways in which it does work, and the challenges that any disconnect between the two—intention and reality—place before us.

Defending Congress during these times—or really any times—is not easy. The percentage of Americans who disapprove of the way Congress is doing its job usually dwarfs the percentage who approve—during the fall of 2018, the ratio was five disapprovers to every approver. Sadly, these numbers are not much lower compared to times past. Indeed, there are times—many times—when we, too, disapprove. But one of us has staked his public reputation and the other his academic reputation on our firm belief in the framers' genius to establish a system of checks and balances that places the Congress in the primary—as in first, not necessarily most important—position.

In this book, we offer our defense of Congress first through a historical lens that illuminates the structure of the government through the framers' eyes and then through the messy practice of politics during the intervening 230 years. To understand the origins and development of Congress requires a mix of politics and careful scholarship. It is the realization that both approaches are necessary for a true understanding of today's Congress. We hope that this dual outsider's perspective and insider's experience provide the insight to persuade you to join our cause in defending Congress, even while you also may disapprove of how it does its job from time to time or even most of the time. Regardless, we believe this book will help you see Congress—and America, as a unique democratic model—in new and deeper ways. Join us as we examine these questions and then, at the end of each chapter, engage each other in a friendly debate about what is, what is not, and what should be.

ACKNOWLEDGMENTS

We have been in a conversation about Congress for almost 10 years. In that time, control of the House of Representatives has passed from one party to another, Presidents have come and gone and so have many members of Congress. But while the names on the office doors may have changed, the public's evaluation of the institution we both love has grown even more critical. In this book, we have combined arguments and evidence to better understand the public's low regard for Congress (it is, after all, the key to citizen control of public policy) and have offered some food for thought about what the people should expect from their representatives and how to improve its performance.

Our debts in this project run deep. This book would not have been completed without the tender care of Jennifer Carpenter, our editor at Oxford. Her shepherding of the project from the original idea to what you're now holding in your hands (or reading on the screen) was done with the perfect balance of pats on the back and kicks in the butt. All the professionals at Oxford made this project both easier and better. Jennifer Lawless, then at American University and now at the University of Virginia, played a vital role in keeping the project on track.

We are thankful to the reviewers whose confidence and critical eye helped us tremendously.

Jeremy Adams
California State
University–Bakersfield

Zachary Baumann
Pennsylvania State
University

Charles Bullock III
University of Georgia

William Byrne
St. John's University

Michael Crespin
University of Georgia

Robert Dove
George Washington
University

Sally Friedman
University at Albany, SUNY

John Griffin
University of Notre Dame

John Grummel
Upper Iowa University

David Hedge
University of Florida

Karen Hoffman
Marquette University

Wesley Hussey
California State
University–Sacramento

Aubrey Jewett
University of Central
Florida

Michael Julius
Coastal Carolina University

Kristin Kanthak
University of Pittsburgh

Nathan Kelly
University of Tennessee

Benjamin Kleinerman
Michigan State University

Glen Krutz
University of Oklahoma

Jeffrey Lazarus
Georgia State University

Jonathan Lewallen
University of Tampa

Robert McGrath
George Mason University

Jonathan McKenzie
Northern Kentucky
University

Scott Meinke
Bucknell University

Hong Min Park
University of
Wisconsin–Milwaukee

Michael Peress
University of Rochester

Jonathan Peterson
North Park University

Jon Rogowski
Washington University
in St. Louis

Gary L. Rose
Sacred Heart University

Josh Ryan
University of Colorado
at Boulder

Jonathan Shuffield
US House of
Representatives

Tracy Sulkin
University of Illinois at
Urbana–Champaign

Diana Tracy Cohen
Central Connecticut
State University

Sarah Treul
University of North
Carolina at Chapel Hill

Ryan J. Vander Wielen
Temple University

Sophia Jordán Wallace
University of
Washington

In combination, we have taught more than 1000 students at Harvard, Princeton, Stanford, Texas, and Georgetown; we are grateful for their inquisitiveness, their interest, and their kindness as we tried many of the ideas in this book on them first. We are particularly indebted to three of Sean's former students who read the book from the first word to the last period. Jonathan Lewallen, Jonathan Shuffield, and Jenson Stevens provided stories to illuminate the themes of the book, corrected factual errors that would have embarrassed us, and suggested "hip" updates that saved us from publishing a book with the word "rolodex" in it. Mickey received particularly valuable feedback from his former Harvard colleague, David King.

While the conversation between us has been ongoing through many different iterations of what Congress is and what it does, the two constants in our life made this project and our very lives much better. We are grateful for Elizabeth Sherman and Anthony Bristol for their interest (sometimes), their support (usually), and their love (always).

Sean M. Theriault
Mickey Edwards

Congress

CHAPTER 1

The Complexity of Congress

How does one introduce a reader to the reality of the US Congress? Perhaps by reflecting that the clearest picture of Congress is its lack of clarity. It is nothing completely and many things in part. It is a clutter of conflicting symbols and conflicting realities. The Congress—535 lawyers, shopkeepers, scholars, engineers, mothers and fathers, Hall of Fame athletes, war heroes, and pacifists (see Table 1.1 for a list of members' occupations prior to their election to Congress)—is the grunge, the grit, and the glory of American self-government. And it is the center, the core, the heart of the American system of government.

Having observed the occasionally oppressive rule of European monarchs, the founders opted instead for a system in which power rested ultimately in the hands of the people themselves. Thus, we elect from our ranks a small number of men and women who both represent us in making decisions and judge for us those matters on which we have insufficient expertise to make decisions. Because most of us choose to be represented by men or women whose backgrounds are similar to ours or who share our beliefs, the Congress is, in many ways, America in miniature, while in other ways it is quite exceptional.

CONGRESS SEEN AND UNSEEN

As we shall see in this book, the Congress is not invariably wise, or consistently noble, or even truly representative. And while it may reflect, especially in the House of Representatives, the dominant political thought of the moment, at least based on the most recent elections, the reflection is primarily intellectual: the Congress of the United States certainly does not look like the United States; if it did, there would be fewer white men, more African Americans, Hispanics, and Asians, and far more women among its members. But neither is it the collection of thieves and scoundrels so often portrayed by reformers and the media.

Table 1.1 The Previous Occupations for Members of Congress, 114th Congress (2015–16)

JOB TITLE	NUMBER	JOB TITLE	NUMBER
Former state or territorial legislator	267	Dentists	3
Congressional staffer	102	Former ambassador	3
Education	100	Police officers	3
Veteran	81	Psychologist	3
Former member of the US House (for senators only)	53	Stockbroker	3
Prosecutor	43	Almond orchard owner	2
Former mayor	39	Sheriff	2
Real estate	36	Venture capitalist	2
Farmer or rancher	29	Vintner	2
Public relations professional	22	Artist	1
Insurance agent	19	Chemist	1
Banker	18	CIA agent	1
Physician	18	Comedian	1
Construction	16	Deputy sheriff	1
Former judge	15	Emergency dispatcher	1
Management consultant	14	Filmmaker	1
Accountant	10	Firefighter	1
Current member of the military reserves	10	Former cabinet official	1
Former governor	10	Microbiologist	1
Broadcasting	9	Optometrist	1
Reporter or journalist	9	Pharmacist	1
Engineer	8	Physicist	1
Former lieutenant governor	8	Letter carrier	1
Social worker	8	Urban planner	1
Congressional page	7	Astronaut	1
Current member of the National Guard	7	Flight attendant	1
Ordained minister	7	Electrician	1
Car dealership owner	6	Auto worker	1
Radio talk show host	6	Museum director	1
Software company executive	5	Rodeo announcer	1
Nurse	4	Carpenter	1
Peace Corp volunteer	4	Computer systems analyst	1
Union representative	4	Foreign service officer	1

Source: Jennifer E. Manning, March 31, 2015, "Membership of the 114th Congress: A Profile," CRS Report.

The saying "What you see is what you get" is only half true with Congress. What you see is what you get, but the things you see contradict each other. And there is much you do not see. Consider these varied images all equally and simultaneously true: For most visitors to Washington, a visit to the Capitol begins with a series of long lines and security protocols, often beginning at the Capitol Visitor Center. Look back across the broad green lawn and see, across First Street to the left, the broad, open entrance to the Supreme Court. Inside, nine men and women direct their clerks through a maze of legal precedents and ponder at length the relationship between the Constitution and life in the raw. At times, what the Congress itself has done or failed to do is evaluated here. Outside, the entrance to the Court is often ringed by citizens exercising their First Amendment right of free speech: with placards and bullhorns, they try to influence Court decisions. Turn to the right and you see the ornate Italianate edifice of the Library of Congress, with its marble and frescoes and statues, and inside, the world's largest single collection of books. The Library of Congress serves the public, but its principal function is to serve the Congress, to see to it that the deciders of public law have access to enough information as possible. Working your way through the Visitor Center (even before entering the Capitol itself), which exhibits your government at work and the documents that changed the course of history, can be awe-inspiring. Emancipation Hall, which recognizes the slaves who helped build the Capitol and the eventual end of slavery, is the first gathering place for the three to five million people from around the world who visit the Capitol yearly. Once inside the Capitol, in the rotunda, ringed with statues and murals, tour guides and tourists alike speak quietly. This is where President Kennedy, Senator John McCain (R-AZ), and Rosa Parks lay in state. It is also where Reagan, on a bitterly cold day, too frigid for an outdoor ceremony, was inaugurated for his second term as president. This is where, in a sealed glass case, America once displayed the borrowed Magna Carta and where, today, a bust of Martin Luther King shares space with statues of George Washington, Andrew Jackson, and the women suffragettes.

All of this is majestic, the rites and the setting, but this is only part of the picture. Self-government is not a Grecian urn to be handled gently and viewed at a distance. Through the rotunda runs a long, narrow carpet, appropriately a runner, along which run representatives, senators, staffers, testifiers, lobbyists, White House legislative liaisons, bureaucrats, and beleaguered reporters all checking their watches, mobile phones, or breast-pocket schedule cards, rushing to meetings, to vote, to persuade, or to report. The foundation of self-government is reflection; the work of self-government is bustle.

Members of Congress rarely enter the Capitol through the Visitor Center labyrinth unless they have been there to meet with constituents or speak at an event. More often they dash up sets of marble stairs leading directly to the House and Senate chambers on the second floor of the Capitol. Or they hurry to votes through underground tunnels or in short-distance underground trams. Running beneath the marble steps, from one end of the Capitol to the other, is a dark, narrow walkway off which senators and representatives can enter the more workmanlike first floor, with its small meeting rooms and administrative offices. If you enter these doors, on the House side, pass through the inevitable metal detectors, continue past the Capitol guards, and turn right at the first crossing hall, you arrive at one of the true crossroads of Congress—a place where the various worlds of Washington politics come together.

To the right is a short flight of stairs—marble, of course—which leads, ulti- mately, to the hall just outside the House chamber. Up these stairs, and down them, rush members who are heading to and from the House chamber to cast votes or take part in legislative debates: Congress as activist, advocate, decision maker. It is fitting that one of the steps remains marked by the blood of a con- gressman who was shot by another in the days when political disputes were waged with more than negative ads and name-calling. A few steps farther, at the end of the hall, are two doors, one to the left and one to the right. The one on the left leads to the House dining room. The House does not recess its work for lunch or dinner. Members continue debating and voting throughout normal meal- times. They often dine on the hot dogs, hamburgers, and egg salad sandwiches served at stainless steel lunch counters in the Republican or Democratic cloakrooms, just off the House floor, but enough eat each day in the dining room to cause long lines outside the two eating areas.

While some eat here with staff members (a good opportunity for scheduling secretaries and legislative assistants to get a few minutes of the members' time) and a few tables are usually filled with members talking to each other (the dining room as social center), most tables are occupied by members visiting with constituents. Here, the local representative—because that is how he or she is perceived—meets with mayors, city council members, realtors, homebuilders, teachers, representatives of senior citizens groups, and visiting high school students.

And then there is Congress as leader. Directly across the hall from the dining room is a small and narrow conference room, spartan by Capitol standards. In the noise and bustle of both hungry and sated diners crowded outside the dining room, the room opposite is scarcely noticed. It has been used for a variety of purposes, ranging from impromptu and informal legislative negotiating sessions to meetings with visiting dignitaries to the regular weekly meetings of small mini-caucuses of members who get together to share information in a social setting. It is, in short, an all-purpose room, one of the Capitol's many centers for the often-invisible informal side of Congress.

Jim Wright walked into that room one day carrying a small package under his arm. Jim Wright was a tall, slender Texan noted both for his thick eyebrows (cartoonists loved them) and for his remarkable speaking ability: reasonableness delivered in a voice as smooth as silk. He was then the Speaker of the US House of Representatives, second in line to succeed to the presidency and a zealous promoter of the Democratic Party's legislative program. Because he believed so strongly in his party's policies, Wright was a fierce and effective opponent of both the Republican agenda and the Republican president, Ronald Reagan. To Democrats, then the majority in the House of Representatives, Wright's was the mellifluous voice of gentle persuasion. To Republicans, Wright was the voice of a snake oil salesman. As the divisions deepened and the stakes grew higher (Reagan's determination threatened the programs that had defined the Democratic agenda since the New Deal; Wright was determined to use his Democratic majority in Congress to stop the Reagan Revolution before it got off the ground), both parties became increasingly belligerent and debate became less civil.

Wright and Bob Michel, the Republican leader in the House, decided it might be a good idea to set up a joint leadership meeting to ease partisan tensions. Wright met regularly in the Speaker's office with the Democratic leadership; Michel and the Republican leaders met on Tuesday mornings at the White House with the Republican president, Reagan, and Tuesday afternoons in Room H-227 of the Capitol, down the hall from Michel's suite of offices. They thought it might be a good idea to get everyone together in the same room. Maybe they could discover areas of common interest, where the Congress could move forward without enmity. Perhaps they could sit together, and even if they could not exactly "reason together," to use Lyndon Johnson's pet phrase, maybe they could simply decide not to face each other as enemies across an increasing divide and come to some agreement about a legislative agenda.

Remember that package Wright carried under his arm? There were fewer than a dozen members in that room—the top members of both leadership groups—and Wright had brought each of them a gift: a blue necktie on which red elephants and donkeys were dancing together (there were then no women in top leadership positions in either party). The tension eased and for a moment, Republicans and Democrats laughed together and enjoyed each other's company. For a moment, at least, members of Congress enjoyed each other's company. But the dance did not last and neither did the laughter. The joint leadership meeting never happened again. Soon the parties were at each other's throats: Democrats were working to scuttle the Reagan program, and Michel was passing out to his Republicans new leisure shirts on which he had had printed the words "Tomorrow's Committee Chairman." At the time, few of the people who received that shirt really thought the Republicans could become a majority. In the intervening years, the various party leaders have attempted the same sort of bipartisan gestures. But without exception—even despite the singing of "America the Beautiful" on the Capitol steps in the hours after the terrorist attacks on September 11, 2001—the hugs and handshakes across the aisle have quickly given way to very public partisan sniping and name-calling.

Despite the political posturing on the House or Senate floor and the finger-pointing and blame-assigning in the offices and meeting rooms, small groups of these public combatants sometimes huddled together over beer and chips, writing and rewriting, suggesting small changes here and there to hammer out, finally, a bill or amendment they could take together to the floor. For each highly publicized flare-up—California conservative Bob Dornan grabbing New York Democrat Tom Downey by the tie, Tip O'Neill, the Democratic Speaker of the House, taking the floor to denounce a speech by Georgia Republican Newt Gingrich—there were dozens of private meetings in which a liberal eastern Democrat like Ted Kennedy and a conservative western Republican like Orrin Hatch worked together in the Senate to find common ground. Since then, the number of meetings across the aisle has diminished considerably and the number of denunciations has grown.

All of these congresses are real: the majesty, splendor, and promise of the grand rotunda; the quick bites of incomplete information snatched on the run to the House or Senate floor; the pleading of constituents; the maneuverings and strategies of party leaders. Is this good? Is this bad? Is this how a congress should act? Is it how we should expect that it would act?

These questions cannot be answered without first deciding what it is that the Congress is supposed to do. If the principal responsibility of the Congress is to ensure the economic welfare of each of the country's citizens, virtuous behavior would be defined differently than if its principal responsibility were to protect each citizen's right to act freely without interference.

Gridlock, the failure to reach agreement to move a legislative program forward, is a bad thing if it is the job of Congress to move efficiently to implement the will of the majority or to achieve what the legislature determines to be in the common good. But gridlock may not be a bad thing if one emphasizes, instead, a Madisonian concern with the need to empower competing factions to prevent dominance by any one of them or to prevent the majority from trampling on the rights of a minority. As James Madison put it in Federalist 51, "It is of great importance in a republic not only to guard against the oppression of its rulers, but to guard one part of the society against the injustice of the other part." At times, one can almost imagine the Founding Fathers looking in on the system they left us, seeing the successful transmission of liberty from generation to generation, watching groups of citizens thwarting the attempts of other citizens to dictate to them, and declaring, "Gridlock! It works!"

But that may be too sanguine a view: clearly, government must still be able to function, to get things done, and sometimes to get things done quickly. In fact, as we will see later, the Congress has sometimes resorted to extraordinary measures to move important legislation with dispatch. Gridlock may be good at times, but it is certainly not good always. Perhaps the answer in each of these cases is somewhere in the middle. Perhaps virtue lies, as Aristotle thought, in the avoidance of extremes. But if we are to find that answer for ourselves, to decide what is, and is not, the essence of a good Congress, and if we are to even understand the Congress as it is, we must first put the institution itself into a greater context. We must examine the Congress in the light of America's social and political contract: the Constitution.

CONGRESS: THE FIRST BRANCH OF GOVERNMENT

Every year, by direction of the Constitution, the President of the United States gives Congress information on the state of the union. On the night of January 17, 1966, just before 9:00 p.m., the heavy double doors at the back of the House opened and a deep voiced boomed, "Mr. Speaker, the President of the United States." It was an important moment. The galleries were packed and television signals beamed the president's entrance to millions of American homes. Over and over, applause welled up from the chamber. Regardless of his standing in the polls, regardless of the success or failure of his programs, regardless of which party controls the Congress, this is the president's moment. Members of Congress—both Republicans and Democrats—reach out to touch him and shake his hand, to wave, grin, and be seen with him.

President Lyndon Johnson basked in the applause and acknowledged his many friends in the audience. He walked to the front of the chamber, stepped onto the dais, and placed his notes on the podium. He turned and shook hands with the Speaker of the House and the vice president, who in this capacity is the president of the Senate. Every motion, every smile, was beamed across the country. And then, in annual ritual, the president told the country and the world the state of the American union.

The picture that was beamed to televisions across the country was perfectly orchestrated by President Johnson because this evening marked another development in the annual state of the union address. For the first time, the president gave the address at night so that he could speak directly to the American people, all while basking in the positive affirmations that only the House chamber can provide.

The minority leader in the Senate, Everett Dirksen (R-IL), who was rather media savvy for his time, recognized the powerful message that Johnson could send with this venue. He demanded equal time so the Republicans could outline their plans for the country. A joint address delivered by Dirksen and the

minority leader in the House, Gerald Ford (R-MI), who himself had the opportunity to give a state of the union address nine years later, was taped from
the Old Senate Chamber to be broadcast several days later. In the years since,
the opposition response has become a more formalized part of the state of
union address immediately following the president's remarks. In 2017, no
fewer than five Democrats gave speeches in response. Representative Joe
Kennedy III (D-MA) gave the official Democratic response, while Virginia
delegate Elizabeth Guzman gave the official Democratic Spanish-language response. Representative Maxine Waters (D-CA) delivered her address on BET.
Senator Bernie Sanders (I-VT) live-streamed his speech on social media.
Former representative Donna Edwards (D-MD) gave a response on behalf of
the Working Families Party.

Johnson's speech, like those of Kennedy and the Roosevelts before him and
Reagan and Obama later, captured the grandeur of America's system of government: a president reporting to the people and their representatives. Dirksen and
Ford's unprecedented joint speech suggested, whether one agrees with its con-
tents or not, that Congress is equally the repository of national power and that
the leaders of the legislative branch are also the leaders of the national government. It was a disconcerting assertion for a people who have become accustomed to thinking of the executive branch as *the government*. It was a question
raised again years later in 2015 when the Speaker of the House, John Boehner,
without informing the president, invited the leader of another government
(Israel's prime minister) to address a joint session of Congress. And consider the

ramifications: if the Congress is as much the government as the presidency, and if the Constitution grants "all legislative power" to the Congress—all power to make the laws, set the priorities, create the policies—then if the Congress acts and the president vetoes, is it the president, not the Congress, who is responsible for gridlock?

Americans have become accustomed to thinking backward: if the Congress blocks a presidential initiative, it is thought to be the Congress that is obstructionist. But since it is the Congress that is supposed to make the laws, the truth is the other way around: if the Congress initiates action and the president refuses to go along with it, it is the president who is the obstructionist. On January 23, 2012, Speaker John Boehner proclaimed that the House had passed thirty employment-related bills that had been blocked by President Obama's party in the Senate acting in concert with the White House. A president may have sound reason for obstructing a legislative initiative, but it is nonetheless in the White House that the blame or credit must lie. That is still not a complete picture. In the real world, responsibilities and authorities are not usually so starkly drawn. Presidents are limited in their powers, but the Congress is, too. How one views these situations very much depends on the politics one practices and the beliefs one holds. In this book, we aim to reassert that Congress has the power—and the responsibility—to serve the institutional interests that it was afforded in the Constitution, apart from what the party leader at the other end of Pennsylvania Avenue thinks.

Despite the pomp and circumstance of the annual presidential visit to Capitol Hill, the Constitution calls for the president to submit an assessment of the national situation only to the Congress, not to the entire country, and for much of the nation's history, presidents dealt with the chore simply by sending a message to the Congress without speech or fanfare. As for the president's majestic entrance onto the House floor, it is a visit that begins with a congressional invitation. And the president's grand visions, rather than being an unveiling of the national future, are often wisps of wishful thinking, ignored by Congress or even at times repudiated. In fact, no president since Johnson has been even partially successful on more than half the requests made during the State of Union address (SEE FIGURE 1.1).

In contrast to the president, Speakers of the House or leaders in the Senate hold national office without national constituency. Their staffs are small compared to the resources available to a president, their information base is more limited, and the diverse nature of the Congress, with its 535 highly individual and independent personalities, makes the actual exercise of national leadership much more difficult than in the hierarchical structure of the executive branch, with one president and tens of thousands of subordinates.

In fact, not only does the very rarity of a national address by the speaker suggest that the Congress is less than the president's equal in terms of media coverage, but also Congress has historically treated itself as less than the administration's equal in asserting the right to exercise leadership and set a national agenda. Observers who discuss America's *presidential system* of government

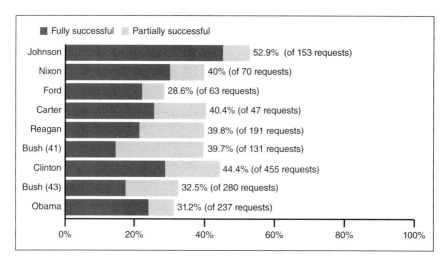

Figure 1.1 State of the Union Address: How Many Get Done?
Presidents ask Congress for many things in State of the Union addresses. Since 1965, only around 40 percent of those requests have been successful to some degree, according to one study. President Obama's record on this count is worse than average. The study's authors evaluated requests starting with Lyndon Baines Johnson's 1965 address, the first aired in prime time. The State of the Union from 1973, when Nixon presented his address as a series of written messages to Congress, is not included.
Source: NPR analysis of data from Donna R. Hoffman and Alison D. Howard.
Credit: Danielle Kurtzleben/NPR.

misstate the comparative roles of the executive and legislative branches; it is just as accurate to suggest that the United States has a *congressional system*, checked and modified by a president who is empowered with a veto and a national platform. But the mistake is not surprising: Congress often fails to assert the primacy the Constitution affords it.

Our view aside, government scholars disagree among themselves as to the relative roles of Congress and the president in national leadership. Many of the most prominent and astute students of the federal system, including Harvard's Richard Neustadt and Harvey Mansfield and the University of Virginia's James Ceaser, have made a strong case for considering the president the de facto leader of American government. James MacGregor Burns refers to the president as America's *chief legislator.* Other political scientists— perhaps most—argue just as strongly that the Congress is the *first branch* of government, not only because it is mentioned first, but also because its powers reach into every area of government, foreign and domestic; it must approve any expenditure, whether for social policy or for defense; and many

of the president's major initiatives—appointing ambassadors, signing treaties, appointing federal judges, naming top military officers—must be
approved by Congress. By contrast, little that Congress does requires presidential approval unless a president vetoes a bill, in which case if the Congress
has enough votes, it can approve the bill anyway. If there is enough support,
whatever the Congress decides can become the law of the land even without
the president's approval. Presidents are sometimes able to change policies
through executive orders, subject to being overturned by Congress if it so
chooses.

One of the clearest signs that Congress may indeed be the dominant branch
of government—and intentionally so—is the fact that while Congress's decisions
automatically become law unless a president acts positively to block them, and
sometimes even then, much of what a president intends is merely empty rhetoric
unless he can persuade the Congress to give him permission to proceed. Presidents have the ability, in a limited number of circumstances, to affect public
policy, but for the most part a president's agenda is dependent on finding congressional sponsors and winning congressional approval, which is why more
astute presidents put great effort into creating an effective program of congressional outreach. Presidents Reagan and George H. W. Bush, for example, assigned
many of their most experienced and capable staff members to work on Capitol
Hill, where they were a constant presence in members' offices or working with
members of the Republican leadership's staff. Furthermore, the Congress can
decide to remove a president from office—but the president has no role in removing a member of Congress. The same is true for federal judges—even Supreme
Court justices.

President Clinton put much of his administration's early efforts into
shaping a comprehensive overhaul of the nation's healthcare system. The Congress refused to go along, and the legislation died. Not until late in Clinton's
fourth year in office did the Congress pass a few small pieces of the original
proposal, and those were parts of the package that had long had bipartisan
support. President George W. Bush fought for a partial privatization of the
social security system in his 2005 State of the Union address. In the sixty days
afterward, administration officials visited sixty cities to put pressure on Congress to act. Bush's bill never made it out of any committee in either chamber.
President Obama pushed hard for immigration reform. When the House and
Senate could not agree on a final version of the bill, Obama gave up and did as
much as he could—much less than he wanted—through executive order.
These anecdotes give validity to the saying "The President proposes; the
Congress disposes."

Many observers—and all presidents—contend that the Congress's dominion over federal policy extends only to domestic issues. Many members of the House and Senate, particularly when a member of their own party occupies the White House, insist on presidential preeminence in foreign and defense policy. During the Reagan presidency, many Republicans demanded that the Congress stop interfering with the president's attempts to shore up the government in El Salvador and topple the government in Nicaragua. These decisions, they argued, were properly presidential. Later, when Bill Clinton, a Democrat, was elected president, Republicans in Congress asserted themselves, and the Congress they controlled, on decisions regarding US involvement in Bosnia, Somalia, and Haiti. Many of the Democrats who had so strongly opposed Reagan's policies in Central America and who had used the Congress to block his initiatives deferred to Clinton's management of foreign affairs. The same story repeated itself with presidents George W. Bush (a Republican) and Obama (a Democrat) and their foreign entanglements in the Middle East and Afghanistan. Both Democrats and Republicans acceded to presidential leadership if the president was of their own party and changed their minds if the presidency changed parties.

The extent of congressional deference to, or resistance to, presidential foreign policy initiatives is often no more than a partisan political judgment: if he is "our" president, we should leave him alone; if he is part of the opposition, we should assert Congress's constitutional prerogatives. On occasion, Congress does assert its independent authority without regard for partisan politics. During the Obama administration's negotiations with Iran over proposals to lift sanctions in exchange for a reduction in Iran's ability to develop a nuclear arsenal, the president insisted on the right to proceed without congressional review; in that instance, many members of both parties insisted that the Constitution required final approval—or disapproval—from Congress. This fight between Congress and the president on the Iranian nuclear deal continued into the Trump administration.

The Constitution makes no clear distinction between foreign and domestic policy. Article I, Section 1, contains the language that creates the Congress and gives the Congress all of the nation's legislative power. Congress, not the president, was given the power to declare war, raise armies, and maintain a navy. Furthermore, the president cannot enter treaties without the Senate's support and cannot appoint ambassadors without the Senate's confirmation, and the Constitution grants Congress the authority over international commerce.

Indeed, the Constitution not only assigned powers to the Congress, but also protected those powers. Just as Section 1 of Article I assigned to Congress all of the federal government's legislative powers, Section 8 gave to Congress the power to impose taxes, to provide for the national defense, to establish the federal courts, and to declare war. The Constitution prohibits the arrest of members of Congress who are attending a legislative session, as well as any action being taken against them for what they say on the House or Senate floor. Presidents cannot prohibit Congress from meeting; the Congress must meet every year and members of the House and Senate can decide for themselves, if they can agree, when and if they will adjourn. In fact, the Supreme Court specifically made that point when President Obama attempted to make an appointment without congressional approval. Arguing that the Congress was then in recess despite its claim otherwise, the Court declared that Congress, not the president, decides when the Congress is in recess. Even when the nation elects a president with imperial ambitions, the Constitution has been carefully crafted to keep power in the hands of the people as exercised by members of Congress.

At times, the Congress has attempted to expand its traditional powers. In some cases, the propriety of such efforts is unclear. For example, when the Congress, through the War Powers Act, reserved the right to intervene in a president's deployment and use of troops, constitutional scholars argued either that the Congress was intruding in an area of presidential prerogative or that it was correctly asserting its control over the military and its authority to determine whether the United States would go to war. It is an arguable proposition. To some, the War Powers Act is an expansion of congressional authority; to others, the decision to let the president make the first move is a surrender of the Congress's responsibilities.

But not all of Congress's efforts to assert itself are subject to such lofty constitutional theorizing. The constitutional system envisions a government in which the people's representatives set policy and the chief executive—the president—implements that policy, using the various agencies and departments under his direction. In recent years, however, critics both within the executive branch and outside government—and even some members of Congress—have assailed the legislative branch for its occasional penchant for *micromanagement*, an attempt through legislation, oversight, or the mere application of threatening pressure to dictate how congressional policy is carried out. In addition, the Congress has been criticized for its initiatives in areas that may or may not be more properly left in the hands of the federal departments. A common example is in the area of defense spending: not only does the Congress set spending limits for defense, determine the relative size and strength of the military services, and establish military priorities (by assigning more money for submarines, for example, than for aircraft carriers), but also it often seeks to determine which aircraft will be built, which pistols will be purchased, or whether a military base in Georgia or Alaska will build a gymnasium instead of a new dining hall. While the Congress may indeed be the heart of American self-government, like a human heart, it is part of an integrated system of interconnecting parts; it must relate to, provide support for, and be dependent on other parts of the nation's governmental body. The Congress limits, and is limited by, the powers of the presidency and the federal courts. Popular presidents who are able to marshal public support can often create pressures that bend the Congress to the president's will, accomplished by presidents as ideologically diverse as Franklin Roosevelt and Ronald Reagan, both of whom, without many explicit powers to dictate national policy, fundamentally shifted the country's political direction.

The Congress approves (through a majority vote of the Senate) all appointments to the Supreme Court and the other federal courts, but what the Congress may or may not do is subject to the interpretation of the Constitution by those courts. Deciding to whom within the US borders the protections of the Constitution extend, mandating the release of state prison inmates, and prohibiting government from interfering with a woman's decision to have an abortion are examples of controversial and powerful court-ordered policies that have constrained the ability of Congress either to support or to defy the majority will of the citizenry.

Federal departments and agencies issue and enforce regulations that may or may not conform to the original intention of Congress when it created the laws those departments are ostensibly seeking to implement. Overturning a federal regulation, however, is not an easy matter, even for a member who wrote the legislation and sees that its purpose is being subverted. The Congress has attempted at times to assert its right to veto administrative regulations, but the courts have held that to do so would be a violation of the separation of powers. Once the powers have been delegated to the agencies, there they remain.

Ours may properly be called a *congressional system of government*, but the Congress is nonetheless only part of a whole. In assessing the performance of the Congress or in determining how it should be improved, it is important to understand exactly what the Congress is, what it is supposed to do, and what its powers are. Is it a usurper, getting in the way of presidential leadership? Or is it the nation's decision maker? How one answers those questions will affect what one thinks of the Congress and its members. Therefore, before we move on to a study of the Congress itself, how it decides, how its members are influenced, and how it relates to the people and the president, we first consider the Congress in a broader context.

EMPOWERMENT AND CONSTRAINT:
THE LIMITS OF POWER

In considering Congress's place in American government, it is important to look to the past. Later, we consider whether the system we now have is as appropriate, and as beneficial, to the America of the early twenty-first century as it was to the America of the late eighteenth century. The world we live in today is far different from the one the Founding Fathers lived in in the 1700s. Today, America is both more urban and more diverse. The problems we face today are different, our knowledge base is greater, and we can communicate and act more rapidly. America's "king," the voter, is different, too: in the eighteenth century, most of the country's African Americans were slaves; each counted, for census purposes, as three-fifths of a person. Women played an insignificant role in commerce and public life, and while they were free to express their opinions, they could not vote. It is true that America is governed today by a system designed for another world.

But two important facts remain. First, if we are to live in an orderly society, there must be common rules of citizenship in which the constraints and proscriptions are knowable and applicable to all. Many scholars and political activists have proposed serious changes in the way we structure government. Some have suggested changing the ways in which we select members of Congress. Others have proposed revising the balance between presidential and congressional powers. We examine some of those proposals in later chapters. But until the Constitution is changed, Congress is what the Constitution says it is.

Second, the framers understood that societies could be complex and that a government could be empowered to intervene in citizens' lives in many ways, both positive and negative. While they did not rule out an activist role for government and early congresses and presidents often acted energetically, the men who wrote the Constitution placed high priority on devising a system that would protect the nation's citizens against two great tyrannies—the tyranny of the majority and the tyranny of the autocrat.

Citizens often complain that the Congress is deaf to their concerns; that it moves too slowly; that it does not act with sufficient dispatch to carry out the majority will; that the legislature seems as though it were wading through a sea of molasses. It sometimes seems to be the common wisdom that the Congress, the people's branch of government, is supposed to act in a representative role and to see to it that the will of the public shapes federal law.

That, however, is not a complete understanding of the Congress's constitutional role. While the Congress is an essential ingredient in ensuring that the government is as representative of the people as possible, the nation's founders were concerned not just with representing the majority view but also with protecting the individual liberties that lie at the heart of the Constitution. The protections were necessarily incomplete: until the adoption of the Fourteenth Amendment, in 1868, individual liberties were protected only against the intrusions of the national government, which alone was regulated by the strictures of the Constitution; the state governments were not so bound.

Nonetheless, insofar as the Constitution could reach, the founders were determined to place constraints on government. To safeguard citizens' freedoms, each of the first ten amendments to the original Constitution specifically limits what government may do. Citizens' rights are protected whether or not they agree with the majority. For the Congress, therefore, it might sometimes be necessary to refrain from imposing the will of the majority, to ensure, in other words, that the will of the majority does not take away from others the right to be different. Unfettered majorities, after all, sometimes make bad decisions. We consider this notion in a later chapter when we examine whether minorities—especially financially self-interested minorities—have been too greatly empowered. But in a nation of diverse citizenship, the protection of minority rights remains an important consideration.

To protect citizens whether or not they are in the majority, the Constitution restricts congressional action. Some of the limitations are not specifically designed to protect individual citizens (for example, the prohibition against appropriating funds to support an army for more than one year at a time), but others very clearly constrain the ability of the Congress to line up with some citizens and against others or to punish citizens who oppose congressional actions. The Congress may not, for example, enact laws declaring actions illegal that were not illegal at the time they took place (Article I, Section 9). It cannot require a candidate for public office to belong to any specific religion or to subscribe to any religious beliefs at all (Article VI).

The first ten amendments to the Constitution, known as the Bill of Rights, are explicit in limiting the federal government's power, including, importantly, the lawmaking power of Congress. Even though Congress is the people's branch of government, presumably reflective of the majority will in the nation, it may not establish a national religion—even one favored by most of the citizens—nor can it prevent a citizen from practicing whatever religion he or she may choose; it cannot stop the public from meeting, even to protest government policies; and even though the role of lobbyists has been seriously questioned (an issue we consider later), the Congress cannot stop the public from petitioning the government. The right to try to affect governmental decision making is at the heart of the concept of self-government.

It is the Constitution itself, in the Second Amendment, that prohibits the government from infringing on the people's right to keep and bear arms. Conscious of the sometimes abusive police power of seventeenth- and eighteenth-century European monarchies, the framers prohibited the government from searching citizens' homes or property, or seizing them, without a search warrant. To protect people against unfair trials, the Constitution prohibits the government from forcing an accused individual to testify against herself.

In short, the Constitution—the very framework for American government itself—severely limits the ways in which government officials, or the public, acting through them, can treat individual citizens. Although people may not agree about the definition of individual rights and how to protect them and although the public will hold a variety of views as to the necessity of governmental action for the common good, it is clear that the founders intended as a general rule to protect citizens in their right to be different, that is, to protect them against both their leaders and their fellow citizens.

Professor Harvey Mansfield addressed this concern in his book, *America's Constitutional Soul*, in which he wrote, "Whereas we (modern Americans) fear a people with too little spirit and activity, they (the founders) feared one with too much spirit and aggressiveness. Whereas we fear an apathetic or dependent majority that does not know how to claim its rights or to exercise them, they feared an overbearing majority faction." Professor Mansfield, in fact, writes that the founders created strong executive and judicial branches of government specifically "to stand up against the people" and "to oppose (their) momentary inclinations."

In considering what one might legitimately ask of the Congress, therefore, it is important to keep in mind that failure to act quickly to carry out the majority will may not, in fact, be a failure at all, but rather the fulfillment of one of Congress's most important duties. There is a second important factor in determining what Congress's role is and what it is not. While the founders enshrined certain rights into the very fabric of the nation, they also significantly tied the hands of Congress to act even when it might be unified to act. Not everything the federal government is permitted to do is within the purview of the Congress.

Some functions of government are expressly reserved to the president (Article II of the Constitution) or delegated to the president by Congress. At the end of 2014, President Obama made a dramatic announcement that his administration would move to ease the tense relationships the United States had had with Cuba for more than five decades. Several anti-Castro members of Congress criticized the decision. In the end, however, it is left to the president to establish diplomatic relations with other countries, to nominate ambassadors

to countries, and to receive ambassadors from those countries. Even if a strong majority in Congress opposed the thaw with Cuba, their hands were tied except with regard to restrictions that had been imposed by the Congress itself. These restrictions do not mean that Congress must sit idly by and watch the president orchestrate the entirety of American foreign policy. The Senate controls who is confirmed to be an ambassador. The entire Congress determines trade policy and appropriates money to run our diplomatic missions abroad. And, as President Trump showed with respect to our policy toward Cuba, the unilateral actions of one president can easily be undone by the actions of his successor.

When President Obama decided to send American troops to Libya in 2011, he had the authority, with Congress reserving only the right to act after the fact to reverse his decision. President Obama went even further. He argued, as have other presidents, that the Constitution, by establishing the president as commander in chief, gives the president the authority to act regardless of Congress's will. Many experts claim this contention ignores the Article I provision placing decisions about whether to go to war in the hands of Congress and traditional uses of the commander-in-chief rank to designate battlefield command, not the authority to decide whether to go to war. The Supreme Court has repeatedly emphasized that a president's foreign policy authority is greatly diminished if Congress opposes his actions. Later, we consider other examples of federal powers that lie outside Congress's authority, but for now it is important to realize that sometimes Congress is either forbidden to act or has simply relinquished its authority.

Even more restrictive of congressional power, and frustrating to advocates of federal action altogether, are the two final amendments of the Bill of Rights: the Ninth Amendment provides that the enumeration of individual rights in the Constitution "shall not be construed to deny or disparage others retained by the people." In other words, when emphasizing that the federal government may not violate certain specified rights, the Constitution does not grant it the authority to violate other liberties: rights naturally remain with the people, whether the Constitution mentions them or not. In addition, the Tenth Amendment provides that government powers not given to the federal government in the Constitution "are reserved to the states, respectively, or to the people." These two amendments, and especially the tenth, have formed the backbone of arguments that the Congress, even with majority support, is sometimes precluded from acting. While the states' rights argument, based on the Tenth Amendment, was once used as a basis for resisting federal civil rights legislation, it is now primarily invoked as a basis for a renewed emphasis on federalism and the return of decision-making power to the states.

As the Tenth Amendment makes clear, much of the governing power in America remains at the state and local levels. And this is the dilemma in which the Congress finds itself. In a world grown increasingly complex, there are more and more occasions for citizens to mumble, "There oughta be a law." Nothing is more disheartening to an angry citizen than to hear an elected official respond to a legitimate complaint or the recognition of a community problem with a denial of responsibility or authority. But because the Founding Fathers were determined to prevent the accumulation of power in a few hands and because the settlers of the various states often followed the federal pattern, both authority and responsibility have been divided and subdivided. Some things only the federal government can do; other things it has neither the power nor the right to do. Within the federal government, Congress can do some things; other things it can do nothing about.

For members of Congress, the constraints on action are one side of a double-edged sword. The Congress is limited in what it can do, but it also has constitutional obligations it may not shirk. While the House and Senate may choose to delegate some of the nation's legislative power to the executive branch, the Congress is not excused from carrying out its oversight responsibilities to ensure that the federal agencies are interpreting and applying the laws in ways the Congress intended. The power and the responsibility were assigned to Congress, and it ignores them only at great peril to itself.

The Constitution, Congress's founding document, is both empowerment and constraint. It sets the framework for the government to act, and it sets the limits to action. Conservatives may generally favor the constitutional constraints on government action while liberals may often prefer a greater level of federal activity, but both are part of a system in which the rules often permit less and the public often demands more.

A MATTER OF PROCESS

Later we consider the politics of Congress—how members of the House and Senate are chosen and how their decisions are affected by political considerations. We will also examine the substantive aspects of legislative action. But any overview of congressional activity must begin with this dictum: process often dictates policy. No matter how strong the ideological drive that propels legislators forward, what they achieve is often determined by the hurdles and sand traps that lie in the path of government action.

We have already referred to one of the cornerstones of the constitutional structure: the balance of powers between the states and the federal government. Some concerns are considered national in scope and on which the federal government is empowered to act on behalf of the entire country. Other concerns, because they are beyond its scope, preclude federal government action.

But the federal government itself is divided and subdivided into so many separate power structures that enacting legislation and getting it faithfully implemented is sometimes a monumental achievement. The system itself becomes a massive roadblock to legislative action. Power is divided among the executive branch (the president and the federal agencies under his direction), the judicial branch (which has assumed the power to strike down both legislation and presidential directive), and the Congress, which itself is divided into two chambers and then divided into committees and then divided even more into subcommittees. In both the House and the Senate, the major parties organize their own governing groups (Democrats call them "caucuses"; Republicans call them "conferences"), which have set up their own research and policy divisions and their own legislative task forces.

The founders meant to make it difficult for the government to raise a citizen's taxes, increase regulation of private activity, or change the laws under which citizens live. That difficulty has been compounded by the complex mechanisms adopted by a succession of Congresses. Today, if a member of Congress wishes to change part of an existing law or write new law, he or she must follow a long and often wrought path.

First, a bill must be introduced, frequently starting in the House. We later discuss the strategies to win support for the bill, including the amassing of legislative cosponsors and outside endorsers, but whether a bill is introduced in the name of one legislator or many, it is normally referred first to the committee of jurisdiction. As we see later, several committees may claim jurisdiction, and the bill may be referred to one of them, or to several, which consider the legislation either at the same time or one after the other. Or several committees may each consider a piece of the proposed legislation. A legislator often attempts to draft a bill in such a way as to increase the chance that it is assigned to a committee thought to be more likely favorable to the desired result. The committees to which the legislation is directed, in turn, assign the legislation, or their piece of it, to a subcommittee—except when they do not. Committee chairs generally have wide latitude to decide a bill's fate, and that includes the ability to simply ignore it altogether, giving it no vote, no hearing, perhaps not even assignment to a sub-committee where it might be considered. If the proposal is significant, the Republican and Democratic leaders in the House and Senate may also review the proposals through their own intraparty task forces and leadership committees, an increasingly common practice as party leaders attempt to exert control over the legislative agenda.

Even if the subcommittee and the full committee approve the legislation, there is no guarantee that it will ever be considered on the House or Senate floor. In the House, this first requires a favorable decision by the speaker or majority leader and approval by the members of the House Rules Committee, who have their own hearings on the bill, and if they want the bill to go forward, they determine what amendments may be offered by other representatives. If the bill survives all these challenges and the House passes the bill, does it become law?

No. It must then go to the Senate, where it may be introduced separately by a senator, sent to a committee, and then to a subcommittee, and the whole process repeats. If the bill is approved by both the House and the Senate, it may still be a long way from becoming a law because the House and Senate must pass identical versions of the bill. If not, the differences between the bills must be reconciled in a *conference committee* composed of negotiators from the House and Senate, after which the approved compromise must also be approved by both houses. Sometimes House or Senate leaders decide to kill the legislation altogether by refusing to appoint any members to participate in a conference committee, an increasingly common process we discuss further in a later chapter.

If the bill then passes that ordeal, it must go to the president for a signature. If the president chooses to veto it and the sponsors want to press the point, they must either attempt to schedule votes to override the presidential veto (again, the leadership may decide not to challenge the president, thus killing the bill) or send the bill back to committee in an attempt to rewrite it to satisfy the president's concerns—in which case the legislation must again be passed by both the House and the Senate and again sent to the president.

At each stage of this process, the bill's advocates must line up support (both within Congress and in the larger community), persuade the leadership to move the legislation forward, contend with possible jurisdictional disputes between committees or subcommittees, counter challenges, and attempt to ease the concerns of potential opponents, often by modifying the bill's original language (being careful not to make so many changes that the original supporters decide they no longer like the bill and refuse to support it any longer). Because this is how the legislative process works, party leaders sometimes subvert the entire process by writing, debating, and introducing a bill within the confines of party leadership. When the Republicans attempted to deliver on their promise to "repeal and replace Obamacare," they did not follow the regular order; rather, they drafted, debated, and redrafted the entire reform within their party conference. Leaders subvert the normal legislative process, though with great danger. Even with majorities in both chambers and a Republican ready and willing to sign a repeal bill, Republicans were ultimately unsuccessful because each member retained the right granted to him or her in the constitution to vote for or against the party's efforts. As of the end of 2018, too many Republicans voted against their own leaders' efforts. And the basic elements of the law, the Affordable Care Act, remained in place, ultimately even surviving a challenge that went all the way to the Supreme Court.

Edwin Feulner, former president of the Washington-based Heritage Foundation, who formerly ran the office of a congressman from Illinois, once observed that getting members to act in concert is a bit like trying to herd cats. It is an apt description, so apt that Trent Lott, a representative who held the second highest position in his party in the House and a senator who was his party's leader in the Senate, used the same phrase—*Herding Cats*—to title his autobiography.

It is not an accident that enacting legislation is so cumbersome and difficult. If America's political system is based on the need to protect individual rights, it must necessarily be difficult to impinge on those rights to take away part of a worker's earnings, to limit what a business owner may and may not do, to send young men and women into combat, or to determine what provisions should be included within healthcare statutes. The system itself has huge barriers to swift action. Citizens whose interests are threatened by government action have time to organize, to marshal support, to petition, to affect elections. Swift action precludes the opportunity to impact what government does: slow, cumbersome action sometimes frustrates the ability to solve problems as quickly as the nation might desire but provides a mechanism to safeguard the citizen against the government. For better or worse, that is our system, and from within, each member of Congress must work day after day after day to see policies change or to prevent proposed changes.

From this, one might conclude that it is a miracle that anything ever gets done. Yet, in most years the Congress has been quite productive: it appropriates money to run thousands of government programs, builds highways and dams, supplies the armed forces, supports international relief efforts, refines the tax codes, and responds to devastating floods and fires—in short, runs (or co-runs, with the president) the federal government. Enacting a law is exceedingly difficult, but in Congress, no less than in other endeavors, where there is a will, there is usually a way. Even in the heavily partisan political environment of recent years, with more members reluctant to work across party lines, legislating remains a group activity that only occasionally results in a law.

A MATTER OF PRINCIPLE

In today's world of partisan fights, Twitter feuds, and the twenty-four-hour news cycle, it is easy for the members' motivations to be reduced to strategy, partisanship, or gamesmanship. Do not lose sight of principles that may have motivated members in the first place. While it is true that sometimes Congresswoman A or Senator B may have introduced a piece of legislation as a favor to a constituent, industry, or special interest group, or because she thought it would be helpful to the economy of her home district, she may well have introduced it because she believed it was the right thing to do. Because each Congress is made up of 535 voting members, representing different constituencies and coming from different backgrounds, it is natural that no single motivation exists for all legislative action. Some members of Congress see themselves as servants, helping their constituents achieve certain ends; some are advocates for causes they believe in deeply; some serve out of a sense of *noblesse oblige*—a belief that they have been blessed and should dedicate their time and effort to repaying the system in which they have flourished. Some may seek office as a means of acquiring power and prestige and may structure their voting patterns to try to increase their own chances of reelection, a pattern that has been tracked by political scientists and that has often led to a general cynicism about the nature of political decision making. Many members of Congress are motivated by a combination of these factors, with different parts of the mix rising to the surface at different times. Thus, a legislator may alternate between being a champion of a party or philosophy and being a dutiful representative of the folks back home, often without considering the two loyalties in conflict with each other.

It is possible to determine whether the loftier motive—that is, commitment to a consistent set of principles—plays a central role in legislative voting patterns. It is possible to learn whether ideology, or certain sets of political values, rather than the search for job security, is central to the decision-making process. If so, the logical result would be less cynicism toward congressional service and the people who choose it, a higher degree of confidence in the legislative system of self-government, and a greater sense that it is possible to steer the nation in one direction or another by choosing one party, or one set of political positions, over another.

Later, we examine in greater detail the proposition that the Congress is largely guided by the philosophies and values of the men and women the voters choose to represent them. Rather than being a collection of self-serving glory seekers, Congress is an arena in which men and women act honestly to shape the kind of society they think best. They must always remember, however, that before they can act on those high philosophies they must be rehired by the people to dispatch the duties and responsibilities of running the government. No single member is a universe. Some members of Congress respond more dramatically to the challenges of reelection or the agenda of the president. But they often exemplify a much loftier ideal: the man or woman who believes in a cause and devotes years of effort to its advancement.

A MATTER OF POLITICS

In any scientific study, one is aware of the exogenous factors, that is, the outside influences that affect outcomes. To some observers, politics is an exogenous factor in the formulation of public policy. In other words, the rational evaluation of options, they believe, is distorted by the injection of irrational considerations such as public opinion polls, legislators' (and elected executives') concerns about reelection, and the influence of *special interests* and advocacy groups. Instead of merely considering possible policy choices from a neutral, best-outcome perspective, these observers complain, policy makers too often refuse to act in a value-neutral way: they clutter up their decision-making processes by injecting irrational preferences into the mix.

But American government is not a technocracy. Important considerations sometimes outweigh the cold calculations of cost and return. One of the best examples is in determining what rules should govern a citizen's interaction with the natural environment. From a market economics standpoint, a certain level of regulation and compliance costs so much that profits evaporate. It is possible to compute, with some degree of confidence, the likely diminution in profit and job creation at various levels of environmental protection. For example, a rational choice would be to discontinue protection limits on smokestack pollution when the cost of providing the benefit exceeds the economic value of the benefit. But in a system of self-government, decision makers do not live or decide in a vacuum. Values other than economic ones must also be weighed. What price does one put on clean air to breathe, seeing the sunrise in the morning, wading in a clear stream? To some, the important issue is whether those protections come at too high a cost. Some argue that protecting a field of prairie grass for the enjoyment of backpackers and picnickers may be nice, but not at the cost of discontinuing drilling or mining operations that provide the principal jobs for a community. Others argue that jobs can be replaced, but natural diversity and beauty, once destroyed, diminishes us all.

The issue is not who is right, but the fact that in a free society, different people come to different conclusions. Because this is their country too—their jobs, their grasslands—they have a right to be heard in the shaping of policy. They make themselves heard through their combined efforts—joining and sup-porting advocacy groups, hiring lobbyists (advocates who represent their points of view to government decision makers)—and through their individual efforts by writing letters to members, speaking up at a legislator's town or neighborhood meeting, or voting for or against candidates for public office.

To the technocrat, these are exogenous influences, expressions of nonrational preference that impinge on sound decision making. But to members of Congress, elected to represent the citizens whose nation this is, they are real, central, vital concerns. The desire for reelection and the fear of defeat—supposedly unworthy and self-serving motivators for public officials—are the levers by which a free people guide the decisions of their government.

The term *politics* covers many activities: the public advocacy of policy preferences, the attempt to influence the outcome of elections (that is, the attempt to influence which persons will be selected to make policy choices), the public spelling out of policy differences, the elected official's responsiveness to the citizen's preferences. But in a society of self-governing free men and women, politics is not exogenous, but central. Politics as the means of free selection between competing policies and potential leaders is the heart of decision making in a democracy. To understand the Congress of the United States, one must first understand that within its walls, politics is not scorned but embraced.

There are various ways to interpret the reaction of elected officials to public input. A member of Congress who tries to vote the way his or her constituents want him or her to vote may be considered *responsive* (a good thing) or be dismissed as *just a politician* (presumably, a bad thing), be praised as a good representative, someone who *listens to us* and *feels our pain*, or be criticized as one who panders and is always checking to see which way the wind is blowing.

But politics is at the heart of the matter, and to marginalize the importance, or the centrality, of politics to the decision-making process—the proper decision-making process in a representative democracy—is to fail completely to understand not only how Congress operates, but also what it is and what it is intended to be. Politics is a central part of the operational nexus of American government. Politics, political philosophy, issue advocacy, and policy are connected inseparably in a system in which policy decision making is not value neutral but value driven.

A MATTER OF PARTY

Politics is increasingly organized by the political parties. This maxim is true both inside the Capitol and *outside the beltway*, the phrase that politicians use to describe the part of the United States outside Washington, DC. Whereas all new members once went through new-member orientation together—without regard for their political party—now they are introducd into their new lives through the lens of their political parties. New-member orientation used to be a bipartisan affair where the new members learned the history of the institution to which they had been elected. Today the parties, separately, in assuming that responsibility, tell them to fundraise at least eight hours a day, from the day they take the oath of office or they will weaken their electoral prospects and to continue fundraising eight hours a day until the day they announce their retirement.

Today, not a single Democrat is more conservative than the most liberal Republican in either the House or the Senate—and it has been that way for more than ten years. The parties were not always so ideologically consistent. While southern Democrats would be more liberal than northeastern Republicans on a few issues, on many other issues they would be more conservative. On a few issues, they would even form a coalition—sometimes with western Republicans, other times with midwestern Democrats—to pass new laws. Such flexibility is rarer today, though on occasion it still happens. Even amid the hyperpartisanship brought about by special counsel Robert Mueller's investigation into Russia's interference with the 2016 election, the Senate reached a compromise on amendments to the Dodd–Frank Wall Street Reform and Consumer Protection Act to limit regulations on small and medium-sized banks. Sixteen Democrats and one independent joined with all the Republicans to pass the measure, 67–31.

Although some members say that leadership in the House and Senate is too powerful and does not allow for the flexibility to cross the aisle to solve problems, we must always remember that anything internal to Congress is established by, can be amended by, or can be ignored by members of Congress. As we discuss later, the words *political party* are not in the Constitution. Neither are the words *committee* and *filibuster*. Each of these concepts has meaning in Congress because members of Congress have given it meaning. Article I, Section 5, gives each chamber the power to determine "the Rules of its Proceedings."

CAUGHT IN THE WEB: CONFLICTING INTERESTS

There is an old joke about the politician who was asked which of two sides in a dispute he would support. "These folks over here are my friends," he said. "Those folks over there are my friends." So which ones would he support? The answer was "I always support my friends." That is precisely the situation in which members of Congress often find themselves. While political activists, generally focused on a single issue or a single group of related issues, may find it easy to break the political spectrum down into (a) the good side and (b) the bad side, it is much harder for a legislator to do that.

Many members of Congress have had the experience of standing before a large group of constituents and having one of them demand, "Why don't you people in Washington listen to us?" While most good politicians do not aggressively confront the potential voter, it is undoubtedly tempting to ask, in return, "Who, exactly, is 'us'? Which of you are we supposed to listen to?"

Take, for example, the situation of a person elected to Congress from a state in which wheat or oil or corn or cotton or coal is a leading product. Many of that official's constituents—the people she represents—earn their living from the production of that product. Many more earn their livings through a peripheral relationship to the product: if a city or town has as its principal employer and revenue producer a mining company, then a host of other people, from schoolteachers to shoe salesmen, earn their livings from the revenue stream generated by that company, even though none of the latter may work directly for it. The mining company starts the ball rolling in an economic process that results in the community having the ability to pave and repair its streets, build and maintain schools, and do the countless other things that help form a modern civilization. If a legislator who represents that state is called on to vote on a measure—a trade treaty, a tax provision, a sales prohibition that would affect the market value of that mining company's shares or the company's sales or revenues—one could expect her to be sympathetic, and probably responsive, to the impact of such a proposal on the company, the jobs of the people who work for the company, and the economic base of the community.

Suppose the action on which the legislator votes results in an increased sales price for the product. Suppose also that the employer produces a product that is consumed directly by many of the people who live in that same congressional constituency. Milk, perhaps. Wheat. Oil. Now there is a conflict. All of the people who live in that constituency, whether or not they work for the principal employer or in the principal industry, will have to pay whatever higher price results. Some constituents benefit directly from the price increase, some benefit indirectly, some do not benefit at all, and all pay the higher price.

Legislators often face such conflicts. If it is an easy decision, it is likely to be resolved long before it attracts congressional attention. Whereas some state legislative districts or city council districts are small and most of the residents of the district are in similar circumstances, members of Congress each represent large and diverse constituencies. In most cases, a member of the House represents more than seven hundred thousand people. Most senators represent many more. Each of California's two senators, for example, represents approximately forty million people. In any of those constituencies—forty million or "only" seven hundred thousand—there are employers and employees, producers and consumers, people of diverse backgrounds and diverse interests. The legislator may choose to be the voice of a part of that constituency, perhaps the part whose interests most closely correspond with the legislator's ideological preferences, or he or she may try to serve as a broker, seeking common ground and compromise. But in a representative democracy, in which legislators are selected from large and diverse constituencies, conflict is inevitable and deciding how to handle that conflict becomes a central part of each representative's burden.

Continuing conflict between competing interests is a central part of the system devised by the framers to ensure the protection of individual rights and liberties. While many Americans can reel off several key provisions of the First Amendment—freedom of the press, freedom of speech, freedom of religion, and some even remember to include the freedom to assemble—even well-educated citizens often forget about the other guarantee in the First Amendment: the right of citizens to petition their government. It is a system designed to empower people to try to prevent the government from doing things that might be harmful to them. Because different people have different interests and different perceptions of their interests, conflict is inevitable. It is a central part of the citizen's interaction with his or her legislature. Members of Congress are literally standing at the intersection of all of America's differing and competing interests.

Economic conflicts are not the only kind. Sometimes legislators must confront the press of conflicting values and priorities between different elements of the legislator's constituency, as well as conflicts between constituent interests (or at least the interests of some constituents) and the legislator's own preferences.

Take, for example, the case in which a group of conservationists wishes to set aside a piece of land to serve as a nationally protected preserve. Often, diverse economic interests are involved—people who want the government to buy their land and others who fear they would be deprived of their livelihood if they can no longer drill, or mine, or cut, or graze, or farm, or build on the land. But members must consider other values as well: the value of conserving wildlife habitat, protecting wetlands, saving species. Some citizens invariably place a higher value on economic opportunity and others place greater priority on safeguarding the common environment. In this case, a legislator must weigh not only economic concerns, but also broader questions about the responsibilities of government, which invariably call into question the legislator's own thoughts about that matter.

Congressional rules call for members of the House and Senate to refrain from voting on legislation if they have a personal interest in the outcome. This conflict-of-interest provision is designed to prevent legislators from using the power of their offices to enrich themselves, perhaps at the expense of others. This prohibition both constrains legislators and protects them: to the friend or partner who urges the legislator to cross the line and create an economic windfall, there is a simple answer: "Love to; but I can't." Unfortunately, no simple protections exist for legislators caught in the web of other conflicting interests.

To ensure that each citizen's liberties are protected, the founders created a system in which conflict is facilitated rather than avoided. The idea is that it is better to have different interests competing for power than to have one interest dominate others. In other words, the noise and confusion of battle—a battle of words, at least—is preferable to the calm and quiet of enforced conformity. Today, other questions must be addressed: for example, while James Madison's determination to empower conflicting interests has worked well to prevent the concentration of power in any single faction or person, we must also consider whether this empowerment of interests has led to a healthy battle between society's more powerful interests and at the same time an unhealthy diminution in the power of the individual citizen. That question is explored more fully later.

One result of all this intentional conflict, however, is clear, especially to any citizen who has taken the time to serve in a legislative role: For any legislator, including members of Congress, sometimes the most difficult task is not representing, but choosing. Over time, some of this choosing has become easier as congressional districts—and even states—have become more politically homogenous. As an example, in the 1980 election between president Jimmy Carter and former California governor Ronald Reagan, the candidate who won a state did so with an average of 55 percent of the vote. Thirty-six years later, when Donald Trump competed against Hillary Clinton, the candidate who won a state did so with an average of 59 percent of the vote. As constituencies have expressed more consistent and more resolute political preferences, the parties have grown even stronger.

THE CULTURE OF CONGRESS

Congress has many realities. For one thing, it is, in many ways, a reflection of the culture that surrounds it and produces it. But the single most striking constant about culture is its lack of constancy. The world around us changes—its norms change, its values change—and in a national legislature, chosen by the people from their own ranks, it is inevitable that those cultural changes find root in the legislative process. The laws change as society changes and so has the means of producing those laws.

A man or woman entering congressional service today finds a completely different House and Senate than he or she might have encountered if their congressional careers had begun a century earlier—or even twenty years earlier. One obvious example of this change is the willingness of the Congress to engage with a much wider variety of issues. Congress today debates whether film producers should be permitted to add color to movies originally filmed in black and white. It considers whether professional football teams should be permitted to move from one city to another, whether the league as a whole should have an antitrust exemption, or whether the league should be held responsible for the concussions that players suffer on the field. In Eisenhower's first congress as president, senators who were present for each roll call would have cast only 270 votes; more than sixty years later, in the first congress of Barack Obama's second term, a senator who was present for every vote would have voted 502 times. A member of Congress lives in an environment in which he or she is required to know about—or at least make decisions about—an almost infinite variety of subjects, many of them issues that would not have been dealt with by congresses of the past.

It would seem probable that if the number of subjects dealt with and votes required has increased, the power of congressional committees and subcommittees would have increased as well. After all, it is in these smaller groupings, each with a narrower responsibility, that one can develop the expertise necessary to deal with subjects who could receive only the most cursory attention from representatives and senators who are sometimes called on to vote dozens of times in a single day.

And yet the *culture* of the modern Congress is one in which deference to expertise has declined. At the same time that much of the nation may desire congressional term limits, essentially filling the legislature with short-term nonexperts, junior members of the House of Representatives are playing a pivotal role in determining policy. The old precept that backbenchers were to sit quietly and speak when spoken to—the idea that first- and second-term members of Congress were the adult equivalent of schoolchildren—has long since vanished.

The public is impatient for solutions to perceived national problems, and it insists that even the newest representative or senator be an active participant in making the right things—whatever they are—happen.

At one time, there was in the Congress a premium on civility. In their relationships with each other, the House and Senate have long proceeded under a civilizing umbrella of comity—equals treating each other with consideration and respect. More than one representative has been gaveled down by the speaker for violating a prohibition against making disparaging remarks about "the other body." Senators refer to each other, in debate, not as "Ted," or "Senator Cruz," but as "the senator from Texas." In House debate, "John" and "Sheila" become "the gentleman and gentle lady from Texas." "Kevin is not "Chairman Brady," but "the distinguished chairman of the Ways and Means Committee." In a setting in which views are strongly held, in which political passions are fervent, rules and traditions enforce a veneer of civil behavior. The idea is similar to that behind the required wearing of uniforms in some public and private schools: the creation of an atmosphere of respect.

But in many ways, that pattern of deference and collegiality no longer represents the real world outside the halls of Congress. The fact that Republicans and Democrats throughout the United States sometimes seem to be living in completely different universes cannot *not* have an effect on Congress. Watching the exaggerated courtesies of bitter rivals seems as anomalous in today's world as old photos depicting men at a baseball game dressed in coats and ties.

CONGRESS IN PERSPECTIVE

In a nation of more than 320 million people—in a nation of 200 people, for that matter—there will inevitably be profound differences of opinion on almost every issue that might potentially involve government action—if not, it is likely that government action is not needed. There will be citizens whose trust in government is high and who would consider declining levels of public confidence in the federal government a sign of something dramatically wrong with American society. There will be others whose trust in government is low, who resist the directives of distant authority, and who would consider a high level of tolerance for centralized decision making a sign of great social sickness.

These differing viewpoints, which are perhaps psychological as well as philosophical, invariably lead to different preferences about a wide range of issues: marginal tax rates, safety regulations, conservation laws, corporate subsidies. The list may not be endless, but it is long, and the items on it, from regulation of the aviation industry to zoo subsidies, form the basis of the debates that engage legislators on a daily basis. Sometimes the choice is between options that are only marginally different; at other times, the choices may be between doing something or doing nothing at all. It is for the legislator to choose between these alternatives or to find, somewhere in the middle, a compromise that can win sufficient support to be adopted.

These choices must be made. A nation may not both do and not do; it may not simultaneously have a high tax rate and a low one, a big military to ensure security both here and abroad and a small one that does not cost an enormous amount of money. It must send troops to preserve American values abroad or not send them to keep the United States from another protracted conflict where American interests are not directly involved. The Congress must choose. This debate between competing alternatives, as well as the mobilization and persuasion that help one side or the other prevail, emerges as the squabbling that so distresses casual observers of the political process. But it is the way a democracy must work.

Passions run high in the choosing process; self-government is not a tidy process. But the other option—a system of imposed decision—is the antithesis of a free society. It is the role of the Congress to make real the 1960s dream of power to the people. That was, after all, the dream of the 1760s as well and the underlying premise of a system of government in which the people's representatives—chosen by them—hold the ultimate power.

COMMENTARY

The Politician's Take on the Foundations of Congress

I have a great reverence for Congress, not because of what it is, but because of what it represents. Many people in recent years have expressed discomfort with the claims of American *exceptionalism*, interpreting the use of the word to claim either some sort of superiority or some sort of exemption. Well, I do not think we Americans are somehow superior to the people of Great Britain or China or Brazil or any other country, nor do I think we are exempt from the obligations that apply to other nations in how we treat each other. But I do think we are exceptional, and what it is that is exceptional is our form of government, unique at the time it was created and even today different than most. And it is the Congress that is the greatest example of that exceptionalism.

These are the two greatest features of the American system of government: first, that almost every major power of government is in the hands of the officials who most directly represent, hear the voices of, and speak for the rank-and-file American citizen. That is because the Constitution requires that every senator and representative be an actual inhabitant of the state from which he or she is elected. And they are dependent on those constituents for their positions of authority; they cannot be selected by a party to represent a community of which they know nothing. Second, American politics is open to all citizens. Sure, there are families that, generation after generation, put such focus on public service that their children grow up inclined toward becoming a candidate, but those well-known names are not typical. I served in Congress with a house painter, a factory worker, farmers, small business owners, military veterans, teachers. I served with Harvard graduates and community college graduates. I was elected to Congress with a journalism degree from a state university and a law degree from a small city university, earned at night while holding down a full-time job. My father sold shoes for a living and my mother worked as a bookkeeper; I was the first member of our family to go to college—including aunts, uncles, and cousins—and I worked my way through college waiting tables during the school year and working at laboring jobs during the summers. This is not about me; it is about a Congress made up of many people just like me, working-class, blue-collar people who have one thing in common: our system of government gives the power to us, not to kings or emperors.

Bernard Crick wrote a book called *In Defense of Politics*. Politics is an awesome responsibility and an honored calling because it is how free people govern themselves. I felt it each time I walked up the Capitol steps and onto the House floor; I felt it later when I taught government and encouraged students to consider entering politics themselves; I feel it every time I give a speech to students, businesswomen, judges, teachers, lawyers, anyone. This is our land and we have no higher obligation than to be good citizens—to care, to participate.

Not long ago, I was on my way to give a talk to visiting students on the House floor. Getting there was a challenge. The traffic was heavy around the Capitol; the sidewalks were so crowded they were difficult to navigate. I saw protesters; I overheard people rehearsing how they were going to make their case in a meeting with their congresswoman; I saw sharply dressed professionals, nuns, Jewish men with yarmulkes, children with their teachers, tourists excitedly posing on the marble stairs—all there for a Congress that is open. I cannot convey how proud I felt to see it and to have been a part of it.

I hope this book gives you a clearer picture of what this thing called Congress is. It is very simple at one level—you choose who to represent you in making the decisions that govern the country—and it is incredibly complex at another level (a mix of laws, customs, rules and regulations, structures, ideologies, personal dynamics). It is sometimes beautiful (the debate over whether to enter the first Gulf War, whichever side you were on, was high-minded and serious on both sides) and sometimes messy (we are a big and diverse country and have many differences to squabble about). And it gives those who participate in it an awesome opportunity to try to do something good for this nation that gives us so much. I hope that at least some of you who read this book decide to offer yourself to this wonderful enterprise; if you think it works well, do your part to make it work even better; if you think it is a mess, get in and help clean it up—because every one of you has a title, too: citizen. Citizen of a free country. Citizen of a country in which the people themselves hold the keys to power. Go for it.

The Professor's Take on the Foundations of Congress

After graduating in 1993 with my bachelor's degree in political science from the University of Richmond, I wanted to work on Capitol Hill. After a month-long job search, I became a staff assistant for the House Office of the Legislative Counsel. The forty or so attorneys in the office are the bill drafters for the House of Representatives. They work for committees, individual members, and leadership. They work for Democrats and Republicans. They can craft a bill in the morning with one set of legislators and plot its demise in the afternoon with another.

In commuting to work in the morning, I took the escalators up from the Capitol South Metro stop on the blue/orange line. As I neared the top of the escalator, I saw the dome of the Capitol. In ninety-degree weather, in rainstorms, and on days when the sidewalk was completely covered with snow and ice, that view never failed to take my breath away. The dome itself is an engineering marvel. Its height is so grand that the Statue of Liberty's feet could be on the floor and her torch would still be twenty feet from the top of the dome.

Even more of a marvel is what is accomplished beneath that dome and in all the rooms around the Capitol Hill complex. Trade pacts are passed, which give the world's poor a fighting chance to emerge from poverty. Education bills are forged, which provide the means for people like Mickey to be the first person in a family to attend college. Taxes are raised and lowered to spur productive activities like homeownership and hinder unproductive ones like smoking cigarettes. And the nation's fallen are remembered and revered.

That anything happens is remarkable to me. These 535 people represent different states, constituents, and viewpoints. They have different experiences and different beliefs and sometimes operate on different sets of "facts." The legislative process rarely hums like a professional orchestra, but the fact that any music whatsoever can emerge speaks to the brilliance of the Founding Fathers and those who have guided and shaped its development ever since. Shutdowns, name-calling, and corruption rear their ugly heads more than we would like, but this set of actors, even at its worst, still produces budgets, tax codes, and trade agreements; sets national policy on who can serve, how much they are paid, and what tools they can use; and oversees the National Institutes of Health, the Justice Department, and the National Parks Service.

While being in awe of the Capitol, its inhabitants, and the decisions it makes is required for all who hold the United States dear, it does not mean that the activities inside should not be studied, criticized, and, at times, overturned. Perhaps the aspect of Congress that leaves me most in awe is the power of the people. It is only with their assent that our Congress is elected and that their wishes, dreams, and nightmares are brought into reality. What we do throughout the remainder of the book is put all of this into a context that can give the Congress a rhythm even when the noise that emerges deafens our ears.

After working on Capitol Hill for a year and studying it for more than twenty, I remain in awe. The more I learn about it, the more amazed I am that anything ever gets done.

CHAPTER 2

The Power of the People

For more than two hundred years, the actors in our political system have attempted to run a government within the dictates of the US Constitution. The Constitution could not spell out all the details, nor did the framers attempt to write a how-to guide for governing. As a result, many questions have arisen— some that could have been predicted at the time of the signing of the Constitution and others only as their words were implemented. For example, while the president was commander in chief, only Congress could declare war. More than two hundred years later, the roles of the president and Congress in the waging of war are still being debated.

This continuing debate—and others like it—suggests some confusion about the role each branch plays within the separation-of-powers system designed by the framers. But that is true in only one sense. Legitimate uncertainty exists about the extent of congressional reach and how entangled the president can get us in hostilities abroad before gaining authority from Congress to act; however, in the broader sense, no confusion exists at all about the fundamental role of Congress. In a multipart, multilayered form of government, Congress's responsibility has remained the same: to be the voice of the people.

This mandate is no minor matter. For much of history, and in many lands, *the people*—that is, the rank-and-file shop owners, factory workers, farmhands, mechanics, clerks, teachers, students, tailors, and bricklayers who made up the bulk of a national population—remained outside the decision-making processes of government. The people set no policies; they were not even consulted as to what policies they might prefer. High-ranking members of the clergy or the military or holders of large estates were sometimes included in power-sharing hierarchies, but for the most part the class system, politically, involved only two classes: those who decided and those who obeyed. Few decided; most obeyed—or were punished for failing to do so.

Increasingly in Europe and America, however, a new, *liberal* idea took hold: citizens began to demand and create constraints on government and new protections for individuals. The Magna Carta, the Constitution, and the Declaration of the Rights of Man all constrained a central authority from acting unilaterally. When the founders drafted America's constitution, infused with the ideals of the European liberals and firsthand awareness of royal abuse, they devised not only a system to limit the powers of the executive, but also one that would empower the people themselves to keep a firm hand on the nation's policies. Article I of the Constitution placed direct lawmaking authority in the hands of Congress.

The framers also worked to ensure that assigning power to Congress would not become a merely symbolic empowering of the citizens. Members of one part of Congress—the Senate—were to be selected by officials of the states they were to represent. But they were not to be appointed by a state executive; they were to be selected by state legislators who had been elected, in turn, directly by the people. The procedure was even more direct in the House of Representatives: citizens were to vote for House members without any intermediary whatsoever. While more than two hundred years of practice make this arrangement seem obvious, at the time of the founding, it was groundbreaking. That ordinary citizens could play such a vital role in the dynamic of governing was, indeed, revolutionary.

The idea that a member of Congress was to serve as the voice of a particular group of citizens—or at least be attuned to their voices—was given further weight by a specific provision in the Constitution. Members of Congress are constitutionally required to be inhabitants of—to actually live in—the states from which they are elected. They are to be selected from among the people themselves. In the United Kingdom, it has historically been the exception rather than the rule for a member of Parliament to be from the district he or she represents in the House of Commons. Today, most members of Parliament have prior ties to their constituency, but a large minority do not, including Theresa May, the current prime minister.

The framers gave the people a critical role in the functioning of their government. The people were expected to keep their elected officials in line. In fact, a great debate during the constitutional convention broke out over who had the authority to determine the monetary compensation for members serving in Congress. Benjamin Franklin thought that they should not be paid at all. Madison, though, was resolute in arguing that members must be given the power to determine their own pay. In the face of criticism that these members could steal from the public treasury for their own benefit, Madison, in Federalist 57, responded that the "vigilant and manly" spirit of the American public would keep members in line. If members attempted to give themselves a pay raise, the American people would decide whether they should keep their jobs. At least three times in American history (1816, 1873, and 1989), the public retaliated with public demonstrations and, ultimately, incumbent defeats. In the modern age, votes to increase congressional salaries invariably draw a full complement of reporters to the Congress's press galleries, and members who vote to increase their pay will soon learn how their constituents feel about it. Both parties caught flak from voters when they agreed to increase salaries and promised their candidates would not use the votes in attempts to defeat those who supported the increase. But because parties exist to win elections, those promises sometimes carried little weight in ensuing campaigns.

Indeed, the people are crucial to the functioning of our government, and yet, the people's record is not as impressive as their responsibilities. In this chapter, we begin by examining how the people view their members and how members view the people. We then outline some of the problems with putting the people in charge. We also provide some solutions for how these lackluster abilities can lead to impressive results. At the end of the day, however, the American people truly do get the Congress that they deserve. After all, they are the only ones who can change it.

THE VOICE OF THE PEOPLE

That members of Congress *represent* is as basic a fact about Congress that exists. Lying behind that basic fact is extreme complexity. How members represent can take two distinct forms. First, members may be *delegates*, who act just as their constituents would act if they were in the same situation. In a modern world, an institution like Congress might not need to exist if all members adopted the true delegate form of representation. With the advent of scientific polling, laptop computers, iPhones, Facebook, Twitter, apps, and other means of rapid, cheap, long-distance communication and information gathering, major issues could simply be put directly to the voters: "for a yes vote, dial 1-800-VOTEYES," or even easier, "text 'yes' to 54321," or easiest, "click here to vote yes!" Determining policy would be a purely administrative matter: rapid computers could simply tally the constituents' votes and direct the various executive branches of government to impose or remove a regulation, to increase or reduce tax rates, to go to war, or even to decide the penalty for a crime. To keep some check on the executive branch, groups of outsiders—independent commissions made up of policy experts—could identify areas of concern and determine which alternative solutions to submit to the public for its electronic vote. Public policy could be made in the same way that the next winner on *Dancing with the Stars* is chosen.

But being a representative may mean more than merely doing the public will; it may—and perhaps should—mean that the holder of that office is a man or woman placed in government to watch out for the citizens' interests. Theorists call this the *trustee* form of representation. Trustees are more concerned with the effects of public policy than they are with the popularity of a given proposal. A member who views her job as a trustee will support a proposal with positive outcomes even if her constituents oppose it. The trustee form of representation rests on members' expertise in guiding their decisions.

The differences between delegates and trustees are profound. In the first case, a representative feels bound to do as the citizens wish, regardless of the representative's own doubts about such a course of action. It is hard to argue with that conclusion. "After all," such a representative might say, "if I don't listen to the people who elected me, they will have no voice in their own government. I have an opinion, but so have they, and if I merely vote as I prefer, rather than as they prefer, I will have usurped their rights as citizens."

A member who votes in Congress as a trustee, however, may take the public's desires into account, but will ultimately rely on his perceptions of the policy's effect on his constituents, whether or not doing so is consistent with their wishes at the time. It is the nature of the job that a member of Congress, who may commission studies, question witnesses, and conduct investigations, will often have better information about a proposal's effects than a citizen who decides based on, at best, newspaper accounts or a Facebook posting.

Most members will employ both kinds of representation during their tenures in Congress, which gives rise to a third type of representation, known as a *politico*. A politico is a member who acts as a delegate on some issues and as a trustee on other issues. Most members are delegates (and, with an eye toward the next election, smart politicians) when it comes to a core issue on which their constituents have firm beliefs such as abortion, capital punishment, or gun control, while being trustees on other issues—those that tend toward more complex policy matters like protecting intellectual property or procuring military defense weapons systems.

Another variant in the representational style is a *Burkean trustee*. While pure trustees would act in their constituents' best interests, a Burkean trustee will act in the country's best interest. Edmund Burke, the eighteenth-century British statesman for whom this variant is named, argued that legislators owed to their constituents not blind obedience but, for two reasons, the exercise of good judgment. First, many issues are complex: the problems being addressed may arise from a variety of interrelated causes (poverty, crime, or homelessness as examples). Second, the alternative means of addressing the problems may have ramifications that are difficult to foresee or differential effects on groups of constituents. Legislators have a responsibility to be alert to the dangers of unintended conse quences. The popular wisdom may call for a *Band-Aid solution* that seldom provides a permanent fix to the problem and often creates additional problems that make matters worse.

Burke thought representatives should independently decide even when their constituents had well-formed and conclusive views on the issue. When an Irish free trade bill was being debated in Parliament, Burke's constituents made their opposition known. Not only were they against it, but also the bill may have been bad for Burke's constituency in both the short and the long run. Both the delegate and the trustee form of representation pointed toward opposing the bill. Burke, though, thought that free trade was an economic good. He supported the bill even if he should "forfeit their suffrages at an ensuing election[. I]t will stand on record an example to future representatives of the Commons of England, that one man at least had dared to resist the desires of his constituents when his judgment assured him they were wrong."[1] In the end, Burke supported the bill and his constituents defeated him at the next election.

Like Burke, many members of Congress may consider it their responsibility to look beyond the narrower, short-term concerns and preferences of their own constituencies. They may choose to focus on the common good, the greater good, the national interest, or the future rather than merely representing the constituents who most recently elected them. Mike Synar, a congressman from Oklahoma, once incurred the wrath of some of his constituents when he told a reporter for the *New York Times* in an interview that he was not "an Oklahoma Congressman" but a "United States Congressman from Oklahoma." It is a significant difference in outlook and one that results in different decisions being reached.[2]

During the course of a single legislative session or even a single day, members may switch roles from delegate to trustee to Burkean trustee and back many times. The role they choose depends on several factors: how strongly constituents feel on the matter, whether the representative's information and understanding of the issue are significantly better than that of the constituents, whether defiance of constituents' wishes is likely to result in defeat at the next election, whether a small constituency benefit outweighs a substantial nationwide cost, and whether the issue is of great enough importance to justify that risk.

Consider the following: Farmers in one state may suffer economic damage if the federal government prevents them from carrying out certain activities on their property. If those activities are carried out, the environmental damage will reach beyond the farmers' property, even beyond the state's boundaries, and adversely affect persons and properties in other parts of the nation, perhaps substantially, in the long run. A factory in another state may be similarly prohibited from continuing some of its activities. Representatives and senators from that state may choose to battle for the rights of their affected constituents. Or they may see their role as one of considering a bigger picture, even if their constituents suffer in the short run.

Or consider this situation: A military base in a third state provides a significant number of jobs. But the Pentagon has determined that the base is no longer needed and that its continued existence is draining resources from other programs that are more crucial to the national defense. Again, that state's senators and representatives may choose to fight the Pentagon and try to save the base. Or they may determine that the nation's security is more important than keeping a base in their state. If scientists proposed federally funded construction of a massive—and expensive—Mission to Mars facility, should a member vote differently on the proposal if the project is in his or her own state than if it is to be located somewhere else? As these examples illustrate, no one form of representation is always right or always wrong. Different constituencies would have different expectations on different issues at different times. Balancing these competing interests is what politics is all about. Members will make their decisions and be forced to justify those decisions both at the time that they are made and during their next campaign as their opponents and the voters scrutinize their voting record.

Now that the ideas of delegate, trustee, and their variants are defined, we next examine what constituents really want from their members of Congress and how members view their constituencies. The answer to these questions will go a long way in providing the rationale for explaining why our system works the way that it does. Understanding Congress requires an understanding of the motivations behind the people and those whom they elect to represent them.

What Do Constituents Expect?

For however many different mixes of representation styles exist, constituents' expectations are more varied and less well defined. Many citizens focus not on specific policy outcomes but on the "direction" of a legislator's activities. These constituents expect a member of Congress to represent their values, to fight for liberal or conservative or business or environmental or feminist causes. These *ideological* concerns generally come as a package containing a variety of more specific issues, such as abortion, gun control, and drug legalization—the kinds of issues for which one may generally find liberals on one side and conservatives on another, or for which constituents may perceive business and environmental concerns to be at odds. Barry Goldwater, an Arizona senator who became the Republican presidential nominee in 1964, was known to ask of a proposal, "Does it maximize freedom?" Others might ask of the same proposal, "Does it reduce inequalities?" To some constituents it is the consistent application of these tests that determines the soundness of a legislator's policy positions. Other constituents take a more pragmatic approach: they will ask legislators to address specific concerns, such as reducing crime or posting appropriate warning signs on a dangerous curve on a highway. These constituents may or may not have a predetermined opinion as to the best approach to solving a problem, but they want it thoughtfully considered, and they want it solved. This view, which gives legislators more flexibility, accepts the premise that many issues are complicated and that their solutions require a more sophisticated understanding than the constituent possesses, which may well be the case with such issues as Social Security and healthcare.

For many constituents, good policy is simply policy with which they agree. For constituents who favor a system of progressive taxation (in which persons with higher incomes pay a higher percentage of their incomes in federal taxes), a change in the tax laws that reduces the burden on the wealthy or increases the percentage of total taxes paid by middle-income taxpayers may be perceived as bad national policy. Even if advocates of the change were able to demonstrate that such a change would increase investment and produce an increase in available jobs, support for a tax code that "favors the rich" would be a serious mark against the member of Congress who voted for such a plan. To constituents who believe that lower taxes on the wealthy create investment incentives and more employment, or that all citizens should be taxed at the same rate, a tax reduction that primarily benefits lower-income taxpayers might be perceived as a bad policy, even if its advocates could demonstrate that such a change would help move families out of poverty or lead to an increase in consumer purchases. For constituents like these, a general reflection of one's values (for justice, for families, for individual freedom) is not enough: a member is expected to represent by casting the votes the constituent would cast if he or she were allowed on the House or Senate floor. Other constituents recognize the expertise that members can develop and evaluate policies more on their effects than on the actual policies.

In addition to legislating—writing laws and shaping policy—members of Congress are expected to provide a link between *government* and *citizen*. This link

takes several forms: providing information about pending legislation, offering opportunities—town meetings, questionnaires, attendance at public events, tweets, and Facebook updates—for citizens to express themselves on public policy issues and assisting constituents who encounter problems with federal agencies.

Most members of Congress maintain a staff of caseworkers, often based in the home state or district, to handle such cases. These staffers develop working relationships with key agency personnel, and in most government bureaus, congressional inquiries and interventions are given preferential treatment; ultimately, they know, those same members of Congress will be voting on the agency's budget request. Members keep close tabs on the number of pending cases and how successfully they are resolved, and it is not uncommon for caseworkers to report directly to a legislator's chief of staff. If the resolution of a constituent's problem depends on the action of a particularly high-ranking agency official or if the normal advocacy intervention has not won results, the member may become involved personally, both with phone calls and with personal meetings.

It should be noted, that even though these interventions are a common practice and well within the accepted definition of a legislator's responsibilities, they do not come without risk. On April 1, 2015, Senator Bob Menendez (D-NJ) was indicted on corruption charges for actions he took on behalf of Salomon Melgen. These actions included acquiring visas for Melgen's girlfriends and pressuring the Dominican Republic to enforce a contract that benefited Melgen's company. Melgen and his family donated $20,000 to Menendez's legal defense fund and an additional $40,000 to the New Jersey Democratic Party victory fund. Furthermore, Menendez took trips on Melgen's private plane, spent three nights at a five-star Paris hotel paid for by Melgen, and vacationed at Melgen's homes in West Palm Beach and the Dominican Republic. Some of these gifts were not properly disclosed on Senate forms. Menendez claimed that he did nothing more than provide services to a constituent and friend. Meanwhile, Melgen claimed that he did not treat Menendez any differently than he did his other friends. After nearly three years of investigations, a trial, and a deadlocked jury, Menendez was cleared of federal corruption charges when the prosecutor decided not to retry the case. As this episode shows, the line is sometimes quite blurry.

Not all constituent service is of a personal nature. Members may be called on to seek financial assistance in the broader community interest—for example, support for the construction or repair of a bridge or highway, the building of a new museum, or the expansion of a local military base or commercial airport. These projects all fall under the banner of *pork barreling*, which occurs when members of Congress try to secure federal funds to support projects in their districts. Since 2011, when such directed targeting of money, commonly referred to as *earmarks*, was banned, members expend more effort securing money from the bureaucrats, who, in turn, are ultimately dependent on these legislators to secure their overall budgets.

What does a constituent expect? To some extent, all of these things—the representing of one's own values or policy preferences, thoughtful consideration of important issues, diligent efforts to resolve a citizen's difficulties in dealing with the massive bureaucracy of the federal government, aggressive advocacy for the economic interests of the local community, and desirable outcomes for the region, state, and country when new policies are implemented.

How Members View the Constituency

Members must be more systematic in how they view their constituents because it is the constituents who decide if the members will retain their jobs. If members do not have a nuanced view of their constituencies, they are likely to be overwhelmed. The sheer number of constituents members have would be staggering to the framers, who mandated in the Constitution that no one member have more than 30,000 constituents. According to the 1790 census, Virginia had the most people (747,610), affording it 19 House members.[3] In the 2010 census, California had the most people (37,253,956), affording it 53 House members. If Congress had not changed its practice of apportionment of the House by capping it at 435 seats in the Reapportionment Act of 1929, California would have 1,308 representatives in the 116th Congress, which would include a House with more than 10,770 representatives in it! Instead of having at most 30,000 constituents, today's representatives have more than 700,000 constituents.

Members would be quickly overwhelmed if they tried to always keep every single one of the seven hundred thousand constituents in mind. A political scientist, Richard Fenno, studied Congress by observing members in their natural habitat both in Washington, DC, and in their districts. He developed a research methodology called *soaking and poking* by only observing a member when she was engaged in official duties (e.g., soaking) and then later asking the member about her actions (e.g., poking). After witnessing many members in their districts, Fenno devised a typology of concentric circles to help explain how members view their districts (SEE FIGURE 2.1).

Fenno called the outermost circle the geographic constituency, which included every constituent in the district. When members think of this level of constituency, they usually describe it in geographic terms—"I represent central Austin—everything north of Lady Bird Lake and south of the county line" or "My district includes the northeast corner of the state, but then has a strip fifty miles south never more than twenty miles from the border." The geographic constituency includes every resident and every structure in the representative's district or the senator's state.

The first circle inside the geographic constituency is a member's reelection constituency, which contains the voters who supported the members in their last general election or expect to in the next election. By virtue of the math in the district, the reelection constituency must include at least half of the voters from the geographic constituency. Those voters who support the members' opponents

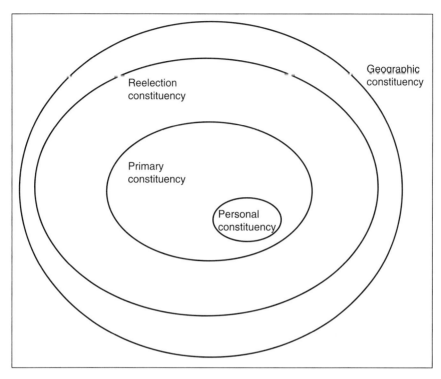

Figure 2.1 Fenno's Concentric Circles for How Members View their Constituencies.

and all those who do not vote are in the geographic constituency, but not the re-election constituency. Because turnout hovers around 60 percent, even during the highest turnout elections, and because few members win without any opposition, almost all members have more people outside their reelection constituency than inside it. The reelection constituency begins with the member's fellow partisans. Only for the luckiest representatives, though will fellow partisans be enough. Most members need to peel off enough independents and voters from the opposite party to retain their seat in Congress.

Fenno found that members' views of the reelection constituency changed over the course of their careers. Members first take an expansive view to the reelection constituency. They begin with their voters from their first election, when they were running either in an open seat or against an incumbent. In the next few election cycles, which Fenno called the *expansionist phase*, members try to increase the number of their supporters. As the members' careers wind down in the *protectionist phase*, the members are less concerned with gaining new supporters than they are with keeping the supporters they have. Knowing the phase of members' careers helps determine whose voice the members listen to most carefully.

The circle just inside the reelection constituency is the primary constituency. A member considers those voters who side with her, even in a contested primary, the primary constituency. Constituencies that include a lopsided number of Democrats or Republicans can prove to be the most dangerous. Members think of their primary constituency as their most loyal voters, which might include people from their ideological bent in their parties (such as moderate Republicans if the member is a moderate Republican or extreme leftwing liberals if the member is an extreme leftwing liberal), residents in their hometown, old business associates, people in the member's old trade, or voters belonging to the special interests particularly favored by the member.

Finally, the innermost circle, the *personal constituency*, contains the members' spouse, family, closest friends, political consultants, and most trusted advisors. Members consult their personal constituency when they are thinking of switching positions on an important issue, figuring out how to deal with negative press, or contemplating a run for higher office. The personal constituency meets to discuss the broad contours that the member follows in both casting difficult and important votes and evaluating future electoral prospects. Some members have a broad personal constituency while others keep it quite small.

How Members Present Themselves

The positions members take on issues are, indeed, important, but perhaps equally important is how members present themselves to their constituents. Depending on the national waves and the partisan breakdowns in their districts, members can begin to gain seniority only to get tripped up in a tough election year because they have not endeared themselves to their constituents.

Understanding how members view their constituencies goes a long way in determining how they present themselves in front of their constituents. Fenno calls this presentation of self *homestyle*. While different members have different homestyles, all take their constituents into consideration. For example, Senator Charles Grassley (R-IA), though he has been in Congress since 1975, not only still owns the family farm, but also continues to till the soil when he is in Iowa. Even his constituents who are liberal Democrats and may disagree with Grassley on many issues appreciate the way that he has maintained his Iowan values. For many years, Grassley served in the Senate with Bob Graham (D-FL), who demonstrated his connection to his constituents in a different way. Graham, who retired in 2005, spent his weekends and legislative recesses on *workdays*, where he would do a different job for an eight-hour shift. Over the course of his career, he did 386 workdays, including days spent as a teacher, a factory worker, a garbage man, a fisherman, and even a gate agent for US Airways! As with Grassley's ideological opponents, conservative Republicans

disagreed with Graham on many issues, but they appreciated the way he placed himself in his constituents' shoes.

Grassley's homestyle is perfectly suited to his state, Iowa, where even people who are not in the farming business grasp what it contributes to the state's persona and economy. Since 1958, Grassley has not lost an election in Iowa. In his first election to the Senate in 1980, he received 53.5 percent of the vote against an incumbent. Since then, none of his opponents in five subsequent reelection efforts broke even 35 percent. Likewise, Graham's workdays perfectly encapsulated the diverse economy of Florida. In his three senate elections, Graham won an average of 61 percent of the vote. Grassley and Graham had successful careers, in large part because their homestyles perfectly fit their constituents.

Other members present themselves in other ways to their constituents. Just as no one style fits all constituencies, no one style fits all members. Homestyles are a function of both the members and their districts or states. What fits an inner-city district may not fit an outlying district encompassing both suburbs and rural parts of the state. The homestyle must constantly be adjusted to fit the member, those she represents, and the time in which she serves—all these factors are fluid and how members present themselves must be fluid as well, lest they hurt their future reelection prospects.

THE VOICE OF THE PEOPLE AND ITS COMPLEXITIES

Having considered how members and their constituents view one another, we can now examine how well the American people perform their crucial responsibility in the practice of American democracy. Their abilities go a long way in determining whether the Congress they get is a good one. Evaluating their proficiency is complicated from the beginning. *The voice of the people* is difficult to define and determine. Furthermore, the American public's ability to exercise it seems at best extremely deficient.

Whose Views Matter?

The phrase *voice of the people* rests on how two critical words are defined: voice and people. We discuss them in reverse order. Who are the people? Should members only consider the views of the constituents who voted for them or are they obligated to consider all their constituents? Because the rich pay more taxes, should their views matter more or should the views of the poor matter more because they are more numerous and more dependent on the government to provide them with sustenance? Furthermore, some people's views are easier to ascertain and still others know more about the government and the society in which they live. Should those who know more count more when members cast votes?

Do members owe their attention to all citizens or only to those who care enough to involve themselves in the political process? Should a citizen who does not contribute, does not volunteer, does not vote, and cannot leave his television or set his smartphone down long enough to take part in preserving the democracy be consulted about national priorities? What if such a citizen did not participate because he or she had no money to spare, worked two jobs, carried the burdens of being a single parent, and could not get off work on Election Day, but would be harmed—or helped—if a particular piece of legislation were to become law? Should this citizen be excluded from a member's decision process? What about the ones who could have voted or volunteered or participated in some other way, but did not want to bother this time around?

Presumably, each member took a position on the issues that surfaced during the campaign that resulted in her election. Many people opposed the positions. They had their say, they attempted to elect someone who thought differently, and they failed. Election campaigns are the means by which the people consider alternative candidates and choose between them. The people who thought like the winning candidate competed fairly and openly on the issues, and they won: the people said they wanted their representative to take the positions the eventual winner promised to take. Scores of people worked in the campaign: the leaders and activists in the political party who provided the nomination and election support, the elected leaders of local communities, the leaders in the various subgroups—chambers of commerce, labor unions, senior citizens groups—all of whom expect the winning candidate to be their voice in Congress.

Shouldn't the sworn-in member now represent, first and foremost, the views of those people who delivered the election? Should they now, after the election is over, have no more voice in their representative's decisions than people whose preferences had been rejected? Would you say the same thing if the election had been extremely close? What about if the election were a landslide? What about the member's votes on issues that were never discussed or debated during the campaign?

Members face another wrinkle in determining how they should represent their constituents. While they all may have an expressed opinion about gun control, some constituents may hold their opinions more fervently than others. Four months after twenty-six students and staffers at Sandy Hook Elementary School in Connecticut were killed, the Senate defeated a compromise gun control amendment, despite achieving two-thirds support in some public opinion polls. Senator John McCain supported the compromise measure because of the overall support it enjoyed among his constituents. His same-state, same-party colleague, Jeff Flake, voted against it because the one-third who opposed the measure felt much more strongly about their opinion than the two-thirds who supported it. Which senator cast the appropriate vote for his or her constituents? Even when polls tilt in one direction, senators can easily justify their votes in the other direction.

Ours is a representative democracy, after all, and if "all men and women are created equal" and the Constitution is careful to guarantee the equal protection of individual rights, cannot one assume that a representative is to represent all his or her constituents equally? But a member who wants to vote wisely, whose vote may tilt the House or Senate toward one policy or another, may see a difficult picture. An answer one way or another on these questions can be justified, but it can also be criticized. Here is where Richard Fenno's formulation of concentric constituent circles comes into play. In their right to vote, all citizens are equal. But members of Congress cannot possibly weigh all constituents' opinions equally.

"Manchin-Toomey would expand background checks far beyond commercial sales to include almost all private transfers—including between friends and neighbors—if the posting or display of the ad for a firearm was made public. It would likely even extend to message boards, like the one in an office kitchen. This simply goes too far."

—Sen. Jeff Flake (R)-Arizona

Facebook post, April 15, 2013

"Is this a perfect solution? No. Would it prevent all future acts of gun violence? Of course, not. Would it have prevented the most recent acts of gun violence? In all likelihood, no. But, it is reasonable and it is my firm conviction that it is Constitutional."

—Sen. John McCain (R)-Arizona

Floor speech, April 17, 2013

Determining the Constituents' Preferences and Interests

We have already seen that determining the voice of the people is difficult for one simple reason: which people should be given a voice. There is an additional problem, too. The most common way for members to determine what that voice is saying involves professional, scientific polling; questionnaires, sometimes conducted on members' webpages; an evaluation of constituent-generated mail, including emails, Facebook comments, and replies on Twitter; and engaging citizens at town meetings (or telephone town halls) or at meetings of community organizations. Members have even developed smartphone apps that allow constituents to access information about the member or federal programs and leave their opinions about public policy problems both big and small. There is no lack of information to be gathered in these ways: a member can count on getting an earful from constituents who take advantage of these opportunities to make their voice heard.

But each of these methods is insufficient. Professional polling, which may provide a high degree of accuracy, is expensive. Polls that seek to learn voter preferences on specific issues are generally conducted during election campaigns and paid for with campaign funds. While candidates often keep tabs on their momentum—behind by ten points on Friday, within the margin of error on Monday—these *tracking polls* rarely ask voters where they stand on the issues the winner will eventually confront in Congress. The nuance that members face in legislation is rarely reflected in opinion polls of their constituents. Whereas members may have to vote on a prohibition on the manufacture and distribution of guns that are made of plastics and cannot therefore be detected by the screening devices in airports and public buildings, their constituents are only ever asked in public opinion polls whether they favor more or less gun control.

Because of the brevity and infrequency of these polls, legislators may know the political will of constituents for only a small percentage of the issues on which the House or Senate votes. In addition, pollsters are usually quick to admit that their surveys provide no more than a snapshot: the preferences of constituents at a given moment in time, shaped by whatever information they may then have on an issue. If a legislator is called on to vote on an issue weeks or months after a poll was taken, and if debates and publicity about the issue had, in the meantime, given constituents more information than they had when they were polled, the "scientific" information on which a legislator relies may need to be updated.

The same limitations apply to other forms of information gathering about constituent preferences. Members who try to derive their constituents' opinions through surveys they conduct through newsletters, unsolicited emails, Facebook messages, tweets, coordinated "AstroTurf" campaigns, and town hall meetings face at least two problems. First, because legislators and their assistants are generally not professionals in survey work and because members of Congress may consciously or subconsciously be seeking responses that fit their own inclinations, the questions they ask may tend to be slanted to produce desired results and the opinions that they hear directly from constituents are self-selected. This may help a member justify why he or she voted a certain way, but it is of no help in arriving at an objective understanding of constituent preferences. The senator may think he or she is being the voice of the people, but if that is the case, it may be a lucky accident.

The second problem is in the sample. A scientific poll is designed to measure accurately the preferences of a large number of people using a small number of responses. Opinions are ascertained from a select group, which may provide a biased view of how the whole district feels. A representative in the House represents approximately three-quarters of a million people. Assume that two-thirds are adults—a voting-age population of half a million men and women. A question that generates even two thousand responses (a good response rate by congressional standards) is providing the opinions of less than 1 percent of the constituency. Because the sample is not scientifically selected, most of the responses might be from white males or Hispanic females or from attorneys or truck drivers. The legislator may be getting the opinion of a narrow segment of the electorate. More important, because responding requires some effort on behalf of the recipient— taking the time to think about the issues, answer the questions, complete the survey, and properly return it—responses are most likely to come from people who feel strongly about an issue or who are most likely to be affected by it—or the constituents with the most time on their hands. In terms of really knowing how one's constituency as a whole feels about an issue, the newsletter questionnaire is of precious little help. Although the internet makes these polls easier to manage,

it does not solve the problems of a biased sample. In fact, it could even exacerbate them because internet users present their own persistent biases.

Finally, face-to-face meetings with constituents, usually in town meetings or appearances before various community organizations, provide members with necessary feedback. Again, the same problem exists. Even if a member of Congress highly publicizes an impending town meeting, the men and women who show up to be heard are likely those who feel most strongly about the issues before Congress, those who are most affected, or those who have nothing better to do. Again, the expressed opinions may not be representative of the general public—the affected and the passionate are most likely to write.

Thomas P. "Tip" O'Neill, the Massachusetts congressman who served as Speaker of the House from 1977 through 1987, has often been credited with coining the phrase, "All politics is local." Whether he was the first to say it or not, the fact is, constituent opinion matters to most officeholders far more than the opinions of newspaper columnists, other politicians (including the President of the United States), or academic studies. But finding out what those opinions are is difficult at best. Most members of Congress try a little bit of everything—questionnaires, town meetings, civic club speeches, reading constituents' letters, conducting professional polls during campaigns, and talking to constituents on the street in supermarkets, bowling alleys, factories, and shopping malls. Ultimately, determining what one's constituents prefer is, like politics itself, more art than science. One gets a feel for the constituency, a sense of constituents' attitudes toward issues in general, perhaps even an assumption that the majority of constituents must share the legislator's preferences or they would have elected someone else. Regrettably, that is as clear as it gets.

The Absence of Committed Political Views

Politicians and the punditry attempt to ascertain the voice of the people through great effort and at great expense. What the most scientific surveys show is an American population that, at best, can easily be swayed from one side of a political issue to another or, at worst, lies. If determining what the people want is so difficult and yet once it is determined we find that they hold those beliefs so fleetingly, the entire democratic exercise is called into question.

In a recent survey experiment, two groups of Americans were asked a fundamental question of public policy: "Are you in favor of or opposed to a big increase in government spending to increase opportunities for poor people?" This question gets to the heart of the raging ideological debate—conservatives oppose this basic proposal and liberals support it. To the first group of people, an extra phrase was tacked on: "even if it means higher taxes." In this group, 44 percent of the people would support increased spending. If this issue were put to a national referendum, the proposal would lose and the government would not increase spending on poor people. The second group is asked about the same fundamental policy, though with a different phrase tacked on at the end: "so they can have a better chance of getting ahead in life." Even though the respondents must decide on the same policy—more spending to help poor people—72 percent of the people support more spending. What seemed under the higher-taxes frame to be a difficult issue in which the American public was almost equally divided becomes an issue that enjoys such overwhelming support that policy makers would wonder why it is controversial. If more than a quarter of the American public can be so easily swayed on this important issue that fundamentally defines the ideology war in the United States, imagine the instability of the American public on less important issues that do not so easily divide the parties. The unfortunate thing about these results is that they do not differ from what political analysts have been finding for more than twenty-five years.[4]

Perhaps even scarier for the voice of the people is that we know that respondents to surveys do not always tell the truth, at least as far as we can determine from what we know the truth to be. In the 2016 presidential election, 60.1 percent of the voting-eligible population voted. And, yet, when surveys ask respondents whether they voted, the number is never close to that amount. According to the National Election Study, which is the bedrock study for much of the political behavior research in political science, 72.2 percent of the respondents in this nationally representative sample responded that they voted. We can imagine that there would be significant social pressure to answer the question affirmatively, so the survey even provides the respondent with socially accepted excuses: "a lot of people weren't able to vote because they weren't registered or they were sick or they just didn't have time." Nonetheless, more than one in seven respondents, if the national turnout figures are to be believed, offered an answer that was not the truth. This gap has increased significantly over time; since the 1950s and 1960s, it has more than doubled.

These issues about survey respondents suggest the difficulty of determining what the voice of the people truly is. The voice offered depends on the question asked, and changes in the question wording can elicit a far different answer. Furthermore, survey respondents frequently give socially acceptable answers instead of the truth. On many issues, members have a hard time determining what their constituents want, even where data exist.

The American Public Does Not Have Faith in the System

In addition to lying on surveys, the American people—at least as those who are surveyed suggest—do not hold firm political beliefs. One political belief, however, is almost universal and is consistent across time. That belief is that the federal government is inept and cannot be trusted (SEE FIGURE 2.2). Except under unusual circumstances, very few people have faith in how democracy is carried out in the United States. In only a handful of Gallup polls conducted since February 2010 have more than 20 percent of Americans approved of "the way Congress is handling its job."[5]

In questions asking about the trust and confidence respondents have in various political institutions, Congress (8 percent responding either a "great deal" or a "fair amount") finished behind the judicial branch (32 percent) and the executive branch (33 percent).[6] While these numbers are lower than normal, they are consistent in at least two respects. First, Congress is always at or near the bottom of the list. Second, the exceptions are when the numbers for all the institutions spike up rather than down. For example, the numbers jumped up after the 9/11 attacks, but within the year, they settled back to where they were before.

While the practice is widely ridiculed, the belief in the system is almost always universal. Americans believe in the Constitution—they even revere it. They approve of separation of powers and a legislative process that makes passing laws difficult. They just do not like the way that these principles are carried out.

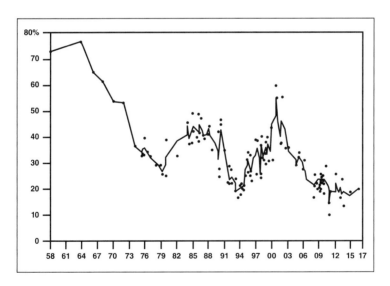

Figure 2.2 Trust in Federal Government. Public Trust in Government Remains Near Historic Lows.
Trust the federal government to do what is right just about always/most of the time.
From 1976 to 2016, the trend line represents a three-survey moving average. SOURCE: Survey conducted April 5–11, 2017. TREND SOURCES: Pew Research Center, National Election Studies, Gallup, ABC/ *Washington Post*, CBS/*New York Times*, and CNN polls. http://www.people-press.org/2017/05/03/ public-trust-in-government-remains-near-historic-lows-as-partisan-attitudes-shift/

The American Public Is Politically Ignorant

In addition to not having firm political beliefs, the American public is also shockingly ignorant when it comes to basic facts about the practice of American politics. An irony from public opinion polling puts these types of representation into clearer focus. For years, surveys have revealed that the American public believes the United States should cut back sharply on foreign aid. Yet when asked what amount of assistance might be acceptable, they usually state a figure much higher than the United States normally provides. Presidents and members from both parties have supported spending on international affairs, including foreign aid, on the grounds that ensuring stability, building new democracies, and using diplomacy to head off potential conflict are important to ensuring America's national security. Yet a member who listens to his or her constituents is under enormous pressure to vote in ways that may not be in the best interests of the nation. In such circumstances, should he or she listen equally to all citizens who have an opinion, whether well informed or ill-informed, or only to those who know what they are talking about?

Beyond their political ignorance about issues, many constituents do not even know who represents them in Congress. In a 2013 Gallup poll, only 35 percent of the respondents could recall who their representative was, let alone their representative's opinions on the pressing issues of the day. About the same percentage could name both of their senators, while an equal proportion could name neither one.

Voter Turnout

No member of Congress doubts that it was the role of the people that set apart the government established under the Constitution in the eighteenth century or that it is the role of the people today that makes the entire system work. The people are critical. And yet, voting in US elections can be anemic. In the 2018 elections, when many argued that the American public sent President Trump a strong rebuke, about five of every ten voters decided not to participate. And it was even worse in 2006 when George W. Bush and the Republicans suffered at the ballot boxes and in 2010 and 2014 when President Obama and the Democrats lost many seats in Congress. Between those midterm elections, when President Trump's name was on the ballot, and Barack Obama's and George W. Bush's before him, about two of every five potential voters stayed away from the voting booth. Far fewer people take part in elections, working for candidates or contributing to campaigns. Only 9 percent attended a political meeting, only 4 percent campaigned on behalf of a candidate or party, 13 percent gave money to a political cause, only 18 percent went so far as to wear a button supporting a candidate, and less than half of the American public tried to influence how others voted. Democracy is not a spectator sport: it requires participation. And yet, the American public is not only not participating, but also not even spectating!

The consistency with which Americans choose not to participate in our democracy suggests that the edifice of the entire democratic experiment in the United States is dependent on workers who are not on the job. And yet, the United States, despite its many democratic shortcomings, still seems to be the standard that the rest of the world uses to measure democracy. How is it that a public that expresses inconsistent beliefs, that can be easily swayed from one side of the debate to the other, that does not participate in the process, that does not have confidence in the process, and that is ignorant in political matters can still hold the key to the functioning of American democracy? We begin to explore how the American public solves this dilemma in the next section.

RESTORING FAITH IN THE AMERICAN PUBLIC'S DUTY

The abilities of the American public to perform their crucial job are doomed from the beginning with the complexity that lies beneath the phrase *the voice of the people*. From a conceptually shaky ground, the record gets worse. And yet, as Madison argued, the people are critical for a properly functioning American democracy. How is it that a theoretically ambiguous concept, combined with the shameful record of the American public, has survived this long? In this section, we recount the genius of the framers of our system. They devised a governmental machine that does not require that expert machinists operate it.

The Vigilant American Spirit

The system designed by the framers and advocated by Madison does not require that the American people aggressively monitor their members of Congress, offering daily doses of rewards and rebukes for how they exercise their public authority. Such a system would fail when so few cannot even name the three branches of the federal government. The system only requires that the people evaluate their members every two years (for the House) and twice every six years (for the Senate). And, during these evaluation periods—what we call elections—the system is set up so that the members' records are described, analyzed, and debated by both the members themselves and those who hope to replace them. The system permits the overseer to be as lazy and unintelligent as possible and yet still exercise a well-informed opinion when that exercise is needed most.

When the American economy is humming along, civil rights and liberties are protected, and the military is keeping America's enemies at bay, the voters return the incumbents to their jobs in overwhelming numbers. As the unemployment rate goes up, as the elected officials get caught with their hands in the cookie jar (or worse), and as our foreign entanglements seem to get more entangled, incumbents stand on shakier ground. The elections of 2006, 2010, and 2018 show that when the American public is not pleased with the direction of the country, they exercise their vigilant spirit. In 2006, the voters gave the Republican Congress and President Bush a strong rebuke. Four years later, the Democrats in Congress and President Obama received, perhaps, an even stronger rebuke. And in 2018, even though Republicans held the Senate, they badly lost the House.

The American public need not always be vigilant; they only need to rise up when they perceive that the country is on the wrong track. Only vague notions of doing better or getting worse and a rough approximation of who is in charge can translate into well-reasoned choices during elections.

Police Patrols and Fire Alarms

The vigilant spirit is aided by the system that the framers designed. Not only can the people become informed through the campaigns of incumbents and their challengers, but also people on the sidelines get—and stay—involved in the process. Oversight comes in two different forms.[7] The first is *police patrol*, where the oversight is constant. Just as the police monitor neighborhoods looking for illegal behavior, so the overseers in American politics should be constantly monitoring their members of Congress for wrongdoing.

The other type of oversight is that done through *fire alarms*. Unlike the police, who are on constant patrol, firefighters only jump into action when an alarm rings. Imagine how foolish it would be for the fire department to send fire trucks out in the neighborhoods to look for fires! It is just as silly for political pundits to expect the American public to constantly monitor members' behaviors. The people need not be well informed; they need only respond appropriately when the alarm goes off. Because other actors in the political process are engaged in police patrol, the American public can be lazy, ignorant, and uninformed.

The two actors that are most involved in police patrol are the media and interest groups. The media is constantly observing members, waiting for one of them to engage in inappropriate behavior so that a reporter can write the next Pulitzer Prize–winning article about another politician engaged in corrupt behavior. Interest groups perform the same function, though they frequently will do it not only on good government issues, but also on public policies. The Sierra Club, the National Rifle Association, and the Club for Growth—and other special interests—are constantly monitoring members of Congress for the American people so that they can turn their attention to much more enjoyable activities, such as voting for the next *American Idol* or their favorite dancing star.

Heuristics

Not only does the system help the American people, but so, too, does the human brain. Psychologists long ago discovered that humans develop mental shortcuts—what they call *heuristics*—to break down complex situations into simpler ones. Political scientists have found that people use these heuristics to make political decisions. As such, the process of voting does not require the people to gather all the information that they know about both candidates and seriously weigh it against the record and the conditions of the country to determine for whom they will vote. The process of voting is usually much easier.

The *likability* heuristic is probably the most important one that helps the people do their job. Voters need only decide who they like and then make political decisions through association. If a person really likes Senate minority leader Chuck Schumer (D-NY), she can simply adopt Schumer's preferences. Individuals can vote for the same people that Schumer would vote for and support the same policies he endorses. On a much larger scale, the American voter can use the likability heuristic when it comes to political parties. If the Republicans support healthcare reform, so, too, does the voter who likes the Republican Party. If the Republicans nominate Martha McSally for an open Senate seat in Arizona, the voter who likes the Republican Party likewise votes for McSally.

The Electoral Process: Adversarial and Competitive

Part of the genius of the American constitutional system is that it established adversarial relationships and that, from time to time, it requires the people to vote. Most of the time, the people can be lazy and inattentive, but because of the frequency of elections in the United States and the campaigns that precede them, the voters are asked to offer their opinions. The challengers must offer a compelling reason to reject the incumbents and the minority party must offer a compelling reason for the majority party to be deposed. If challengers in individual elections or the minority party across elections do not make the case, the legislative process continues as before. If, however, they do make the case for change, those in power lose power and those previously not in power gain it. The American people need not understand the minutiae of the legislative process, have the most profound understanding of how all the various features of the American government work, or have the most complex understanding of the ramifications of a two-thousand-page bill recently enacted into law; they just need to weigh in from time to time on how they think things are going. This constant recalibration of how Congress functions is all based on the adversarial nature of politics as structured by the constitutional framework.

Potential Preferences

The last and perhaps the most important way that an uninformed, distrusting, and lazy American public can still perform its very important duty in American democracy is because the elected officials think that the American public can do its job, and so they act in accord with the public's wishes. When member of Congress cast votes, accept campaign contributions, or meet with lobbyists, they are not usually under the attentive stare of the media camera or under the strict scrutiny of an interest group and, yet, they typically act as if they are. Members tend to develop a rationale for their every action, so that if this is the one action that makes it into a newspaper, they have a plausible story to explain it.

Although members know that their constituents do not have well-formed opinions about many public policies, they usually act in accordance with what they perceive their constituents' *potential preferences* to be.[8] If their constituents were well informed about a particular vote, what would they think? Members are afforded some latitude in how they construct these preferences, though the more realistic members are in thinking about their constituents' potential preferences, the less trouble they are likely to find themselves in during their next reelection campaign.

CONCLUSION

Writing the Constitution was only half the battle—perhaps even the easier half. Getting it ratified was at least equally difficult. The two framers who advocated most vociferously for its ratification were James Madison and Alexander Hamilton. The two shared many political beliefs, but one important belief that divided them was how the new government would gain legitimacy. Madison believed that the system needed to provide for constant consultation of the American public to be sure that its views were being implemented into policy. Legitimacy could only be ascertained if the American public had a stake in the process. We could think of Madison as having a *bottom-up* approach to government.

Hamilton, in contrast, thought that legitimacy could only be secured through the proper functioning of the government. If the American public approved of the effects of the policies its political leaders enacted, the system would be legitimized. If they disapproved, it would not be. Hamilton took a *top-down* view. What both leaders agreed on is that the acceptance of the American public was critical for the democratic experiment to work in the newly formed country. What they and their colleagues in Philadelphia put in place was a system with characteristics for both a bottom-up and a top-down approach to securing the American public's acceptance. Regularly held elections that include campaigns reaching out to the populace and a system where the ambition of incumbents was counteracted by the ambition of their challengers set the democratic experiment down a path that has continued to evolve and develop even today. The internet, blogs, Twitter, and Facebook each function as an outlet for the American public to express its outrage and desires. Political parties, interest groups, and the media provide the crucial constant oversight that keeps all members of Congress in line.

To be sure, the system is not perfect. But, given that the "workers" in our democratic operation rarely show up, do not know much about the machinery, do not care to learn about it, and are easily persuaded to jump from one side of a debate to the other, the system seems to do much better than the worker would suggest it does. The facts that Democrats point to the 2006, 2008, and 2018 elections as proof that democratic accountability is alive and well, that some ridicule the 2010 and 2014 elections as a sign of democratic failure, and that some Republicans view the 2006, 2008, and 2018 elections as illegitimate, but the 2010 and 2014 elections as an appropriate midcourse correction, underlie the durability and success of the American system. We the American people, however, must protect what we have been given. More than two hundred years of experience has shown us that if the system fails, it is only because we have failed the system.

COMMENTARY

The Politician's Take on the People

It is tempting—and reassuring—to note that the people themselves control the nation's destiny. The members of Congress, after all, are the employees of the national enterprise; the people form the board of directors. In a way, that is true. One of the best examples in my memory came after Ronald Reagan moved into the White House in 1981. The people had selected him to lay out a vision for the future, and more than thirty years later, many of the changes he brought to government continue to resonate. So, too, do the changes that came—this time against his wishes—in 1982, when voters decided his administration had read too much into his victory and gone too far in reshaping public policy; they gave the Democrats a stronger hand in Congress and thus did a little reshaping of their own.

But members of Congress understand *people power* somewhat differently than ordinary citizens might. As politicians who must gain the voters' approval to win seats in Congress, they (we; I did it, too) divide the people into classes. Here, those classes are not based on wealth or family or prestige; they are based on participation. Most politicians are neither cheered nor deflated by seeing poll results that show their popularity rising or slipping because they know that (a) those voters who have the strongest feelings about the issues will have far more of an impact on election results than other voters, even if the most committed are in the

(Continued)

minority; this is the *intensity factor* and it limits the power of the majority. A corollary (b) to the intensity factor is the turnout factor. Here is the hard truth about the limits of people power: for a candidate, it does not really matter whether the majority of voters favor his or her candidacy or that of another candidate; all that counts is which candidate is preferred by those people who actually show up to vote on Election Day. That will be a subset of the whole constituency and often, in a party primary, a very small subset. Two years before my first successful election, I appointed a coordinator of my Election Day get-out-the-vote activities—many months before the first campaign ads were written or the first doorbell rung or the first campaign speech given.

Yes, there is power in the people, but only in those who engage seriously in the process.

COMMENTARY

The Professor's Take on the People

The last nine congressional elections (2002–2018) classically show how in control the American voters are of the political system. In the aftermath of the extremely competitive 2000 presidential race between Republican George W. Bush and Democrat Al Gore, only decided by a slim 5–4 vote in the Supreme Court, the entire system could have devolved into a constitutional crisis. The deep reservoir of confidence that the Supreme Court enjoyed and the class with which Gore handled his defeat steadied a ship of state that could have had to weather much more tumultuous waters. After the attacks that the United States endured on September 11, 2001, the system again could have faltered. Instead, the two sides of the partisan war, together, passed legislation to secure our homeland. In the 2002 and 2004 elections, the Republicans were rewarded with continued, though certainly not overwhelming, majorities.

In 2006 and 2008, when Americans began questioning our involvement abroad and the lack of economic growth at home, the Republicans were thrown out and the Democrats, in the wake of Obama's election, controlled the House, Senate, and presidency for the first time since Clinton's first two years in office (1993–4). The American public scaled back the Democratic dominance in the 2010 elections by returning the House to Republican hands. In 2012, those in power (Democrats in the White House and Senate and Republicans in the House) remained in power as the American economy—perhaps a bit too slowly for some—began to recover. In 2014, Republicans captured the Senate, which they had lost eight years prior. In 2016, A Republican was returned to the White House, and two years later, that party lost many seats in Congress.

Despite the influence of special interests, the media, congressional district line-drawers, and all the other threats to American democracy, the American voters' voice was not diminished. The closeness of the 2002, 2004, 2012, and 2016 elections sent the signal to those in power that they could continue exercising their power, but they needed to be cautious else they lose it. The overwhelming victories for the Democrats in 2006, 2008, and 2018 and for the Republicans in 2010 and 2014 showed that nothing short of all-out corruption could have kept their overwhelming sentiment from being realized in the political process.

In the United States, even if the American voter lacks confidence, does not know much about the process, does not participate much, and has fickle views, the system works. Truly, we get the government that we deserve. While Democrats may lament the uncompromising nature of the Tea Party Republicans, no one is surprised that the victors in the 2010 and 2014 elections are not compromising— they were elected precisely because they told the voters that they would not compromise. Democrats may want to blame congressional procedures, the institutional leadership, or even the entire framework, but the voters got exactly what they wanted. As the calendar turned to 2013, Republicans may have complained that the tax compromise reached to avert the *fiscal cliff* involved too many capitulations by Republicans and not enough on Obama's part as the tax rates expired for the richest Americans, but the election results from two months prior made clear that Democrats held the upper hand on taxes. Indeed, the power of the people remains strong!

CHAPTER 3

Getting Elected to Congress

Above all, politics is about ideas. The greatest misunderstanding about politics—and the people who become actively involved in politics—is the belief that most of the people who seek elective office are interested only in accumulating power. But while most Americans are studiously—perhaps determinedly—nonideological, most of the men and women who run for public office or actively engage in political campaigns do so because they hold relatively strong beliefs about some aspect of the relationship between citizens and the government.

Whether it is a belief in less government and more individual choice or a belief in more government and greater numbers of constraints on individual behavior, it is political belief that rouses passions and instigates both candidacies and election activism. If the Congress is, among other things, the arena in which competing values are debated, then political campaigns are the first step in determining which positions will ultimately prevail. Most members of Congress arrive in Washington with predetermined attitudes toward whole ranges of policy questions.

Many of these issues—and disagreements about them—play a central role in our elections and help to determine which candidate will ultimately be elected to Congress. Central to each issue is the candidate's view of the proper role of government or whether one should be concerned primarily with protecting the rights of the individual or more with advancing the interests of the society as a whole. These questions are central to determining who will sit in the House or Senate, debating alternatives and deciding the laws that we will all live under.

In 1993, a gunman killed Carolyn McCarthy's husband and injured her son as they were riding the Long Island Rail Road commuter train. Five other passengers died. McCarthy, who was then a licensed practical nurse, became a strong advocate for gun control. When her congressman, Daniel Frisa (R-NY), a former marketing representative for Johnson & Johnson, voted for the repeal of the assault weapons ban, she turned her anger into action and challenged him in the 1996 election. She won by 16 percentage points. After serving in the House for more than ten years, she was still known as the gun lady in her district. In an effort to expand her legacy in 2009, she introduced a bill to implement President Obama's promise to expand the AmeriCorps program. The House quickly passed the bill. Despite opposition from Senate minority leader Mitch McConnell (R-KY), a former Jefferson County judge who thought the price tag was too large, more than half of the Republicans—and all Democrats—supported it. One supporter, Orrin Hatch (R-UT), who worked as a janitor and construction worker while paying his way through law school, suggested that the bill be renamed in honor of Senator Ted Kennedy (D-MA), who enlisted in the Army after being kicked out of Harvard for cheating on a final exam, because of his lifelong commitment to volunteer service; Kennedy died less than six months later.

The story of the AmeriCorps expansion illustrates that the people pulling the levers of government in the United States come from various backgrounds with differing levels of interaction with the government in their previous jobs. How does one join this circle of power? How does one get the authority to help set the national agenda? How does one become the government? In this chapter we examine the electoral process: Who decides who will run? What determines who will win? We will study the roles of money and volunteers and examine the effect of the high cost of modern campaigns on the political process. In reading this chapter, a student should ask, is the system fair? Does it fulfill the national promise of self-government or does it perpetuate the concentration of power in the hands of the wealthy few? Does an outsider have a realistic chance of being elected to Congress?

A HISTORICAL PERSPECTIVE ON CONGRESSIONAL ELECTIONS

The election system in place today was not born fully mature from the Constitution. In fact, the Constitution is remarkably silent about some of the basic particulars of congressional elections. Article I, Section 4, gives the state legislatures the power to determine the time, place, and manner of holding congressional elections, but grants Congress the right to alter these regulations except for the choosing of US senators, which, according to the Constitution, was reserved for the state legislatures. Article I, Section 2, which established the House of Representatives, prescribes the electorate for congressional elections. Rather than establishing national standards that would pit one state with an expansive view of enfranchisement against another state that severely restricted it, the Constitution dictated that whoever could vote in the more numerous body of the state legislature could also vote in US House elections. This compromise kept the constitutional convention from having to engage in the painful debate about who ought to have the right to vote—a question that surely would have paralyzed it. Article I, Section 5, gave the respective chambers of Congress the power to resolve disputed elections. The Constitution provides little beyond these three dictates for the running and management of congressional elections.

Early Congressional Election Contests

Upon the ratification of the Constitution, it became the responsibility of the political leaders to determine how the mandates of the Constitution could be carried out. Within a few short years, the newly formed political parties became the dominant players in congressional elections. The party would determine who would run for which seat in which legislative body. Self-starters faced insurmountable odds of winning an election—or even standing for an election—without the blessing of the party leaders. The political career of nineteenth-century Speaker Henry Clay demonstrates the fluidity of politicians' careers during the party-dominated system. In 1803, Clay was elected to the Kentucky General Assembly. Three years later, he was chosen by the Kentucky legislature to fill a vacancy in the US Senate. When he returned to Kentucky in 1807, he was elected Speaker of the Kentucky House of Representatives, a position he kept until 1810, when the legislature again chose him to fill a vacancy in the US Senate. The following year, he was elected to the US House, where, on its first day in session and his first day of serving in the body, he was elected Speaker. In 1815, he resigned his seat so that he could serve as a peace commissioner to help draft the Treaty of Ghent, which officially ended the War of 1812. Upon his return to the United States, he won his House seat and, again, the Speaker's chair, where he remained for the next three congresses. He took a hiatus from the House in 1821 and 1822, but returned—again as Speaker—for one additional congress in 1823. He ran for president in 1824 and lost, but was decisive in swinging the election to John Quincy Adams, who named him secretary of state. He held the position for the entirety of Adams's presidency. In 1831, he returned to the Senate, where he remained until 1842. At the beginning of this twelve-year stint, he again ran unsuccessfully for president in 1832. Twelve years later, he again was defeated for president. In 1848, the Kentucky legislature again elected him to the Senate, where he served until his death in 1852. Over the course of his career, he served two disjointed terms in the Kentucky

General Assembly, three disjointed terms in the House, and four disjointed terms in the Senate and unsuccessfully ran for president three times.

During this era, the parties—not the individual candidates—organized precincts, recruited candidates, provided volunteers, offered expertise, and contributed the money required to run campaigns. It was not atypical in many states for party officials to direct every stage of a candidate's campaign, from issue selection to the design and placement of billboards and placards. In some ways, this system was similar to the election process used today in nations with a parliamentary system of government. In a typical parliamentary system, voters essentially choose between competing parties. After elections, the leaders of the prevailing party take over management of the government. The party's legislative leader is chosen to serve as prime minister. Because the party leader, the prime minister, and the majority in parliament are all from the same political bloc (the leader and prime minister are, in fact, the same person), dissatisfied voters can show their displeasure at the next election by simply voting against the party that formed the government. In these systems, party, rather than constituency, dominates. Frequently, the candidate running for office from a particular district is not even from the district. They are selected to run in that district to serve the larger needs of the party. The candidate's campaign is essentially a tag-along to the national campaign of the party and its candidate for prime minister.

While the United States has never had a parliamentary system of government, it has at times operated as if seats in Congress were the private patronage of local party bosses. The twentieth-century examples of the Pendergast machine in Kansas City (credited with launching Harry Truman's political career), the Daley machine in Chicago, and the powerful Tammany Hall in New York earned national notoriety. Less noticed, but equally powerful, were the various city and county political bosses, often serving as the local leadership of the parties. Candidates were not chosen because of their legislative acumen or their policy expertise, but because they were loyal to the machine. In turn, once they were members of Congress, they would return the spoils of office to the parties that selected them and ran their elections.

The Seventeenth Amendment to the Constitution changed one of the three constitutional mandates of congressional elections by making the people directly responsible for the election of senators. Even before ratification in 1913, the states implemented a variety of different voting mechanisms to give the people a voice in the process, though most of these were nonbinding. Within two years of its passage in Congress, the amendment was ratified by three-fourths of the states, giving the people even more power in choosing their members of Congress.

Candidate-Centered Elections

While the party domination of congressional elections survived the collapse of the Whig Party, the birth of the Republican Party, and the waging of the Civil War, it began to lose steam in the second half of the nineteenth century with the adoption of the Pendleton Act of 1883, which forbade parties from forcing their elected and appointed officials to contribute to the political parties' coffers. It also made merit, instead of party loyalty, the basis for receiving a civil service job. The Progressive Era reforms further diminished the power of parties. The secret ballot provided voters with an easy mechanism to vote for individual candidates rather than entire party slates. It also opened up the primary system, which reduced the party's power by closing the smoke-filled backrooms where nominations had typically been sought and granted.

As these reforms took root and became more entrenched, candidates became more responsible for their own careers. As television made communications easier and the money to fund campaigns became more tightly controlled and monitored, individual candidates became even more responsible for their own elections and careers. The political career of Clay's modern-day counterpart—Speaker Paul Ryan—illustrates the effect of candidate-centered elections and careers. After winning a seat in the House of Representatives, Ryan fulfilled his political goals by gaining seniority in the chamber and eventually rising to its most important position. Like his recent predecessors, he did not use the Speaker's chair as the base for a higher political office. Although he may harbor higher political office in the future, he would be the first Speaker to use that position for a higher office since Speaker John Nance Garner, who was elected vice president in 1932, sharing the ticket with Franklin Roosevelt.[1]

The transformation from a party-centered congressional election system to a candidate-centered system had consequences above and beyond the careers of the politicians. First, the party-centered system re-warded loyalty, whereas the candidate-centered system rewards ingenuity. In the earlier period, candidates would be provided with all the resources they needed to run a credible race. In the later period, only candidates who obtained those resources could run credible races.

Second, the members of Congress had differing levels of accountability. In the party-centered system, the members were first and foremost accountable to the party. Many members were denied their party's renomination. Only after receiving the blessing from the party could a member seek renewed approval from their constituents. In the candidate-centered system, it became rarer for members to be defeated for their own party's nomination.

Third, the types of candidates that emerged under the systems differ. In a party-dominated system, the individuals who received the nomination were the candidates who could win the general election. This meant that the Democratic Party leaders would nominate a fiscal and social conservative for a conservative southern district and the Republican Party leaders would nominate a liberal Republican in a liberal northeastern district. The party leaders' first responsibility was to win elections. In a candidate-centered election, however, electability is only one consideration primary voters have when they cast their ballots. Usually the primary voters' biggest consideration is ideology. Under a candidate-centered election, it is more common to see candidates running to the extremes in the primary and to the middle in the general election.

In a candidate-centered system, the political parties, then, can be an asset or a detriment. As recently as the late 1970s, in the South and Southwest, candidates who ran for office on a Republican ticket often decided not to list their party identification on billboards and yard signs. They tried to win despite, not because of, party affiliation. On the other hand, those same candidates received important help from their parties, as did Democratic candidates. While most candidates had to raise the majority of their funds on their own and recruit their own volunteers as well, the parties provided training schools for candidates and campaign managers, lists of potential contributors, and access to such volunteer-rich, party-affiliated organizations as the local Federation of Republican Women or the Young Democrats clubs. Political parties often maintain staffs of experts in fundraising, polling, organization, and advertising design, all of whom are available to supplement the candidate's own team of specialists.

Because the candidates have taken control of the congressional election process, the number of ordinary citizens who have thrown their hat in the ring has grown enormously. In the 2014 elections, for example, 279 people who ran during the general election for a seat in the House had never held public office—14 of them won their election. As FIGURE 3.1 shows, getting on the ballot is not the same as winning a seat because many more candidates lose than win, but a central feature of the system established by the framers was that in the United States, we would be a government of the people. In the 2014 election, 1,841 candidates spent funds in excess of $5,000, which required them to file campaign expenditure reports with the Federal Election Commission. Of those who filed reports, 858 won their primaries. Eventually, 435 of those candidates won seats in the House.

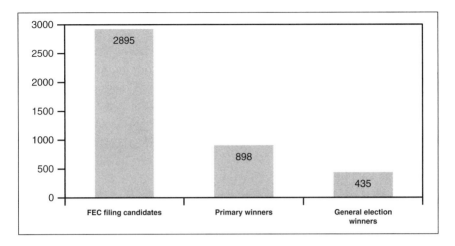

Figure 3.1 Candidates for the US House of Representatives, 2018.
Source: www.opensecrets.org/overview/index.php?cycle=2018

THE FOUR FACTORS OF CONGRESSIONAL ELECTIONS

With days to go before an election, newspapers, televisions, and blogs are filled with analysis of who is up and who is down. Pundits speculate about which party will control which chamber and what that will mean for negotiations between the White House and Congress. Such times are filled with excitement, anticipation, and anxiety. Political scientists, too, get caught up in the exhilaration. While the last commercials, Election Day weather, and last-minute surprises can tilt an election in one direction or the other, the broad scope of who wins and who loses is determined long before the first ballot is even cast. To gain leverage on what decides election outcomes, political scientists break up the factors into four broad categories: fixed, long-term, medium-term, and short-term.

Fixed Factors

The fixed factors of congressional elections have their roots in the Constitution or US law. These dictates include the date of the election and the length of term for the members. We think of these factors as being fixed—that is, they do not change from one election cycle to the next. While the actual date may change, it has been since 1845 and will always be the Tuesday after the first Monday in November (supposing that Congress does not change the law). The winner of the election will always be the candidate with the most votes, who will then serve a two-year term in the House or a six-year term in the Senate. The fixed factors are the broad factors that set up the logistics and dynamics not only for one election cycle, but also for all future cycles.

Long-Term Factors

While the long-term factors are not necessarily spelled out in the Constitution, individual candidates in any particular race can think of them as being fixed—at least for a given election cycle. The difference between fixed factors and long-term factors is that the latter can change from election cycle to election cycle. The most obvious long-term factor that helps to explain election outcomes is the district boundaries. According to the US Constitution, the number of seats that each state gets in the House of Representatives must be reconfigured to minimize the population variation across the states. This process is known as reapportionment. After the seats in the House are reapportioned to the states, each state with more than one seat must undergo redistricting to minimize population variation across districts in their state. While reapportionment was faithfully carried out since the nation's founding, it was only in the 1960s that the Supreme Court, through a series of opinions, mandated that states redistrict. Until then, some states redistricted every ten years (or even more frequently), while other states rarely redistricted.

District lines change, but rarely do they change within an election cycle. While Texas's 10th district in 2018 may look different than it did in 2008, for the candidates running for the 10th district in 2018, the lines are fixed—they do not change over the course of the election, except in rare circumstances when the court system has mandated changes to comply with federal law or when new political majorities implement lines more favorable for their party. District lines for senators are a fixed factor because those lines do not change except in extraordinary circumstances, such as when Maine separated from Massachusetts in the Missouri Compromise of 1820 or when West Virginia broke away from Virginia during the Civil War.

Another important long-term factor is party registration numbers. While voters may change their official party affiliation over the course of the election, broadly speaking, the ratio of Democrats to Republicans in a district or state does not dramatically change from the beginning of the campaign to the end. That is not to say that the number of votes for the Democrats and Republicans does not change, just that the party registration numbers do not change that much. On Election Day, only 40 percent of Democrats may show up and only 70 percent of them may vote for the Democratic candidate. In contrast, 55 percent of Republicans may cast a vote and the Republican candidate may get 95 percent of their votes. Regardless, the underlying ratio of party-registered Democrats to party-registered Republicans stays essentially the same throughout an election cycle.

The other large set of long-term factors includes all the laws that define the electorate and implement the logistics of an election. States are continuously tweaking who can vote and the manner in which they do it. As an example, many states now permit early voting. State law can change the early voting period, though that change is likely to occur long before the campaign gets under way. States can also change the enfranchisement law—whether felons can vote, for example. Last, states can change the requirements for voting, such as voter identification cards, absentee ballot requirements, or the opening and closing times for the polling stations (see Table 3.1). While all of these factors can change within an election cycle, they are likely to remain constant once the real campaign starts.

Table 3.1 Changes Since the 2016 Election That Made Voting Easier or Harder

STATE	CHANGE TO STATE LAW	EFFECT
Arkansas	Reinstate voter identification	Harder to vote
Florida	To make it easier to vote without showing up to the polls on Election Day	Easier to vote
Georgia	To make voter registration more difficult	Harder to vote
Idaho	Modified voter identification law less burdensome	Easier to vote
Indiana	To make it easier to register	Easier to vote
Iowa	To require voter identification, restrict voter registration efforts, and impose new burdens on Election Day registration and early and absentee voting	Harder to vote
Kansas	To make it easier to vote without showing up to the polls on Election Day	Easier to vote
Montana	To prevent civic groups and individuals from helping others vote absentee by collecting and delivering their voted ballots (not yet approved by voters)	Harder to vote
New Jersey	To make it easier to vote without showing up to the polls on Election Day	Easier to vote
North Dakota	Reinstate voter identification	Harder to vote
Tennessee	To make it easier to vote without showing up to the polls on Election Day	Easier to vote
Utah	To make it easier to vote without showing up to the polls on Election Day	Easier to vote
Virginia	To make it easier to vote without showing up to the polls on Election Day	Easier to vote
Wyoming	To restore the right to vote for people with criminal convictions	Easier to vote

Source: The Brennan Center, https://www.brennancenter.org/analysis/voting-laws-roundup-2017, accessed April 26, 2018.

Medium-Term Factors

Medium-term factors can change within an election season, but the individual candidates do not have control over them. Examples of medium-term factors include the unemployment rate, the president's approval rating, and, during times of war, the number of casualties. The candidates are very much expected to react to these changes, but have no control over changing them. As the 2008 election season wore on, the economy faltered. On September 29, approximately five weeks before the election, the stock market fell 777.68 points, the largest drop in history, wiping away $1.7 trillion in market value. No congressional candidate had any control over this cataclysmic plunge, but every candidate had to react to the news.

Short-Term Factors

The short-term factors are those things that individual candidates can control. These include campaign commercials, fundraising strategies, visits from high-profile politicians, and debate strategies—in a word, we can think of short-term factors as the *campaign*. The short-term factors are the things that receive media coverage in the days leading up to the election because they are the only factors that are changing, which make for better and more interesting stories.

Good debate performances or compelling commercials have made political strategists extremely important in the running of congressional campaigns. On occasion, congressional campaigns create just the right commercial to fit the times and their race. In her 2014 race for an open Senate seat in Iowa, Joni Ernst used a commercial that parlayed her experience of castrating pigs on her family farm to her abilities to cut pork in Washington to come from behind to win the Republican nomination and, eventually, the general election. While an ad like hers

is relatively rare, it happens frequently enough that political scientists and pundits must always keep an eye on what is happening with candidates during a campaign.

Which Factors Matter Most?

Although politicians, journalists, pundits, and bloggers focus most of their attention on the short-term factors, most political scientists agree that these factors are the least important in predicting who wins and who loses on election night. No doubt, these factors can play an important role in the very close elections that could tilt a chamber toward one party or the other, but in the broad scope of understanding congressional elections, most winners and losers are determined before the first ballot is cast or even before the first campaign commercial is aired.

Consider for a moment the 2018 election cycle. It was one of the most dynamic and unpredictable in a generation. Nonetheless, well more than 75 percent of the seats were never—not even for the slightest minute—in play. While Senate seats are typically more competitive, on average, than House seats, more than half were not in play. At the beginning of the cycle, prognosticators deemed seventeen Senate seats safe for one party or the other. Of those, only 3 slipped into a more competitive category (*safe* to *likely, lean,* or *tossup).*

Political scientists generally think that medium-term factors are not as important as long-term and fixed factors. Again, consider the 2018 election. Trump's approval stood at 40 percent (while 54 percent disapproved) and Congress, which had Republican majorities in the House and Senate, was even less popular—only 13 percent of the American public approved of the job Congress was doing; 53 percent disapproved. The conditions for the majority party were as bad as they had been for Republicans since 1974. And, yet, on Election Night, more than 200 Republicans still managed to win. If medium-term factors were the most important, that number should have been much lower.

Nonetheless, the tilting of districts or states in one direction or the other frequently determines which party controls which chamber. These district-by-district and state-by-state tilts have very important consequences. These *tilts* are what campaigns are all about. But, if you want to know which candidates will win, you will do far better in your predictions if you know the long-term factors affecting the candidate than if you know only the medium- and short-term factors. For example, if a candidate produces the perfect campaign commercials, delivers flawless debate performances, and receives all the best endorsements, but is running in a district where her opponent enjoys a two-to-one party registration advantage, all her efforts will be wasted come Election Day.

For much of the time since World War II, overall outcomes were not in dispute. Even while they regularly won the presidency, Republicans could not figure out how to secure majorities in both chambers of Congress. Ronald Reagan's election in 1980 ushered in a Republican majority in the Senate; fourteen years later, Republicans finally achieved a majority in both chambers for the first time since 1952. Since then, the majority party's margins have been lower, meaning that 10 percent of the close races on Election Day can swing the majority across the aisle. This closeness exacerbates the focus on short-term factors because how these factors play out determines which party will have a majority in the House and Senate. As Election Day draws near and the horse race media coverage escalates, never forget that 90 percent of the elections will not be close because fixed, long-term, and medium-term factors have already pointed to a winner. Because the other factors are durable and rather straightforward and because of the competitiveness between parties today, in the next section we break down the short-term factors, otherwise known as the campaign.

THE CAMPAIGN

Although the medium- and short-term factors are the least important in understanding which candidates will win and lose, political scientists match pundits and bloggers in the amount of time that they spend analyzing these factors. While the remainder of this chapter focuses on the campaigns, students of congressional elections must not lose sight of the importance of fixed and long-term factors if they want to understand the broad landscape of outcomes on Election Night. Up to now, we have talked about *the* campaign, but we should distinguish between the primary and the general election. In the following description, we will make explicit when the factors only affect one or the other of these campaigns.

The Candidates

The diversity of the United States is reflected to some degree in its congressional candidates. Because there is no typical congressional district, it is hard to describe a typical congressional candidate. Nonetheless, to get analytic leverage on thinking about congressional candidates, we break them down into two broad categories: challengers and incumbents. An incumbent is a member of Congress who is running in a district that he or she currently represents. A challenger is any candidate who is not the current member for that district. Challengers, in turn, come in two forms: those who challenge an incumbent and those who run in open seats, which are defined as those races in which no incumbent is running. The overwhelming number of congressional contests includes incumbents. In this section, we first describe the recruitment process and then the role of incumbents.

Recruitment

Candidate recruitment has come a long way since party bosses, meeting in a smoke-filled room, hammered out lists of candidates for the general election. More remnants of that process likely exist than most politicians and political observers would like to admit. Recruitment is probably the most important and least studied aspect of congressional campaigns. Recruitment is crucial because the right candidate can make a seemingly noncompetitive race competitive. Consider the vacancy created when Robert Byrd (D-WV) died in 2010. During his

long tenure in Congress, West Virginia became increasingly reliably Republican. While Barack Obama in 2008 had received 53 percent of the vote nationwide, he only received 43 percent of the vote in West Virginia—it was his thirteenth worst state. In the days leading up to the special election for the vacant West Virginia Senate, Obama's statewide approval rating had fallen to 28 percent.[2] Only one Democratic candidate in the entire state had even a chance of holding on to Byrd's seat: the popular governor Joe Manchin. When Manchin decided to enter the race, Byrd's seat went from being forecast as a Republican takeover to a Democratic hold. Despite the Republican strategy of showing a famous hug that Manchin shared with Obama at Byrd's funeral, Manchin won the special election to finish Byrd's term with 54 percent of the vote. Two years later, Manchin received more than 60 percent of the vote for a six-year term, even while Obama only received 36 percent in the state. Despite Hillary Clinton's poor 26 percent showing in West Virginia in 2016 (her second worst state behind Wyoming), Manchin's success in the state continued and he won his 2018 election by 3.2 points.

Likewise, the wrong candidate can snatch defeat from the jaws of victory. Within six months of Manchin's victory in West Virginia, a House seat in New York became vacant when its occupant, Anthony Weiner, sent sexually suggestive photographs of himself via his public Twitter account. In 2010, Weiner defeated Bob Turner by 18 percentage points. Despite Weiner's scandal, the Democrats were expected to hold on to the seat, which, in part, exacerbated the calls for his resignation in the immediate aftermath of the offending tweet. The Democrats selected David Weprin, a member of the New York Assembly, to run in the special election. After running a lackluster campaign and despite holding a three-to-one advantage in party registration numbers, Weprin lost to Turner by 6 percentage points.

Manchin and Weprin represent not only most of the continuum from good candidate to bad, but also a continuum of the party's role in selecting candidates. Manchin, for all intents and purposes, was the Democratic Party in West Virginia. He chose to run for that office and orchestrated the mechanics behind the election to smooth his transition from the governor's mansion to the Senate. At the other end of the continuum, Weprin was chosen by the leading Democrats in New York City to run for the seat. His candidacy was predicated on his selection. The rank-and-file Democrats had very little influence in Weprin's selection. To infer from Weprin's race that party bosses choose bad candidates is to make a rash judgment from one case. In many other cases, bosses choose good candidates and, likewise, voters choose bad candidates. The candidates can have a significant effect on a race, but the way in which they are selected rarely does.

Influential people in the party can recruit good candidates in many ways. Sometimes merely mentioning to someone that she or he would make a good candidate propels the person's candidacy. Other times, party officials promise help through campaign donations, campaign strategies and experts, or clearing the field of other potential candidates. Each district is different, with a different mix of influential people in it that can change from election cycle to election cycle.

The ability of the average citizen to choose one of his or her neighbors to make the laws, or to go to Washington personally as a member of Congress, creates the ultimate safeguard: the ultimate empowerment and constraint. This ability to select oneself for a role in American politics is a key element in the formation of a government of the people. In America, anyone can be elected to anything. The seats of power are open to one and all. A man or woman may simply decide one day while mowing a lawn, taking a shower, dressing a child, or cursing the evening news that something needs to be done, and he or she is just the person to do it. The founders placed much of the nation's power in the hands of the people by establishing a system in which the Congress   the people's representatives— would have the ultimate authority over the laws and taxes that affected them. The founders envisioned a governmental system that combined both empowerment and constraint and brought the system to life by empowering ordinary citizens to take the reins of federal decision making and by giving the citizens, through their representatives, the ability to constrain governmental power.

Many candidates simply select themselves for the job and jump into the race feet first, often with no experience as a candidate and few initial advantages. They do so regardless of family, wealth, education, connections, gender, race, age, religion, or sexual orientation. To become a candidate, a person typically must simply pay the required filing fees or gather the necessary signatures to have his or her name entered in the more than a thousand races that take place every year to determine who will sit in the Congress. They need not be anointed; they need only have a strong desire to have an effect on the system. While some men and women who run for public office may do so for the prestige or for the ego gratification that comes with holding high office, most are, by nature, doers—the kinds of people who want to effect change. Running for office gives them the opportunity to do that.

The day after President Trump was inaugurated, the largest single-day protest in US history took place in at least 408 marches throughout the United States and at least another 168 marches in eighty-one countries. In total, around five million people took part in marches around the globe—the largest of which, the Women's March on Washington, had around half a million participants. The activism spurred by Trump's victory and inauguration persisted. Representatives of Emily's List, which seeks to elect pro-choice female candidates, talked with 920 women in the 2016 cycle. In the 2018 cycle, more than 15,000 women, from every walk of life, contacted Emily's List about running for office. In 2016, President Barack Obama named Jahana Hayes the "Teacher of the Year." Two years later, she entered the race to replace her congresswoman, who had recently announced her retirement. After winning her election in 2018, she will continue her desire to improve her students' lives, but instead of doing so from the front of the classroom, she will be doing it from the floor of the House of Representatives.

The Congress also has its share of industrialists and inheritors of both name and wealth. Romneys and Udalls take seats in the Senate as Kennedys and Cheneys have taken seats in the House of Representatives. Only after earning millions in software, car alarms, and online cards did Greg Gianforte (R-MT), Darrell Issa (R-CA), and Jared Polis (D-CO) begin their career in public service. Congressional candidates with pedigrees and their own resources can have an easier time getting to Congress because they have the means to estab-lish themselves in the early stages of a campaign, whereas candidates without money and a family organization struggle. Nevertheless, the roll of congres-sional candidates who have lost includes the names of many rich people.

Newt Gingrich (R-GA), who rose to be Speaker of the House, Paul Wellstone (D-MN), elected to the Senate from Minnesota, and David Brat (R-VA), who defeated the then House majority leader in a primary, were college professors who decided to run against well-entrenched incumbents and filed for office with little encourage-ment from leaders in their communities. Curt Weldon, from Pennsylvania, was a fire chief before he was elected to Congress. Al Franken (from *Saturday Night Live*), Fred Thompson (from *Law and Order*), and Sean Duffy (from *Real World*) were television personalities; Jim Bunning, Heath Shuler, J. C. Watts, and Jon Runyan were profes-sional athletes. Patty Murray, a housewife who had never run for office before, nom-inated herself based on her experience as a mom in tennis shoes; today, she sits as a three-time-reelected US senator and one of the real power brokers for the Democrats in the Senate. This pattern is repeated election cycle after election cycle.

The parties have taken an increasingly active role in recruiting candidates. In fact, a key person in both parties takes on the responsibility of finding com-petitive candidates in every race. These members of Congress will vote by day and talk to local citizens, community leaders, and party volunteers back in the districts by night to ensure that their parties will have as many good candidates as possible running throughout the country.

Sometimes these recruitment efforts pay off. In 2012, the mom-in-tennis-shoes-turned-senator, Patty Murray, chaired the Democratic Senatorial Cam-paign Committee. Her primary role was to find good candidates and ensure that they had the resources to run competitive races. When her colleague, Kent Conrad (D-ND), announced his retirement, most pundits moved that state from solid Democrat to safe Republican. It was thought that no Democrat could make the race competitive during a presidential election year in a state that Obama lost in 2012 by almost 9 percentage points. Murray enticed Heidi Heitkamp, a former North Dakota attorney general, to make the run. She struck the perfect balance of policy moderation and homespun personality to win the race by less than 1 percentage point—a result that was unthinkable even a couple of months prior to the election. In 2018, the partisanship of her state finally caught up to her when Heitkamp lost by about 10 points, in a state that Hillary Clinton lost by 36 points.

Other times, the strategy to get behind a candidate before the primary back-fires. Senate Jim Bunning (R-KY) had long been a feckless campaigner and an unpredictable senator. The Republican establishment successfully got him to an-nounce his retirement in July 2009. The same establishment rallied around the candidacy of Trey Grayson, who was then serving as Kentucky's secretary of state.

Even before Bunning's announcement, the grassroots Tea Party movement pushed Rand Paul, an ophthalmologist and son of Congressman Ron Paul (R-TX), to run. He did. During the campaign, Paul portrayed Grayson as the embodiment of establishment in an election cycle where voters were looking for outsiders. Paul won the nomination by 23 percentage points and the general election by 12 points. One can be anointed to run, but as Grayson can attest, winning is something else entirely.

For some candidates, it is fulfilling just to run and be an active part of the process. They have no intention of winning. Some want to push a particular issue. Cindy Sheehan, whose son, Casey, died in the Iraq War, famously established Camp Casey outside president George W. Bush's ranch in Crawford, Texas. To keep the spotlight on the antiwar movement, Sheehan ran against Nancy Pelosi in the 2008 election. In a seven-person race, Sheehan finished second, with 16 percent of the vote. Others want to gain some name recognition to further their law or medical practice. Still others want to run a credible race so that when a future opening presents itself, they have some experience and early name recognition. In 1996, businessman Mark Warner opted to run against popular incumbent Senator John Warner (R-VA). No one, including Mark Warner (who is not related to John), thought that the incumbent would lose. Mark Warner ran a respectable race and did better than many pundits expected. Five years later, Warner became the presumptive Democratic nominee for governor and won the election by about 5 percentage points. When John Warner opted for retirement in 2008, Mark Warner was easily elected to the Senate, nearly doubling the number of votes his Republican challenger received.

The Incumbents

Party officials are happiest if they do not have to engage in any recruitment effort whatsoever. For numerous reasons, the best candidate for almost all congressional races is the incumbent. First, incumbents usually win. Second, incumbents are usually better at securing campaign resources. Third, incumbents are usually well known by their constituents. Fourth, incumbents are not as likely to have primary battles that irreparably tear a party apart. Fifth, incumbents are less likely to have competitive general election contests. Luckily for parties, incumbents choose to run for reelection about 90 percent of the time, and when they run, 90 percent of the time they win.

Sometimes, though, incumbents choose against running for reelection. Ultimately, the decision to retire indicates either an attempt at a promotion to a higher office or a decision to recede from public life. Every election cycle, House members try to become senators, senators and House members try to become governors, and some try to move from Article I (the legislative branch) to Article II (the executive branch).

Other incumbents opt to retire not only from the House, but also from political life all together. Political scientists have discovered that several factors cause retirements, including old age, scandal, perturbations in their districts brought about by redistricting, electoral vulnerability, and reaching a *career ceiling*, which happens when a member's power in the legislature stagnates. In the 2018 cycle, five House Republicans retired because they had reached the end of their terms as chairs of committees. These retirements initiate the recruitment stage to the process and a new cycle of a congressional career.

The Power of Money

While it is a truism that anyone running for office can win, there is another more realistic truism: it is much harder for some candidates to win than others. Students of the political process have observed that potential candidates often decide whether to run based on an early assessment of their prospect for victory. Men and women who have thought about entering the political arena attempt to evaluate the likely opposition in terms of several factors: whether the probable opponent is an incumbent, which party the president belongs to, and how the president's popularity or lack thereof might affect the races of other candidates, whether the economy is strong and growing or weak and stagnant, how the public perceives the Congress and the government, and whether a district has a demonstrated willingness or reluctance to support a particular type of candidate.

But a candidate assessing his or her prospects for election must also take into account a more immediate consideration: How much money can the candidate raise? An answer to this question can be decisive in convincing even the most ambitious would-be politician not to run (not to mention the potential candidate's natural worries about media scrutiny, background investigations by opponents, and the general loss of privacy that follows when filing for public office).

While money is important for the explicit purpose of paying for campaign posters, television commercials, mail pieces, polls, campaign experts, and the supplies necessary to make a credible run, money plays an equally important implicit role in showing others that a candidate can make a serious run. If even the most qualified candidate stumbles in securing campaign contributions, the major players in the parties, unions, and businesses will remain on the sidelines. Only when a candidate can demonstrate that she can raise money will the other political actors notice and then act. Indeed, in contemporary campaigns, it takes money to raise money. Raising money is the best sign that outside actors can read in evaluating the seriousness of a campaign.

Several factors in recent years have combined to make it harder and harder for candidates to gather the resources necessary to run an effective congressional campaign. First, congressional districts continue to expand as the national population grows and the size of the House of Representatives remains fixed at 435 members, a size first set in 1913. In the reapportionment that followed the 1910 census, each House district had about 200,000 people in it, roughly the same number of people represented by the forty New Jersey state senators. Since the 2010 census, each House district has roughly 710,000 people in it, which was just less than the entire 1910 population of Florida, a state that now has 27 House seats. The growth in the US population means that candidates must raise more money to reach more voters than even a generation ago.

Second, the American population has become increasingly urban. In 1910, 54 percent of Americans lived in the rural areas of the country. By 1970, that percentage was halved. In the 2010 census, it dropped below 20 percent for the first time. The concentration of voters in urban clusters forces candidates to spend more money on mass media, which is a much less efficient way to advertise because the media markets are not coterminous with the congressional district lines. In 2018, when congressman Roger Williams (R-TX) ran television campaign commercials in Austin, Texas, they were seen not only by voters in his congressional district (the 25th), but also by those in the 10th, 21st, 27th, 31st, and 35th congressional districts. Williams had to either inefficiently spend money on television commercials or engage in the expensive and labor-intensive strategy of microtargeting potential voters.

Third, the level of expertise candidates require of their campaign consultants has grown. As the majority party margins in the House have decreased, the outcome of each race has become more important, so the demands on candidates to have the right experts in place is increasingly important. Polling has become a regular part of congressional campaigns. Fundraising experts, media experts, debate consultants, and social media experts have all driven up the costs of running a credible congressional campaign.

Not surprising, the costs of congressional campaigns have skyrocketed. In 1990, the midterm election during president George H. W. Bush's term, the average general election contest in the House cost $582,492; the average for a Senate seat was $4.3 million. In 2014, a House contest cost about $2.2 million and Senate races cost $15.6 million. Even after controlling for inflation, the contests in 2014 cost 60 percent more in the House and 34 percent more in the Senate than they did even just twenty years prior (SEE FIGURE 3.2 for a depiction of how the costs have grown).

In 2014, House candidates, on average, were given $1,093,405 to wage their campaigns. Approximately 53 percent of that money came from individuals, 37 percent from political action committees (PACs), 5 percent from the candidates themselves, and 1 percent from the parties (the remaining 4 percent came from unknown sources).[3] Senate candidates were given $7,827,052, and their breakdown differs a bit from that for the House. Senate

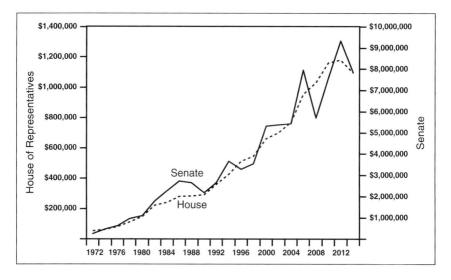

Figure 3.2 The Average Amount Raised by Congressional Candidates.
Source: Jacobson and Carson (2016).

candidates received 71 percent from individuals, 13 percent from PACs, 6 percent from the candidates themselves, and 4 percent from political parties, which means that 6 percent of the sources are unknown. These breakdowns have been consistent since the late 1970s, never wavering more than a few percentage points, even in years where Democrats did well and incumbents were overwhelmingly reelected.

Congressional candidates can spend their money on many different activities. Just as there are no typical districts or candidates, there are no typical campaigns. A broad assessment of several campaigns over time suggests that candidates spend 53 percent of their budget on communication, almost a third of which is on television ads. Forty percent of their expenditures go to overhead, including staff salaries (14 percent), fundraising (12 percent), and travel (4 percent). They spend the remaining 7 percent on research, which is approximately split between polling and opposition research.

The adage in analyzing how money is spent in elections is that half of the money is wasted. The problem for candidates and political scientists is that no one knows which half, and it has become exceedingly difficult to determine. If the world were a laboratory and political scientists were bench scientists, we could have Candidate A spend 80 percent of his budget on television advertising and Candidate B spend 20 percent of her budget on television advertising. We could see how they do and then speculate about the relative advantage of advertising on television. The problem is that congressional candidates want to win races; they do not want to help political scientists determine the ideal spending formula for congressional campaigns. As such, the adage is likely to continue in perpetuity.

Campaign Finance Laws

Regulating the money in congressional campaigns is a bit like playing Whac-A-Mole at the county fair. As soon as you stop too much money coming from one source, it finds an outlet in a different source; the consistency in percentages of campaign contributions that comes from individuals and PACs is evidence of this. Two key components in the previous sentence have been the ingredients of all campaign finance laws since the 1970s: *too much* and *source*. Until the reforms that were enacted in the early 1970s, the campaign financing laws were a patchwork of four laws. The Tillman Act of 1907 and the Smith–Connally Act of 1943 banned corporations and labor unions, respectively, from contributing to political campaigns. The Corrupt Practices Act of 1925 instituted reporting requirements for both political organizations and congressional candidates. It also placed a spending limit of $2,500 for House candidates and $10,000 for Senate candidates, although these limits could be raised to as much as $5,000 and $25,000, depending on the number of votes cast in the previous election. The 1940 amendments to the Hatch Act of 1939 established $5,000 contribution limits by an individual to any single individual or political committee. Political committees were limited to giving a total of $3 million in any single year. These laws contained numerous loopholes and exceptions, which candidates and political organizations easily exploited in practice.

As the amount of money that federal candidates spent on campaigns rose from $140 million in 1952 to $400 million in 1972,[4] members attempted to gain control of the financing system by passing the Federal Election Campaign Act of 1971, which contained five major provisions:

1. Limited the total amount candidates could spend on media advertising (which would be adjusted annually based on the Consumer Price Index)
2. Forced radio and television stations to offer political candidates the lowest unit costs for advertising time
3. Prohibited promises of employment in exchange for support
4. Limited the amount of their own money that candidates (and their families) could contribute to their campaigns
5. Instituted strict financial reporting requirements

The strict reporting requirements mandated by the Federal Election Campaign Act of 1971 were instrumental in providing the sunshine necessary for breaking and investigating the Watergate scandal. Watergate, then, fueled the most comprehensive campaign finance reform bill in congressional history. As then Senator Walter Mondale (D-MN) argued in early hearings on the bill, "The present system is not bad, it is rotten."[5] Passed as amendments to the 1971 act, the Federal Election Campaign Act of 1974 included the following provisions:

1. Established contribution limits ($1,000 per individual and $5,000 per organization per election)
2. Set spending limits ($100,000, or 8 cents per voter, for Senate primaries, $150,000, or 12 cents per voter, in Senate general elections and $70,000 for House primaries and general elections)
3. Repealed the media expenditure limit established by the 1971 act
4. Limited party spending to $10,000 in House elections and $20,000 in Senate elections
5. Strengthened the disclosure requirements
6. Established the Federal Election Commission
7. Instituted public financing for presidential contests

Although the Supreme Court, in its 1976 *Buckley v. Valeo* decision, struck down the Federal Election Campaign Act's spending limit provisions by equating political money to speech, the remaining provisions governed the campaign financing activities for candidates in both presidential and congressional elections for twenty-five years.[6]

To correct for abuses that began to creep into the financing system in the 1990s, Congress again passed reform. In 2002, the Bipartisan Campaign Reform Act, known also by its sponsors' names (McCain–Feingold in the Senate or Shays–Meehan in the House), became law. It had two major provisions. First, it banned soft money, which is defined as money that does not need to be reported to the Federal Elections Commission. Second, the act limited issue advocacy ads paid for by corporations or nonprofit organizations in the days leading up to the election.

In 2009, the Supreme Court, in *Citizens United v. Federal Election Commission*, struck down the latter provision, effectively nullifying the first provision as well. As a result, the amount of unaccountable money in campaigns is essentially without restriction. The Supreme Court ruled that the Bipartisan Campaign Reform Act unconstitutionally restricts the political speech of corporations, labor unions, and other associations. Since the decision, these groups have played an increasing role in American elections. Typically, these groups form super PACs to carry out their election-related activities. Though these super PACs have less stringent reporting requirements than candidates, they are still restricted from coordinating activities with the candidates or the candidates' official campaign organizations.

At issue with all these laws is a fundamental balance between fairness in elections and the fundamental principle of free speech. Some would limit the total amount of money a candidate could spend on his or her election; some would turn all campaign financing over to the federal government; some would require candidates to raise the bulk of their campaign funds from small individual contributions or from citizens who live in the district the candidate seeks to represent.

But citizen involvement, including financial support, is critical to the process of self-government. Citizens who believe deeply in the importance of certain issues, or in the general relationship between citizens and their government— whether they favor a more active government or a more limited one—ought to be involved in helping to shape the community's decisions. Observers have argued that all the nation's congressional candidates put together spend less on their campaigns than Americans spend for cigarettes or cheeseburgers. Many of the citizens who oppose spending limitations or federal financing of elections argue that the limitations would reduce the flow of information to the voters and federal financing would decrease still further the already low level of citizen participation in elections.

The Power of Organization

While money is important in congressional campaigns, it is not the only thing that matters. Organization, too, is of great consequence. Money and organization have a funny relationship in congressional campaigns. While a good organization can lead to more money and money can buy an organization, a good organization can also decrease the importance of money.

Campaign volunteers, like campaign money, have greatly evolved since the end of World War II. Candidates running for Congress forty years ago could usually count on a large supply of volunteers drawn primarily from the ranks of retirees and women, who then did not work outside the home in great numbers. It was common for a campaign to have an organized women's group—the Bellmon Belles (for Oklahoma Senate candidate Henry Bellmon), the Gibson Girls (for congressional candidate Glenn Gibson), and the like—who would show up in colorful uniforms to hand out brochures at public events, sign up volunteers at campaign coffees, and spend hours every day immersed in the camaraderie of the campaign headquarters. Those days have passed, but campaigns still heavily rely on volunteers—workers drawn from among a candidate's church or social friends, members of the local Democratic or Republican clubs, or interest groups that perceive a big impact on their issue dependent on the outcome of the race.

Given a choice between a large bank account and an army of volunteers, any knowledgeable candidate will choose the people, not the money (although all would probably prefer to have both). In 1974, voters in Milwaukee elected to Congress a young man named Robert Kasten (R-WI). Throughout the entire campaign, Kasten trailed his opponent. Polls continued to show him losing, even on the eve of the election. Yet on Election Day, Kasten won and went on to serve in both the House of Representatives and the US Senate. Kasten's secret was a campaign strategy that later came to be known among political operatives as the *Kasten plan*. Simply put, it assigned to each precinct in the congressional district a specified vote target based on an assessment of how many votes each precinct would have to produce to result in a district-wide victory. The targets were based on compilations of precinct-by-precinct election results in previous campaigns between Republican and Democratic candidates. In some precincts, this required a Kasten victory margin not of one vote, but of forty, or fifty, or seventy-three—whatever was required to offset projected losses in other precincts. In other precincts, the target was not victory—assumed to be an impossible task—but a loss by no more than a specified number of votes. So a Kasten worker in charge of one precinct might have a goal not of 50.1 percent, but of 57 percent, and a worker in another precinct might have a goal of 42 percent. Instead of trying to win even in precincts where winning was highly improbable, Kasten determined the outcome needed in each precinct to achieve an overall victory.

Robert Kasten did not come from a poor family: he and his relatives had access to the money needed to wage an effective campaign. But his opponent, an incumbent, also had access to money. For practical purposes, Kasten was in the same position as a candidate with no resources whatsoever: he could not win the election with dollars. His strategy, therefore, was simple: he would trump dollars with people.

Kasten's plan was completely dependent on volunteers. To make it work, he had to have a large and dependable campaign organization capable of reaching into every precinct. Every voter had to be contacted personally to determine which ones were likely to vote for Kasten on Election Day. Then, on that day, each favorable voter had to be contacted again—several times, if necessary—to ensure that each potential Kasten supporter went to the polls. Rides had to be provided to voters who could not get to the polls on their own. Kasten campaign workers had to be stationed at each polling place to keep track of which voters had arrived and which had not.

Years later, a candidate of the opposite party in the same state used a modified version of the Kasten plan to win an improbable election. In 1998, Scott Klug (R-WI) opted for retirement. Democrats figured that flipping the district was crucial in their effort to take back the House majority. Tammy Baldwin, a member of the Wisconsin Assembly, took on a state senator and the county executive of the district's biggest county in the Democratic primary. In securing only 37 percent of the vote, she barely won the race. What she did not have in money she made up for in an army of volunteers from the University of Wisconsin. In hoping to become the first openly gay or lesbian nonincumbent candidate to win election to the US House, she relied on the same strategy in the general election. She won with 53 percent of the vote. Two years later, she won the general election by just 8,902 votes. Of the nine counties in her congressional district, she secured more votes than her opponent in only one—luckily for her, it was the one with the most people in it. Baldwin successfully used the Kasten plan, which she more easily implemented because of the increased availability of technology. Like Kasten, after a few terms Baldwin ran for and won a seat in the Senate.

Unlike money, which is quantifiable, organization is harder to assess. As such, good organizations have led to some of the most surprising primary results in congressional elections. Although House Majority Leader Eric Cantor (R-VA) had a campaign war chest of $5.5 million dollars he was defeated by Dave Brat, a little known college professor who spent a mere $200,000, in the 2014 elections. Four years later and in the other party, Alexandria Ocasio-Cortez defeated Joe Crowley (D-NY), the fourth-ranking Democrat in the House, even though she was vastly outspent. What Brat and Ocasio-Cortez lacked in money, they made up for in an army of volunteers.

The Kasten, Baldwin, Brat, and Ocasio-Cortez victories prove that elections are not won by the candidate who has the most financial support; sometimes a well-run organization can trump even money in congressional elections. The key to election victory is voter turnout, which is made easier with an organization and an ample campaign treasury. Although the landscape of congressional campaigns had changed dramatically between the 1970s and today, the fundamentals are the same—money and organization.

While volunteers may be harder to find today, with more and more families sending two or more adults into the public workplace, there remain nonetheless rich fields for the mining of a volunteer army. In recruiting campaign workers, creative candidates and campaign managers attempt to mine the connections between the candidate's campaign platform and those segments of the electorate most likely to be supportive of such a platform. Thus, a candidate who opposed the North American Free Trade Agreement between Mexico, Canada, and the United States might turn for help to members of labor unions, who also opposed the agreement. A candidate who opposed restrictions on private gun ownership might seek volunteers from the membership of the National Rifle Association.

Candidates frequently build volunteer organizations based around individual support groups. They may, for example, ask Union A, Club B, or Employer C to provide the campaign with a telephone team or precinct walkers on Tuesday evenings between 6:00 and 9:00 and another group to provide workers during the lunch hour on Fridays. Not only does the volunteer save the campaign money, by providing services a candidate might otherwise have to pay for or providing a counterweight to an opponent's advantage (persuasion by phone rather than by advertising), but also the campaign worker's personal involvement may provide an additional persuasive element—passion—that is missing from a paid-for campaign. In 1992, Ernest Istook, an Oklahoma state representative was elected to Congress by enlisting large numbers of volunteers from his church. Others relied on former classmates and friends from their softball league.

If it was the founders' intention to constrain the power of government by empowering individual citizens to determine who would make the nation's laws, nothing more surely secures that outcome than the ability of the nonwealthy outsider to find a way to compete, and win, in the political arena. The key to a truly democratic system of governance is maintaining a process in which, ultimately, power rests with the people—not just their power to vote, but also their ability to shape an election's outcome. A process that encourages political participation is the ultimate guarantor of self-rule; a process that makes it more difficult for individuals to participate in elections inevitably swings power to the wealthy and the powerful and reduces the ability of the average citizen to sustain or alter the direction of government. In this sense, the health of the political environment may well be measured by the extent to which volunteers, rather than hired experts and craftily designed commercials, shape election outcomes.

Primaries versus the General Election

People who are the most passionate about ideological differences are also the most likely to take part in elections as campaign workers and as voters. The lower the turnout, the more likely that the ultimate decision will be made by people who have strong feelings about one or several issues. Because smaller numbers of voters participate in intraparty primary elections, and because those voters are more likely searching for a candidate who meets certain ideological criteria, primaries tend to pull voters away from the political center. In Republican primaries, candidates are pulled toward the right; in Democratic primaries, they are pulled toward the left. The danger for the candidates who emerge from primaries is that they will have moved so far in a conservative or liberal direction to assuage the concerns of committed activists that they will no longer appeal to the less ideological center in which most general election voters are found, but because this pull toward the edges is sometimes true in both parties it may ultimately lead to the election of legislators who are more extreme in their positions—either more conservative or more liberal—than the people they were elected to represent.

This polarization endangers the winning candidate. Ideas are central to campaigns, as they are to decision making in Congress, but when candidates take positions on controversial issues, they may be embracing a double-edged sword: the positions one takes to win a party primary may bring defeat in November; a centrist position designed to win in the general election may bring defeat in the primary. Ideally, a candidate will only take positions in which he or she truly believes, but each campaign is designed to highlight a few major issues, and the choices one makes can be crucial to the chances for victory both in the primary and in the general election.

After resounding victories in 2008, the Democrats enjoyed the power of unified party control. Two years later, and despite losing sixty-three seats and the House majority, Senate Democrats held on to their majority. Two years after that, they again held on as the Republicans maintained their control in the House. What many political commentators pointed to as the difference between the two chambers was the weak set of Senate candidates nominated by Republicans in 2010 and 2012. When extreme ideological candidates are victorious over more moderate candidates in the primaries, the general election dynamics get interesting—and dangerous—for the parties. With great peril, primary voters ignore the advice of William F. Buckley, who said a Republican primary voter should nominate the most conservative Republican who could still win the general election.

In 2018, President Trump was very helpful in securing the nomination for two Republican women. In the open Senate seat in Tennessee, Trump campaigned for Marsha Blackburn, a conservative House member who pulled out a tough primary win. She defeated a former popular governor in the general election in a state Trump won in 2016 by 26 points. In South Carolina's First Congressional District, President Trump campaigned for Katie Arrington in her primary election against the incumbent, Mark Sanford. Although she won the primary, Arrington lost the general to Joe Cunningham, in a district that Trump won by only 14 percentage points.

WHO WINS?

The winners of congressional elections are simply the candidates who do the best job of blending money, organization, and ideas to fit the fixed, long-, medium-, and short-term factors of the election cycle. This is a bit like saying that the winner of the Super Bowl is the team that generally plays the better game, while capitalizing on its opponent's blunders and minimizing its own mistakes. Unpacking both statements is the subject of many a Monday morning quarterback. In this section, we try to come up with a more meaningful answer to the question, Who wins?

Incumbents Win!

Perhaps the best truism of congressional politics is that incumbents win. Regrettably, this statement is about as helpful as the first sentence of the previous paragraph. Again, it is akin to saying that the better team wins. First, it should be noted that the better team does not always win. Sometimes a team that is outplayed for three quarters ends up with a chance to win in the final minutes of the game, gets lucky, and wins. Such is the case with candidates who challenge incumbents. Nonetheless, even in *anti-incumbent* and *wave* election cycles, more than 90 percent of House incumbents win and 80 percent of Senate incumbents win (see Table 3.2). Enough challengers win though to scare all incumbents into working very hard for their reelections.

The easiest explanation for why incumbents win is that, by virtue of being an incumbent, they have demonstrated that they can blend money, organization, and ideas to fit the fixed, long-, medium-, and short-term factors of the election cycle. Having won one election, the incumbent must simply modify his or her winning campaign from the previous election cycle to fit the new election cycle. If the incumbent can handle that deftly, more often than not, he or she will again be victorious.

Beyond a proven track record, incumbents have five distinct advantages in congressional elections.[7] First, and most important, the duties and responsibilities of the job required by members of Congress are generally what voters seek. In an election, voters want a candidate to represent them and to legislate on their behalf. Members of Congress, as it turns out, do represent their constituents and legislate on their behalf. To continue with the sports analogy, it is a bit like a football coach trying to decide who is going to be the quarterback in the next game. The default option is always to go with the quarterback from the previous game, especially

Table 3.2 Incumbency Reelection Rate, 1974–2018

| | HOUSE OF REPRESENTATIVES | | | | | SENATE | | | | |
YEAR	INCUMBENTS RUNNING	PRIMARY LOSSES	GENERAL ELECTION LOSSES	TOTAL LOSSES	REELECTION RATE	INCUMBENTS RUNNING	PRIMARY LOSSES	GENERAL ELECTION LOSSES	TOTAL LOSSES	REELECTION RATE
1974	374	8	38	46	87.7	26	2	2	4	88.0
1976	385	3	12	15	96.1	25	0	9	9	64.0
1978	270	8	9	17	93.7	22	0	7	7	68.0
1980	387	6	30	36	90.7	29	4	9	13	55.0
1982	384	10	28	38	90.1	30	0	2	2	93.0
1984	391	3	15	18	95.4	29	0	3	3	90.0
1986	395	3	6	9	97.7	27	0	7	7	78.0
1988	409	1	6	7	98.3	27	0	4	4	85.2
1990	406	1	15	16	96.1	32	0	1	1	96.9
1992	368	19	24	43	88.3	28	1	4	5	82.1
1994	387	4	34	38	90.2	26	0	2	2	92.3
1996	384	2	21	23	94.0	21	1	1	2	90.5
1998	402	1	6	7	98.3	29	0	3	3	89.7
2000	402	3	6	9	97.8	29	0	5	5	82.8
2002	390	8	8	16	95.9	28	1	3	4	85.7
2004	404	2	7	9	98.0	26	0	1	1	98.0
2006	400	2	22	24	94.0	29	0	6	6	79.3
2008	404	4	16	20	95.0	29	0	5	5	82.8
2010	399	54	4	58	85.5	26	2	2	4	84.6
2012	390	13	23	36	90.8	24	1	1	2	91.7
2014	376	5	13	18	95.2	29	0	5	5	82.8
2016	387	5	8	13	96.6	29	0	2	2	93.1
2018	378	4	29	33	91.3	30	0	5	5	83.3

Sources: www.rollcall.com/politics/casualtylists/108thcasualtylist.html, www.opensecrets.org/bigpicture/elec_stats.php?cycle=2004

if that quarterback brought home a victory, as all incumbents, by virtue of their being an incumbent, must have done. On occasion, that quarterback will be unavailable (if the incumbent retires) or is traded to another team (seeks to become governor, for example). On still other occasions, the quarterback may have played badly in the game, but his team may have won despite his poor play. In that instance, the coach (or constituents) could opt for a new quarterback (or candidate). Other potential quarterbacks may have some of the same skills, but none will have been the quarterback in the game last week when the team won.

Second, incumbents' ability to do their job is subsidized by American taxpayers, which is necessary since the Congress is not composed solely of rich people who can volunteer their time and effort. Members receive a salary, health insurance, and an expense account, which in 2014 averaged almost $1.4 million, to help them represent their constituents and legislate on their behalf. Doing a good job as a member of Congress automatically increases the incumbents' prospects in their reelection efforts.

Third, members, simply by virtue of being a member, gain certain privileges such as name recognition and free media. Members must court their local media, and if they do so successfully, the local media reports on the activities of their members of Congress because that is their job. If members are doing a good job, the local media will shed light on how they are representing their constituents and legislating on their behalf.

Fourth, incumbents have easier access to campaign contributions than their challengers do. Once an incumbent has a demonstrated record of accomplishment on a particular issue, special interests that care about that issue will be more likely to donate money to the incumbent because the incumbent is more likely to win. Challengers may have the right position on an issue but, relative to the incumbent, have a much lower chance of winning. *Keeping* someone in power who casts the right vote is much easier for campaign contributors than *putting* someone new in power who would cast the right votes.

Fifth, in congressional races, party cues frequently dominate the election. On occasion, a voter will vote for a particular candidate rather than the party. In such cases, because of the other four advantages, a split-ticket voter is much more likely to side with an incumbent who has done a good job and who enjoys name recognition in the district rather than the challenger, who has a shorter track record and is less well known.

Political scientists use different models to try to calculate the benefit these advantages provide the incumbent in presidential elections. Most models suggest that since the 1970s, it has been worth between 5 and 8 percentage points, though in a few election cycles (1986 and 1988) it jumps above 10 points. This finger on the scale—or is it a whole hand?—goes a long way in explaining why incumbents usually win.

Let us offer one last note about the incumbent's reelection record. Another reason that incumbents win such a high proportion of their races is because

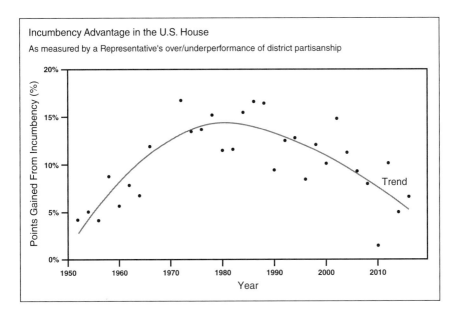

Figure 3.3 The Rise and Fall of the Incumbency Advantage in Congressional Elections, 1950–2016.
Source: Adapted from G. Elliott Morris, *TheCrosstab.com,* based on data from Gary Jacobson, Geoffrey Skelley, and Carlos Algara.

incumbents are politically savvy and smart. At times, members will acknowledge that their reelection efforts are unlikely to be successful. Rather than subjecting themselves to electoral defeat, some incumbents opt to retire. While the #MeToo Movement propelled many women to run for office, it caused one to resign. In early 2018, Congresswoman Elizabeth Esty (D-CT) was harshly criticized for keeping her chief of staff on the job despite allegations of sexual harassment and threats of violence to women on her staff. Even after he left her office, she wrote a positive letter of reference for him. It became clear that this scandal put in jeopardy her once safe reelection. Within weeks, she announced her retirement. Had she instead run for her seat and lost, the proportion of incumbents who won would have decreased. Political scientists have struggled with how to handle the calculation of the incumbency advantage in the face of such strategic retirements. Such a high proportion of incumbents win precisely because the ones that will not win frequently retire instead.

Quality Challengers

When candidates have previously won an election to any other public office, we call them *quality challengers* for a congressional race. These candidates are more likely to win than those who have never won an election. From 1946 to 2010, political scientist

Gary Jacobson found that only 5.9 percent of challengers to incumbents win. When former officeholders run against an incumbent, they win about 19 percent of the time.

As former officeholders, they accrue some of the advantages enjoyed by incumbents, but clearly not all of them. For example, a city mayor is familiar with representing her constituents and acting on their behalf. The job description for mayor is close to that for representative. She is also likely to enjoy higher name recognition and easier access to money, but again, not to the same degree as an incumbent. Furthermore, by virtue of being mayor, she has proven that she can run a campaign, get voters to the polls, and win. While a race for Congress is certainly different, it utilizes some of the same skills she has developed in her mayoral experiences.

Despite Hillary Clinton's 10-point margin over Donald Trump in her district, Barbara Comstock (R-VA) held on to her seat by almost 6 points. In 2018, the Democrats nominated Jennifer Wexton, a state senator who represented much of northern Virginia's congressional district, to run against Comstock. In part because of her high name identification, Wexton was able to neutralize Comstock's incumbency advantage and win the seat by 12 points.

Really Lucky Candidates

Sometimes a golfer hits a hole in one. Sometimes a pitcher will toss a perfect game. And some candidates who have never won an election to anything win a seat in Congress. This happens frequently enough that many candidates who have never run for anything—let alone won anything—throw their hats in the ring. Some of these candidates run exceptional campaigns that hit all the right notes—think of just-a-mom-in-tennis-shoes Patty Murray in 1992 or Jahana Hayes in 2018. They both had the right message for the right time and were rewarded with a seat in Congress.

Other times, candidates are lucky to win simply because they are not the incumbent. In 1994, Ways and Means Committee chairman Dan Rostenkowski, who was indicted on seventeen counts of corruption of various sorts between the primary and the general election, lost to first-time candidate Michael Patrick Flanagan. In 2008, Kwame Kilpatrick was forced to resign his office as the mayor of Detroit because of what a federal prosecutor described as a "pattern of extortion, bribery and fraud." Though his mother, representative Carolyn Cheeks Kilpatrick (D-MI), was never implicated in the scandal, her once-safe seat became very unsafe. In 2010, when her son was sentenced, she lost her seat to Hansen Clarke in the Democratic primary. As an indication of how lucky they were in their initial contests, neither Flanagan nor Clarke survived their first reelection efforts.

Although the 2018 election included some candidates who were either under indictment or had recently been under indictment, the freshman class of the 116th Congress does not seem to include any really lucky candidates. Certainly, election night contained a few surprises, such as a Democrat winning a House seat in Oklahoma for the first time since 2010. Even though Donald Trump won the district by more than 13 points in 2016, two years later, Democrat Kendra Horn, who had never held political office, beat one-term incumbent Steve Russell by 1.4 points. Her task of holding on in the 2020 election will be difficult, but she is not pegged for certain defeat like some of the other lucky winners.

WHO VOTES?

The stakes in the 2008 election were massive. The economy was barely sputtering along and economists from across the ideological spectrum worried that a credit freeze might trigger a worldwide depression. United States forces were involved in protracted wars in Afghanistan and Iraq. The debt was reaching new heights and unemployment was beginning to rise. Americans had the chance to elect the first African American president or a former prisoner of war who lived a life honored by all Americans. They differed on fundamental policies that would steer the American government through a minefield the likes of which many Americans had not seen in their lifetime. Under the most compelling set of circumstances in at least three generations, more than two of every five registered voters decided not to participate in this election of a lifetime. Two years later, when the new president's policies were under intense scrutiny, three of every five registered voters stayed home. In Obama's reelection campaign, when economic growth was still stagnant, an even lower percentage of Americans voted than in 2008. It was lower still in the 2016 election. These tepid turnout numbers beg the questions of who votes and why.

Congressional races generally draw far fewer voters than a presidential race. Since the Congress ultimately determines what laws we live under and recent congressional elections have led to major directional changes in public policy, there may be greater reason for concern about low voter turnout in House and Senate races. Voter turnout in the presidential race between Richard Nixon and Hubert Humphrey in 1968 exceeded 60 percent, after which it dropped steadily until, in 1988, Ronald Reagan's reelection turnout barely topped 50 percent. Turnout rates went up a bit, to around 55 percent, in 1992, but by 1996 were down to 49 percent. As bad as this seems—democracy, after all, depends on an active citizenry—presidential contests were raging successes compared to congressional races. House elections in presidential election years, when interest is at its peak, dropped steadily from about 55 percent in 1968 to about 45 percent twenty years later, nudging back over the 50 percent turnout rate again in 1992. In the years when the Congress was the focus of voter attention—the *off-year* elections, or *midterm* when no presidential contest helped to drum up voter interest—voter turnout was just under 45 percent in 1970, and by 1990, it was under 35 percent.

Even in 1994, when Republicans waged a major national campaign to recapture Congress and took control of both the House and the Senate for the first time since 1954, voter turnout jumped to just over 35 percent.

Clearly, elections are not being decided by the entirety of the public. So the question is: Are the citizens who do vote representative of the public as a whole? Or are certain kinds of voters dominating the process? Whether it is inevitable or not, good or not, governing has usually been the province of a community's more successful citizens, at least when success is measured in material terms. That remains the case, even in a political system in which participation is ostensibly open to all. In 2016, for example, 32 percent of the least-educated citizens—those with eight years or less of education—turned out at the polls. That same year, 52 percent of high school graduates, 63 percent of citizens who had had some college courses, and more than 74 percent of citizens who had completed four years of college voted. Nor is educational achievement the only sign that the community's elite citizens decide who will serve in Congress.

Throughout the 1980s, white voters consistently voted in larger percentages than black voters. In 1980, the year in which a conservative Republican, Ronald Reagan, took the White House away from the Democrats, just over 50 percent of voting-age blacks went to the polls; more than 60 percent of voting-age whites voted in the same election, magnifying the impact of the larger white population. These days, the turnout rate for African Americans almost equals that of Caucasians, though that does not mean that all races and ethnicities vote at the same rate. While the non-Hispanic white turnout was greater than 64 percent in 2016, Hispanic turnout was 33 percent. Wealthy citizens are also more likely to vote than people with lower incomes. In 2016, more than 80 percent of all Americans with annual incomes above $150,000 went to the polls. The lower the income level, the less likely the citizen would vote. Even though low-income citizens might be seriously affected by changes in government support policies, only 41 percent of persons who earned less than $10,000 went to the polls that year. The same disparity exists in age: 73 percent of citizens between the ages of 65 and 74 went to the polls in 2012; among the youngest citizens—aged eighteen to twenty-four—about 43 percent voted.[8]

The picture is clear: it is the older, richer, whiter, better-educated Americans who disproportionately decide who writes the laws. The obvious question becomes: Is this unfair? Should decisions be made equally by both the well informed and the poorly informed? Should a high school dropout have as much to say about the nation's policies as a man or woman who has spent years becoming well educated? This goes to broader questions of governance and the perennial debates over government by the masses versus government by elites. For our purposes, however, it is enough to ask whether voter turnout is a clear indicator of voter interest.

Being aware of these data, candidates for Congress—the people concerned with *getting there* and taking a seat in the House or Senate—will invariably focus their election efforts on those elements of the populace that are most likely to participate in the election. Republicans tend to campaign among more conservative voters and Democrats among liberals, but both focus their efforts not only on citizens with specific areas of concern (doctors, factory workers, farmers) but also on the populations that are most likely to vote, such as senior citizens and upper-income professionals. What this means is that the segments of the population who do not vote because the candidates are not speaking to them will guarantee that candidates will not ever speak to them by not voting. It is a vicious cycle that is hard to break. The surest way that those who feel unrepresented can ensure that their issues have a more prominent role in campaigns is to increase their group's turnout.

The citizens who do show up to vote in elections have many different motivations for the decisions they make. Although the proportion of voters who call themselves independent continues to rise, many voters still rely on the candidates' partisan affiliation to determine their vote. In fact, the proportion of the electorate that votes for one of the parties for all races rather than individual candidates from different parties across races continues to grow. Beyond partisanship, voters frequently opt for candidates whose names they recognize. Voters are exceedingly more likely to recall the incumbents' names than they are the challengers', which helps explain the incumbency advantage. Other voters are single-issue voters, which means that they research all the candidates' positions on a particularly important and salient issue and cast a ballot for the candidate whose position is closest to their own. Interest groups will frequently make this research rather easy by making an endorsement or giving money to a favored candidate.

These decision rules suggest that voters are systematic in their decisions. Some are. Many other voters make their decisions based on yard signs, bumper stickers, and a catchy radio commercial. Still others rely on personal appeals from friends, relatives, and coworkers. And other voters rely on a mix of different cues to help them complete their ballot.

CONCLUSION

Clinton Rossiter, a history professor at Cornell, wrote that government must be not only constitutional, but also representative. In evaluating who gets to Congress, it is fair to ask whether the current election system in the United States provides a national legislature that is, indeed, representative. What is the effect of the openness of the modern system, in which party bosses are rare and parties, at least in the electoral arena, have diminished power? Does the ability of concerned citizens to select themselves as candidates help create a more representative

Congress? Does the high cost of modern campaigning freeze out potential candidates? (If so, how can this barrier be removed without diminishing the ability of citizens to participate and the ability of candidates to get their messages to the voters?) Do volunteer-based candidacies overcome, at least partially, the handicap of inadequate campaign funds? Should all views be represented in Congress or only the views that seem to enjoy a large measure of public support? Does the ability to raise money and enlist volunteers indicate that degree of support? If campaigns are a contest between competing ideas about the role and nature of government, shouldn't the majority view prevail?

In future chapters, we will look at how the Congress functions, how its members decide what positions they will take on the issues, what pressures legislators feel, and what changes might make the system better, but the whole process begins—and perhaps ends—with the Election Day selection of the people's representatives. How well that system works determines, in the long run, how well America's democracy works.

COMMENTARY

The Politician's Take on Elections

Elections matter: they determine who sits at the control board pulling the levers and turning the dials that make our government work. To some extent, they set the nation's course because they empower or withhold power from those who advocate a certain approach to public policy and the role of government in our lives. But there is a limit to what those elections can accomplish, even beyond the obvious point that nonvoters (usually the majority of those who are eligible to vote) have no say in what transpires after the votes are counted.

The reality is that in even the most hotly contested races, many of the issues members of Congress vote on, or advocate for (or against), are not discussed during the election campaign. Elections revolve around personalities, general philosophical inclinations, and a few specific issues—jobs, war, immigration, abortion, attitudes toward labor unions, etc. But every member of the House and Senate votes hundreds of times every year on issues that played no role in their having been elected. Members of Congress vary in how well they gauge, or attempt to gauge, constituents' attitudes on those issues as they arise during the legislative term.

In addition, while the voters get one day every two (or six) years to express their preference, other voices have the congressional ear much more frequently: party leaders, presidents, organized factions (chambers of commerce, labor unions, organizations of teachers, healthcare workers, veterans, the elderly, etc.). This, by the way, is probably as it should be: as time passes, those men and women who cast their votes on Election Day may get more information and change their views. To that extent, Election Day results are a snapshot in time, reflecting how an issue or a candidate is perceived at a given moment. Elections matter tremendously; they determine the players, but beyond that, they become a part of the mosaic, not the final word.

COMMENTARY

The Professor's Take on Elections

On most issues, I am an optimist. Perhaps on no issue is my optimism more at odds with the conventional wisdom than on congressional elections. I do not think that money is the be all and end all of elections, nor do I think that special interests play the corrosive role that so many deride. My research and my gut tell me that *vox populi*—"the voice of the people"—wins out.

Before I lose all credibility for voicing such optimism, I will say that special interests and money can matter in extremely close and competitive elections. The experts can always point to a race where an incumbent was able to hang on because he had a five-to-one spending advantage over his challenger, or where the Club for Growth or Move-on provided the crucial organization that defeated one candidate or another. I look at these noted results as the exceptions that prove the rule.

Lest I engage in the same kind of cherry-picking that I fault the experts with doing, let me examine the spending from a bigger pool. In 2010, the year that the Democrats lost sixty-two House seats, their Democratic Congressional Campaign Committee outspent the National Republican Congressional Campaign Committee by $31.5 million. In losing five Senate seats, the Democratic Senatorial Campaign Committee spent almost twice as much as the National Republican Senatorial Committee ($129 million compared to $68 million). As evidence that the argument works for both parties, as the Republicans were losing twenty-seven House seats in 2006, they were outspending the Democrats by $37 million! The amount of money that a candidate raises can be both a sign of strength and a sign of desperation.

Sure, money helps. And, members of Congress probably spend too much of their day trying to raise it and too much time worrying about how a vote on one bill hurts them with an interest group, but at the end of the day, what matters is an articulated message that resonates with the voters. Neither an influx of money nor a parade of volunteers from the Club for Growth in 2006 could have saved the Republicans from losing the House, and neither an influx of money nor an army of volunteers from the unions in 2010 could have saved the Democrats from losing the House. Indeed, the voice of the people, so long as the voice is distinct, will trump even money and special interests!

Before moving on to the job of being a member of Congress, I must point out one other interesting fact about the 2006 and 2010 elections. Even though the Democrats won by a landslide in 2006 and then were swept out in a landslide in 2010, 185 districts in the House sent Democrats to Congress in both 2006 and 2010; likewise, 195 districts sent Republicans in both election years. Such high numbers reinforce the point that the factors that matter most are those that do not change from election cycle to election cycle. Sure, a swing of fifty-five seats from one party to the other was enough to swing the House from Republicans' hands to Democrats' hands and then back to Republicans' hands, but if you want to make the best prediction about who will win congressional elections, you are far better off knowing and analyzing the fixed and long-term factors of congressional elections—in these two wildly divergent election years, they account for 88 percent of the results!

CHAPTER 4

Being a Member of Congress

In the 1972 movie *The Candidate*, Robert Redford plays Bill McKay, the idealistic son of a former governor who is persuaded to run for the US Senate against a popular incumbent. As the race tightens, McKay's campaign is no longer about principle but simply about winning, which, in the end, he does. The movie ends with a provocative line that McKay speaks directly to the camera: "What do we do now?"

For some members of Congress, winning is the primary goal. But for most, winning a congressional seat is a step toward fulfilling a vision of what government should be, whether that is specific to a set of policy goals, a vague desire to make government work better, or simply to be an advocate for the winning candidates' interests. Whatever the goal, almost every new member of Congress faces that same question: What do I do now? That is partly because getting elected is only a first step; almost all new members of Congress, even those who have served for years in state legislatures, find that the congressional experience—the pace, the range of issues, the unique rules, the number and intensity of competing interests—is unlike anything they have known before. And it is also partly because issues that seemed simple when one was on the outside looking in are revealed in all their true complexity. Here is where the words of the Constitution are transformed into the actual government of, by, and for the people of the United States. So now that we have considered how the Congress fits into the overall picture of American government and how its members are selected, it is time to look more closely at who members of Congress actually are, what they do, and why they make the decisions they make.

DESCRIBING THE MEMBERS OF CONGRESS

In 2008, Republican Joseph Cao, the fifth of eight children who escaped Vietnam three days after Saigon fell in 1975, was the surprise winner of the US House seat based in New Orleans. He was able to triumph in a district that gave

Barack Obama 75 percent of its votes by criticizing the ethics of the incumbent, William Jefferson. Three years before Cao's surprising victory, federal agents discovered $90,000 wrapped in aluminum foil in the freezer of Jefferson's garage. Upon assuming his seat in 2009, Cao became fast friends with representative Don Young (R-AK), a member first elected twenty-five years before Cao, who was then only six years old and still living in Vietnam. Their districts were four thousand miles apart. About the only thing the pair had in common was their party registration. In a Congress made up of lawyers, doctors, editors, teachers, and even the occasional pharmacist and farmer, where the scions of America's wealthiest families share committees with the sons and daughters of maids and bartenders and where the range in ages may cover as much as fifty or sixty years, the relationship between Young and Cao is not uncommon. The House of Representatives, though not as diverse as the American population at large, brings elected officials of all sizes, stripes, and ages together. Their common situations and challenges frequently forge the most unlikely of friendships. In this section, we explore the demographic changes that have come to characterize the modern House and Senate.

Race, Ethnicity, and Sex of Members of Congress

As Cao's election can attest, Congress is no longer filled completely with old white men, though plenty are still around. Although they continue to comprise around 75 percent of the total membership, almost without exception their proportion declines every election. The members of the 115th Congress are the most diverse in the institution's history. Among their ranks in the House are forty-seven African Americans, forty Hispanics, thirteen Asian Americans or Pacific Islanders, and two Native Americans. The Senate includes five Hispanics, three African Americans, and three Asian Americans. Eighty-four women serve in the House and twenty-one serve in the Senate. Although representation of women and

Table 4.1 Racial, Ethnic, and Gender Diversity in the 115th Congress (2017–8)

	US POPULATION	HOUSE (%)	DISPARITY	PROPORTION OF POPULATION REPRESENTED (%)
Black	12.3	10.8	1.5	87.8
Hispanic	12.5	9.2	3.3	73.6
Asian	3.7	3.0	0.7	80.8
Native American	0.9	0.5	0.4	51.1
Female	51.0	19.3	31.7	37.9
	US POPULATION	SENATE (%)	DISPARITY	PROPORTION OF POPULATION FILLED (%)
Black	12.3	3.0	9.3	24.4
Hispanic	12.5	5.0	7.5	40.0
Asian	3.7	3.0	0.7	81.1
Native American	0.9	–	0.9	–
Female	51.0	23.0	28.0	45.1

minority racial and ethnic groups is increasing, none of these groups has reached the level of representation they have in the general population. African Americans in the House are the closest to fulfilling their proportion—while African Americans make up 12.3 percent of the US population, they comprise 10.8 percent of the House (see Table 4.1). As such, they are 87.8 percent of the way toward having their representation in the House equal their population in the United States. However, African Americans are woefully underrepresented in the Senate. The number of African American senators would need to quadruple before their proportion in the Senate equaled their proportion among the US population.

While African Americans, Hispanics, and women remain underrepresented in both chambers, their numbers today are higher than they were even twenty years ago (SEE FIGURE 4.1). The big jump came in 1992, although not for the same reason for all three groups. The increase for Hispanics and African Americans was mostly a result of redistricting changes taking place after the 1990 census. President George H. W. Bush's justice department mandated that wherever a minority district could be created, it must be created. In Georgia, the legislature created two districts and the justice department forced them to draw another one; the same occurred in North Carolina and Florida. Not surprisingly, in November 1992, twelve additional African Americans and six Hispanics took seats in the House. Hispanic representation continued to increase most markedly in the years just after redistricting. While the increasing growth of Hispanics mirrors their increasing growth in the general population, the proportion of African Americans in the United States and Congress has remained more stable.

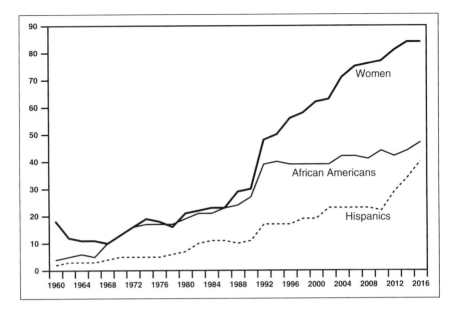

Figure 4.1 The Growth of Women, African Americans, and Hispanics in the US House, 1960–2016.

The 1992 elections, in addition to bringing more African Americans and Hispanics to the House, also brought many more women to Capitol Hill (twelve additional women in the House and four in the Senate). What could not be manufactured through redistricting was accomplished through the treatment of a woman – law professor Anita Hill, when she accused a nominee to the Supreme Court, Clarence Thomas, of sexual harassment during his confirmation hearings in 1991. The spectacle of fourteen white men sitting on the Judiciary Committee casting judgment on Anita Hill—and ultimately dismissing the accusations—propelled many women to run for office; many, including just-a-mom-in-tennis-shoes-turned-senator Patty Murray (D-WA), for the first time. In 2018, elections also saw a surge of female candidates among the newly elected members of Congress. Donald Trump's inauguration on January 20, 2017, set off one day later the Women's March, the largest one-day protest in U.S. history. From that day until the election nearly two years later, women participated in electoral politics at a much greater rate, including an unprecedented proportion of candidates and election day winners.

Most members of Congress from these underrepresented groups are Democrats. In fact, for the first time in history, white men constituted a minority of the Democratic caucus beginning in the 113th Congress (2013–14). Even today, white men comprise around 90 percent of the Republican Conferences in the House and Senate. It should be noted that all African American representation in Congress prior to 1935 was in the Republican Party. During Reconstruction, when African Americans joined with white Unionists in the South to form a governing majority, twenty-one African Americans were elected to the House and two were elected to the Senate. Even after Reconstruction ended in 1876, six more African Americans represented the South in Congress (the last one left the House in 1901). The first African American elected in the North was Oscar De Priest, a Republican, who represented Chicago from 1929 to 1935. His successor, Arthur Mitchell, elected in 1934, was the first African American Democrat elected to the House. It was not until

1991 that another African American Republican, Gary Franks, was elected. Today, only one Republican in the Senate and one in the House are African American.

Other Member Characteristics

Each new Congress contains not only fewer white males, but also usually fewer lawyers, fewer adherents to mainline churches, and a wider range of ages—both young and old. In the 2016 House elections, for example, six members under thirty-five years old were elected, as well as eight members over age eighty. In 2006, Keith Ellison became the first Muslim and Hank Johnson (D-GA) and Mazie Hirono (D-HI) became the first Buddhists elected to Congress. In 2012, the first Hindu, Tulsi Gabbard (D-HI), was elected to Congress. In the 2018 election, Rashida Tlaib (D-MI) became the first Muslim woman and the first Palestinian woman in Congress. As Vietnam veterans have been leaving the House, those members with military experience have also waned, even while the wars in Afghanistan and Iraq are creating more veterans. Senator Daniel Inouye (D-HI), who died in 2012, and representative John Dingell (D-MI), who retired in 2014, were their chamber's last serving World War II veterans.

As the American public has become more accepting of gays and lesbians, their numbers in Congress have grown. In 1983, Gerry Studds (D-MA) became the first member to come out as gay or lesbian and only then because he was mired in a sex scandal. In 1998, Tammy Baldwin was the first nonincumbent openly gay or lesbian to win a congressional election. She reprised that role in 2012, when she became the first open gay or lesbian—incumbent or not—to win a senate election. Each election brings more LGB members to Congress.

Our emphasis on race, gender, ethnicity, and sexual orientation in this section highlights the *descriptive* representation of members. Constituents who share these characteristics can see that their representatives look like them in some fundamental ways. Some theorists argue that this descriptive—or *symbolic*—representation is critical for Congress's legitimacy. Certainly a Congress today composed of all white men—as it once was—would be appropriately viewed skeptically by US citizens.

Other political theorists argue that descriptive representation is not as important as *substantive* representation. They suggest that a pro-choice woman is not the best representative for a pro-life female constituent. If it is policy that concerns the constituent, a male pro-life member would be a better representative. As with most things in the study of Congress, the correct answer is probably a mixture of both. A descriptively accurate Congress to the exclusion of substantive representation would probably be viewed as skeptically as a Congress made up of only white men. Balancing these interests can be difficult. Since 2007, Steve Cohen, a Caucasian and the first Jewish member of Congress from Tennessee, has represented the Memphis district in Congress even though it is 39 percent African American and 37 percent Hispanic. Although some have criticized him for not being a racial or ethnic minority, on his webpage Cohen argues that his constituents could not be better represented on the issues that concern them or have a bigger fighter in Washington, DC, for local projects.

MEMBER GOALS

A member's day is filled with hundreds of decisions: Should I have breakfast with the Chamber of Commerce from a hostile part of my district or my regular member prayer group? Should I vote to increase funding to fight the highly contagious ebola virus in Africa? Should I meet with a rich contributor who has different policy goals than my party's leadership? Should I exercise at the House gym or call ten potential donors to my campaign? While many of them are easy decisions—for example, Should I vote to support my party on a procedural vote?—many others are hard. We cannot begin to understand the decisions members make unless we understand what motivates them. In this section, we consider different goals that members juggle in carrying out their jobs.

Reelection

By virtue of their seats in Congress, we know that all members have been selected by their constituents, except for those few senators appointed to serve the remainder of another's term because of a vacancy. To keep their seats, they (including recently appointed senators) must be reelected. David Mayhew (1974), a political scientist from Yale, famously wrote that all members of Congress were "single-minded seekers of reelection." He argued that if we assumed it, we could begin to analyze the decisions members make. In that light, he called his famous axiom "an abstract simplifying assumption," that is, an analytic shortcut congressional observers can make to understand Congress and the behavior of its members.

Mayhew readily admitted that members have many other goals, but he called reelection the *proximate* goal—none of their other goals could be satisfied unless they were first reelected. To portray members as single-minded seekers of reelection necessarily casts them in a negative light until one analyzes more closely what it means to seek reelection. For example, members who care about reelection are likely to cast votes consistent with the preferences of their constituents, to send newsletters to inform the constituents about their activities both in Washington, DC, and in the district, to engage in moral and ethical behavior, and to help their constituents find resolution with the federal bureaucracy on a social security claim, immigration problem, or small business loan. No one would say that a member doing those things is doing anything inappropriate—in fact, it is exactly those activities that we would want from our members of Congress. So, the fact that members of Congress care about their reelection is an indication of how brilliantly the framers of the Constitution structured our government, even after two hundred years of practice!

We are not so naive as to think that reelection-focused members always engage in the best possible behavior. For example, members who care about their reelection are likely to spend many hours on the phone asking for campaign contributions from people inside and outside the district, to try and engineer a series of votes so that they do not have to cast a difficult vote between raising taxes or cutting Medicare, and, on occasion, to put their finger to the wind to determine the popularity of a position before casting a vote. While we might prefer that members spend less time fundraising, make difficult votes transparent, and exercise good independent judgment, we recognize that the system cannot be perfect. Furthermore, even less than admirable activities are constrained by the demands of constituents.

For some members, the goal of reelection may be the highest goal, but for most, it is simply, as Mayhew argues, the goal that must be satisfied first before attempting to fulfill other goals. Many political pundits argued that Eric Cantor (R-VA), who then was the House majority leader, lost sight of the proximate goal (reelection) as he was crafting policy and strategy for his fellow House Republicans. In 2014, he lost by more than 10 percentage points in a primary to an opponent whom he outspent forty to one. Although many members are motivated for their reelections so as to satisfy some of their other goals, Cantor's loss, according to fivethirtyeight.com, was an earthquake felt all around Washington, DC. It is to some of those other, nonreelection goals that we now turn.

Providing Good Constituent Service

Members of Congress aim to provide a link between *government* and *citizen*. This link takes several forms: providing information about pending legislation, offering opportunities—town meetings, Facebook polls, attendance at public events—for citizens to express themselves on public policy issues. Other times, constituents seek the intervention of members of Congress to resolve disputes that arise between the constituents and the federal government.

These constituent problems come in many forms. For example, if a constituent has failed to receive a social security payment to which he or she is entitled, or if a military veteran has failed to receive an earned citation, the member may become an *ombudsman*, intervening to speed up the process or increase the level of agency responsiveness. While some citizens write or call the federal agency, others turn to their legislators to provide constituent service—or in congressional lingo, *casework*. Members encourage this practice because they can thus win the gratitude—and support—of constituents whose cases have been satisfactorily resolved or who recognize that their legislators have made a serious effort on their behalf. As opposed to staking a position on a public policy problem, which can draw both support and opposition from constituents, casework provides members with the opportunity to garner only support for their efforts.

Much of the hard work in these cases is performed by a member's personal staff. Members are not reluctant to step in if they think that the resolution will be quicker or more complete. While they know that they cannot personally help enough people to secure their reelection, they hope that the constituents spread the word of their helpfulness. One good deed done by a member can spread to an entire community of grateful potential voters. Former congressman Tom Steed (D-OK) would welcome new members of the state's House delegation, regardless of party, by pointing to his file drawers full of folders detailing his office's work for constituents, something he said was both good representation and a good way to stay in office.

Formulating Good Public Policy

Most members of Congress run for Congress because they want to accomplish something. They are driven to a political career because they have a view as to how things should be done. Some of these members view good public policy through an ideological or issue-specific lens. They fight for liberal or conservative policy or for business or environmental or feminist causes. These ideological concerns generally come as a package containing a variety of more specific issues, such as abortion, gun control, and affirmative action—the kinds of issues on which one may generally find liberals on one side and conservatives on another, or on which constituents may perceive business and environmental concerns to be at odds, for example. Senator Barry Goldwater (R-AZ), who became the Republican presidential nominee in 1964, was known to ask of a proposal, Does it maximize freedom? Others might ask of the same proposal, Does it reduce inequalities? To some constituents it is the consistent application of these "tests" that determines the soundness of a legislator's policy positions.

For many, whether a vote is considered good is simply determined by whether one agrees with it. For members who favor a system of progressive taxation (in which persons with higher incomes will pay a higher percentage of their incomes in federal taxes), a change in the tax laws that reduces the burden on the wealthy or increases the percentage of total taxes paid by middle-income taxpayers may be perceived as poor national policy. Even if advocates of the change were able to demonstrate that such a change would increase investment and produce an increase in available jobs, support for a tax code that favors the rich would be a serious mark against the member of Congress who voted for such a plan. To constituents who believe that lower taxes on the wealthy will create investment incentives and more employment or who believe all citizens should be taxed at the same rate, a tax reduction that primarily benefits lower-income taxpayers might be perceived as poor policy, even if its advocates could demonstrate that such a change would help move families out of poverty or lead to an increase in consumer purchases. For constituents like these, a general reflection of one's values (for justice, for families, for individual freedom) is not enough: a member is expected to represent by casting the votes the constituent would cast if allowed on the House or Senate floor.

Other members take a more pragmatic approach: they may address specific concerns such as reducing crime or ensuring that healthcare is affordable and accessible. These members may or may not have a predetermined opinion as to the best approach to solving a problem, but instead they will thoughtfully consider the alternatives that best solve the problem. This view accepts the premise that many issues are complicated and that their solutions require a more sophisticated understanding than a strict ideological lens can provide. This, for example, may be the case with such issues as Social Security and Medicare.

Finally, good public policy can be entirely void of ideological content. Members of Congress may fight about the appropriateness of the federal government instead of private banks delivering loans to students, but once the decision is made that the government will deliver the loans, all members of Congress—and all Americans—believe that the delivery of the loans should be done without waste, fraud, and abuse. The design of an efficient delivery service can be deemed good public policy even if members had preferred private banks.

Furthering Their Political Careers

While some members are driven by policy goals, others are driven by the desire for power. For some members, that means rising from the ends of the row on a committee dais to the center, where the chair of the committee sits. For other members that means joining the whip organization in hopes of someday climbing the party leadership ladder. Other members are content to be permanent backbenchers so long as their pet issue is not ignored.

Some members want to gain prestige within the institution while others want to use their congressional seat as a stepping-stone to some other office. An adage in Washington, DC, claims that all representatives fashion themselves a future senator and all senators fashion themselves a future president. While it is certainly true that some representatives are content to stay in the House and more than a handful of senators maintain no ambition for the White House, these cases are noteworthy because of their infrequency. As an example, the 2016 presidential race included four currently serving senators and two former senators.

Still others yearn for a position in the administration or their state's governorship. Others use their seats in Congress to leverage jobs in which they can better showcase their talents. Two Republicans in the 113th Congress stunned their colleagues when they announced that they were leaving the House. Mike Rogers, the chair of the House Intelligence Committee, announced that he was retiring from the House to become a radio talk show host. In an interview with the *Washington Post*, Rogers argued, "If I can move the needle on the 2016 elections and the conversation and the dialogue about America's future, then I'm equally excited about that than I am about the work I'm doing right now."[1] Representative Jo Bonner did not even wait to the end of the congress to leave the House to become the vice chancellor of government relations and economic development for the University of Alabama system. In his words, "While I had every intention of completing this term, sometimes opportunities come along that are so rare— and so special—that it forces you to alter even your best-made plans."[2]

Having Majority Party Status

As Congress has become increasingly partisan, the minority party has had fewer opportunities to influence the crafting of legislation, especially in the House. As we will see in later chapters, the majority party frequently tries to marginalize the minority party through a series of legislative process innovations and developments. To retort, the minority party frequently tries to gum up the legislative process so that passing even noncontroversial bills becomes exceedingly difficult. This cycle makes the passing of any legislation more difficult, which only makes it more difficult for members of the minority party to see their ideas implemented into law.

Because party polarization has made serving in the minority much less fulfilling than being in the majority, the fight over that status has increased so much that political scientists have increasingly included it among members' primary goals. A member of the majority party has a better chance of influencing the legislative agenda, a more prominent role in passing legislation, and an easier time raising money. In a 1999 study, political scientists Gary Jacobson and Eric Magar found that majority party status was worth about $36,000 in additional campaign contributions (when winning candidates, on average, spent less than $600,000). Certainly that figure has increased in the intervening years.

Having majority party status, however, comes with tremendous burdens. The responsibility of governing in a highly polarized environment has become exceedingly difficult. When the economy is humming along and Americans feel secure, the best the majority party can do is to maintain its status as the majority. When the economy struggles and the military is involved in quagmires abroad, the American people are frustrated and that frustration is directed toward the majority party.

These member goals are neither mutually exclusive nor exhaustive. Many other motivations may underlie members' actions and any one member always has a mix of goals that he or she is simultaneously trying to fulfill. It is exceedingly rare that members would only be motivated by one goal—even the much-heralded reelection goal. Members may possess more of one goal than another goal and to a different degree than their fellow members. It is the mix of 535 members simultaneously pursuing their goals that makes studying Congress so interesting—and so difficult.

THE PERKS OF SERVING IN CONGRESS

Having laid out what members of Congress look like and what motivates them, we now describe the perquisites—often abbreviated as *perks*—that members have at their disposal simply by serving in Congress. What these benefits were and who would decide what they were caused much debate at the constitutional convention. As James Madison, who at the time was serving in the House, argued on floor in 1789: "There is a seeming impropriety in leaving any set of men, without control, to put their hand into the public coffers, to take money to put in their pockets."[3] Nonetheless, it was exactly the knowledge that members would face this difficult dilemma that convinced the framers to leave them with the power to determine exactly what their benefits would be upon their election. The balance that was so critically achieved cautioned members against digging too far into the public coffers, lest they risk a backlash from the electorate.

The perks of serving in Congress are distributed remarkably equally. Unlike almost any other job in the United States, members make the same amount of money whether they are serving their first year or in their thirtieth year on the job. The only characteristics that differentiate the perquisites of serving are the number of constituents (to account for the office personnel needed to respond to constituent requests) and the distance from Washington, DC (to account for travel expenses).

Salary and Health Benefits

One of the first acts of Congress in 1789 was the establishment of members' pay at $6 per day. Since then, members of Congress have increased their pay thirty-seven times. Today, members of both chambers receive an annual salary of $174,000. In 1999, members instituted automatic cost-of-living adjustments in their pay, which grew out of frustration with constituent opposition to any congressional pay raise at all even to keep up with rising costs. The only way for them not to receive the automatic adjustment is for both chambers to reject it, which they do with regularity. Nothing in the Constitution mandates that members of both chambers receive the same salary, but by convention they normally do.

By virtue of their employment in Congress, members forgo many opportunities to earn outside income. Members can earn only an amount equal to

15 percent of their annual salary as outside income and none of it can come from serving on corporate boards or working for firms, partnerships, associations, or corporations. Furthermore, they cannot be paid honorariums for giving outside speeches or attending corporate or interest group meetings. This outside income can come from publishing books or utilizing the skills they developed before their congressional careers, such as farming or practicing medicine or law. Members are not restricted in receiving income unrelated to their work, such as stocks paying dividends or the sale of real estate. Members only receive retirement benefits if they have served more than five years in Congress; the actual amount of benefit is dependent on their age and their years of service, but can never exceed 80 percent of their final salary.

Like other civil service employees, members of Congress can participate in the Federal Employees Health Benefits Program. If they chose to participate, they must contribute to the program. With the passage of the Patient Protection and Affordable Care Act (otherwise known as Obamacare), members are restricted to the plans created under the act.

Offices and Other Expenses

Members of Congress are also given offices on Capitol Hill. While all members get an office, some offices are better than others. After an election in which many members are defeated or retire, Capitol Hill is turned upside down as the newly vacant offices are first offered to the continuing members along a strict seniority basis before the newly elected members draw lots for determining the order in which they choose the remaining offices.

All members of Congress have an office in one of the three House office buildings—Cannon, Longworth, and Rayburn (named for the Speaker who presided when the building was approved)—or one of the three Senate office buildings—Russell, Dirksen, and Hart (named in honor of important senators who served during the twentieth century). Some party and committee leaders in the House also have offices in the US Capitol, though these are strictly concerned with legislative or party affairs. Almost all senators also have a small office somewhere on the Senate side of the Capitol—some of these no bigger than a closet. These offices, of which there is no published list of room assignments, are called *hideaways* because senators frequently try to escape the pressure of meeting with constituents or lobbyists—or even other senators—between votes on the Senate floor.

Members also have offices in their districts and states. In contrast to the Capitol Hill offices that are geared almost exclusively to legislative affairs, the district offices are consumed with constituent services or managing the members' time when they are in their constituencies. The magnitude and number of these offices vary depending on the size and spread of the population. Yvette Clark (D-NY), whose district is entirely contained with Brooklyn has only one district office, whereas Liz Cheney (R-WY), whose district is one of the largest, encompassing the entire state of Wyoming, has four offices. When Congressman Mickey Edwards won in 1976, he set up five district offices even though his district was entirely contained within one county. Given that his district had far more Democrats than Republicans in it, he focused his attention on local issues, and having so many district offices ensured that his constituents had easy access to his staff, among whom over half remained in Oklahoma, a proportion rare then and equally rare today.

The district offices must be the member's eyes in the district. They provide the critical link between government and citizen. This link takes several forms: providing information about pending legislation; offering opportunities for citizens to express views on public policy issues through town hall meetings, questionnaires, and attendance at public events; and assisting constituents who encounter problems with federal agencies. District offices perform a variety of important functions for the representative, including the handling of constituent services (casework); serving as the visible face of the member in the community

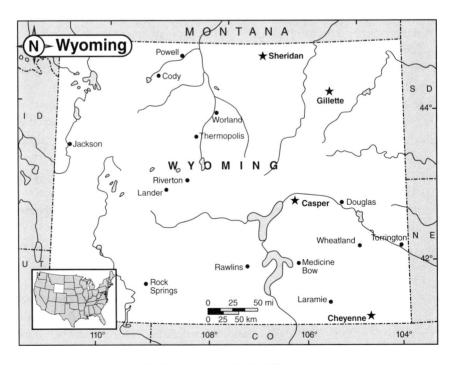

Figure 4.2 Representative Liz Cheney's Four District Offices.

(a function that includes keeping tabs on happenings in the community like high school graduations, bar mitzvahs, Eagle Scout awards, deaths, or anything that may call for a representative to send congratulations or condolences); representing the member at public events (chamber of commerce meetings, civic club luncheons, award ceremonies); arranging for constituents to meet with the member either in Washington, DC, or in the district; arranging local press conferences or monitoring local media coverage; and maintaining contact with community organizations. All these functions are necessary for the legislators to effectively carry out their very broad job description. Well-functioning district offices help secure a member's reelection. Poorly run district offices present members in the worst possible light, which makes it exceedingly hard for them to endear themselves to their constituents. These offices are central to the member–constituent linkage and some of these local staff members eventually end up in Congress themselves. In 2012, congressman John Shimkus's project manager, Rodney Davis (R-IL), sought and won the seat in the neighboring district.

Members structure their staffs similarly, though it can vary by member. A typical office is headed by a chief of staff (formerly known as an administrative assistant), who directs the work of the legislative, administrative, communications, and casework staff members, manages the office accounts, and, in conjunction with a scheduler, often acts as a gatekeeper, managing the member's time (although the amount of gatekeeping varies greatly by member: some want as much free time as possible to work on legislative priorities while others seem eager to talk to almost any visitor who drops by). Other senior staff in members' offices include the legislative director, who is responsible for all legislative affairs for the member, and the district director, who is in charge of the member's offices back in the district. Congressman Tom Cole (R-OK), for example, previously served as district director for Mickey Edwards before first winning statewide office in Oklahoma and then winning a House seat himself. Members' offices also include a scheduler and a press secretary, often a former journalist. Hiring congressional staff is sometimes a tricky business. A press secretary taken from the ranks of newspaper reporters may have difficulty making full use of television news opportunities; former television reporters may not be up to speed on the use of internet media. Schedulers familiar with the new member's district may not understand the importance of a legislative event and those with experience on Capitol Hill may schedule back-to-back meetings in district communities a hundred miles apart. Legislative assistants with strong political opinions may be inclined to skew their reports to prompt members to vote accordingly. Congressional staff members have the ability to wield enormous influence and the hiring process is sometimes an intricate dance. Meanwhile, much of the important work in a congressional office is done by more junior staff assistants, legislative aides who oversee specific areas of policy or legislative correspondents who oversee the members' responses to mail from constituents. Most offices usually include interns, but their exact roles vary by office and by intern. An individual congressional office is a good replica of a small business, although legislation and constituent services are the focus rather than sales or consumer products. These basic job descriptions are adhered to more closely in senators' offices, where more staff requires specialization, than in the House, where smaller staffs must be nimbler.

The funds for operating these offices are allocated in the annual legislative branch appropriations bill, which also provides money for staff salaries, travel, mail, office equipment, district office rental, and other general office expenses. Incidentally, none of the allocated funds can be used for campaign purposes, which means staffers who wish to work in members' reelection efforts must leave the federal payroll and do their work outside the members' offices.

Representatives receive their allocation as a Members' Representational Allowance, which is composed of four parts: personnel, official office expenses, travel, and official mail, which is sent via a member's signature—the *frank* in congressional parlance—in place of a stamp. In 2016, Members' Representational Allowances average $1,268,520 but range from $1,207,510 to $1,383,709. Senators receive their allocation through the Senators' Official Personnel and Office Expense Account. The senators' average in 2016 was $3,263,940 but ranged from $3,008,288 to $4,760,211.

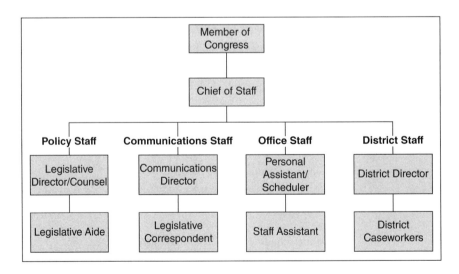

Figure 4.3 Office Structure for a Member of Congress.
Source: Eric Cantor, "Hit the Ground Running," 112th Congress edition, http://www.governmentattic.org/4docs/HitGroundRunning2011.pdf, accessed August 3, 2016.

THE DAILY LIFE OF A MEMBER

Because the Congress deals with the most important issues the nation faces—how much to spend on national security, how much to take from citizens in the form of taxes, the extent to which a citizen's private behavior is subject to regulation by the federal government, even whether troops should be sent into battle or whether an elected president should be removed from office—one might assume, and hope, that much of a member's daily activity is focused on study and thoughtful discussion. Unfortunately, members, like the people they serve, live within the time constraints of a twenty-four-hour day. And because their job descriptions are so complex and the demands on their time so varied, it is seldom that any one task receives a member's full attention for long.

What is true is that members have very difficult jobs and work very long hours. When Congress is in session, members, on average, work seventy hours a week; when it is not in session, the weekly hours only decrease to fifty-nine.[4] How members spend that time varies greatly depending on whether they are in Washington, DC, or in their districts. When they are in Washington, roughly one-third of their time is spent on legislation and policy and only one-sixth on constituent service. When they are in the district, the percentages are almost reversed. Consistent across both locations, members of Congress spend just less than one-fifth of their time on political or campaign work (SEE FIGURE 4.4).

The hours that members spend on various activities do not begin to scratch the surface of the difficulty in structuring a member's day. One of the problems is the legislative schedule itself. Not only are many votes to be cast, but also they are scheduled in the midst of many other activities that also demand the legislator's time and attention. It is not a new problem: as long ago as 1979, when Richard Gephardt, later the House Democratic leader, was still serving in his first term, he told Alan Ehrenhalt of the *Washington Star* about the hectic nature of life in the House of Representatives: "One reason we don't have a consensus on more things," Gephardt said, "is that we don't have time to think about them." Gephardt had been interviewed after his fourth round trip of the day between the Capitol and his congressional office a block away. Another first-term member, David Stockman, who later became President Reagan's budget director, made a similar complaint: after voting for the 648th time that year, Stockman complained that "the legislative products being reported to the House are terribly shoddy and incomplete. . . . It's due to the schedule and the zoo-like atmosphere."

The schedule and "zoo-like atmosphere" are even more chaotic today than they were when Gephardt and Stockman served. Rather than technology easing the conflicts of time, it has exacerbated them. In addition to the several committees and subcommittees on which members serve, several often meeting at the

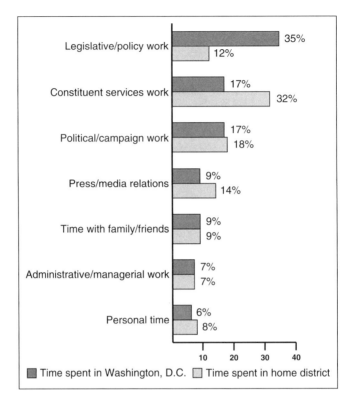

Figure 4.4 How Members Spend Their Time in the District and in Washington, DC.
SOURCE: "Life in Congress: The Member Perspective," released by the Congressional Management Foundation and the Society for Human Resources Management in 2013, http://www.congressfoundation. org/storage/documents/CMF_Pubs/life-in-congress-the-member-perspective.pdf, accessed June 6, 2013.

same time, many also participate in a variety of other official and unofficial congressional activities, including party or policy committees and whip organizations, issues-related task forces and strategy groups, regional caucuses, state delegation meetings, and more private and personal activities such as bible study groups and members-only social groups. Caught in such a heavy schedule, many try to carve out time regularly to work out briefly in the members-only House or Senate gyms (like private citizens with gym memberships, they pay annual dues to belong, at a fee comparable to that of most public gyms). One of those dues-paying members who often sought out the opportunity to exercise with friends was George H. W. Bush, who continued to use the House gym even when he was president (members knew he was there when they encountered secret service agents stationed outside the doors). Bush was able to use the gym, unlike President Clinton, who succeeded him, or the younger President Bush, because neither were former members of Congress.

The schedule is made more complicated, and the day more hectic, by the uncertain nature of the daily voting schedule. While the Senate tends to be more organized, with senators given a general indication of when votes may occur, procedures in the House are more uncertain. Even when debate on a bill is limited to a predetermined duration (for example, one hour for the bill's supporters and another hour for opponents), the minutes may resemble the last minutes of a basketball game, in which two minutes may stretch to ten. Debate may even be interrupted by an intervening quorum call, which is a recorded vote to determine how many, and which, members are present (usually to help a bill's sponsors or opponents plan their strategies, to stall for time to bring one's supporters to the floor, or to determine whether enough members are present to allow legislative business to continue under House or Senate rules). Members have often remained in the Capitol, or in their offices, well into the evening hours waiting for a vote, only to learn that the matter had been decided by a simple *voice vote* of the members who were present on the House floor at the time, none of them having called for a recorded vote. At other times, proposals that were generally considered noncontroversial and likely to be decided by a voice vote have triggered demands for a roll call, catching members away from the Capitol.

All these time pressures are at least as bad for senators, who represent many more constituents (in the case of California, fifty-three times as many), have many more important state interests to consider, and have more media demands on their time. Even worse for senators is that they do not have the luxury of electronic voting. Each roll-call vote happens only by calling the entire membership roll, which can take up to thirty minutes for each vote.

Despite all the other demands on their time, members prioritize their meetings with their constituents. The First Amendment to the Constitution guarantees each citizen the right to petition the government, which frequently takes the form of a constituent meeting with their member. Day after day, House and Senate corridors are jammed with groups of constituents making their way to congressional offices, usually armed with materials outlining their concerns and legislative goals. Labor leaders, school board members, builders, physicians, operators of child-care centers and nursing homes, auto dealers, environmental activists, members of senior citizen organizations—all make their way to Washington (in addition, of course, to scheduling meetings with their representatives in their home states and districts).

Constituent meetings also take place over meals: at breakfasts, lunches, dinners, and afternoon and evening receptions. Sometimes the meetings are local (for example, realtors from a congressional district for dinner with that member); sometimes they are statewide (realtors from an entire state will hold a dinner for all the members from that state); sometimes they are national (members of a state's congressional delegation will meet with constituents from throughout the state as part of a much larger dinner bringing together many members of Congress in a single room, each of whom will meet with his or her own constituents).

In addition, a variety of institutions and organizations sponsor events to which they invite all members of the House and Senate in an attempt to increase the legislature's awareness of a particular group's concerns and interests. On a typical day, a House member received the following invitations: an Alaskan king crab feed, a reception hosted by an Alaska congressman to help promote the concerns of Alaska fishermen; an installation ceremony for members of the National Advisory Council on Women's Educational Programs; a reception for the new vice president of the Educational Testing Service; a reception sponsored by a group of European airlines that were going to exhibit at a state fair in the member's home district; a reception hosted by the Council on Legal Education Opportunity; a reception celebrating the anniversary of the Republic of China; a reception for the World Fellowship of Religions; a dinner for a high-ranking Chilean government official; a luncheon sponsored by the United Fresh Fruit and Vegetable Association; a reception in honor of a newly published book; a banquet hosted by the Forum for the Arts; a reception honoring a Puerto Rican pianist; a reception at the new Washington offices of a major industrial corporation; a reception to view an automaker's new line of cars; a music festival; a state fair; a golf tournament; a party hosted by the State of Texas, and a reception for the American Paper Institute. Again, the number of invitations and conflicts only increases for senators.

At the end of a long day, members are rarely able to retreat to a normal family life as their predecessors did. With increasing regularity, more members leave their families behind in their constituencies and spend the night in their offices. By one count, as many as fifty members sleep in their offices. Even when Speaker Paul Ryan ascended to the Speaker's chair, he still spent his nights in Washington, DC, in the Longworth House Office Building. He continued to take his regular shower in the House gym. Some members have traded living with their families for living with their colleagues. While he served in Congress, George Miller famously rented the extra bedrooms in his Capitol Hill home to his other colleagues. Chuck Schumer and Dick Durbin continued to live in the home even after they moved from the House to the Senate. Leon Panetta had to move out of the house (and the House!) when President Clinton appointed him to head the Office of Management and Budget. While the Constitution forbids a person to hold two federal jobs, ethics laws prohibit a White House official from paying rent to a member of Congress.[5]

DISTRICT WORK PERIOD

Thursday, June 9, 2011

6:15 a.m. CT – 9:00 a.m. ET	(time zone change) Travel
9:00 a.m. ET – 9:45 a.m. ET	Groundbreaking for Greene County Waste Water Treatment Plant at WestGate at Crane Technology Park (speaking)
10:00 a.m. ET – 10:50 a.m. ET	CACI Ribbon Cutting and Open House at WestGate at Crane Technology Park (speaking)
11:00 a.m. ET – 12:30 p.m. ET	Meeting with RADIUS Indiana at Crane Federal Credit Union
1:00 p.m. ET – 2:00 p.m. ET	Meeting and Tour of URS at WestGate at Crane Technology Park
2:15 p.m. ET – 3:15 p.m. ET	Meeting and Tour of SAIC at WestGate at Crane Technology Park
3:15 p.m. ET – 4:30 p.m. CT	(time zone change) Travel
5:00 p.m. CT – 6:00 p.m. CT	Constituent meetings in Evansville District Office

WASHINGTON, D.C. WORK PERIOD

Wednesday, June 22, 2011

8:00 a.m. ET – 8:30 a.m. ET	Meeting with 2011 Congressional Art Competition winner for the 8th District
8:30 a.m. ET – 9:30 a.m. ET	Republican Conference Meeting
9:30 a.m. ET – 12:00 p.m. ET	Transportation & Infrastructure Committee Full Committee Bill Markup
10:00 a.m. ET – 12:00 p.m. ET	Education & the Workforce Committee Full Committee Bill Markup on H.R. 2218, "Empowering Parents through Quality Charter Schools Act"
10:00 a.m. ET – 12:00 p.m. ET	Science, Space, and Technology Full Committee Hearing on "NOAA's Climate Service Proposal"
11:30 a.m. ET	Legislative Business begins on the Floor of the US House of Representatives (votes throughout day)
12:30 p.m. ET – 1:30 p.m. ET	Republican Study Committee weekly staff meeting
2:00 p.m. ET – 2:30 p.m. ET	GOP Doctors' Caucus Press Conference
3:00 p.m. ET – 4:15 p.m. ET	Department of Defense Value Engineering Awards at the Pentagon where Naval Surface Warfare Center, Crane division received two awards
4:15 p.m. ET – 5:15 p.m. ET	Constituent Meetings in Office
5:30 p.m. ET – 7:00 p.m. ET	Votes

Figure 4.5 Congressman Larry Bucshon's (R-IN) Typical Daily Schedule.
Source: https://bucshon.house.gov/sample-daily-schedule, accessed August 3, 2016.

At the end of a long week, members usually rush home to their constituencies. Once they arrive at the airport, they are subject to the same Transportation Security Administration scrutiny as any other person in the flying public.

Although members may have access to first-class seats because of their status with the airlines or their office allowance accounts, many opt for flying coach out of fear of being seen by one of their constituents in the first-class cabin. One perquisite that members still utilize is free and convenient parking in the Washington, DC, airports.

The pace is no slower at home in their districts and states. Because members of Congress are expected to remain in close touch with their constituents, most return frequently to their home states. Younger members and those elected by narrow margins may return home on most weekends—in fact, most members return home at least forty weekends a year. The congressional schedule is generally compressed into four days a week: they remain in Washington when the House or Senate is in session and leave for their homes on Thursday night or Friday morning, returning late Monday night or early Tuesday morning. These long weekends are generally as hectic as days in Washington, filled with town meetings, civic club speeches, ribbon-cuttings, parades, factory visits, and, as always, countless meetings with individuals or constituent groups. What is more, the weekend pattern is frequently repeated, for longer periods, during congressional recesses—breaks for Easter, Christmas, and for as long as a month during the summer. The pace seldom slows, especially for newer members, who invariably try to attend every possible function in an attempt to build a solid relationship with constituents to whom they may still be relatively unknown.

The heavy schedule of involvement in the home community does provide the members with needed feedback. Members can generally count on getting an earful from morning until night as constituents take advantage of these interactions to let their presumed spokespersons in Washington know what they are expected to do. But this gathering of information, as important as it is to representative government, comes at a high price. Because members of Congress are expected to fill many roles—legislator, ombudsman, representative, caseworker, public speaker— the time that might otherwise be spent on deliberation and study is often frittered away in dribs and drabs in a daily schedule that produces more information than reflection. The multiplicity of tasks creates long workdays and long workweeks, leaving members of Congress exhausted and forcing them to make crucial decisions on the run, eating, talking, and deciding in short bursts of time and attention.

Members of Congress spend time at places other than in Washington, DC, and in their districts. The most systematic use of this time is congressional delegation trips (or CODELs), which are official trips taken abroad by members of Congress. Some of these trips are fact-finding trips when members go to a world hot spot to gain firsthand knowledge of the situation on the ground. In May 2013, John McCain (R-AZ) snuck into Syria not only to assess the ongoing struggle, but also to apply pressure on the Obama administration to step up its support for the Syrian rebels. Other trips are more benign, such as two months earlier, when then Speaker John Boehner sent ten House members to Pope Francis's installation mass as Pope in St. Peter's Basilica. These trips can be criticized by journalists and constituents, especially when they take place in sunny resort destinations. Most trips abroad, though, are to strong US allies or troubled hot spots (see Table 4.2). These trips are an important way for members to obtain the independent information they need to legislate US foreign policy rather than being dependent on whatever the executive branch wishes to tell them or on what they read in the morning newspapers or see on television. Foreign policy is not an exclusive presidential power—in fact, much in the foreign policy arena, from approval of treaties to confirmation of ambassadors to determining the amount of foreign aid and deciding whether to go to war, is specifically within Congress's jurisdiction. Failure to get the firsthand information necessary to make those decisions would be a dereliction of duty. For example, congressional trips overseas led to a cut-off of funds for rebels fighting the Nicaraguan government in the 1980s (and later to a partial resumption of that funding) and to a sharp reduction in aid to the United Nations' International Fund for Agricultural Development (when traveling legislators discovered a significant lapse in the organization's oversight regimen).

Table 4.2 Most-Visited Countries and Total Number of Days Spent There by Members of Congress, 109th–112th Congresses (2005–12)

COUNTRY	DAYS
Germany	1211
Kuwait	1043
Afghanistan	1010
Italy	972
Israel	929
United Kingdom	893
Iraq	766
France	731
Belgium	674
China	656
Remainder	18,178

Source: Alexander Alduncin, Sean Q. Kelly, David C.W. Parker, and Sean M. Theriault, "Foreign Junkets or Learning to Legislate? Generational Changes in the International Travel Patterns of House Members, 1977–2012," *The Forum*, December 2014, 12(3):563–577.

From 2005 to 2012, members of the US House spent 18,178 days abroad.[6] Approximately 60 percent of House members will take at least one CODEL trip over the course of a congress. Some members, though, spend an inordinate amount of time abroad. Congressman Stephen Solarz, who was the chair of the Asian and Pacific Affairs Subcommittee of the House Foreign Affairs Committee, spent 144 days abroad in the 96th Congress (1979–80) and 106 days abroad in the 99th Congress (1985–6). In 1980, Solarz became the first American public official to visit North Korea since the end of the Korean War. In the 112th Congress (2011–2), the chairman of the Rules Committee, David Dreier, spent 124 days abroad. Most members, however, spend about a week abroad per year (SEE FIGURE 4.6). The overwhelming percentage of trips include members from both parties (bipartisan), though an increasing amount are solitary trips or those trips composed of members from only one party (partisan).

All these invitations, meetings, events, and trips abroad are part of the members' official job function. Add to that the normal demands of daily life—children's soccer games, dinners with spouses and coworkers, haircuts, and doctor appointments—and the members' schedules are as complex and demanding as any other citizen's life, but magnified tenfold. Voters who think

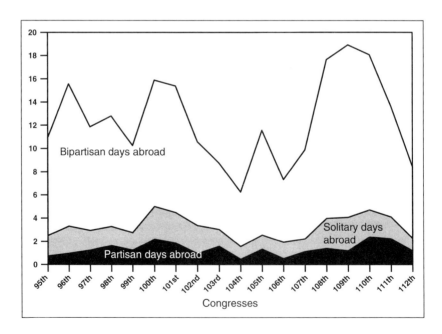

Figure 4.6 The Number of Days That Members Spend Abroad, from the 95th to the 112th Congresses (1977–2012).

members of Congress lead a cushy lifestyle have never seriously contemplated the myriad demands on their time. No doubt, some may lead cushy lives (there are rich members of Congress, just as there are those who come from working-class jobs), but even they would be leading much cushier lives if they did not face the multitude of pressures to which members of Congress are subject.

HOW MEMBERS VOTE

The most important thing that a member does hundreds of times a year is vote. Voting not only sets US policy on college loans, trade with Mexico, and federal spending on roads, bridges, and rivers, but also showcases how members represent their constituents. In other words, voting is the most frequent and best exemplification of members, simultaneously legislating and representing. Political observers have long puzzled over the motivations that cause legislators to vote for or against certain proposals. Some suggest that the motivation is simple, transparent, and self-serving: legislators put their fingers to the wind, decide which course of action will most likely guarantee their reelection, and vote accordingly. Others presume a loftier motive: when members of Congress support the same policies their constituents support and oppose the positions their constituents oppose, they are increasing their chances of reelection, but they are doing so by doing exactly what they were elected to do: represent the people who elected them. Another variant of this interpretation is based on the assumption that the views of the representative and the constituent are identical, or at least very similar, or the voters would have chosen someone else (SEE FIGURE 4.7 for potential influences on how members vote).

In a democratic society, the environment in which we live is at least partially shaped by the decisions of the people we elect. It is important to understand how those decisions are made. And some truth exists in each of the conclusions stated previously. But they are incomplete and may also be misleading. The first of these three interpretations assumes that the men and women who are elected to office are empty vessels with no opinions of their own, or at least that they hold those opinions lightly and dispense with them easily. Yet the most cursory reading of the *Congressional Record*, stump speeches, campaign brochures, Facebook posts, tweets, and advertising scripts reveals that the Congress is generally made up of men and women with strongly held political views.

The second interpretation is based on the assumption that legislators view their jobs primarily in terms of the so-called delegate function of representation: they

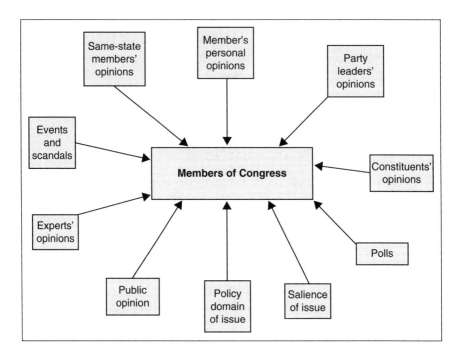

Figure 4.7 The Various Cues Members of Congress Use in Deciding How to Vote.

find out what their constituents want and vote accordingly, more as rubber stamps than as thoughtful legislators. Yet ample evidence shows that legislators vote against their constituents' wishes when to do so seems important to the national interest. In fact, John Kennedy wrote an entire book about such *Profiles in Courage*, and his daughter wrote a follow up, *Profiles in Courage for Our Time*, in 2002.

The third interpretation assumes that legislators are philosophical mirrors of their districts or states, yet countless examples demonstrate that members are concerned about other attributes—a reputation for integrity, attentiveness to local concerns, dedication to constituent service. What is more, since members of Congress vote hundreds of times in each legislative session, a good many of the votes they cast are on issues that were never seriously discussed during their election campaigns: the voters do not know what to expect from the members, and the members do not know where the majority of voters stand.

While it is true that most Americans are not strongly ideological, it is equally true that most of the men and women who run for high public office hold some very strong opinions about the important issues of the day. Given the high cost of campaigning and the toll it takes on one's personal life, a citizen must have a strong motivation to jump into the political waters. As a result, candidates—and this is the pool from which we eventually get the women and men who will serve in Congress—tend to be what the media calls *true believers*, people who have adopted, and are deeply committed to, specific points of view on the important social, cultural, and political issues of the day. Campaigns are fought—and often fought bitterly—over such controversial and divisive issues as gun control, abortion, balanced budget amendments, votes to go (or not go) to war, tax increases, and welfare spending. It would be amazing if the men and women who espouse strong views on these issues during their campaigns were to simply set those views aside after being elected and instead become neutral in the great debates swirling about them.

A pattern of shifting coalitions can evolve based on case-by-case evaluation of legislative proposals. Because the men and women who serve in Congress recognize that, they rely on the more or less predictably liberal or conservative tendencies of their colleagues. Indeed, it is this ability to know where members are likely to align themselves that allows the party leadership in Congress, as well as the thousands of lobbyists who attempt to influence legislative outcomes, to devise effective strategies to develop coalitions to pass or to defeat legislation. By knowing in advance how most members are likely to vote on key economic, social, or defense issues, party whips and their assistants can simply do a quick check to identify potential defections (related, perhaps, to the specific concerns of a member's home district) and then concentrate most of their attention on the smaller number of undecided or *persuadable* members whose votes are necessary to produce a legislative victory.

Members of Congress are sometimes criticized for being overly concerned with their own self-preservation, a suggestion that helps to create among those who hear it a harshly cynical attitude toward the American practice of self-government. Such criticism overlooks the great consistency with which most members of Congress vote. For the most part, if one were to trace a conservative (or liberal) senator's votes over a period of eighteen or twenty-four years (three or four terms), in years when that senator's political philosophy was popular among the voters and in years when it was not, in years when the senator faced tough opposition or relatively weak opposition, in years when his or her party's presidential nominee was strong and when that nominee was relatively weak, one would find that his or her conservative and liberal vote ratings, determined by ideology-based activist groups, would remain within a very narrow range year after year. Conservatives would remain conservative; liberals would remain liberal. It has been argued that members of Congress "die with their ideological boots on."[7]

As the political parties have become ideologically sorted—both inside and out of Congress—teasing out an ideological motivation for casting votes on the chambers' floors from a partisan motivation has become exceedingly difficult. These motivations have not always so conveniently overlapped. In the 1950s and 1960s, southern Democrats were often torn between doing what their fellow partisans from the North wanted and what their fellow ideologues—the conservative Republicans—wanted. On matters of policy, they frequently sided with their ideology. On matters of organization or procedure, they would side with their party. The defeat and retirement of southern Democrats helped propel the aligning of ideology and party in Congress, which, in turn, helped align the ideology and party in the electorate.

More so today than at any point in congressional history, elections have consequences, not because of how they affect the members of Congress—though they certainly do that—but because they determine who is a member of Congress. When the House switched from Democratic control to Republican control in 2010, the House became more conservative, not because Democrats changed their minds but because fewer of them were around; as it turned out, most of those who remained continued to vote as they always had. This consistency in voting by our representatives is important because a strong Congress—a legislative system in which the people themselves, acting through their representatives, make most of the rules they live under—is the key to self-government. If politicians are no more than the self-serving lowlifes so often pictured by skeptics, one could not expect—and should not expect—the system to work very well. Anyone who really wanted a government that worked, that solved problems, that heard the citizens' voice, that cared about the national interest, might very well opt for a system that vested power in a few strong men and women. But if the congressional system works—if the people choose legislators who represent strong beliefs about the nation's priorities and if the legislators they choose can be expected to be true to the values they claim to represent—then the citizen, using his or her vote, can move the nation in one direction or another. It is a critical difference.

Decisions made in Congress are the result of legislators choosing among, or compromising between, differing ideas about what is most important: a stronger defense, for example, or more programs to help the elderly? In most cases, all legislators voting on a proposal to cut defense spending agree that it is important to maintain a strong national defense and that it is important to ensure that the elderly not suffer. But because the supply of available dollars is finite, they ultimately must choose where to draw the line: Does one increase the ability to protect against all possible dangers if doing so means there is less to spend on programs for senior citizen centers? Does one continue to improve senior citizen facilities even at the risk of providing a less effective defense against a potential security threat?

CONCLUSION

Members of Congress must simultaneously oversee the bureaucracy, represent their constituents, and decide on public policy. In this chapter we have explored the cast of characters who are given this awesome burden and how it is they go about doing it. The genius of the system is that members can only continue to do it so long as they are returned to office. Even if members are not motivated solely by their reelection, if they fail to act as though they are, they are likely to be turned out of office.

COMMENTARY

The Politician's Take on the Member's Job

Most of the chapter you have just read reflects a view we both share; that is because we have written this book and its chapters together, editing each other's work. But differences remain.

Professor Theriault cites with some approval Yale professor David Mayhew's argument that members of Congress are motivated primarily by a desire for reelection. Obviously, no member of Congress wants to lose his or her job any more than your professor wants to lose his or her job, or your parents, or, if you are employed, you. And Sean does a good job of attempting to skate around Mayhew's formulation—an exaggeration for effect, a grain of truth, etc. But the fact is that Mayhew, because his colleagues and younger political scientists read his work and grant it credibility, deserves a great deal of the blame for the perception spread in many classrooms that members of Congress care only or at least primarily about getting reelected, a claim that leads to the obvious conclusion that votes on important policy issues—votes that invariably impact the lives of many Americans—are merely the result of a callous, self-serving calculus rather than being based on a member's actual assessment of the merits of the legislation he or she is being asked to vote on. The fact is that most members of Congress have accumulated a history of votes, speeches, and campaign materials that demonstrate long-standing political beliefs. And most members remain true to those beliefs whether or not they face tough opponents or relatively easy reelection races, whether or not their party is popular with the electorate, and whether or not their party's nominees at the top of the ticket (for governor, say, or president) are popular. Rather than being malleable, as a cold reelection calculus would suggest, members of Congress, for better or worse, remain fairly fixed in their political views.

Here is why it matters. If I believe you care only about self-advancement or self-interest, my natural reaction is to distrust what you say and what you do; I believe, as some reporters appear to, that any comment made by a member of Congress is not an accurate reflection of what he or she believes but a way to try to win favor. Soon, any statement by any public official is automatically distrusted. In a democracy that cares about individual liberties, a certain amount of skepticism

(Continued)

is important, but democratic governance also requires some degree of trust in the government one has elected. Arguments like Mayhew's undermine that trust and turn all members of Congress, and all government officials, into self-serving liars in the public's eye.

It is precisely because being a member of Congress gives the men and women who occupy those seats a chance to advance the ideas they believe to be in the best interests of the country that the job is, for most, the most important nonfamily role they ever play. It was for me. Every day when the House was in session, I walked up the stairs Abraham Lincoln walked on, sat where JFK, LBJ, and George H. W. Bush sat before me, and, like them, got to represent tens of thousands—today, hundreds of thousands—of Americans in deciding the most important government issues of the day. Members of Congress, whether they are in Washington or at home, are on seven days a week; it can sometimes be exhausting, but just as often it can be exhilarating.

COMMENTARY

The Professor's Take on the Member's Job

On almost every issue having to do with Congress, the two of us are in complete agreement. While we may differ on policy, we both see the institution of Congress through similar eyes. Put simply, both of us revere Congress.

The one issue that gave us the most concern in writing this book together is Mayhew's reelection motivation assumption. Prior to our joint effort on this book, Congressman Edwards had been meeting with my students in DC for almost ten years. He was always quick to correct what he knew I taught in my class, MOC = SMSR (members of Congress are single-minded seekers of reelection). While the certainty of my presentation of that equation is overstated, I do think that such a simplification for understanding Congress has tremendous merit.

Some may be repulsed by the raw self-interest that it reveals, but I take it as a badge of honor that the framers of the Constitution should wear proudly. Asking members to not be focused on their reelection is the equivalent of asking a football coach to not be focused on winning games or the chief executive officer of General Motors to not be focused on selling cars. Of course, we do not want coaches to win games at all costs or chief executive officers to make profits at all costs, but these fundamentals must drive them or else they are unlikely to be successful. So it is with members of Congress. It is only in seeking reelection that we can evaluate how members are performing their duties.

In his commentary, the Honorable Mickey Edwards says that if members only cared about reelection, they would not be such loyal party members or hold such consistent views even while public opinion vacillates. I think Mickey is both correct and incorrect. Loyalty matters and members too frequently remain loyal even when it hurts them: loyalty not only to their parties, but also to their views. Mayhew's derivation of MOC = SMSR is so beautiful because it encompasses that stability that Mickey so admires in members of Congress. Voters, like members, have many goals in their heads when they cast their ballots. Among those is predictability. If a member's opinion changed with the wind, the voters would simply opt for another candidate in the next election. Reliability, predictability, and consistency matter to voters.

So, when are members likely to be critical of their own party? When are they likely to admit that they have evolved on a particular issue? I would propose that members are likely to be consistent until that consistency becomes too big a burden to bear. The reelection motivation can keep members consistent, but it can also propel adaptations, adjustments, and flip-flops when remaining consistent with a previous position would cause electoral defeat.

CHAPTER 5

The Legislative Process

It is a common enough expression: "There oughta be a law." And laws there are, often hundreds of new ones enacted every year. Public concerns are translated into public action. Housing discrimination is outlawed; protections against too much government intrusion are secured; federal agencies are established to ensure that food and medicines are safe and effective; environmental protections are put in place; taxes are adjusted to encourage saving or to reduce the deficit or to spur economic activity. And new and existing laws are supplemented by appropriations, enacted every year, to provide money for the national defense at home and abroad, to fund America's space program, and to support medical research.

Not all of the public's concerns are addressed, not all of the bills that members introduce are enacted into law (in fact, only about one of ten—in some years, one of thirty—will eventually make it successfully through the entire process), and some of the laws that are passed have a direct effect only on relatively small portions of the population or are thought to be of benefit to only so-called special interests, whether they be dairy farmers, college students, auto manufacturers, or the elderly. So what is it that determines which causes are addressed by Congress, which needs are met, and which programs are funded? How, in other words, does somebody's idea, or concern, make that long and difficult transition from mere thought to public law?

The legislative process is always changing. In this chapter, we provide the broad contours of how legislation has weaved through the process for more than two hundred years. Each step along the way can be both difficult and complicated. There are numerous educational pamphlets, and even films, that describe, in clear, simple, and often cartoonish fashion how a bill becomes a law, but in truth the process is often anything but simple. These descriptions of the legislative process can be thought of as the classic process. In the next chapter, we consider some of the changes that have occurred in the legislative process over the past forty years.

THE TEXTBOOK CONGRESS

The Constitution is surprisingly silent about how a bill should ultimately become a law. It merely mandates that identical bills receive majority support in both chambers of Congress and that the president sign the bill into law; furthermore, it stipulates that each chamber can override a presidential veto with two-thirds support. Almost all other steps in the legislative process are subsumed under the right of each chamber to establish the necessary rules to govern the legislative process in its respective chamber. The legislative process used by the early congresses changed quickly. By the time the country started dealing directly with the scourge of slavery, the legislative process was well established; it had become so regularized that by the mid-twentieth century, political scientists described it as the *Textbook Congress* or the classic process (SEE FIGURE 5.1). While even the Textbook Congress was not immune to alterations and developments, the broad contours, to which we now turn our attention, were fairly consistent.

Introducing a Bill

The first step in the process—generating an idea that should be enacted into law—can be the most difficult. Usually, behind an idea lies a deep-seated passion or an initial spark that propels a person to engage in the legislative process. Someone—a member of Congress, a congressional aide, the President of the United States, a cabinet secretary, a constituent, a manufacturer, someone who works for an association, a college professor, an employee of a federal agency, or even a college student—decides that something ought to be done about a particular problem, in other words, *there oughta be a law.*

If the member of Congress decides to investigate the idea in hopes of formulating legislation, frequently the staff works with policy experts to crystallize the idea into legislation. Additionally, Congress has created two nonpartisan offices to help determine whether the idea has merit and, if so, how to transform the idea into legislation. First, the Congressional Research Service, which is part of the Library of Congress, is filled with policy experts who can tell the members and their staffs what laws currently exist and how they are carried out. Second, the Office of the Legislative Counsel contains lawyers who transform these ideas into the legal language that is used in legislation. Both offices adhere strictly to nonpartisan activities; they do not provide expertise on constructing a political argument surrounding the law, though members certainly have access to many of these kinds of experts as well.

Once a bill has been formally drafted, it can be introduced by—and only by—a member of Congress. Other legislatures permit the president, governor, or some other nonlegislative actor to introduce bills. In the US Congress, only bills that have been signed by a duly sworn-in member of Congress introduced in that member's chamber while Congress is in session are considered to have officially

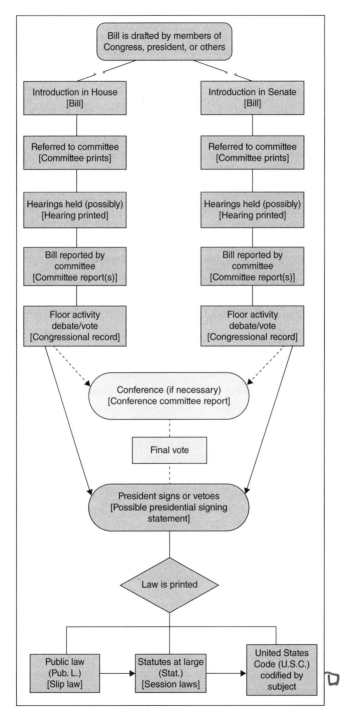

Figure 5.1 The Legislative Process Under the Textbook Congress.

been introduced. In the House, this is done by placing the bill in the hopper, a basket on the Speaker's rostrum. In the Senate, a senator can introduce a bill by taking it to the clerk at the rostrum or by seeking recognition to introduce the bill verbally. In whatever method chosen, the member who introduces the bill is called the *sponsor*. To showcase broad support for a piece of legislation, the sponsor will frequently seek many or several powerful members to *cosponsor* the legislation. If the cosponsor *signs on* to the bill prior to introduction, the member is called an *original cosponsor*. After the bill has been introduced, any member can sign on to it. The members who sign on after introduction are called simply cosponsors. The signature of the member is the only formal requirement for the bill: members could introduce a bill that they wrote out on a napkin the previous night at a local pub—so long as the napkin contains their signature. The bill can even be in the language spoken by baseball players on a diamond rather than the legal language that most bills take. Again, the only requirement is that the bill contains the member's original signature.

When the bill is introduced, the parliamentarian in the respective chamber refers the bill to the appropriate committee for action. Although the parliamentarians work at the pleasure of the Speaker of the House and the Senate majority leader, they use the rules of the chamber and precedents rather than politics in making their decisions. One of the first acts of a new House of Representatives is to adopt an outline of each committee's jurisdiction; in the Senate, the jurisdiction rules from the previous congress remain in place, though the Senate can amend them whenever they like. As with the Congressional Research Service and the Legislative Counsel's Office, the parliamentarian is not an operative of a political party. For this reason, when the majority switches from one party to another, the employees of these offices usually remain the same; they do not flip-flop like party leadership offices, committee staffs, or even some administrative staffs such as the clerk of the House or the secretary of the Senate, though they can be replaced because they each serve at their patron's pleasure.

Merely writing a bill and introducing it is unlikely to yield much further action. The sponsors of legislative proposals, if they are to be successful in creating new laws, must undertake aggressive, and sometimes lengthy, campaigns to win support for their ideas, often beginning long before their proposals are scheduled to be considered in any formal or official way. As soon as the legislation is introduced (and sometimes even much earlier), its sponsors undertake the effort to build support in two distinct ways: among their congressional colleagues, whose votes they need for passage, and within the greater public community—the constituents, contributors, and policy advocates whose views may play a significant role in each member's voting decisions. Inside the Congress, this effort is usually done first in personal conversations between members who share similar

===== **EXAMPLE 5.1** =====

Introducing a Bill

The 1960s and 1970s saw an explosion in the laws protecting various groups from discrimination, most famously the Civil Rights Act of 1964, which protected women and racial, ethnic, and religious minorities from discrimination in employment and public places. This legislation, however, did not include persons with mental or physical disabilities. To rectify this exclusion, advocates pushed for similar protections for those groups and Congress responded with several additional laws. The 1973 Rehabilitation Act prohibited discrimination against disabled persons in federal jobs and programs. The 1975 Education for All Handicapped Children Act required free public education for disabled children with as few restrictions as possible (it continues to exist today as the Individuals with Disabilities Education Act). The 1988 Fair Housing Amendments Act prohibited discrimination in selling or renting housing on the basis of a disability. Many advocates for the disabled felt additional legislation was needed to prevent disabled persons from being discriminated against in private-sector jobs and public accommodations. To codify these protections into law, Senator Tom Harkin (D-IA) introduced S.933 on May 9, 1989, with a bipartisan mix of original cosponsors (9 of the 33 were Republicans). Before it passed the Senate, an additional 30 senators become cosponsors, 10 of whom were Republicans. On the same day Harkin introduced his measure, representative Tony Coelho (D-CA), who struggled with epilepsy himself, introduced a companion measure in the House. The list of cosponsors in the House had a more Democratic tilt—only 40 of the 250 cosponsors were Republicans (14 of whom were original cosponsors).

Although similar bills had been introduced the previous year, no action had been taken before the 100th Congress (1987–8) ended, requiring the bills to be reintroduced in the 101st Congress. The bills prohibited discrimination against disabled persons in hiring and in services and accommodations like transportation, restaurants, and other public places. They also required the federal government to issue new accessibility guidelines for public places built after the law's enactment and for modifying existing buildings.

One of the provisions ensured that public transportation was accessible for all. Because many areas of public life, including public transportation, were already the subject of countless federal laws and regulations and because federal agencies and even judges must be able to know specifically what a law is meant to do (or not do), the drafting process may turn out a legislative product that seems like legalistic gobbledygook to the casual observer. Instead of mandating that "public transportation be accessible for all," the legal language is more specific and, well, more legalistic (SEE FIGURE 5.2).

Because such precision is required to eliminate ambiguity in the law, a great deal of attention is paid by Congress's nonpartisan legislative drafting offices to the wording of legislative proposals. Getting the language precise enough that it cannot be misconstrued by either the bureaucrats who are charged with enforcing the law or the judges who are charged with interpreting the law is both an art and a science.

(Continued)

SEC. 403. PROHIBITION OF DISCRIMINATION IN PUBLIC TRANSPORTATION SERVICES PROVIDED BY PRIVATE ENTITIES.

(a) GENERAL RULE: No individual shall be discriminated against on the basis of disability in the full and equal enjoyment of public transportation services provided by a privately operated entity that is primarily engaged in the business of transporting people, but is not in the principal business of providing air transportation, and whose operations affect commerce.

(b) CONSTRUCTION: As used in subsection (a), the term 'discriminated against' includes—

  (1) the imposition or application by an entity of eligibility criteria that identify or limit, or tend to identify or limit, an individual with a disability or any class of individuals with disabilities from fully enjoying the public transportation services provided by the entity;

  (2) the failure of an entity to—

   (A) make reasonable modifications consistent with those required under section 402(b)(2);

   (B) provide auxiliary aids and services consistent with the requirements of section 402(b)(3); and

   (C) remove barriers consistent with the requirements of section 402(b)(4); and

  (3) the purchase or lease of a new vehicle (other than an automobile) that is to be used to provide public transportation services, and for which a solicitation is made later than 30 days after the date of enactment of this Act, that is not readily accessible to and usable by individuals with disabilities, including individuals who use wheelchairs.

Figure 5.2 The Legal Language for the Provision Banning Discrimination in Public Transportation.

At times, the words chosen in a draft have drastic consequences as to the legislative path the bill takes. Although each committee and subcommittee of the Congress has an assigned area of jurisdiction, the line separating those jurisdictions is often fuzzy and porous. By changing a few words in the drafting of a bill, a member can ensure that his or her proposal is sent to a committee where the sponsor knows that the chair or other influential members are inclined to support passage, rather than to another committee where the bill is more likely to be ignored or even actively opposed. In the House of Representatives, for example, simply calling a charge a *user fee* (in which case jurisdiction could fall to several different committees) rather than a *tax* (the purview of the Committee on Ways and Means) may make the difference between ultimate success or failure in trying to maneuver an idea through the legislative process. Knowing the proclivities of the committee members, a bill's sponsor may also try to include language or provisions that increase the chances that the proposal is favorably received.

When Senator Harkin introduced his bill, he gave a speech highlighting its importance: "The [Americans with Disabilities Act] is, without exaggeration, the most critical legislation affecting persons with disabilities ever considered by Congress."[1] In his floor speech accompanying the bill's introduction, House sponsor Tony Coelho (D-CA) briefly explained, "The bill will go a great distance toward eliminating discrimination against the disabled in employment, public accommodations, transportation, communications, and public services."[2] By giving these floor speeches, the influential sponsors signaled to their chambers that they considered the Americans with Disabilities Act an important legislative priority.

---

interests. A special effort is made to win support from members of the committees and subcommittees that initially determine the legislation's fate. Chances for passage are greatly enhanced if the sponsor persuades the chair or another influential member of the relevant committee to agree to support it. At the next step, the sponsor will attempt to enlist the help of as many other members as possible. This step is usually undertaken by the circulation of a "Dear Colleague" letter in which the primary supporters spell out the legislation's intent and arguments for its adoption and ask for other members' support. Some get involved in the fight for passage, becoming allies in trying to gain a public hearing and favorable votes in committee. Others, who may simply agree with the premise of the proposed legislation, but not rank it high among their own legislative priorities, may nonetheless agree to be listed as cosponsors (most members, in fact, cosponsor many bills, including large numbers of proposals that are quickly buried and forgotten, simply because it is a way to show their support for an idea or do a favor for a colleague, even if it is an idea whose time clearly has not come).

Because of the number of bills that get introduced, the introductory phase of a bill's path through Congress may drag on for months, some even with additional "Dear Colleague" letters. What's more, because the legislative struggle is as much an effort to defeat "bad" ideas (bad, of course, being in the eye of the beholder) as to enact "good" ones (also in the eye of the beholder), members often read these letters to learn of initiatives they may wish to actively oppose. Thus, another letter may be generated, this one warning of the dangers of the proposed legislation. Controversial proposals may generate a flurry of letters back and forth, pressing arguments and rebuttals. Thus, the battle rages, outside the view of either the press or the public literally as a fight for the minds of one's colleagues.

Upon introduction, the member can engage in activities that can enhance the bill's prospects for future success. If members give a speech on the floor announcing the introduction of the bill, they send a signal to their colleagues that they take the legislation seriously and advocate for further action. Members can also play to an outside audience. Giving a press conference sends a stronger signal than simply offering a press release. Members' time is their most valuable resource. If they expend time on a task, other members are more likely to take notice. Most bills are introduced without a speech on the floor or even a press release. In the 114th Congress (2015–6), senators introduced 3,548 bills and representatives introduced 6,536.

Committees

After the parliamentarians in their respective chambers refer the bills, it is up to the appropriate committees to act on them—or not. The committee procedures in the House and Senate are analogous. Each committee and subcommittee has on its plate a wide range of issues, and however valuable a member's time is, committee time is that much more valuable. The chair is ultimately responsible for setting the committee's agenda. Only through much effort—and at the considerable risk of damaging the relationship with the chair—can other committee members wrestle even part of a committee's agenda away from the chair. Obtaining the chair's support for a bill is therefore crucial for it to move beyond the referral stage.

Whether a bill receives any action is almost entirely left up to its chair, who can refer the bill to subcommittee or simply start full committee deliberations— or the chair can simply not act on the bill whatsoever. If the bill is referred to subcommittee, it undergoes a process similar to that in the full committee. At the request of the (sub)committee chair, the (sub)committee can hold hearings on the bill. During hearings, members, lobbyists, chief executive officers, political activists, and even ordinary citizens can offer analysis or insight into the bill. The chair has sole authority to call witnesses, either individually or as a panel. Usually by agreement, the ranking minority party member can also call witnesses, but rarely is the minority given as much time as the majority in presenting its arguments. These witnesses make their own brief statements, though they frequently reserve the right to submit a much longer statement to the committee. After the statement is entered into the record, each member on the committee is given the opportunity to question the witness or panel of witnesses. Hearings are frequently more about establishing a public record than changing minds. The statements by experts are repeated and cited as evidence for the bill's approval or disapproval, in precisely the same way that a lawyer draws on witness testimony to persuade a judge or jury of a client's innocence or guilt.

=== **EXAMPLE 5.2** ===

Committees

Although most House bills are sent to a single committee, the parliamentarian referred the House draft of the Americans with Disabilities Act to four different committees; because of the expansiveness of the legislation, Judiciary, Public Works
and Transportation, Energy and Commerce, and Education and Labor each were
given a part of the bill. Within weeks, each committee, in turn, referred the bill to
at least one of its subcommittees, where extensive hearings were held and compromises between the chairs and ranking members were forged. In turn, each of
the committees acted on its portion of the bill. In the end, each committee overwhelmingly reported to the floor its part of the bill.

The House Education and Labor Committee unanimously approved the bill
in November 1989. The Energy and Commerce Committee had jurisdiction over
the bill's telecommunications and railroad provisions and approved the bill by a
40–3 vote in March 1990. The committee also amended the bill to require Amtrak
and other commuter rail providers to provide at least one disability-accessible car
per train within five years and to make all newly purchased or built trains similarly
accessible to the disabled. The Public Works and Transportation Committee, which
had jurisdiction over the other transportation provisions, approved the bill by a
45–5 vote. The final House committee with jurisdiction, Judiciary, spent two days
marking up the bill and adopted several compromise amendments to make the
bill more favorable both to business groups and to disabled rights advocates. The
committee finally approved the bill by a 32–3 vote.

Because of the compromises struck along the way, the bill that would be debated on the floor had changed dramatically from the one Coelho introduced.
Not only had the bill changed, but also its primary House patron changed—
representative Steny Hoyer (D-MD) took over the bill when Coelho, who was em-
broiled in a financial scandal, resigned from Congress in June 1989.

Unlike in the House, the Senate bill was referred to only one committee—
the Labor and Human Resources Committee, which within a week began holding hearings. Several business groups, including the US Chamber of Commerce,
testified against the bill, citing the costs of implementing the employment
protections. To assuage the concerns of business and to retain the support of
president George H. W. Bush, who had publicly endorsed the bill as a presidential candidate and again a few days before being inaugurated as president, the
committee compromised its way to a unanimous vote in reporting the bill to
the full Senate.

Many more bills are never given a hearing—they simply are filed away and
forgotten, never to be acted on. After hearings, if the (sub)committee wants to
further the legislative process, it conducts a *markup* in which the bill is presented to members of the (sub)committee for debate and the offering of amendments. During this stage, the members have the opportunity to literally mark

up the bill—that is, make all sorts of changes, both great and small. Members supporting the legislation usually view proposed changes skeptically; members opposing the bill almost certainly attempt to amend it either to make it less bad, from their standpoint, or to inject material that makes it harder either for the proponents to pass the bill when it gets to the floor or for the bureaucracy to enforce the provisions of the new bill. If the bill's sponsor is a member of the (sub)committee, he or she attempts to orchestrate the debate, making clear to supporters which, if any, amendments are acceptable (most, being less familiar with the issue, tend to follow the sponsor's lead). If the sponsor is not on the (sub)committee, he or she must find an ally to lead the battle at the committee level. So long as the amendments garner a majority vote, they become part of the bill. At the end of the markup, all the members of the (sub)committee take a vote on whether to *report* the bill. If the bill has not been changed, they take a vote to report the bill. If the bill has been changed in markup, they take a vote to report the bill as amended. Sometimes the bill has undergone such radical changes that the original bill is barely recognizable. In these cases, the committee may just decide to consider reporting a *substitute* to the bill—if so, a vote to report the bill in the nature of a substitute is taken. If the motion to report a bill receives majority support at the subcommittee level, the bill is reported to the full committee, where it can go through the same process. If the motion to report a bill received majority support at the committee level, the bill is reported to the chamber from whence it came prior to its referral. If a majority at the (sub)committee disapproves of the bill, it is consigned to the congressional trash can in the same way that a bill that never had a hearing was.

Throughout this process—which may take many months—the bill's sponsors and supporters continue to pursue their efforts to line up additional endorsements from persons or organizations outside Congress and from colleagues in the House and Senate. Now, however, the focus of support is more carefully targeted. If the Sierra Club or the Chamber of Commerce, for example, supports a proposal, it encourages its supporters who live in the home districts or states of the members who serve on the committees to which the bill has been assigned to write to, or visit, the targeted member of Congress. The most important and most effective *pressure group* for any member of Congress is his or her own constituents, and it is to them that a bill's sponsors turn to increase the pressure for supporting the proposal. In addition, groups like the Sierra Club or the Chamber of Commerce are urged to publish news of the proposal in their newsletters, to write articles for newspapers, as well as contacting members of Congress with whom they have close relationships.

For major bills, the process of winning approval, from the subcommittee level to the committee level to the House and Senate floor, becomes a continuing escalation of pressure on the members who will ultimately decide the bill's fate.

While the Sierra Club or Chamber of Commerce is galvanizing its members, so too are the interest groups on the other side of the issue. Even bills of lesser scope and less controversy are subject to the same sort of campaign, though on a smaller scale. Any member that hopes to have her idea enacted into law must be proactive in corralling support. Rarely does legislation move through the process based solely on the power of the idea; even the smartest, most efficient, and most obvious ideas require substantial energy to triumph through the legislative process. As such, most bills never move beyond the referral stage of the legislative process. In the 114th Congress, only 532 senate bills and 849 house bills survived committee deliberations and were reported to their respective chambers.

The Floor

Even for those bills that make it through the early stages—finding cosponsors and outside supporters, persuading committee leaders to allow hearings and conduct markups—the legislation now has only begun to wind its way through the arduous process of being transformed from an idea into a law. It is not uncommon for legislation to make it successfully past the hurdles posed by the subcommittees and committees of the House and Senate and yet proceed no farther.

Through the committee stage, both chambers have similar processes, though the House typically relies more on its committees than the Senate does, which is more likely to skip the committee and directly consider a bill on the floor. Once a bill is reported from the committee, the chambers have very different processes. These different processes have come about as a consequence of each chamber deciding its own rules. Nothing in the Constitution mandates that the House follow one prescribed path while the Senate follow another. In fact, if the Senate so chose, it could adopt the House rules for its chamber, but neither chamber can eliminate its respective constitutionally designated presiding officers, the Speaker of the House and the president of the Senate (the vice president). House and Senate rules can go beyond the Constitution, but they cannot go against it. Regardless of the chamber, it is crucial to obtain the support of legislative leaders—the majority leader in the Senate and the Speaker in the House of Representatives—who hold enormous power in deciding which bills are considered on the floor and when.

The House of Representatives

In the House of Representatives, the reported bill goes to the all-important Rules Committee, which is stacked with members who are loyal to the Speaker and where the majority party usually has twice as many committee members as the minority. In a large chamber with many members, the biggest advantage the majority party enjoys over the minority party is its ability to structure debate, and its dominance on the Rules Committee is the surest way to maintain this advantage.

=========================== **EXAMPLE 5.3** ===========================

The Floor

The Senate took up the unanimously approved Senate Labor and Human Resources Committee's Americans with Disabilities Act bill in September 1989. For the first time, the Senate debate featured a sign-language interpreter. During the debate, which took place all on one day, the Senate considered sixteen amendments: one was withdrawn, one was defeated by roll-call vote, one was agreed to by roll-call vote, and twelve were agreed to by voice vote. The remaining amendment, which Senator Grassley (R-IA) offered, was perhaps the most interesting from an institutional perspective. He tried to have the law apply to Congress, which, at the time, was exempt from most civil rights laws. While no senator was interested in exempting Congress from the law, several were reluctant to support the amendment because they believed it would be unconstitutional to give the executive branch authority over the legislative branch to enforce compliance. Finally, the senators agreed to Grassley's amendment via standing vote, but also to another amendment by Senator Harkin (D-IA) that protected the rest of the bill by making the amendment severable, which means that if a court ever struck down the provisions in the Grassley amendment, the remaining portions should still be enforced, rather than the entirety being declared unconstitutional. The Senate passed the bill, 76–8, via roll-call vote on September 7.

The House considered the bill the following May. The rule (H.Res.394), which established two hours of debate and listed the amendments that would be considered, passed 237–172 when all but eighteen Democrats voted for it and all but fourteen Republicans voted against it. The House considered eight amendments: two were approved by voice vote, two were approved by roll-call vote (one of them unanimously) and four were rejected by roll-call vote. For each of the amendments except the unanimously approved one, a majority of Democrats voted against a majority of Republicans, but the parties did not vote as a block—far from it. At least twenty-three members defected from their party's majority on each of the votes. The most controversial amendment, adopted on a close 199–187 vote, allowed employers to transfer food workers with contagious diseases to other jobs, even if the disease could not be transmitted through food. The amendment's supporters said that the provision was needed to give employers flexibility in the face of public perceptions about how AIDS could or could not be transmitted. Opponents of this amendment, including the Bush administration, charged that it was discriminatory because all relevant science suggested that AIDS could not be spread through the handling of food.

Having dispensed with all the amendments, the House considered a motion to recommit the bill to committee, which serves as a last chance for the minority party to change the legislation. The House overwhelmingly defeated the motion (143–280) before even more overwhelmingly approving the bill; only 3 Democrats and 17 Republicans voted against the 403 supporters.

The House has very particular rules, which it adopts at the beginning of each new congress, that dictate the order in which the bills shall come up for debate on the floor of the House. To supersede that strict regimen, the Rules Committee must write a *special rule* for a particular bill for it to have priority status on the floor. In so doing, the rule also outlines how the debate proceeds in the House. It dictates the amount of time that shall be consumed on the House floor, which members control the time, which amendments are to be considered and in which order they shall be debated on the floor, and even whether members are allowed to raise points of order to protest a violation of House rules (for example, allowing proposals to authorize new programs in a bill to appropriate spending).

The Rules Committee, its chair, and the majority of its members serve theoretically as traffic cops, ensuring that the House's systematic consideration of legislation is not bogged down by trivial side issues or by attempts to delay the smooth progression of legislative action. What the Rules Committee does in reality, however, is much simpler: it operates to ensure that legislation the majority party supports has the best chance of passing and that legislation it opposes has far worse chances of success. At this stage, it does this primarily by controlling the amendment process. The Rules Committee can provide the members much discretion on the House floor. It could permit any member to make any amendment to any part of the bill, so long as it is consistent with the House rule that the amendment is germane—which is a fancy way of saying it is relevant to the bill. Such a rule that allows a broad level of participation is considered an *open rule*. Likewise, the Rules Committee can declare that no member can make any amendment to any part of the bill. Such a rule is a *closed rule*, because it closes the bill to alteration. Between these two extremes, the Rules Committee offers many variants. Some rules permit one or two amendments; other rules permit any member to offer an amendment so long as the amendment has been printed in the *Congressional Record* prior to the debate (called *modified open rules*); still other rules close off certain titles from amendment while opening up other titles to any amendment (known as *modified closed rules*).

Upon the special rule's adoption on the House floor, debate proceeds according to the dictates of that rule. After debate on the bill, the minority party typically has one last chance to change the legislation—even under a closed rule. This last chance is a *motion to recommit* the bill to committee. The language of the motion suggests that the bill would be referred to a particular committee with some suggested change; however, the practice of the motion, if it is agreed to, is often that the language is automatically changed "forthwith" and reflected in the bill prior to a final passage vote that usually happens shortly after the recommittal motion—in other words, the committee to which the bill is formally *recommitted* does not officially act on the bill—the changes to the bill happen automatically upon the adoption of the motion.

In the House, members can take votes in several different manners. First, and easiest, they can take a voice vote, whereupon members who support the proposal collectively say "aye," members who oppose the proposal say "nay," and the presiding officer announces which side had more *voices*. If any member thinks the presiding officer has made an incorrect judgment, she can ask for a division of the assembly, in which members' explicit intentions are counted. Typically, the presiding officer asks members to stand at the appropriate time to indicate which side they support. These *standing* votes are not recorded. Only the people inside the chamber or watching on CSPAN can determine which member supported which side. Though the rules require that a certain number of members request it, in practice, the presiding officer simply grants a standing vote without counting hands. Only on recorded votes are each member's intentions explicitly recorded individually. All members wishing to vote must record their preference by inserting a specially encoded card (the size of a credit card) into the numerous voting boxes on the House floor within the amount of time prescribed by the rule setting up the bill's debate. The presiding officer is responsible for cutting off the time in which members can vote. Even when the members agree to take a fifteen-minute vote, the presiding officer—not the time clock—decides when the "fifteen minutes" has expired. Whatever method is used, the side with the most votes wins.

Speaker Paul Ryan has tried vigorously to redefine "fifteen minutes" as fifteen minutes. Within a few months of becoming Speaker, Ryan closed the vote on an important Iran sanctions bill even though more than 130 members had yet to vote. Amid calls to extend the vote, Ryan retorted, "Voting within the allotted time would help with the maintenance of the institution." And with that, because of their own tardiness, nearly a third of the representatives' voices were silenced on an important foreign policy issue.[3]

The Senate

The Senate follows a different floor process altogether. Because each senator has more individual power than a representative in the House, little happens in the Senate without every senator's consent. Whereas the House operates under special rules, the Senate operates under *unanimous consent agreements*, which are usually hammered out by the majority leader and the minority leader. These agreements are not about the wording of the bill as much as they are about the manner in which the bill would be debated on the Senate floor. The leaders work in consultation with their entire party membership because even if the leaders have decided on an agreement, any senator, by virtue of it only taking effect on the unanimous agreement of the entire Senate, has the power to object, which would seriously derail the legislation.

Once all senators have agreed upon a unanimous consent agreement, the bill is usually debated and amended in a much more informal way than in the House, though the agreement can dictate rather strict procedures for the debate on the Senate floor. At the conclusion of the Senate debate, if a majority of the senators vote in favor of it, the bill is considered passed in the Senate.

Because each senator has the power to seek recognition on the Senate floor, the legislative process in the Senate can become cumbersome. First, an individual senator can object to a unanimous consent agreement, which can stall or obstruct the process. Second, during debate, a senator, once recognized to speak, can speak indefinitely, which is called a *filibuster*. The only recourse that the other senators have against a senator who objects to a unanimous consent agreement or who holds the floor indefinitely is to *invoke cloture*. Cloture can stop these filibusters, but it requires the consent of sixty senators. Because of the importance and now frequency of these filibusters, most pundits speak as though passage of legislation in the Senate requires sixty votes. To be clear, passage only requires a majority, but frequently a supermajority is required to cut off debate, which is necessary for taking a final passage vote. Third, as opposed to the House, the Senate permits nongermane amendments. In fact, nongermane amendments are frequently the easiest way to move forward legislation that has otherwise stalled. Senators, if they desire, can strip a bill of all its words except the bill number and replace it with an entirely different piece of legislation. Or, a senator can offer a completely unrelated amendment to a bill being debated on the Senate floor. If the amendment passes, both the original bill and its amendment are then considered bound together. The House, with its germaneness rule, could only consider an amendment if it was in some way related to the bill on the House floor.

But it is important to note that in most cases, and especially on controversial issues, a bill's supporters do not merely toss their proposals onto the floor and hope for the best. To develop a workable strategy, therefore, one must have a good sense of what other members are thinking. One must know how members are planning to vote and what changes in the proposed legislation might change their minds, making them more or less inclined to support the bill. It is not enough merely to have in hand a headcount of who plans to vote which way; a member who has put a great deal of effort into winning passage of a legislative initiative must also know what amendments would improve chances for passage and which ones must be opposed. On the one hand, a proposal's staunchest opponents may strongly resist passage of an amendment that might, in their view, make the legislation less bad on the grounds that the improvement may cause some who might have opposed it to decide that the bill was now at least marginally acceptable, thus hurting the opposition's chances of bringing about the bill's defeat; a bill's supporters, on the other hand, may reluctantly agree to support amendments that would modify their proposals if they felt the change was something they could live with and might improve the chances of the legislation's ultimate passage—or they might oppose the changes in the belief that they would simply destroy the bill's intended effect. In addition, the principal advocates of the legislation must also know which of the available arguments would be most effective in floor debate and which members would be most effective in delivering those arguments. Thus, managers of a floor debate often spend considerable time appealing to the concerns of members *across the aisle*. Republicans, for example, citing the words of Democratic presidents, respected Democratic legislators, or people important to the Democratic political base (union leaders, environmentalists, civil rights activists) if suitable quotes can be found. Although members spend a great deal of time crafting their message, the audience most of the time for most of the floor speeches is not their fellow members, but the press, interest groups, and people who are watching the proceedings from outside the chambers.

It is not only the debating procedures that are different in the Senate; so, too, are the voting procedures. One commonality is the use of voice votes. If one-fifth of the senators insist, a roll-call vote can be demanded. Instead of voting electronically as the House does, the Senate takes votes by calling the roll. The clerk calls each individual senator by name and records the position that the senator announces. While the House does not forbid the calling of the roll, the Senate simply does not have provisions by which they could even take an electronic vote; as with almost everything, though, the senators could implement electronic voting if they so desired.

By the time it survives committee and finds its way to the floor, a bill has traveled a significant way down the path to becoming a law. If member time is precious and committee time is even more precious, floor time is the most precious of all. Party leaders are reluctant to use floor time except for bills that have a good chance of passing. Nonetheless, the sponsor and proponents of the legislation must tread carefully. While the success rate of a bill surviving the floor is much greater than the success rate of a bill surviving the committee, it is still not 100 percent. The Senate passed 172 of the 532 bills that were reported from committee in the 114th Congress. The House passed 633 of the 849 committee-reported bills.

Passage in one chamber or the other only marks the halfway point for legislation. When a chamber passes a bill, it informs the other chamber of its action. From there, the legislative process in the second chamber starts from the beginning. The bill is subject to the same committee and floor trials and tribulations that it experienced in the original chamber. Because the chamber of original jurisdiction typically gives a bill the full legislative process, the second chamber to act can, but does not always, skip or shorten the legislative paths to passage. Nonetheless, many bills in every congress surpass the hurdle of one chamber, but fail in the other. Because of all the steps required in the legislative process, sometimes a bill in one chamber will have a *companion* bill in the other chamber. That means that both the House and the Senate can consider pieces of related legislation at the same time. They cannot, however, simultaneously act on the same piece of legislation.

Acting simultaneously on bills that cover similar topics—or even that contain identical language—can improve the chances of passing a law, but certainly does not guarantee it. In the 114th Congress, the Senate passed 268 House bills and the House passed 132 Senate bills. Incidentally, the Senate did not pass 137 bills that the House did pass and the House did not pass 33 bills that the Senate did.

Action After the Floor

The Constitution requires that both chambers pass an identical bill before being sent to the president. More often than not, the chambers pass two different bills. Sometimes the differences arise because one chamber makes changes to the other chamber's bill; other times, the House passes its version of a bill and the Senate passes a companion bill (or vice versa). However the changes happen, these House-passed and Senate-passed versions must be *reconciled*—that is, both chambers must pass the identical bill before it can be presented to the president.

The chambers have used multiple processes to iron out the differences in the legislative language. The easiest process is for one chamber to adopt the changes made by the other chamber. For example, if the Senate makes minor changes to a House-passed bill, it is relatively straightforward for the House to adopt the Senate's changes. If so, both chambers will have passed the same bill and it will then be subject to a presidential signature or veto.

A more complex version of the same basic process is for the chambers to negotiate as entire chambers the changes needed for the legislation to become identical. Suppose the Senate makes three changes to a House-passed bill. The House could agree on the first and third changes, but insist on the original language with respect to the second change. The Senate could then agree to drop the second change. If so, then the bill, in identical form, passed both chambers and is subject to presidential action.

The process usually used by the Textbook Congress was for the chambers to establish a conference committee whose purpose it is to iron out the differences between the chambers' bills. The members—or, in the language of Congress, *conferees*—are made by the presiding officer, but usually in consultation with the party and committee leaders. As a general rule, the conferees are chosen from the committees that held hearings on the bill, sent it on to the floor for final passage, and managed the debate in favor of the bill on the House and Senate floors. That is not always the case. Leaders in both chambers have considerable power over the naming of conferees and may, in effect, predetermine the outcome of the deliberations simply by choosing which members participate (or by refusing to name any conferees at all, thereby dooming any chance of the bill ever becoming a law). Furthermore, conference committees have great powers. They can alter language that is consistent between both bills; they can even delete the exact same language

---

EXAMPLE 5.4

Action After the Floor

The controversial food service amendment and the different provisions regarding applicability to Congress were the two biggest changes made during floor deliberations of the bills. To reconcile not only these two big differences, but also the relatively minor differences in the bill, the House requested a conference committee with the Senate, which subsequently agreed. The conference committee convened in June 1990, and conferees came to agreement over the course of a single two-hour meeting. The conference committee agreed that the House and Senate would set up different internal procedures for dealing with discrimination claims. The food service provision proved trickier, as Senator Jesse Helms (R-NC) had offered a motion to instruct Senate conferees to accept the House's amendment, which the Senate then approved by voice vote. Motions to instruct conferees are nonbinding, so the Senate negotiators were not required to adopt the food service amendment, but now majorities in both chambers had gone on record supporting the provision. In the end, conference committee chair Edward M. Kennedy (D-MA) convinced the Senate conferees to oppose the provision, while House conferees voted to strike it 12–10. As a result, the food service amendment was dropped from the conference report. When the conference committee report went back to the two chambers, Democrats had hoped to have the House approve the bill first, but a few Senate Republicans blocked action out of fear that the House would reject another attempt to add the food service provision, which then would prevent the Senate from being able to amend the conference report in a similar way. A month later, in July 1990, the Senate sent the bill back to conference to change the way that Senate employees could file for discrimination. Senator Helms once again filed a motion to instruct conferees to adopt the food service provision, but this time the Senate rejected his motion by a 39–61 vote. Instead, the Senate approved a compromise sponsored by Senator Orrin Hatch (R-UT) that required the Health and Human Services Department to develop and disseminate a list of infectious diseases that could be transmitted through handling food and to allow employers to transfer workers with the diseases on that list to other positions. This motion was approved 99–1 in the Senate, and the conferees from both chambers quickly adopted the new provision. The House approved the conference report on July 12 by a 377–28 vote, with Senate approval coming the next day by a 91–6 vote.

---

that both chambers passed. They have the power to do whatever they want to the entire bill. Their only constraint is that what they do is subject to a vote in both chambers. Thus, even after legislation has passed both chambers, a bill's sponsors must continue to lobby congressional leaders to ensure that the bill is, in fact, sent to conference and that a sufficient number of the bill's supporters are included to ensure a positive result. For the bill to be reported from the conference committee, it must enjoy majority support from both the House conferees and the Senate conferees independently. The conferees take separate votes by chamber and both must approve the legislation before it is sent back to their respective chambers.

In the conference committee, most relatively minor differences are easily disposed of by staff members, who meet by themselves to reach a preliminary compromise. Major differences, however, may lead to hours of contentious debate between the members themselves across party and chamber. Because most such deliberations are open to the public—meaning that both reporters and interested parties may be present—compromise is difficult (politicians are not eager to be seen as selling out those whose interests they have been championing). Thus it may be that sometime after midnight, or close to it, the member chairing the committee (a role that alternates between the House and Senate) declares a brief recess, during which the key players (the chair and ranking member from each chamber, perhaps accompanied by a representative of the White House and the bill's leading proponent) step into a separate room, out of public view, and quickly agree on the compromises necessary to reconcile the bills. When the conferees are called back together, agreement can often come quickly.

But because committees are generally not representative of the House or Senate as a whole, the agreements reached by conferees may not be acceptable to the full House or Senate membership. After a conference committee concludes its work, the compromise version must go again to both chambers since both the House and the Senate must, in the end, pass identical bills. At this stage, neither chamber can amend the language decided on by the conference committee—the only option is to approve it or defeat it. Even here, another challenge looms. Amendments that were defeated in the House, for example, but passed in the Senate and are agreed to as part of the final conference compromise may doom the entire legislation when it returns to the House if enough of the bill's original supporters consider the amendment (which they had already defeated once) to go beyond what they are willing to accept. In addition, the intervening time (many months may pass between the time a bill passes one or both chambers and the time it goes to, and returns from, a conference committee) gives opponents time to mount intensive lobbying campaigns that can persuade a senator or representative to change his or her vote. Because the conference committee's compromise version invariably contains provisions that were not included the first time the member voted for the bill, it can be easy to explain a changed position. The lobbying, the persuasion, and the public debate thus continue well past the time when a bill is actually voted on. Again, each chamber determines its own procedures and process, including the right to simply ignore the conference committee's compromise. If a chamber does refuse to act on the bill and if—as a last-ditch effort—the other chamber refuses to accept the first chamber's bill, the legislation dies at the end of the congress even though it almost got all the way through the process. In the 114th Congress, the House and Senate only passed 338 identical bills.

On to the White House

Although the president formally only enters the legislative process at the end, his hand is felt throughout the process. The president has a congressional liaison team whose job it is to meet with key congressional leaders, a bill's leading supporters or opponents, and individual members whose decisions may affect the outcome. This team stresses the president's positions and often attempts to determine whether some presidential action might sway members' votes. On any important piece of legislation, the White House issues a printed memorandum, available to members during the debate, outlining the president's position on the bill under consideration, including his reasons for support or the principal arguments against passage. If the president is strongly opposed to the bill, the memorandum may include a threat that the president will veto the legislation unless it is substantially altered. Because it is difficult to override a presidential veto, such threats are taken seriously and a bill's advocates may continue, even at this late stage, to negotiate with the administration, seeking a compromise that will allow the president to eventually sign the legislation. This description assumes that it is the principal goal of the bill's sponsors to see the proposal eventually enacted as a public law; however, that is not always the case. When the Congress is controlled by the president's opposition, bills may be introduced, passed, and sent to the White House in full awareness that they will never become law, but in the hopes that the president's veto will create a political issue to be used against him, or against his party, in the next round of elections. The House of Representatives made at least seventy attempts to repeal the Affordable Care Act (otherwise known as Obamacare).[4] Members considered this primarily political posturing because they knew that Obama would veto the legislation, which he did in early 2016. When Donald Trump became president, Republicans had a much harder time passing a repeal bill because they knew that it would be signed by Trump, who had campaigned on its repeal. Because of that, six Republican senators who supported repeal in 2016 voted against repeal in 2017.

If the president does eventually receive the bill, the president can sign it, veto it, do nothing, or place it in his "pocket." If the president signs the bill, it becomes law. If the president vetoes it, the Congress can then vote to override his veto. If two-thirds of the members in both chambers agree to override the president's veto, the bill becomes law. If the president does not act on the bill and Congress remains in session for ten days (not including Sundays), the bill becomes law. If Congress, during those ten days, adjourns and the president does not act on the bill, the bill dies. In essence, the president kills the bill, not actively by vetoing it, but passively, by sticking it in his pocket.

The End of a Congress

Bills in Congress face many opponents. Committee chairs can ignore bills and never hold hearings on them. Party leaders can sabotage the legislation in a

---

EXAMPLE 5.5

On to the White House

Because the president's legislative team had been involved in the bill since even before its introduction, no drama accompanied the bill's final step in the process. President Bush, surrounded by all the bill's champions, signed the bill into law on July 26, 1990. He described the behind-the-scenes work to get the bill through the legislative process: "It's been the work of a true coalition. A strong and inspiring coalition of people who have shared both a dream and a passionate determination to make that dream come true. It's been a coalition in the finest spirit. A joining of Democrats and Republicans. Of the Legislative and the Executive Branches. Of federal and state agencies. Of public officials and private citizens. Of people with disabilities and without."[5]

The Americans with Disabilities Act of 1990 faced some challenges to its enactment, but it also illustrates the classic, or textbook, legislative process at work. Companion bills were introduced in each chamber after several years of developing a particular policy idea, in this case, prohibiting discrimination against people with disabilities and ensuring that they have equal access to transportation, communication, and public spaces. The bills first received subcommittee action, and then the full committees got involved. While this was going on, committee leaders, administration officials, and interest groups worked together to forge compromises over how the law would eventually be implemented. Members of both chambers who did not sit on the relevant committees were given the opportunity to offer amendments on the floor. Large bipartisan majorities supported the bill both in the committee setting and on the chamber floors, and a conference committee was given the opportunity to reconcile the differences between the two different versions. In short, the Americans with Disabilities Act's path through the legislative process shows how rules, order, and structure were important for success in the Textbook Congress.

number of different ways. Special interests can lobby members to oppose legislation. The president can issue veto threats or vetoes themselves. These are all great opponents. But none of them is as pervasive as any legislation's greatest opponent: time. Committee chairs may be favorably disposed toward legislation. Party leaders, from both sides and both chambers, might support it. It may even have support from interest groups and the president, but the time and effort to ensure that a bill clears all the legislative hurdles may simply be too great. If bills could exist in perpetuity, time might not be as formidable an opponent. But, bills only exist as bills until Congress adjourns *sine die*, which literally means "without day," or in the parlance of the legislative world, "without assigning a day for further meeting."

While Congress can adjourn several times during a congress, it only adjourns *sine die* at the end of a congress. When it does so, it intends to adjourn until the next congress begins. At that point, all the legislation from the previous congress ends and must start from the very beginning in the next congress. Even a bill that has only a word difference between the House-passed bill and the Senate-passed bill must start at the beginning with a member signing a bill and placing it in the hopper. Very few bills are ever actually defeated, either by a majority in committee or by a majority on the floor. All but very few bills simply die at the end of a congress because they have never been acted on.

DIFFERENT PIECES OF LEGISLATION

Until this point in the chapter, we have only considered bills, the type of legislation most of us think of when we think of Congress. Bills can be public—that is, they apply to everyone in the United States—or private—that is, they apply only to named individuals. In 1971, the bureaucracy was given more power to deal with the matters that had previously only been addressed in private bills. Since then, private bills are normally restricted to grants of citizenship, alleviation of tax obligations, or military matters.

Bills—private or public—are abbreviated with the first letter of the originating chamber. So, the first bill in the House of Representatives is called H.R.1. The first bill in the Senate is called S.1. But bills are only one type of legislation considered in Congress.[6] Like bills, joint resolutions—abbreviated H.J.Res. or S.J.Res.—require majority support in both chambers before being presented to the president for his disposition. Successful bills and joint resolutions both have the status of law, but Congress typically uses joint resolutions for things that do not have the permanency of law. For example, Congress creates temporary commissions, such as the 9/11 Commission, with joint resolutions. It also uses joint resolutions for continuing appropriations (when one fiscal year ends before Congress has appropriated money for the following fiscal year), making irregular appropriations (such as the funds made available for recovery after a disaster), establishing the date for convening of Congress, and adjusting the amount of money the government can borrow. It also uses joint resolutions for two important pieces of legislation—to declare war and to amend the Constitution.

Unlike bills and joint resolutions, concurrent resolutions—abbreviated H.Con.Res. and S.Con.Res.—are not presented to the president, but continue to require majority support in both chambers. Congress uses these mostly for congressional housekeeping matters like adjourning, recessing, creating joint committees (as opposed to commissions), and providing for a joint session of Congress. Importantly, the congressional budget resolutions, which provide the broad contours of the congressional budget, are also established by a concurrent resolution.

Simple resolutions—abbreviated H.Res. and S.Res.—are specific to each chamber. Because the Constitution gives each chamber the power to establish its own rules, the assent of the other chamber is not required. So, changes to the Senate Rules are accomplished through an S.Res. Simple resolutions also are used for the adoption of special rules in the House (for the outlining of legislative debate on the floor), the expulsion of members (which requires a two-thirds vote), the disposition of a contested election (each chamber decides its own contested elections), expressing the *sense* of the chamber (which can relate to specific legislation or to stake a general belief contained in the chamber's membership), and the ratification of a treaty (Senate only; requires a two-thirds vote).

IMPLICATIONS OF THE TEXTBOOK CONGRESS

The legislative process in the Textbook Congress was neither born into existence overnight nor is it changed with each new majority that sweeps into the Capitol. Rather, it is a process that Harvard political science professor Kenneth Shepsle says has come to balance the three competing interests of committees, parties, and constituents.[7] This semistable process included the necessary components for obtaining aggregate success in a legislative body: congressional experts on the issues (committees), the coalitions that form to win elections and govern the country (parties), and the members' desires to satisfy the demands of those responsible for electing them (constituents). Members, recognizing the process, adapted their individual behavior to succeed at this legislative game.

Under the Textbook Congress, three rules of thumb came to dominate their behavior inside the Capitol. First, members recognized that rules, order, and structure are critical for success. A bill was not heard on the floor before it had a full vetting in committee. Differences in the House bill and the Senate bill were resolved in conference committee. The majority leaders and the minority leader in the Senate regularly provided for the broad contours of debate in the Senate.

One step of the process was not taken until the previous step was accomplished. If the bill failed at one step, the process stopped. Although even in the Textbook Congress rules and structures could be abrogated, a strategy that relied on unconventional moves usually backfired. In fact, the process in the Textbook Congress was so orderly that it was called a *ladder* process—no rung on the ladder could be attempted until the previous rung has been accomplished.[8]

Second, a sponsor of a bill recognized the importance of the committee and its chair because of the crucial role it played in setting the legislative agenda. The easiest route to getting a bill signed into law was to get the committee chair's support. Although legislation in the Textbook Congress could pass without the chair's approval, a strategy that tried to go around the chair was much less likely to succeed.

Third, members who had expertise were valued in the legislative process; those who sought publicity were not. Because of the importance of committees in the process, a sponsor of a bill was likely to get much further in the legislative process if she pursued the support of the committee's chair than if she pursued the support of the *New York Times* editorial board. In the language of Capitol Hill, *workhorses* were rewarded for thoroughly learning a policy area and becoming an indispensable voice in the minutiae of law; *show horses*, who were more concerned with their next media appearance, had a more difficult time seeing their ideas turned into laws.

CONCLUSION

In the classic legislative process as described in this chapter, more than perhaps almost anywhere else, the founders' plan is clearly seen. For the most part, neither the president nor the Congress can act without winning at least the tacit consent of the other—a system that inevitably forces compromise and prevents extreme positions from dominating the legislative process.

Lawmaking in the United States—that is, placing new taxes on the people, providing new rules and regulations that limit the individual's freedom of action, or merely wiping old laws off the books—is a difficult exercise, designed to maximize the ability of citizens to influence the legislature's actions and to force some degree of consensus before new burdens can be imposed. If the American system of government is intended to both empower and constrain the nation's elected officials, it is in the arduous process of considering proposed laws that the dual purpose is most clearly seen. An idea can become a bill and a bill can become a law—the public's concerns can be addressed and many of its collective problems alleviated—but not easily and, for the most part, not quickly. The process of transforming a raw idea into public law requires the leaping of one high hurdle after another, which is why the winning of the congressional version of Olympic gold—standing beside the president as he signs your bill into law—is for most legislators a remarkable professional triumph.

By separating the powers of government into various political units, the framers of the constitution deliberately placed many roadblocks between the formulation of an idea and the enactment of a new federal law. It was their intention that it should be exceedingly difficult for the federal government to impose a new tax on the citizenry or to subject the nation's citizens to new laws telling them what they may or may not do. Many of the framers, including leaders of the Revolution, spent a considerable portion of their later lives as officials of the federal government, an exercise in the relatively new idea of self-government, a means of ensuring that the people themselves would have ultimate control over the laws they would live under and the taxes they would be required to pay.

While dividing authority into three branches, the Constitution is quiet about the exact legislative process a bill should follow before being implemented into law. Within a few years, however, a standard model developed that came to be thought of as the Textbook Congress for the methodic manner in which it can be explained. A bill does, in fact, become a law, eventually, by the same process so often depicted in cartoons and film strips: an idea becomes a bill, the bill is sent to committee, the committee sends it to the full House or Senate, then to the other body, then to conference, then to the president, and, voila, there is a new law on the books.

The model is just that, a model. It does not describe the legislative process for every bill. Not every law passed goes through all the steps described in this chapter—there are only a few essential steps (passage by both chambers, for example). In fact, in more recent congresses, the regular order has become rather irregular. We discuss these irregularities in the next chapter.

═══════════════════ **COMMENTARY** ═══════════════════

The Politician's Take on the Legislative Process

You have not read Sean's take on this yet because mine comes first, but I have read it, and as you will see, this chapter in particular—looking at the Textbook Congress and the evolved (devolved?) Congress—gives us a chance to show how the prism through which one sees things can lead to both congruence (Sean and I agree on much) and divergence.

Sean is right in at least two very important particulars. The first is that the Textbook Congress now so lovingly recalled was not all sweetness and light, nor was it truly reflective of the society at large. He is right that the number of women and minorities in Congress was so small that their absence almost certainly affected both policy decisions and funding priorities in both the House and the Senate. He is also right that we had some real battles, fiercely waged, throughout that time.

But I suggest that there are other factors to take into account; on the surface they contradict each other but that, in fact, is the nature of Congress: it has more facets than the Hope diamond.

One factor is that the battles were intense and over fundamental issues—tax rates, foreign policy, environmental regulation, the whole panoply of divisive public policy questions, including conflicts about the government's role in affecting what had long been private matters (some version of the Hyde Amendment, opposing the use of federal funds to pay for abortions, found its way into hosts of other unrelated policy debates). America was supporting governments against rebels (El Salvador) and supporting rebels against governments (Nicaragua). Newt Gingrich unleashed vicious attacks against Speakers Tip O'Neill and Jim Wright, and then O'Neill's words were stricken from the public record in a rare rebuke after he attacked Gingrich in return. Those who see those days as supremely stable remember a time that never existed.

But here is what did exist: at the end of the day, things got done, and often in a bipartisan manner. Here is a personal example. My liberal friends hate this, but I believed the rebels fighting the Sandinista government in Nicaragua were in the right and that supporting them was the right thing to do, a decision I reached after many trips to Central America to meet with priests, labor leaders, farmers, and government leaders. Tip O'Neill and most of his fellow Democrats were convinced that the rebels (the Contras) were the bad guys. After the Congress had cut off funding for the Contras, defying the Reagan administration, I offered an amendment to restore part of that funding (for nonlethal support). Democrats had a large majority in the House and O'Neill, who controlled the Rules Committee, was strongly opposed to my amendment, as were a majority of his party members. But Tip and his Rules Committee allowed my amendment to be offered and allowed a full and fair debate, and in the end, I won. In addition, the final three speakers on behalf of my amendment were three of the most powerful Democrats in the House, even though O'Neill spoke passionately in opposition to it. Not only did the Speaker allow an amendment that he and most of his party opposed, but also Democrats as well as Republicans felt free to support me. That is what was different.

In sixteen years in the House, especially after I was elected to a senior party leadership position, I spent countless late-night hours huddled with Republican and Democratic negotiators hammering out compromises on difficult issues. Like other members of that time, I had numerous friends on the other side of the aisle. So in that sense, the Textbook Congress—now viewed either as something unfortunately lost or as something that never really existed—did exist. And it was different. And it was better.

COMMENTARY

The Professor's Take on the Legislative Process

In today's highly polarized Congress, the Textbook Congress is deified. According to conventional wisdom, the Congress of the mid-1900s knew how to compromise, solve problems, and get along with each other. While party competition existed, it did not paralyze the legislative process. Furthermore, the American public trusted Congress, voter participation was high, and public service was respected. Again, according to conventional wisdom, the war raging between the parties brought all of that to an end and ushered in the ugly side of politics.

Wisdom cannot become conventional unless it contains elements of truth. While the Textbook Congress certainly had its attributes—especially looking at it from the present—political science does a disservice when it fails to point out the legislative losers during the Textbook Congress. In the congresses of the 1960s, the House included a handful of African Americans, half as many Hispanics, and never more than eighteen women. Legislative compromise was forged by white men who had a much more common path to Congress than those of their twenty-first-century counterparts.

While the New Deal began the sewing of the social safety net, it took the demise of the Textbook Congress to bring about real civil and voting rights legislation. The conservative demeanor exercised by members of Congress was matched by their conservative approach to the legislative process. Pressing problems advocated by newly active and engaged faces required bold leadership—all of which the Textbook Congress obstructed.

The Textbook Congress accentuated order, rules, and structure. In today's chaotic politics, those attributes are sorely needed. Nonetheless, order, rules, and structure make achieving other positive qualities such as responsiveness, accountability, and mass participation more difficult. No historical era of Congress should be evaluated by simply scrutinizing its strengths or its faults. A comprehensive analysis requires an examination of both assets and liabilities. Only then can we get an accurate picture of where things stand prior to offering reform proposals.

CHAPTER 6

Modern Developments in the Legislative Process

Newt Gingrich's tumultuous reign as Speaker came to an end when the Republicans lost seats in the 1998 midterm elections, the first time since 1934 that the president's party gained seats in the midterm. When representative Denny Hastert (R-IL) took over for Gingrich, he promised to take the House in a different direction under his speakership. Rather than delivering his inaugural speech as Speaker from where the presiding officer stands, he went down to the House floor to deliver his inaugural speech, which included this passage:

> Serving in this body is a privilege, it is not a right, and each of us was sent here to conduct the people's business. I intend to get down to business. That means formulating, debating, and voting on legislation that addresses the problems that the American people want solved. In the turbulent days behind us, debate on merits often gave way to personal attacks.
>
> Some have felt slighted, insulted, or ignored. That is wrong. That will change. Solutions to problems cannot be found in a pool of bitterness. They can be found in an environment in which we trust one another's word; where we generate heat and passion, but where we recognize that each member is equally important to our overall mission of improving life for the American people. In short, I believe all of us, regardless of party, can respect one another, even as we fiercely disagree on particular issues.[1]

Nancy Pelosi, after two years of serving as Speaker with President Bush in the White House, sounded a similar theme of letting the will of the House majority work its way, but only after she strong-armed the passage of President Obama's economic stimulus package. She promised to abide by the *regular order* after her leadership team received a letter signed by sixty-eight members of her Democratic caucus asking leadership to loosen its grip on the legislative process.[2]

In the months before he became Speaker, John Boehner (R-OH) made the same promises as Hastert and Pelosi:

> So instead of clamping down even further, it's my view that we should open things up and let the battle of ideas help break down the scar tissue between the two parties. Yes, we will still have disagreements. But let's have them out in the open. Yes, we will still try to outmaneuver each other. But let's make it a fair fight. Instead of selling our members short, let's give them a chance to do their jobs. Let's let legislators legislate again.[3]

Voicing the same sentiment, Speaker Paul Ryan made the same declaration: "We need to let every member contribute, not once they earn their stripes, but now. . . . The committees should take the lead in drafting all major legislation: If you know the issue, you should write the bill. Let's open up the process. . . . In other words, we need to return to regular order."[4]

The regular order that was so admiringly described by each of the last four Speakers of the House is the process described in the previous chapters as the Textbook Congress. It was the process that valued rules and order, recognized the importance of committees (and their chairs), and rewarded members for becoming policy experts. Each of the Speakers, upon assuming the power to ascertain the will of the majority in the House, to varying degrees, ignored the regular order in an attempt to achieve legislative victories for their party. Upon gaining the ability to control the levers of the legislative process, the majority party leadership usually opts for efficiency, which frequently runs counter to the Textbook Congress's more deliberative regular order.

In addition to the party leaders' attempts to more efficiently achieve legislative success, members' individual prerogatives struck at the core of the Textbook Congress. Leaders—in conjunction with individual members—no longer wanted to invest in a system that encouraged rules and structure, that empowered committees, and that punished members for seeking the media's spotlight. Moves outside of the institutional Congress, though not entirely outside of the members' own hands, helped bring down the regular order.

This chapter first outlines some of the forces that transformed the regular order into the *irregular order*. Then we discuss some of the tricks members and party leaders have innovated to pass their ideas into laws. These unorthodox procedures—as political scientist Barbara Sinclair (2011) calls them—have at times become more regular than the regular order they replaced. After reviewing some of these unorthodox changes, we discuss the implications that they have had on the legislative process. Suffice it to say from the outset, the members serving with Speaker Ryan no longer follow the same rules of thumb that the members followed when Speaker Sam Rayburn presided over the Textbook Congress in the middle of the past century.

FORCES THAT BROUGHT ABOUT THE IRREGULAR ORDER

The Textbook Congress, which took shape in the middle of the twentieth century, balanced members' interests in passing good policy, in maintaining good relations with their constituents, and in utilizing political party to help them achieve their goals (Shepsle 1989). If Congress were not responsive to the people, the Textbook Congress may have continued in perpetuity. But, in the lead-up to and the recovery after the American involvement in World War II, the nature of representation between members of Congress and their constituents changed and, with it, its politics. The norms that had dictated member behavior during the Textbook Congress began to break down. In this section, we outline some of the forces that chipped away at the Textbook Congress before examining the changes in procedures in the following section.

Individual Member Enterprises

Though they lost some power with the Progressive Era reforms in the late 1800s and early 1900s, political parties were still primarily organizing congressional elections. Most members of Congress remained on the job as long as their constituents and their parties consented. These dynamics persisted even through the Great Depression, World War II, and the beginning of the Cold War. Although most Americans continued to approve of President Eisenhower, his personal popularity never fully transferred to the Republican Party, which he had only officially joined a year before being elected president.

Republicans were able to achieve bare majorities in both chambers when Eisenhower was first elected in 1952, but promptly lost it two years later. By the sixth year of the Eisenhower presidency in 1958, the Republicans in Congress feared that while the president remained popular, the American public was looking for change. In recognizing that the Republican label was wearing thin, Republican incumbents decided to run their campaigns as individuals rather than as a team as the parties had done since the two-party system had been established in the United States. The weakening of parties in combination with the increasing availability of radio and television permitted the incumbents an alternative route to Congress. As such, the Republican descriptor was missing from campaign paraphernalia in hopes that the voters would go with the name they recognized instead of the opponents of the party that they had grown weary of. The strategy ultimately failed in stemming Republican defeats when they lost forty-eight seats in the House and fifteen seats in the Senate, though it may have succeeded in keeping those numbers down from what might have otherwise happened. We will never know how the Republicans would have done had they run, as they had done before, as a team. Despite the Republicans' poor showing, the strategy of running as individuals rather than as members of the team took hold and would be repeated whenever candidates perceived that their party label was electorally weak.

As members' ties to the fortunes of their parties decreased, they became increasingly responsible for their own elections. With time, and with an increase in financial and technological resources, members would become more and more electorally independent from their party. As members were able to raise more money, develop their own campaign strategies, and run on their own messages, they became less willing to abide by a system that rewarded orderly play and, in some respects, stifled individuality in the legislative process.

In short, none of the implications of the Textbook Congress fit with the members who were increasingly in charge of their own electoral enterprises. Members were less willing to go along with a structure and order that would not give them an immediate role in the process. They were less willing to cede their power to a committee chair who may or may not share their priorities and values.

They were less willing to do the work of legislating in lieu of raising their profile, which more directly helped them achieve their next electoral victory. While the implications of the Textbook Congress may have been good for passing legislation, they were not good at helping members, especially newly elected, vulnerable members, keep their seats in Congress. The individual member enterprises offered an additional route to Congress that became increasingly popular among incumbents.

The Stalling of Civil Rights Legislation

Despite their best efforts to minimize their losses in the 1958 elections, Republicans lost many seats to liberal Democrats. Two years later, Democrats enjoyed unified government when John F. Kennedy entered the White House. During these two elections, the South had remained as Democratic as it had been since the end of Reconstruction in the late nineteenth century. The national change in politics was that more urban centers in the North began to vote for Democrats at higher levels. These new Democratic voters and the candidates they elected expected action on the most pressing issue of the late 1950s and early 1960s: civil rights.

Each chamber had a feature that kept civil rights legislation from passing. In the House, chairman Howard W. Smith (D-VA) and his fellow conservatives dominated the Rules Committee. Even when the Judiciary Committee reported a civil rights bill, it was never able to secure the rule required for debate on the House floor. In the Senate, the conservatives were able to filibuster it, which required both a supermajority of votes and time on the Senate floor to break. These features helped to weaken the Civil Rights Act of 1957, which pleased neither the opponents nor the supporters of civil rights, though, to its credit, was the first civil rights bill enacted into law since Reconstruction.

The members who campaigned on and fought for civil rights grew frustrated with a system that thwarted their efforts. They began applying an increasing amount of pressure on their party leadership to permit a full debate on civil rights. In 1961, Speaker Sam Rayburn engineered a compromise for his caucus that would retain Smith as the chair of the Rules Committee, but expand the number of seats on the committee so that it could finally have a pro–civil rights majority. After a long struggle that included the death of a president, the energies of his successor, and, perhaps most crucially, changing the fundamental rules of the game, Congress finally passed the Civil Rights Act of 1964 and the Voting Rights Act of 1965. In so doing, however, the Textbook Congress, which rewarded rules and order, committee power, and workhorses, necessarily had to be weakened.

Supreme Court Opinions

While the representatives among the states have been consistently reapportioned every ten years following a census, as dictated by the Constitution, redistricting within the states has been much more sporadic. For nearly two hundred years under the Constitution, the drawing of congressional district lines was an activity left almost entirely up to the states. Through several Supreme Court decisions in the 1960s, however, a new requirement was added to the mapmakers' requirements—an equal number of constituents in every congressional district within a state. In the 1962 case *Baker v. Carr*, the Court struck down the malapportioned districts by instituting a *one person, one vote* standard. Two years later, the Supreme Court clarified that opinion in *Wesberry v. Sanders* by requiring the congressional districts in a state to be as nearly equal as possible.

By requiring districts within a state to have equal population, the Court implicitly forced congressional districts to become more heterogeneous. Prior to this Supreme Court mandate, states often prioritized district homogeneity instead of population equality. An urban district might have more constituents and a rural district might have fewer constituents in the interest of keeping like-minded constituents within one district. To achieve population equality, congressional districts frequently cut across communities of interests.

What the implementation of this standard meant for members was that they needed to be involved in multiple policy areas to satisfy the multiple demands of their constituents. Prior to the 1960s, a member from a rural part of the state could afford to focus all of his energy on agriculture policy. As the districts came to have an equal number of constituents, a rural member with a segment of their population based in the suburbs of a big city split her time between agricultural policy and roads because some constituents demanded price supports for their crops while others wanted more efficient commutes to their jobs in the big city. As a consequence, members had a desire to get involved with the legislative agenda on committees to which they were not appointed. Again, the rules and order and the sovereignty of committees (and their chairs) were sacrificed on the altar of a politics in transition.

Northernization of the South; Southernization of the North

Since the earliest days of the Republic, the northern states and the southern states had different priorities and interests. It took Thomas Jefferson and Alexander Hamilton brokering a deal to bring the US Capitol from the far North in New York City to the border between the two in its current location of Washington, DC. Later in the nineteenth century, the divergent interests of the regions exploded into the Civil War. The Reconstruction of the South after the war did little to align the two regions' differing interests. What the location of the Capitol and the resolution of slavery did not do, television and the growth of the national news media did. When broadcast journalists from the 1950s and 1960s, such as Edward R. Murrow and Walter Cronkite, gave the news of the day for the entire nation, they forged a national identity and national standards for acceptable behavior in a way that regional newspapers simply could not. In part, it was the national news media coverage of the deplorable treatment of African Americans in the South that shook the consciences of northern liberals and gave rise to a national civil rights movement and, eventually, the laws that encapsulate it.

As the news media began telling a national story, transportation and infrastructure greatly improved, which increased both travel and migration across regions. As people from the North moved south to take advantage of the warmer weather and the more hospitable business climate, Southerners moved north for improved job prospects in the industrialized labor force. What at one point were distinct regional issues became national priorities. Northerners who moved south created the demand for increased education funding in the South just as the influx of African Americans to the north put issues like busing and affirmative action on the agenda in the North.

As the issues within the regions became more diversified, so did members' desires to address them. A system that prioritized rules, order, and committee autonomy could not easily be adapted to meet the growing number of issues demanding members' attention.

The Fiscalization of Politics

Two months after President Kennedy was assassinated, president Lyndon Johnson declared, in the 1964 State of the Union address, a war on poverty in the United States. At the same time, Johnson escalated spending on the conflict in Vietnam. In combination, these two "wars" greatly increased the federal budget. These two spending sprees slowed, at least in the interim, the engine of economic growth in the United States. During the same period, the debt grew because the federal government did not simultaneously increase the amount of revenue it was collecting even while it was spending more.

President Richard Nixon attempted to restrict government spending simply by withholding the money from congressionally approved projects that he opposed. Congress passed a law in 1974 that strictly forbade this impounding of funds. A year later, the Supreme Court decided in Congress's favor.

In the 1980s, the deficit grew even more as a result of a compromise between President Reagan and Congress. House Democrats supported Reagan's defense increases so long as he would support their increased spending on social domestic programs. When Reagan proposed the tax cuts on which he campaigned, it was too tempting for him and Congress to cut revenue and, simultaneously, to increase spending on their pet projects. When tax rates went down and spending increased, big deficits got even bigger.

By the late 1980s, members of Congress could no longer achieve compromise by spending money on both Democratic and Republican priorities. In breaking his "no new taxes" pledge, president George H. W. Bush, Reagan's successor, ushered in a new era where the conflict between the parties could not be settled by spending money on both the military and domestic social programs. When large deficits and the growing federal debt entered the legislative agenda, bargaining and compromise between the parties became more difficult.

By their very nature, budget politics did not align with the existing committee system. To control the raging debt, the lawmaking system needed to view the entire budgetary situation simultaneously, which automatically linked issues that were previously considered independently. Because neither the rules and structures within Congress nor the committee system could contain the fiscalization of politics, the Textbook Congress seemed ill suited to deal with pressing problems of the deficit and debt.

The Sorting of the Parties by Ideology

In the 1950s, the American Political Science Association made a rare foray into the real world of politics by decrying the functioning of the political parties at the time. It issued a report calling for parties to be more internally homogenous so that the voters could face a clear choice in elections and the winning party's platform could more easily work its way through the legislative process. At the next election, the voters could more easily reward or punish the party based on how its programs addressed the major issues of the day.

Although not immediately realized, the desires of the American Political Science Association committee have been increasingly satisfied. The conservative southern wing of the Democratic Party, although waxing and waning, has been on a downward trajectory since Johnson signed the civil rights bill into law. The progressive wing of the Republican Party, which had always had its base in the New England states, has almost entirely disappeared.

When both parties had a liberal and a conservative wing, compromising across the aisle was more easily accomplished. In today's politics, competition between the parties is heightened because the parties today are as divergent as they have ever been. As a result, compromise across the parties today is reached only on relatively insignificant issues or by expending much effort. The Textbook Congress had little role for political parties, and as party leadership in Congress has gotten stronger, the Textbook Congress has increasingly suffered.

Party Competition

In more recent American politics, neither the liberals nor the conservatives have enjoyed a long-run clear majority. The ideologues have always been tempered by the so-declared moderates. The only way that the Democrats ever fashioned a *permanent majority* in the Congress in the years after the stock market crash of 1929 was because they were able to hold a significant portion of the liberal vote along with most of the South, which had always been conservative. As this coalition began to fall apart, American politics increasingly became divided along party and ideological lines that reinforced each other. While the sides in the partisan war have diverged, the battleground has become more equally divided. Between Kennedy's election and Clinton's, the Republicans—even those inside Congress—knew that they would be in the minority after the election. Everyone was surprised when they managed to win the Senate on Reagan's coattails in 1980 and hold it until his six-year-itch election in 1986. But for that one hiccup, Republicans knew that for them to have an influence in the legislative process, they would have to work with Democrats.

Newt Gingrich thought that the Republicans could become a majority in the 1994 election. In the beginning of that election cycle, most everyone disagreed. By the end of the cycle, the Republicans had, indeed, won a majority of seats in not only the House, but also the Senate. Ever since 1994, both parties have entered the election cycle believing that they could win a majority of seats. In the ensuing years, the majority party has had a significantly smaller majority than the Democratic majorities of the 1960s through the 1980s.

What this intense electoral competition has meant is that both political parties try to gain electoral advantage wherever they can. The Textbook Congress, in privileging rules and order, sought, first and foremost, solutions to public policy problems. Today's Congress, in contrast, seeks, first and foremost, electoral victory. In so doing, today's minority party tries to thwart the majority party at every turn. Furthermore, party leaders seek to win not only the legislative game, but also the electoral game by portraying their opponents in the worst possible light. The values and features of the Textbook Congress were ill suited to deal with parties that use the legislative process to score electoral points.

The Imperial President

When the United States entered World War II, president Franklin Roosevelt dominated politics. In each military exercise abroad since that time, the American public has rallied behind its president, at least initially. Johnson's efforts in Vietnam only became unpopular as the war raged on. President George H. W. Bush enjoyed unprecedented approval when the United States defended Kuwait in the Persian Gulf. His son achieved his highest approval numbers in the wake of the September 11, 2001, terrorist attacks; only when the War on Terrorism continued to rage did they began to fall.

Since the 2001 attacks, the United States has lived under a constant terrorist threat, which has increased the stature of the president relative to the Congress. In the Textbook Congress, the president's primary legislative role was to dispose of legislation once it reached his desk. As the president's agenda has increasingly become the legislative agenda and as the party leaders of the president's party have increasingly taken their cues from the president, the Textbook Congress and the heightened importance of the president in the legislative process have proven to be incompatible. Rules, order, committee power, and congressional workhorses do not readily adapt to presidential prerogatives.

THE IRREGULAR ORDER

The stability that the Textbook Congress enjoyed in the middle of the twentieth century confronted trends toward the end of the century that it could not easily withstand. As a consequence, members, leaders, and parties adapted the legislative process to more easily operate in an ever-changing political environment. These changes, then, helped fuel the evolving political environment. The Textbook Congress entered a vicious cycle that ultimately would transform the regular order into the irregular order. Not all of the features of the irregular order happened at the same time or were a result of the same causes, but they are all deviations from the Textbook Congress. We outline some of them here.

Multiple Referrals

The Textbook Congress put a premium on order and sequential steps in the legislative process. The next step after bill introduction was referral to committee. If the committee chair decided not to hold a hearing on the bill, the legislation had a slim chance of advancing, let alone becoming law.

In 1975, the Democratic caucus gave the Speaker the ability to refer bills to multiple committees. This simple move dramatically cut into the autonomy that committees had come to enjoy. Before multiple referrals, a committee chair who objected to a piece of legislation could simply ignore it. Under multiple referral, another committee could move the legislation along. The committee that ignored it not only lost the ability to amend it during committee, but also could be shut out of changing it on the floor or even in conference committee, which usually is composed of members from the committee of original jurisdiction.

Multiple referrals can take many forms. First, a bill can be sent to two different committees at the same time, which is called a *joint referral*. Usually joint referrals have strict guidelines dictating when a committee must address the bill lest they lose the ability to shape the legislation. If one committee tries to defeat the bill by not acting on it and the other committee reports the bill, it is as if the first committee was never given the referral. If both committees report the bill, but not the identical bill, the Rules Committee decides which of the bills (or which combination of the bills) is the legislative vehicle for floor debate. At the time that the House adopts the special rule written by the Rules Committee outlining the parameters of the debate, the House also adopts the decision of the Rules Committee as to what the legislative vehicle is. In 1995, the Republicans curtailed the use of joint referrals by designating one of the committees as *primary*.

EXAMPLE 6.1

Joint Referral

In January 2003, President George W. Bush announced his intention of the United States to enter into a trade agreement with Singapore, the negotiations over which had begun in 2000 under President Clinton. As part of the agreement, the US trade representative had negotiated an immigration provision that would carve out H-1B temporary worker visas for professional workers who entered the United States through the trade agreement. Bush and Singaporean Prime Minister Goh Chok Tong signed the free trade agreement on May 6, 2003. For it to go into effect, Congress had to approve it.

The tax committees—Ways and Means in the House and Finance in the Senate—typically have jurisdiction over trade agreements, but the Singapore agreement's temporary worker provision also gave the Judiciary Committee an important role. The Senate version of the bill to implement the United

(Continued)

States–Singapore Free Trade Agreement (S.1417) was introduced in July 2004 and jointly referred to the Senate Finance and Judiciary Committees. Both committees reported the bill, but not without resistance. Several Judiciary Committee members objected to changing US immigration law through a trade agreement. Their critique was strategically tricky, because had the committee decided not to report the bill, its voice would have been silent even as the Finance Committee moved the bill along the legislative process. It is possible then, that despite the Judiciary Committee's objection, the bill still could have been brought to the floor of the Senate without the input of the Judiciary Committee.

Second, a bill can be referred to different committees sequentially. In this type of referral, which is still regularly used, the first committee has a set amount of time to work with a bill before it goes to the second committee. Instead of using the introduced bill as its legislative vehicle, the second committee uses the bill reported from the first committee. If the first committee does not address the bill, the second committee receives the introduced bill after the time for the first committee has run out, and the process appears as if the first committee was never given jurisdiction over the bill. The last committee that reports the bill has the advantage of its legislation being the one considered by the Rules Committee, which could then fashion a special rule for the bill's floor consideration.

Third, a bill's referral can be split between multiple committees. One committee might have jurisdiction over the first half of the bill and a second

---

EXAMPLE 6.2

Sequential Referral

Legislation to reauthorize the Federal Aviation Administration and related programs has evolved in recent years and become integrated into the irregular order. Dubbed the Vision 100—Century of Aviation Reauthorization Act by its sponsor Don Young (R-AK), the 2003 law (H.R.2115, Pub. L. 108-176) covered multiple aspects of aviation, including safety, airport security, noise and emissions pollution, and research, but the bill was only referred to the House Transportation and Infrastructure Committee, which Young chaired. When the agency and its programs came up for reauthorization again in 2011, the Transportation and Infrastructure Committee received the initial referral in February. After they reported the bill (H.R.658) the following month, it was subsequently referred to both the Science and the Judiciary Committees. Even though neither committee acted on the bill before it went to the House floor, the sequential referral process gave more members access to change the bill prior to floor consideration.

=== EXAMPLE 6.3 ===

Split Referral

The Violence Against Women Act illustrates how the split committee referral process has dramatically changed as part of the irregular order. The original act was passed as part of a larger omnibus crime bill in 1994 (H.R.3355, Pub. L. 103-322). Even though the Violent Crime Control and Law Enforcement Act of 1994 addressed a variety of different smaller topics, such as police corps grants and training programs, substance abuse treatment, violent offender sentencing, and rural crime, the entire bill was referred to one committee in each chamber—Judiciary. When the Violence Against Women Act provisions were up for reauthorization in 2013, the House version (H.R.11) was referred to four different committees—Judiciary, Energy and Commerce, Education and the Workforce, and Financial Services—with each panel considering only those provisions within its jurisdiction. The bill's multiple referral not only reflects the program's expansion (and proposed expansion) to include protection for immigrants and American Indian women, but also reflects how Speakers are able to exert more control over the legislative process by sending various parts of a bill to different committees and then reassembling the bill during Rules Committee deliberation.

---

committee might have jurisdiction over the second half. Under such a referral, the Rules Committee is again responsible for putting the bill back together and presenting the floor with the parameters of debate as well as the legislative vehicle to be considered on the House floor.

Senate bills can also be referred to more than one committee, though it is done far less frequently than in the House, where an increasing percentage of major legislation is referred to more than one committee (SEE FIGURE 6.1). Without regard for the type of referral, the only way that the House floor can disapprove of how the Rules Committee handles the question of preparing the legislative language for floor consideration is for the House to defeat the rule—a step that could lead to the bill's ultimate demise, though it usually only results in a revised rule that can obtain majority support.

Subcommittee Bill of Rights

Some features of the irregular order came about informally as members adapted to existing rules or institutions. Other features emerged explicitly because Congress wanted them. The subcommittee bill of rights is an example of the latter. It arose from the Hansen Committee, named after its chair, Julia Butler Hansen (D-WA), recommended, and the Democratic caucus adopted, a subcommittee bill of rights in 1973, which granted individual powers to subcommittees, which until that time

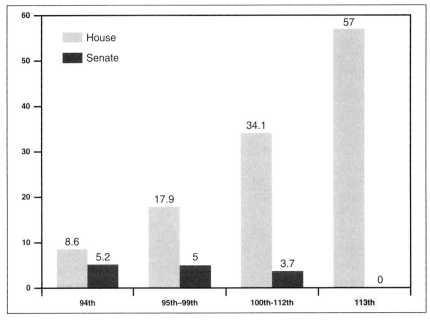

Figure 6.1 Proportion of Major Legislation Referred to More Than One Committee, 94th–113th Congresses (1973–2015).   SOURCE: Barbara Sinclair, *Unorthodox Lawmaking: New Legislative Processes in the U.S. Congress* (Thousand Oaks, CA: Sage CQ Press, 2017).

════════════════════ **EXAMPLE 6.4** ════════════════════

Subcommittee Bill of Rights

Representative Dana Rohrabacher (R-CA) served as the House Foreign Affairs Oversight and Investigations Subcommittee chairman in the 112th Congress (2011–2), and the media attention his position afforded him gave his fellow congressional Republicans occasional discomfort. Rohrabacher introduced a bill in 2011 that would cut off US aid to Pakistan and a resolution in 2012 that would state that Balochistan, an area split among Afghanistan, Pakistan, and Iran, had the right to choose whether it should become a sovereign nation. If subcommittees were not independent sources of power, it is unlikely that his actions would have had much of a ripple in Congress. But as a consequence of his status, Rohrabacher had a bigger platform that drew more media attention.

His actions elicited reactions. Rohrabacher was prevented from entering Afghanistan as part of an official 2012 congressional delegation after he made a series of controversial statements about Afghanistan's president, Hamid Karzai, and undertook an investigation into the Karzai family finances. His controversial statements and actions in part led the Foreign Affairs Committee to eliminate its Oversight Subcommittee altogether in 2013. The committee instead conducted oversight and investigations in the full committee, where new chairman Ed Royce (R-CA) could exert more authority. Rohrabacher was reassigned to chair the committee's Europe Subcommittee.

had to act in concert with the preferences of the full committee chair. The subcommittee bill of rights gave subcommittees named jurisdictions, power to hire staff, and the ability to hold hearings and markups with the approval of the full committee chair (see Table 6.1 for an example of how the House Armed Services Subcommittees' names changed).

While full committee chairs did lose some power, they continue to work their will within the committees. Subcommittees hold hearings and report bills, but the full committee can ignore these actions. Full committees can still hold hearings and markups on bills even if the subcommittee chair disapproves. As such, a subcommittee chair's easiest path to power and legislative influence continued to be working well and in tandem with the full committee chair.

Table 6.1 The Names for the House Armed Services Subcommittees

92nd Congress

- Armed Services, listed with no subcommittees[1]

93rd Congress

- Armed Services[2]
  - Legislative subcommittees
    - Subcommittee No. 1
    - Subcommittee No. 2
    - Subcommittee No. 3
    - Subcommittee No. 4
    - Subcommittee No. 5
  - Special subcommittees
    - Intelligence
    - Human Relations
    - Armed Services Investigations

94th Congress

- Armed Services
  - Research and Development
  - Seapower and Strategic and Critical Materials
  - Military Compensation
  - Military Installations and Facilities
  - Military Personnel
  - Investigations
  - Intelligence (Special)

[1]*Congressional Directory: 92nd Congress, 1st Session*. 1971, page 269, https://babel.hathitrust.org/cgi/pt?id=mdp.39015032388350;view=1up;seq=305.
[2]*Congressional Directory: 93rd Congress, 1st Session*. 1973, page 289, https://babel.hathitrust.org/cgi/pt?id=mdp.39015038055771;view=1up;seq=334

Discharge Petitions and the Threat of Discharge Petitions

As part of the 1910 revolt against Speaker Cannon, the House adopted an early version of a discharge petition, which dislodges a bill from a committee uninterested in advancing a bill. In 1935, the number of signatories required to discharge a bill from committee increased from one-third of the total House membership to one-half. Indeed, it was the very threat of the discharge petition working that eventually got Rules Committee Chairman Smith to report a rule for the bill that ultimately became the Civil Rights Act of 1964. As initially written, the signatories of the discharge petition only became visible when the discharge was executed. If a petition never reached the proscribed amount, all the signatories remained secret. This lack of visibility was powerful. A majority of members could claim to have signed the petition, but if a true majority was never reached, no one would ever know which members had signed and which had not.

In 1993, in response to pressure from conservatives who accused members of proclaiming support for legislation while failing to sign the petition that would allow it to be considered, the House changed the rule so that the signatories become public immediately upon their signature. This rule change made discharge petitions much more powerful instruments, which, in turn, made the

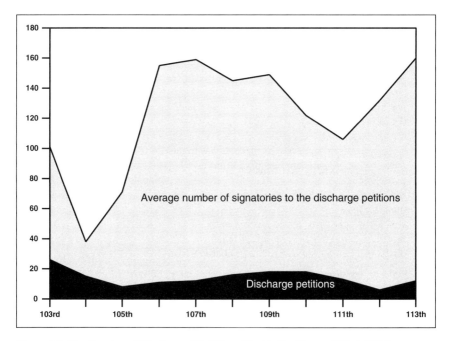

Figure 6.2 The Number of Discharged Petitions Filed in the House, 103rd–113th Congresses (1993–2014).

=== **EXAMPLE 6.5** ===

Discharge Petitions and the Threat of Discharge Petitions

The Bipartisan Campaign Reform Act of 2002 is commonly known as McCain–Feingold after its Senate sponsors. The House version that became law (Pub. L. 107-155), named Shays–Meehan after its sponsors, took the long road to the House floor, including multiple discharge petition attempts, before finally being enacted in 2002. Representative Chris Shays (R-CT) and his primary cosponsor, representative Martin Meehan (D-MA), introduced comprehensive campaign finance overhaul legislation in 1996, and House minority leader Dick Gephardt (R-MO) led a push to discharge it from committee, but that petition received only 186 signatures, short of the 218 necessary to put the bill on the House's schedule. Republican leaders put forth their own version of campaign finance legislation in response; a year later, it was rejected. After Shays and Meehan reintroduced their bill in the 105th Congress, representative Carolyn Maloney (D-NY) filed a petition to discharge the new Shays–Meehan bill from committee. Maloney's petition received only 8 total signatures (which included Meehan but not even Shays), but another petition to discharge Scotty Baesler's (D-KY) campaign finance bill received 191 signatures; both Shays and Meehan signed this petition, but Shays later withdrew his support. The two House sponsors again reintroduced their legislation in the following congress and again a discharge petition was filed. Though this petition, sponsored by Tom Campbell (R-CA), received only 3 signatures (which included Shays but not Meehan), Republican leaders again felt pressure to bring campaign finance legislation to the floor. The House Rules Committee agreed to, and the House later adopted, a debate rule for Shays–Meehan in 1999 (H.R. 417). Despite the House passing the bill (252–177) after almost ten hours of debate, it languished in the Senate.

Although the House had passed their campaign finance proposal, the Shays and Meehan bill (H.R.380) died in committee the following congress. The Senate, however, took up the McCain–Feingold companion (S.27) in March 2001 and passed an amended campaign finance bill, 59–21. The Senate bill was sent to the House three months later, but languished in committee. Rather than wait for another new congress, Shays and Meehan introduced an updated bill ten days after the Senate-passed version made its way to the House. The House Rules Committee approved a debate rule for this new bill (H.R.2356), but the House rejected the resolution on the floor. Jim Turner (D-TX) filed a petition to discharge H.R.2356, which received the necessary 218 signatures six months later. The House debated the most recent iteration of Shays–Meehan in February 2002, passing the bill by a 240–189 vote. The Senate subsequently invoked cloture on and cleared the Bipartisan Campaign Reform Act. On March 27, 2002, more than six years and four discharge attempts later, the bill finally became law.

threat of using a discharge petition much more real. Bills could not be marked up by committees from which they were discharged. For a committee to maintain power over the bill, the committee has to act on it before the discharge petition achieves the necessary number of signatures.

Omnibus Bills

As regional hostilities escalated in the lead-up to the impending Civil War, Senator Henry Clay (Whig-KY) tried to broker peace in 1850 just as he had done in 1820 when he spearheaded the legislative effort that became known as the Missouri Compromise. Using the lessons from his earlier effort, his 1850 plan included a variety of policies that balanced those benefiting the North with others benefitting the South. Clay reasoned that if he could get the advocates for the various parts to support the entire package, he could cobble together majority support for the entire package. It was a legislative strategy that came to be called an *omnibus* bill because all the disparate parts of the agreement would be joined in a common legislative vehicle—a bus, if you will. Ultimately, Clay's strategy failed in 1850, but peace, however temporary, was secured when Senator Stephen Douglas (D-IL) steered the various parts of the omnibus through Congress as separate pieces of legislation.

Perhaps because of Clay's failure, the omnibus legislative strategy was not regularly used for more than a hundred years. But once it started being used, it was so with a vengeance. The omnibus is not the most irregular legislative

============================ **EXAMPLE 6.6** ============================

Omnibus Bills

Senator Tom Coburn (R-Oklahoma), an obstetrician, was often referred to as "Dr. No" for frequently objecting to unanimous consent requests and placing holds on myriad bills and nominations. The House passed approximately 70 public lands bills during the 110th Congress (2007-8) and most enjoyed large majorities. The Senate Energy and Natural Resources Committee approved approximately 90 more, but Coburn objected to passing all of them, citing concerns about costs to the government and restriction of private property rights. Energy and Natural Resources Committee Chairman Jeff Bingaman (D-NM) attempted to combine the bills as an omnibus package, but again Coburn objected, so all 160 bills died when the 110th Congress ended. Bingaman reintroduced an omnibus measure (S.22) at the beginning of the following congress that included all the previously written House and Senate public lands provisions and had the bill placed on the Senate's legislative calendar without a committee hearing or markup. Senate Majority Leader Harry Reid (D-NV) then filed a cloture motion, and the chamber voted 71–29 to move forward on debate and then, subsequently, to pass the bill.

When the measure moved to the House, Democratic leaders placed the bill on the suspension calendar, which requires two-thirds of current House members to approve legislation, but also restricts debate to forty-five minutes with no possibility of amendment. During House consideration, Representative John Culberson (R-TX) decried the bill's lack of committee hearings and limited debate time, using language that potentially violated the chamber's rule against inappropriate or insulting language. Representative Nick Rahall (D-WV) asked that Culberson's words be taken down, which would have prohibited Culberson from speaking on the floor for the rest of the day; Culberson, instead, moved to strike his words. The bill did not reach the necessary two-thirds to pass.

This defeat, however, was not the end of the bill's life in the 109th Congress. Reid added the omnibus public lands measure to a smaller House bill (H.R.146). This time, Coburn was allowed to offer a handful of amendments. The Senate passed the amended bill, 77–20. Because the bill originated in the House and the Senate amended it, House Democratic leaders only had to offer a motion to concur with the Senate amendments, to restrict the possibility of additional amendments, and to prohibit any points of order against the motion. The House agreed to the motion, clearing the way for the bill to become law. Packaging the hundreds of public lands measures as one omnibus bill allowed the congressional majority party to more easily navigate an individual senator's objections and limit the amount of time spent on debate compared to trying to deal with each bill individually.

---

innovation because even though it is a big bill, it can still work its way through the legislative process of the Textbook Congress. Nonetheless, omnibus bills put more power in the hands of the party leadership, which usually takes a direct role in fashioning them, and the Rules Committee, which decides their procedures for floor consideration. Additionally, the larger the bill, the less scrutiny that rank-and-file members can give to each additional provision, especially when the omnibus bills are considered urgent, which most of the time they are. Indeed, it has become a popular refrain from the minority party to complain about how omnibus bills are rushed through the process without giving members proper time to consider their various parts.

Continuing Resolutions

The Appropriations Committee is tasked with spending the money to run the federal government. It divides the entire budget into thirteen pots of money and its subcommittees are tasked with writing and passing a bill to fund the agencies and programs under their jurisdiction. If the new fiscal year starts before Congress passes all the subcommittee bills into law, the agencies and programs under their jurisdiction do not have the money to continue functioning. To avoid the government coming to a screeching halt, the Congress frequently passes continuing resolutions, which continue the funding of the programs and agencies usually but not always at their current level (SEE FIGURE 6.3 for the duration and number of continuing resolutions that were required for the funding of the government).

Because of the dire consequences of not passing these continuing resolutions, party leadership frequently has a more prominent role in developing and passing them than they do in the individual subcommittee bills. When Congress fails to pass these continuing resolutions in a timely manner, the government can shut down, which, by raising the stakes of the legislation, empowers leadership

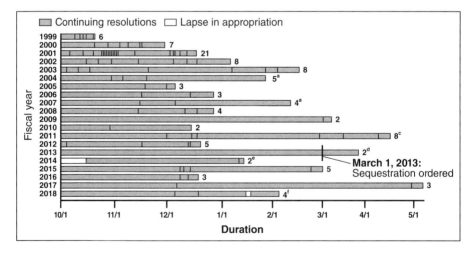

Figure 6.3 Duration and Number of Continuing Resolutions, 1999–2018.
SOURCE: https://www.gao.gov/products/GAO-18-368T

═══════════════ **EXAMPLE 6.7** ═══════════════

Continuing Resolutions

Congress has increasingly used continuing resolutions to fund government agen cies and programs. With an impending March 27, 2013, deadline for the previous stopgap measure's expiration, both chambers moved to incorporate new appropriations bills into the next continuing resolution, which on Capitol Hill is referred to as a C.R. The Education, Labor, Health and Human Services, Housing and Urban Development, Interior, State, and Transportation Departments, the Environmental Protection Agency, legislative branch agencies, and energy and water development, financial services, and foreign operations programs saw their fiscal 2012 appropriations levels roll over into the fiscal 2013 year. The Agriculture, Commerce, Defense, Homeland Security, Justice, and Veterans Affairs Departments, NASA, and other science programs all received new fiscal 2013 appropriations funding levels. House leaders brought the continuing appropriations measure (H.R.933) to the floor under a closed rule that prohibited any amendments or points of order and originally would have provided new funding only for the Defense and Veterans Affairs Departments. In contrast, the Senate debate included ninety amendments and expanded the number of programs that would receive new funding levels. Including fiscal 2013 appropriations in the C.R. gave agencies greater flexibility in determining how federal money should be spent. The spending bill was enacted into law on March 26, 2013, a day before the previous round of agency funding was set to expire.

---

even more. When the normal appropriations process is used, the Appropriations Committee exercises the greatest amount of power.

Ad hoc Working Groups and Task Forces

Nothing in the Constitution or the rules of the House or Senate requires legislation to go through a committee. Whether or not a bill is first sent to committee, it can be brought up for consideration on the Senate floor. Because this procedure is normally accomplished with a unanimous consent agreement, any senator may object and choose to filibuster the motion to proceed to consideration of the bill. In that case, supporters of the bill can seek sixty votes to invoke cloture (thus, ending debate) over that senator's objection, so the bill can still obtain floor consideration. If a House majority approves a special rule for consideration of a particular bill, then the bill is debated on the House floor even if that bill did not go through a committee. The only thing that stops the chamber leaders from subverting the committee process is a dedicated minority in the Senate comprising at least forty-one senators or a bare majority of House members. For a variety of reasons, party leaders sometimes avoid the committee process. Some bills cut

---

EXAMPLE 6.8

Ad hoc Working Groups and Task Forces

Speaker of the House Newt Gingrich (R-GA) relied heavily on task forces early in the 104th Congress (1995-6) for different purposes, but particularly to help draft legislation related to the Republican agenda as established in the Contract with America. Gingrich set up a budget task force consisting of himself, majority leader Dick Armey (R-TX), and several committee chairmen to draft a budget resolution that would balance the federal budget within seven years. Gingrich also bypassed several committees to create a Medicare task force and was credited with drafting the bill, devising an outreach strategy to seniors and other groups, and making deals with other members to gain support for the bill. By creating these task forces, Gingrich did not have to rely on or even consult with the appropriate committee chairs, thereby centralizing the development and passage of these Contract with America pieces of legislation.

Borrowing a page from Gingrich's playbook, the new Speaker of the House in 2007, Nancy Pelosi (D-CA), also turned to task forces to bypass recalcitrant committee chairs. Congressman John Dingell (D-MI), who proudly boasted that he was the congressman of General Motors, was not an ally in considering legislation to address global warming. Pelosi attempted to create a new task force to highlight global warming and energy issues, which Dingell and other committee chairs opposed. In a battle that pitted the committee chairs against the new Speaker, the opposing sides finally agreed to create the task force as the new Select Energy Independence and Global Warming Committee, which, to gain the support of the committee chairs, did not have the power to report legislation. In essence, the task force became a study group rather than the powerful task forces that Gingrich created.

Pelosi and then Minority Leader John Boehner (R-OH) largely appointed members to the select committee who had experience dealing with the issues from their perches on the Energy and Commerce, Natural Resources, and Science and Technology Committees. The committee's ranking member, James Sensenbrenner (R-WI), initially opposed the committee's creation, but wrote an editorial a few years later arguing that Republicans (who had just won back the House majority in the 2010 elections) should retain the committee as a valuable oversight forum. The Republican leadership did not heed his advice, and the panel suffered an ignominious death when its authorization expired in 2011.

---

across too many committees' jurisdictions for the committee deliberation to yield helpful information. Other bills may be opposed by the committee chairs or even a majority on the committee while still maintaining sufficient support in the chamber to pass the bill. Other problems require quicker action than the committee process could give.

In these instances, the chamber leaders have a variety of strategies under which the members can acquire sufficient information to draft legislation. The

Table 6.2 Examples of Task Forces

YEAR	TOPIC
1989	Democratic task force on tobacco and health
1992	Democratic task force to investigate the release of the hostages in Iran during the 1980 presidential election
1995	Republican antipoverty task force called Project Hope and Opportunity
1995	Republican Medicare legislation task force called Design Group
1995	Democratic task force to develop a comprehensive welfare reform proposal
1998	Bipartisan task force to deal with problems associated with Y2K
1998	Senate task force on China's most favored nation status
1999	Bipartisan task force on Alzheimer's disease
2001	Bipartisan task force on brain injuries
2015	Bipartisan task force on transgender equality
2018	Bipartisan heroin task force

leaders can establish a task force to deal with a problem or to write a bill. The leaders name members, presumably with different views on the subject, to develop a compromise. The advantage for party leaders in using these ad hoc groups is that they can control their membership more easily than they can the membership of committees. Furthermore, while committee chairs are given wide latitude in committee deliberations, the leaders of these ad hoc groups have even more discretion. These task forces have been created in different ways and they possess different powers. What they all do—by their very existence—is weaken the autonomy of the committees and strengthen the party leadership that created them.

Gangs

In addition to top-down ad hoc groups that party leaders establish, members have been increasingly developing a bottom-up approach to solving problems through the establishment of *gangs*, which, unlike task forces, are never formally created. These gangs have neither the power of committees nor the power of task forces, but if they can develop a solution that cuts across different perspectives, they may be able to persuade party or committee leaders to consider their solution.

Gangs' popularity increased in 2005 when fourteen senators—called the Gang of 14—were successful in striking a compromise in which the Republicans would refrain from using the "nuclear option" to change Senate rules by bare majority and the Democrats would refrain from filibustering judicial nominees. Because enough senators from each party were part of the gang, they had the

---

=== **EXAMPLE 6.9** ===

Gangs

As deficits began to climb in the wake of increased government spending to combat the Great Recession of 2008, the volume and frequency of calls by both economic and political leaders to cut the federal government's budget increased. Amid parallel talks within parties, within chambers, between President Obama and Speaker Boehner, and between Vice President Biden and House Majority Leader Eric Cantor (R-BA), Senators Mark Warner (D-VA) and Saxby Chambliss (R-GA), in a brief chat on the Senate floor, found that they largely agreed on the economic path forward. Within a couple weeks, their informal conversations expanded to new participants—Senators Dick Durbin (D-IL), Kent Conrad (D-ND), Mike Crapo (R-ID), and Tom Coburn (R-OK)—and a more formalized structure.

As the issue of the increasing debt collided with a possible government shutdown and the hitting of the debt ceiling, the talks around Capitol Hill became more intense. When the White House and party leaders were engaged in serious negotiations, the Gang of Six stepped out of the spotlight, but as the negotiations between the institutions at opposite ends of Pennsylvania Avenue faltered, the gang's discussions intensified, along with media scrutiny. In the end, the gang struck a tenuous deal, which ended up sabotaging the talks between President Obama and Speaker Boehner, who almost simultaneously struck a deal. The gang's deal was closer to the Democrat's position than the Obama–Boehner deal. When Obama tried to use this turn of events to his benefit, Boehner balked and walked away from the table. The breakdown in negotiations poisoned the atmosphere of cooperation and ended up killing the gang's deal as well.

The quadruple threat of the rising debt, a government shutdown, the end of the Bush tax cuts, and the breaching of the debt ceiling ultimately culminated in the so-called fiscal cliff that paralyzed Capitol Hill at the end of the year. Each of these threads ultimately was unraveled—if only temporarily—at the end of the year and the beginning of 2012. The story of the Gang of Six nicely illustrates the complexity of trying to strike a deal outside the leadership channels.

---

numbers to overcome either filibusters from Democrats who did not agree with the compromise or use of the nuclear option by the Republicans. The Gang of 14 reconstituted itself to smooth the confirmation process for Samuel Alito, whom President Bush had nominated to fill the Supreme Court seat made vacant by Justice Sandra Day O'Connor's retirement.

Because gangs frequently subvert their institutional power, party leaders and committee leaders generally view these gangs skeptically. Although no formal rules exist for the creation of gangs, they are mostly used in the Senate and they usually contain an equal number from both parties. Sometimes the number is important, as it was in the Gang of 14, but other times the number is solely dependent on who claims membership in the gang.

Table 6.3 Examples of Gangs

YEAR	NAME	TOPIC
2005	Gang of 14	Judicial nominations
2009	Gang of Six	Healthcare
2011	Gang of Six	National debt
2013	Gang of Eight	The impending fiscal cliff
2013	Gang of Eight	Immigration
2018	Gang of Six	Immigration

Commissions

At times, party leaders try to draft former members or policy experts into the process by establishing commissions, which are usually established by a law with mandates as the law prescribes (see Table 6.4 for some recent examples of commissions that Congress has created). Sometimes they are tasked with investigating a particular problem and issuing a report to Congress. Other times, they are even given the ability to write legislation that is then submitted to Congress with expedited rules for their consideration. Sometimes they are composed of nonmembers only; at other times, Congress creates commissions that include some of their own members.

These commissions serve two important purposes for members of Congress. First, by establishing a commission, Congress shows that it is responsive to a particular problem it believes needs addressing. Second, by including congressional outsiders, the commission is at least one step removed from the political process, though its findings can become fodder for subsequent electoral campaigns. Because

Table 6.4 Examples of Commissions

YEAR	NAME
1990	Defense Base Closure and Realignment Commission
1994	National Commission on Crime Control and Prevention
1997	National Bipartisan Commission on the Future of Medicare
1998	Trade Deficit Review Commission
1998	National Commission on Terrorism
2000	Commission on Ocean Policy
2002	National Commission on Terrorist Attacks Upon the United States
2008	Commission on Wartime Contracting in Iraq and Afghanistan
2009	Financial Crisis Inquiry Commission
2013	National Commission on the Structure of the Air Force
2016	Commission on Evidence-Based Policymaking

═══════════════ **EXAMPLE 6.10** ═══════════════

Commissions

The question of whether to raise the federal debt ceiling—a statutory limit on the amount of debt that the US Treasury Department can issue to pay for past federal appropriations—had been a formality in Congress for decades since the contemporary budget process arose in 1980. In 2010, Senate Budget Committee Chairman Kent Conrad (D-ND) and Ranking Member Judd Gregg (R-NH) introduced legislation to create a bipartisan federal deficit and debt commission. When Senate defeated the proposal, President Barack Obama created the commission by executive order.

The National Commission on Fiscal Responsibility and Reform, colloquially known as Simpson–Bowles after its two lead members, needed the support of fourteen of its eighteen members to be approved. Only eleven members ultimately agreed on what the panel's recommendations for balancing the federal budget should be, so the Simpson–Bowles Commission's proposals did not move forward, though the ideas it supported continued to affect the congressional debate.

Although similar in design, intent, and structure, there is a key distinction between the Conrad–Gregg proposal and the commission established by Obama. The latter could only make recommendations to Congress, which could ignore them. The former, because of how it was written, would have forced Congress to address it. Because the White House cannot dictate to Congress how it shall conduct its affairs, Obama could not write these provisions into the executive order that created the commission.

---

of the variety of structures that Congress creates for these commissions, it is difficult to assess how commissions affect the power dynamics on Capitol Hill. Because the alternative for these commissions is thorough investigations and hearings conducted by committees, it is unlikely that commissions enhance committee power. If they are given the power, commissions that draft legislation usually see their proposals debated under strict guidelines established by the party leaders. As such, commissions most likely weaken individual members' ability to influence the process and enhance party leaders because they are ultimately tasked with structuring the debate over the commissions' proposals.

Restrictive Rules

The Rules Committee has ultimate discretion in establishing the parameters for debate in the House. In the Textbook Congress, the Rules Committee more often than not gave the bills open rules, which meant that any member could offer any germane amendment to any part of the bill. The real power of the Rules Committee came from its ability to kill legislation by refusing to grant it any rule whatsoever. The regular order, then, was for a bill to have an open and fair debate on the floor of the House.

━━━━━━━━━━━━━━ **EXAMPLE 6.11** ━━━━━━━━━━━━━━

Restrictive Rules

Perhaps the most famous restrictive rule in the past fifty years in the House of Representatives came in 1998 when the House was deliberating the impeachment of President Bill Clinton. Few Democrats wanted to be seen as supporting a president who had lied about an inappropriate relationship with an intern. Even fewer Democrats wanted to vote for impeaching the president over the affair and its aftermath. Furthermore, many Republicans felt uncomfortable voting to impeach the president, though none was interested in supporting him.

Following the 1998 congressional elections, in which the Republicans lost seats, most members simply wanted the impeachment debacle to go away. Most pundits thought that the Republicans would pursue some middle option castigating the president, but not impeaching him. House Majority Whip Tom DeLay (R-TX) objected to such an easy resolution. As such, he convinced the Rules Committee to write a strict closed rule where members were only given one choice on each of the four articles of impeachment: they could either vote to impeach the president or acquit him—no middle option was offered. In the end, the House adopted the restricted rule, which forced up or down votes on each article of impeachment. Two of the four articles passed, which precipitated a Senate trial in which Clinton was ultimately acquitted.

Over time, the majority party leadership in the House learned that open rules could result in changes to legislation that they did not support. Perhaps more damaging, open rules could put their vulnerable members in a difficult position where they would have to support either their leadership or their constituents. Increasingly, the rules governing House debate written by the Rules Committee restricted members' abilities to amend bills (SEE FIGURE 6.4 to see how restrictive rules have grown over time). As minority parties faced fewer opportunities to amend bills and put their electorally vulnerable opponents in difficult positions, they took advantage of the few opportunities they were given, which, in turn, led to even fewer opportunities to offer amendments.

A popular refrain from the minority party is that democracy in the House is being threatened because it is being denied the opportunity to offer amendments. In fact, the refrain is true. The hypocrisy of the refrain comes when yesterday's minority becomes today's majority and then advances as many closed rules as yesterday's majority. The regular order put a premium on debate and having the House work its will. The irregular order sacrifices debate and discovering what the will of the House is in favor of protecting vulnerable members of the majority party and ensuring majority party legislative success.

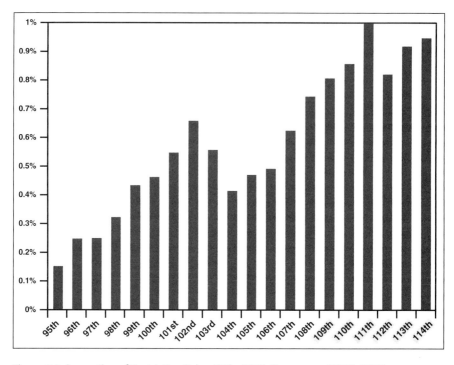

Figure 6.4 Proportion of Restrictive Rules, 95th–115th Congresses (1977–2018).

Special Special Rules

The Rules Committee is usually thought of as deciding the restrictiveness of amendments that a bill is subject to on the floor of the House by writing special rules. On occasion, the Rules Committee decides other features of the floor debate that can be even more consequential through the use of special special rules, which include *queen of the hill* and *king of the hill*. The standing rules of the House forbid text in legislation that has been amended in its entirety to be subject to further amendment. At times, party leaders want legislators to be able to vote on multiple different solutions to the same problem. The Rules Committee can write a special special rule that allows for these multiple versions to compete against one another. A king-of-the-hill special rule, first used in 1981, dictates that the last alternative to receive a majority vote, even if it does not receive the greatest number of votes, is the alternative that is considered passed by the House. Between 1981 and 1994, the House used eighty-eight king-of-the-hill special rules as dictated by sixty-four special rules written by the Rules Committee and adopted by the House. Beginning in 1995, the Rules Committee opted for a queen-of-the-hill special rule, which dictates that the alternative with the highest number of votes, so long as it is at least a majority, is the alternative that

---

EXAMPLE 6.12

Special Special Rules

The congressional budget resolution is often a statement of policy priorities, and so its consideration has become more contentious as the two parties in Congress have become more polarized. Over time, different groups within the House of Representatives have been given the opportunity to offer their own budget alternatives even though the majority party knows that none of these alternatives will be adopted. The fiscal 2014 budget resolution included a prime example of a special special rule (H.Res.122) that allowed House members to vote on budget proposals that their constituents might support while preserving the majority party's control over the final outcome. The rule permitted debate on five budget alternatives: the Senate's budget resolution; a substitute amendment offered by the Congressional Black Caucus that would increase funding for domestic policy programs; a substitute amendment offered by the Progressive Caucus that focused on increasing employment; a substitute amendment offered by the Republican Study Committee that would lower taxes and discretionary spending; and a Democratic Caucus substitute that prioritized Democratic programs. The rule set out not only the amount of time for debate on each amendment, but also the order in which they were debated. If any of the substitute amendments had been adopted, debate would end and any amendments that had not yet been considered would not be considered. Immediately, the House would move to adopt the (now-amended) budget. The majority party (Republicans) was able to maintain control over the final outcome in part because members who might have wanted to vote for one of the earlier amendments had to weigh that alternative against the possibility of not being able to vote for a later amendment that they or their constituents might like even more.

---

is considered passed by the House. The 104th Congress used this rule on only three occasions and the 105th Congress used it twice. The last time it was used was in the 107th Congress, though it was included as part of an unsuccessful discharge petition to dislodge a comprehensive immigration reform bill in 2018.

These special special rules can give the Rules Committee and the majority party leadership even more power than they have with special rules. By providing members with the opportunity to vote in favor of multiple alternatives, they can give members the opportunity to vote for one alternative that their constituents may favor and a different alternative that their party leaders favor. Because the party leaders determine the sequencing of the alternatives, they have wide latitude in rigging the results so that the party-preferred policy wins.

Complex Unanimous Consent Agreements

Managing the floor of the Senate is much more difficult because each senator during the proceedings has the prerogative to object, which can bring debate to a halt. To more efficiently manage the Senate floor, the leaders from both parties

---

======= **EXAMPLE 6.13** =======

Complex Unanimous Consent Agreements

Whereas UCAs in the Textbook Congress might have simply outlined the time that the Senate would start debating a bill, complex UCA dictates not only when the Senate will debate, but also who controls the time, what amendments can be offered, and what happens on disposition of the various moving parts of the legislation (SEE FIGURE 6.5 as an example). Sometimes managing the Senate floor can be a bit like juggling balls. In the 113th Congress (2013–4), Majority Leader Harry Reid (D-NV) offered a UCA to schedule floor time for two high-profile bills: S.744, immigration overhaul legislation, and S.954, agriculture program reauthorization.

MR. REID. Madam President, I ask unanimous consent that following any leader remarks on Friday, June 7, tomorrow, the Senate resume consideration of the motion to proceed to Calendar No. 80, S. 744; that the time until 1:30 p.m. be divided as follows: Senator *Sessions* or designee controlling 3 hours, and the majority leader or designee controlling the remaining time; further, following any leader remarks on Monday, June 10, the Senate resume consideration of the motion to proceed to S. 744; that the time until 5 p.m. be divided as follows: Senator *Sessions* or designee controlling 2 hours, and Senator *Leahy* or designee controlling the remaining time; further, that at 5 p.m., the Senate resume consideration of S. 954, the farm bill, with the time until 5:30 p.m. equally divided between the two leaders or their designees; that at 5:30 p.m., all postcloture time be considered expired and the Senate proceed to vote in relation to the Leahy amendment, with no amendments in order to the amendment prior to the vote; and upon disposition of the Leahy amendment, the Senate proceed to vote on passage of S. 954, as amended; that upon disposition of S. 954, the Senate resume consideration of the motion to proceed to S. 744, with Senator *Sessions* or designee controlling 1 hour of debate on Monday evening; that following any leader remarks on Tuesday, June 11, the Senate resume consideration of the motion to proceed to S. 744, with the time until 12:30 p.m. equally divided between the proponents and opponents; further, Senator *Sessions* or designee controlling up to 1 hour of that time; that at 2:15 p.m., on Tuesday, June 11, the Senate proceed to vote on the motion to invoke cloture on the motion to proceed to S. 744; finally, if cloture is invoked on the motion to proceed, the time until 4 p.m. be equally divided between the proponents and opponents; and at 4 p.m., the Senate proceed to vote on the adoption of the motion to proceed to S. 744.

THE PRESIDING OFFICER. Is there objection to the request? Without objection, it is so ordered.

Figure 6.5 A Complex Unanimous Consent Agreement   SOURCE: 113 Cong. Rec. (June 6, 2013).

have been implementing increasingly complex unanimous consent agreements (UCAs), which have some of the same features as restrictive rules in that they outline who can offer amendments and when they can be offered. The trick for the majority party leader, is that prior to implementing a UCA, he (in time, perhaps she) must obtain, at least, the passive acceptance of all senators, a requirement that makes complex UCAs benign in comparison to the restrictive and complex rules of the House.

As with restrictive rules, complex UCAs take power from the individual senators and place it in the power of the party leaders. Complex UCAs limit all senators' freedom on the floor of the Senate to more efficiently move legislation along. In essence, senators' agreement to these complex UCAs is an agreement to tie their own hands. Senators agree to such hand tying up until the costs of doing so outweigh the benefits. It only takes one senator's objection to the complex UCA to preclude it from dictating what happens on the Senate floor.

Self-Executing Rules and Postcommittee Adjustments

In the Textbook Congress, the Rules Committee decides the conditions under which the House floor would consider a committee reported bill. In addition to restrictive rules and special special rules, the Rules Committee in the era after the Textbook Congress has increasingly been writing self-executing rules, which upon adoption not only sets up debate for a bill but also deems that the House, by virtue of its adoption, has taken some other action. These other actions take many forms. First, the rule could prescribe the automatic adoption of some amendment—that is, the rule can change the words of the legislation after the committee reported it and before its debate on the floor. Second, the rule could combine two bills for the purposes of debate on the

---

EXAMPLE 6.14

Self-Executing Rules and Postcommittee Adjustments

Self-executing rules serve both administrative and policy purposes. They can be used to correct typos and other errors made in a bill's text or to drastically alter a substantive provision. As an example of the former, in the 112th Congress (2011–2) when the House was about to take up a bill that would restrict the enforcing of regulations in economic downturns, an error was discovered that made reference to the "employment rate" instead of the "unemployment rate." In the rule (H. Res.741) setting the particulars for floor debate on the bill, the House corrected the error even before they could debate the bill. Upon adoption of the rule, which the House agreed to by voice vote, it automatically changed the bill to read "unemployment" without a separate vote taken on amending the bill.

An example from the same congress of a self-executing rule that had a more substantive effect came in the rule for the 2012 Interior Department appropriations

(Continued)

bill. The bill, as approved by the Appropriations Committee, contained a ten-year extension to the Forest Service's stewardship contracting program, which involves private groups and individuals managing federal lands in ways like maintaining trails, setting controlled fires, and restoring watersheds and animal habitats. The special rule for the bill (H. Res.363) struck the extension from the bill, which had the effect of deleting the program when its authorization expired in September 2013. By adopting the rule, the House automatically struck the provision, which eliminated the program's future authorization without debating or voting separately on the program's merits.

House floor. Third, the rule could deem some other legislation as being automatically passed.

For the most part, these self-executing rules are done to create a more efficient legislative process. At times, the majority party may also use them for partisan advantage. Through self-executing rules, the Rules Committee is given more discretion over the legislative process. Self-executing rules reduce the autonomy of the committees vis-à-vis the majority party leadership. The only recourse that a committee has against their implementation is to encourage enough members to vote against the rule, which sends the bill back to the Rules Committee.

Avoiding Conference Committees

In using the regular order, if the Senate passed a bill with different legislative language than the House, the respective chambers appoint conferees to negotiate and compromise away the differences between the two bills. The conferees frequently come from the committees that had jurisdiction over the original bill. Increasingly, the party leadership has chosen to bargain directly between the two chambers rather than using a conference committee. This procedure has been described as ping-pong because just as a ping-pong ball travels continuously across the net, so the bill travels across the Capitol from chamber to chamber.

Such a process ensures that the party leadership stays in control of the process until the two chambers have passed identical bills. This irregular procedure is another way party leaders subvert the power of committees. So long as conference committees, which were composed of members from the committees of original jurisdiction, controlled the legislative endgame, committee preferences were advantaged over the party leaders' preferences. By avoiding conference committees and by bargaining between the chambers, the party leaders stay in control of the entire legislative process until the end of the game (SEE FIGURE 6.6 for the declining use of conference committees).

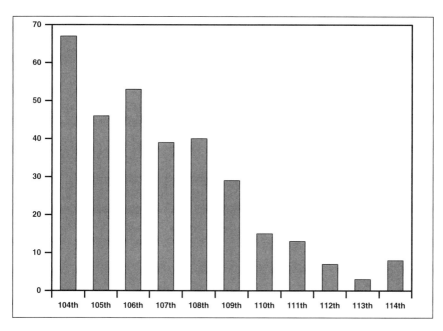

Figure 6.6 The Number of Conference Committee Reports, 104th–114th Congresses (1994–2016).

=== EXAMPLE 6.15 ===

Avoiding Conference Committees

Members of Congress and their staffs often have access to information about legislation that would affect US and foreign businesses, financial institutions, and government regulators to which individuals outside of government do not have access. This private information has caused concern for many that members or congressional staff could use their knowledge to engage in insider trading, or making deals and investments that benefit them financially based on information that the general population is not privy to. Some members of Congress wanted to address this issue by explicitly banning insider trading by members and staff, but legislation that would do so languished in committee for years. Then in November 2011, the television news program *60 Minutes* aired an episode about recent allegations of insider trading among members of Congress, drawing public attention to the issue. The Senate quickly moved to introduce and pass the Stop Trading on Congressional Knowledge Act in early 2012. Only three senators voted against the bill's passage.

The House then moved to pass the bill under suspension of the rules in early February. The bill passed easily, with only two House members voting against it, but members of Congress from both chambers and both parties also criticized House Majority Leader Eric Cantor (R-VA) for bringing an amended version to the floor that eliminated the Senate's provisions regulating "political intelligence-gathering" by lobbyists and redefining which public acts would be eligible for prosecution under public corruption statutes. Nevertheless, the Senate agreed to adopt the House's amendment by unanimous consent rather than convene a conference committee that would resolve the two chamber's different versions. Doing so kept negotiations between House and Senate leaders from undoing Majority Leader Cantor's action. Furthermore, the establishment of a conference committee only would have drawn attention to an issue that party leaders wanted to keep away from the spotlight.

Fast-Track Authority

The Constitution specifies that all legislative power resides in Congress. In this era of the irregular order, Congress has on occasion and with increasing frequency decided that it is incapable of performing its constitutional mandate, so it cedes part of that mandate to actors outside the legislative branch. Congress retains the ability to either approve or reject what the other actors decide, but at the outset ties its hands from amending it.

As American diplomacy has developed, the president has taken the lead on negotiating trade agreements with other countries. These agreements, on occasion, are *fast-tracked*, which means that the executive branch can negotiate agreements that Congress must approve or reject in total. By doing so, Congress deprives itself of the power to amend the agreement. Such a restriction allows the president to more efficiently negotiate the agreement. Without fast-track

---

EXAMPLE 6.16

Fast-Track Authority

Congress cleared trade agreements with Colombia, Panama, and South Korea in 2011 without giving itself the opportunity to amend any of them. The House rule (H.Res.425) for the three agreements did not allow any amendments and only allowed one motion to recommit the Colombia agreement, which was rejected. Both the House and the Senate approved each of the three trade promotion bills with large bipartisan majorities: the Colombia agreement (H.R.3078) passed 262–167 in the House and 66–33 in the Senate; the Panama agreement (H.R.3079) passed 300–129 in the House and 77–22 in the Senate; and the South Korea agreement (H.R.3080) passed 278–151 in the House and 83–15 in the Senate. While the White House had negotiated each of these agreements for at least four years, the House debated each bill for ninety minutes and the Senate spent less than nine hours debating all three, reflecting the fast-track nature of these agreements.

authority, the president's agreement is subject to congressional amendment, which if adopted would force the president to reopen discussions with the other countries, leading to even more changes, which would also require congressional approval

Filibusters and Holds

Most of the changes to the irregular order described above have taken greater root in the House, where only a simple majority is needed. Because of the individual powers that its members retain, the Senate has been more impervious to some of these changes. Nonetheless, it, too, has experienced some modern developments in the legislative process. In addition to complex UCAs, two other changes to the regular order—filibusters and holds—have, at their roots, the ability of any senator to object to a UCA.

EXAMPLE 6.17

Filibusters and Holds

Senators of both parties, from many different states, often place holds on nominations as a bargaining strategy for some other substantive issue. Senator James Risch (R-ID) placed a hold on President Obama's Interior Secretary nominee Sally Jewell until a deal could be reached to keep the sage-grouse off the endangered species list. Senator Mary Landrieu (D-LA) had often placed holds on executive branch nominations to force action on issues important to her state. During the George W. Bush administration, she held up several nominations until her state received additional funding to rebuild levees after Hurricane Katrina. Landrieu later placed a hold on president Barack Obama's Treasury Secretary nominee Jack Lew until the administration agreed to lift its moratorium on deep-water oil drilling, which had been instated following the BP *Deepwater Horizon* oil spill in the Gulf of Mexico. Landrieu's same-state Republican colleague, David Vitter, engaged in similar tactics, such as when he placed a hold on a military promotion in 2010 because the nominee, who was the head of the Army Corp of Engineers at the time, had not approved hurricane recovery projects on the Louisiana coasts. A pair of other same-state senators, Republicans Pat Roberts and Sam Brownback of Kansas, teamed up in 2009 to hold up President Obama's Army Secretary nominee until the administration agreed not to send Guantanamo Bay detainees to a Kansas prison.

Senators must be careful in how they use their power of holds. While any individual hold can slow down legislation, giving that senator a great deal of power, if all senators freely exercise their hold powers, the Senate can quickly become paralyzed, which would make all senators worse off because none could achieve any legislative accomplishment. Placing too many holds on legislation or nominations comes with a reputational cost. Each successive hold weakens the power of the next hold.

A filibuster is when a senator or group of senators tries to delay action in the Senate by endlessly debating either a procedural move or an actual piece of legislation. Individual senators derived the right to filibuster in 1806 when the Senate eliminated the previous-question motion. Without such a motion, senators are incapable of procedurally terminating debate. The House retained its previous-question motion, which both chambers had established in their first set of rules in 1789. Because the House retains the previous-question motion even today, a simple majority can mandate the settling of the question on the floor. In 1917, the Senate adopted cloture, which is a means to cut off debate. At the time of its adoption, it required the support of two-thirds of the senators voting. In 1975, the Senate lowered the requirement of support to 60 senators (regardless of the total number of senators).

Prior to the commencement of debate on the Senate floor, a senator may place a hold on a piece of legislation or a nomination. This hold has the effect of letting his or her party leadership know that if a UCA is offered, the hold-placing senator will object. A senator places a hold on a bill or nomination by informing the party secretary of her opposition. The hold is secret unless the senator chooses to make her name public. Because the objection to a UCA portrays the whole Senate in a negative light, party leaders typically respect the holds placed by their fellow senators. On January 27, 2011, the Senate voted 92–4 to require senators to enter their holds in the Congressional Record if the hold was to last more than two days. To circumvent the rule, senators can rotate their holds on a particular bill so that no one senator ever holds a nomination or bill for more than two days. Just as the two-day limit is reached, one senator releases the hold while another senator places a new hold on the bill or nomination. Just as this hold reaches its two-day limit, the second senator releases the hold and the first senator again places a hold on it. This cycle can repeat itself indefinitely, which means that the legislation does not move forward and no senator is ever required to make her hold public. Because so many holds remain secret, it is difficult to get an accurate number of holds for each congress.

When the holds become too cumbersome or are attached to legislation that is too important, the leadership can try to overcome the hold by forcing the hold-placing senator to object to the motion to proceed on a bill or nomination. If the senator persists in obstructing legislative progress, the leadership can try to invoke cloture and move the legislation or nomination over the objection of the senator. Such a process is cumbersome and time-consuming. It is usually more efficient for the leadership to negotiate with obstructing senators to ease legislative consideration. While it is difficult to get an accurate number of holds, it is easier to count the times that the objection leads to a filibuster, which triggers the cloture process (SEE FIGURE 6.7).

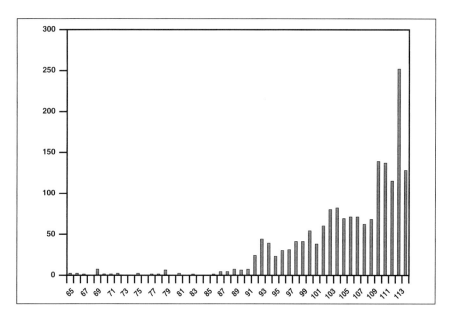

Figure 6.7 The Number of Cloture Petitions Filed in the Senate, 65th–114th Congresses (1917–2016).

Death by Amendment and the Filling of Amendment Trees

In addition to holds and filibusters, senators can also slow, stall, or even kill legislation by endlessly offering amendments to a bill once it has reached the Senate floor. As the number of amendments on a bill grows, the time that it takes to get to a final passage vote likewise grows. By offering many amendments, senators can signal their opposition without having to engage in the high-stakes strategies of placing a hold or engaging in a filibuster. Even as holds and filibusters have grown, so, too, has the strategy of offering increasingly more amendments.

The easiest way for leaders to restrict the power of amending a bill is through a complex UCA, but such a strategy requires the consent of every senator. The highest-stakes strategy of defeating the death-by-amendment strategy is for the party leader to file a cloture petition even before debate on the bill has begun. A more nuanced strategy for the party leader is to *fill the amendment tree*.

By virtue of his position, the majority leader has the right of first recognition, which means that he has the ability to be recognized before any other senator. By being recognized first, the majority leader can offer a first-degree amendment (i.e., an amendment to the legislation) and a second-degree amendment (i.e., an amendment to the amendment), which blocks all other senators from offering

---

EXAMPLE 6.18

Death by Amendment and the Filling of Amendment Trees

In 2011, the Senate considered a bill that would impose tariffs on countries that deflated their currency to gain unfair trading power over the United States. On October 3, in a 79–19 vote, the Senate invoked cloture so that it could proceed to consideration of the bill. On the next day, Senate Majority Leader Harry Reid (D-NV) offered five amendments and one motion to recommit the bill, which precluded any other senator from offering any other amendment to the bill. At the end of the day, Reid offered a cloture motion to preclude extended debate on the subject. Two days later, the Senate invoked cloture (62–38) on the bill; five days later, it passed the bill (63–35).

---

amendments because Senate precedents prohibit third-degree amendments. As with most strategies that fight fire with fire, filling the amendment tree exacerbates legislative warfare.

CONSEQUENCES OF THE CHANGES

Just as the Textbook Congress had consequences on the legislative process, so do the perturbations of the regular order. The most obvious consequence of the irregular order is that committees, the once-described fiefdoms of Congress, have lost much power. Their ability to squash bills that they do not like has been greatly weakened through multiple referrals, discharge petitions, and task forces. The sovereignty of their work has been compromised by the creation of omnibus bills tackling issues across committee jurisdiction lines, postcommittee adjustments, the decline in conference committees, and the increased use of fast-track authority to noncommittee actors. At almost every step, the party leadership has gained the power that committees have lost.

The second consequence of the irregular order is that at one time the legislative process could be described as a ladder; now it is characterized as a tree.[5] In the Textbook Congress, if a chair refused to call a hearing on a bill, it died. Under the irregular order, that same committee chair can intend to kill a bill by refusing to provide for a hearing on it, but the bill can be resurrected in several ways. A different committee could get jurisdiction over the bill, or the Rules Committee could make postcommittee adjustments so that the features of the once-dead bill could be incorporated into a different bill heading to the floor. And, to add insult to injury, the Speaker could try to depose the recalcitrant committee chair. In short, the committees are no longer the power bases that they were even thirty years ago, let alone sixty years ago when the Textbook Congress flourished.

The third consequence is that Congress has lost power to the president. Increasingly, the president sets his party's agenda. The leadership of the president's party have increasingly taken their marching orders from him. The opposition party to the president increasingly devotes its time and energy to thwarting his agenda. As congressional action has stalled in the face of the growing polarization between the parties, the executive branch has increasingly centralized the unitary action of the president. No change in the irregular order better encapsulates this transfer of power from the Congress to the president better than fast-track authority. Presidents, as a consequence of congressional inaction, frequently build strategies to combat congressional paralysis. President Obama's strategy of "We Can't Wait," implemented in 2012, is just one example. Rather than waiting for Congress to pass his jobs bill or reform immigration, Obama took every action that he could to get the executive branch to move on these policies through executive actions. Although constitutional scholars debate the legitimacy of such actions, so long as they did not contravene existing law, they did not receive serious opposition. Nonetheless, what works for one president can work for another. As soon as Donald Trump became president he rolled back many of Obama's actions with the same tool Obama used to create them—his pen—without any congressional action whatsoever.

CONCLUSION

The legislative process, with the implementation of all the recent innovations, is even more complicated than it was in the Textbook Congress. Even more so, it involves an intricate dance of compromise and brinksmanship, a careful drafting of language and strategy, a marshaling of support both within the Congress and outside in the general public. That dance, however, is being choreographed increasingly by the majority party leadership in the House and Senate. It is doubtful that the framers of the Constitution would approve of these recent innovations. The new system has sacrificed the prized slow and methodical process that might someday result in legislative enactment and replaced it with a system that rewards party team-playing and legislative efficiency—two concepts that the framers viewed skeptically.

The examples of irregular order, however, cannot be easily grouped and dismissed as corrupting the framers' pure vision of democracy. As previous chapters outlined, the Textbook Congress had some flaws, at least as seen by today's advocates for swifter action. The long thwarting of civil rights legislation and the monopoly power that long-standing congressional committee chairs exercised hurt Congress's standing with the American public. As witnessed by the irregular order tactics, today's party leaders have implemented changes that in turn cause them much consternation once the political winds change direction.

========================== **Commentary** ==========================

The Politician's Take on the Modern Developments

Democracy is about conflict—the accommodation of differing views. But it is also about how those conflicts are resolved peacefully, and that is a matter not of policy, but of process—not what decisions were made, but whether they were made fairly.

The worst thing about the loss of regular order is that without it, the credibility of the political system is legitimately called into question. Here is an example: Sean and I have used the willingness of Congress to grant presidents (of both parties) fast-track trade authority as one example of the problem. To many (that is, of the few who have ever heard of it), giving the president the power to insist on a simple take-it-or-leave-it vote on a trade agreement is common sense: after all, only a president is constitutionally authorized to negotiate treaties, and if Congress meddles by taking out or adding provisions, other countries are likely to pull out of the agreement altogether rather than renegotiate. So what is wrong with giving the president the ability to say, "Take it all or you get none of it?" Only this: In the 2016 presidential election, there was a powerful voice not heard from in recent years, and it was a very angry voice. It was the voice of blue-collar workers frustrated by the fallout from trade agreements that they blamed for the loss of American jobs and, for those who had jobs, a narrowing of opportunities for their children. Senator Bernie Sanders built much of his campaign around that complaint. So did Donald Trump. In the end, Hillary Clinton, too, moved in their direction.

Congress had surrendered its constitutional obligation to determine what the laws are; in the case of trade agreements, it had surrendered the ability to insist on maintaining standards it had put in place. And eventually, American workers rebelled.

The point is not whether those who complained about the agreements were right or wrong—that is a matter of debate—but whether in the acquiescence to presidential demands, members of Congress had done more than simply abandon the procedures the Constitution envisioned; they had also abandoned the American people who had sent them to Washington to make wise decisions on their behalf. In football terms, they punted.

I have written this book with Sean and share these comments because I served in Congress. If I had told the voters that, if elected, I would promise to do whatever the president or my party leaders told me to do, I would never have been elected. Regular order is not merely some mumbo jumbo insider terminology: it is essential to the workings of a democracy. And its abandonment is responsible for much of the justified anger so many Americans feel toward the first branch of government.

=========================== **Commentary** ===========================

The Professor's Take on the Modern Developments

As the dynamics within the country changed, reelection seeking incumbents adapted the Textbook Congress to suit their needs. The structure, institution, and rule-based Congress became too incompatible with the individual members' desire of electoral security in a changing political environment. The members themselves determined that they were better placed and, more important, better motivated to achieve their individual goal than a rigid system constructed to negotiate policy changes. Ironically, the breakdown of the Textbook Congress only substituted a rigid legislative process for powerful party leaders, though not all at one time.

At least initially, members of Congress broke down the Textbook Congress to pass legislation that would help in their reelection efforts. As the process increasingly broke down, the political parties, both in the electorate and inside Congress, began to sort so that the number of members who were cross-pressured by their ideology and party—that is, conservative Democrats and liberal Republicans—declined. Instead of individual members gaining power when the Textbook Congress broke down, the party leaders did as the Republican conference and Democratic caucus began to get more distinct from each other and more internally cohesive.

The developments occurring within both chambers these days are steps along the path to parliamentary parties. A unified majority party, with time—and rule change if need be—will ultimately work its will. The Senate's filibuster rules only retard this process; they cannot stop it. The maneuver orchestrated by Harry Reid and the Democrats forbidding filibusters on executive branch nominations and federal judges in 2013 was only the first step toward the filibuster's ultimate demise. Part of Reid's motivation, apparently, was that his party might as well benefit from the move because it was assumed that the Republicans would have taken it the first time that a filibuster-proof margin opposed a Republican president and a Republican majority. And, indeed, that is what Majority Leader Mitch McConnell did when he could not otherwise get sufficient votes to overcome a filibuster over Neil Gorsuch's nomination to the Supreme Court.

These developments make the legislative process more complex and more manageable for the majority party. The natural endpoint of this path is unfettered domination of the majority party over the minority party in both the House and the Senate. While the legislative process will be less cumbersome, the ability of a strong minority will be powerless to stop it, a result that would cause great concern for Madison and those who are leery of unencumbered government action.

CHAPTER 7

The Committees

Just as Apple hires some employees to work the Genius Bar and other employees to design the software to power iPhones, so Congress does its job by dividing up the policy areas for which it is accountable. Every employee at Apple cannot weigh in on every decision the company makes, and so it is with Congress. Some members are experts in defense policy while others are experts in tax code. Most of the action of Congress and most of the important decision making within Congress takes place not on the House or Senate floor, but in thirty-six separate committees in which expert witnesses are heard, issues are debated, policy alternatives are developed, and compromises are reached.

Though committees were not mentioned in the Constitution, each chamber retained the right to develop its own legislative process as it saw fit. As the role of the federal government grew, so, too, did the demand for and development of the committee system. In 1812, representatives took 219 roll-call votes and senators took 109. By 2012, with the federal government having expanded its involvement in many areas of American life, representatives voted 654 times and senators voted 250 times. It is hard to imagine any representative or senator having the time, energy, or inclination to master the details of hundreds of thousands of pages of legislation or review countless volumes of testimony supporting or opposing changes in child-care legislation, flood relief, highway construction, defense spending, and international trade policy. Congressional committees, each charged with a specific part of the public policy terrain, allow members to focus their concerns on fewer issues and to develop the expertise needed to make decisions. More often than not, this expertise is directly tied to the members' constituents.

Over the years, the jurisdictions, responsibilities, and powers of individual committees have been expanded and reduced; new committees have been created while others have been consolidated or eliminated; the names of the committees have changed to reflect changes in jurisdiction or the different priorities of new congressional majorities. Through it all, the importance of the committee structure has endured. In this chapter, we first provide a brief history of the congressional committee system. Next, we explain in more detail the system operating in today's Congress. Third, we describe the internal structure of the committees. Fourth, we categorize the committees according to how members view their importance. Fifth, we outline how committees do their jobs. We end the chapter by describing how political scientists have viewed and studied the committees.

THE HISTORY OF COMMITTEES

In early congressional history, the committees existed only on an ad hoc basis, usually being created for the sole purpose of processing a single bill. The broad contours of a bill were first agreed on by the whole membership before an ad hoc group of members were asked by their respective floors to develop the words necessary to carry out the agreed-on policy. If this ad hoc committee produced results consistent with the chamber's preferences, the chamber would pass the bill, commend the committee for its work, and then disband it. During this period, the House or Senate, by acting as a *committee of the whole*, created a very floor-centered legislative process. That is, the committee that decided on the policy consisted of the whole membership of the chamber.

The House slowly began to rely on a committee system, though after more than twenty years in operation, a majority of the legislation was still processed by these temporary committees. When Henry Clay (Whig-KY), who had previously served six months in the Senate, showed up for his first days of service in the House of Representatives in 1811, he was elected Speaker because his hawkish views toward England united various political factions that were eager to repel the British threat surrounding the newly formed nation. Clay exercised great discretion and power so long as the British threat was real. As the war faded from the political agenda, the preferences of his grand coalition began to splinter, with each subgroup rallying behind a different leader. Clay tried to hold his coalition together by appointing his loyalists—or, as he may have seen it, potential rivals—to chair newly created *standing* committees, whose jurisdictions were codified and whose existence not only transcended the individual bills on which they were working, but also remained in existence from one congress to the next. By giving other powerful members the ability to act on pieces of the legislative agenda, Clay may have held his coalition together much longer than their common preferences could have. By the time he left the House for the last time in 1825, the number of standing committees had more than doubled—increasing from ten to twenty-seven—and the amount of legislation that they processed increased from 47 percent to 89 percent (SEE FIGURE 7.1).[1]

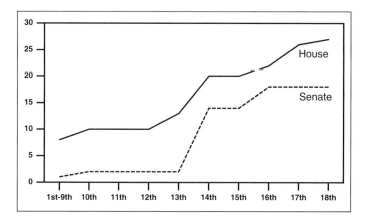

Figure 7.1 Growth in the Number of Standing Committees, 1789–1824.
SOURCE: Walter Stubbs, *Congressional Committees*, 1789–1982 (Westport, CT: Greenwood Press, 1985).

While the House standing committee system came into existence in fits and starts, guided by Clay's political acumen, the Senate created its standing committee system in one fell swoop. In the first 13 congresses, senators created only two standing committees. In the 14th Congress (1815–17), they created 12 more. In the first session of the 14th Congress, the Senate considered only one bill (of 379) in standing committees. In the second session of the same congress, the Senate considered all but 36 bills (of 283) in standing committees. Within a couple of years, the Senate went from two standing committees to fourteen and from considering less than 1 percent of the bills in standing committees to more than 87 percent. The House and Senate committee systems that existed in 1825 look much more like today's committee system than the committee system used even as late as 1810.

While the development of the committee system was engineered by the leaders in Congress, it was perfectly consistent with the growth, in terms of both size and population, that the nation was experiencing. While the Senate's membership was only increasing by 2 members with each new state's admittance to the union, the House's membership grew when the population grew. Between 1789 and 1825, the Senate added 22 seats to their original 26; the House more than tripled, going from 65 to 212 members. The House, whose growth was more rapid, developed the committee system earlier than, and implemented it more completely than the Senate, which then and now enjoys its advantage of having fewer members. Even today, the House is much more dependent on its committees than the Senate.

Ironically, even though committees have their origins in party leadership, the two institutionalized features of Congress trade off with one another. Sometimes party leadership is more powerful than the committee system and at other times the dynamic is reversed. Members made two key decisions that gave committees the ability to compete with party leaders. First, after Speakers Thomas Reed (R-ME) and Joseph Cannon (R-IL) greatly expanded the power of party leaders in the late nineteenth and early twentieth centuries, the rank and file rebuked Cannon in 1910, when forty-two of his fellow Republicans sided with the Democratic caucus in removing him from the Rules Committee and stripping him of his power to make committee assignments. Party leaders can only be powerful if they have the support of their chambers; committees are the repositories of that power when party leadership fades.

Second, the committee system became more defined when Congress passed the Legislative Reorganization Act of 1946. By restricting the number of standing committees from forty-eight to nineteen in the House, the Speaker marginally lost power to refer bills to favored committees while ignoring other committees that were stacked with members opposed to the Speaker's agenda. No longer could Speakers skirt difficult committee chairs by naming a new and more compliant committee. Rather, the party leadership was forced to work through the nineteen existing channels to pass legislation. When the committees' jurisdictions became better defined, the committees themselves began exercising even more independent power. The committee chairs were based not on the party leadership's preferences, as they were just fifty years before, but by being awarded to the person in the majority party who had served the longest on the committee, which placed the power once exercised by the Speaker directly inside the committees themselves. As a result of the seniority system and well-defined jurisdictions, the committees grew stronger and more autonomous.

As the Senate's membership increased and as the federal government grew, the Senate in time became dependent on their committees as well. The chairs of both House and Senate committees, because they were difficult to depose, often became autocratic, ruling their committees as if they were personal fiefdoms and controlling the fate of legislation that fell within their purview. Because the Democratic Party dominated the South, southern members were more likely to survive repeated elections and accrue more seniority. Over time, they came to control a disproportionate number of committees. House Speakers and Senate party leaders were forced to negotiate with these chairs rather than leading them, as they had done for most of the nineteenth century.

This strong committee system was the bedrock of the Textbook Congress. Because of the importance and centrality of committees to the work that Congress could accomplish, a series of norms soon developed. New committee members, who were ostensibly the equals of their more senior colleagues, were treated as apprentices until they had acquired enough expertise to meaningfully engage the legislative process; committee members were expected to concentrate on issues that came before their committees, a degree of specialization that kept members from involving themselves in policies beyond the jurisdiction of those committees; and members were expected to be available for long hours of committee work at the will of the chair. Although the adherence to these norms varied by committee and by chamber, the three norms reinforced the importance of the chambers' senior members and the relative weakness of the junior members.

The tensions between committee chairs and their less senior colleagues began to rise as increasingly conservative Democratic committee chairs exercised incredible power in a Democratic caucus that was getting increasingly progressive. Perhaps most famously, conservative Democrat "Judge" Howard Smith, the chair of the Rules Committee, best exemplified the powers of strong committee chairs when he refused to have his committee consider civil rights legislation that had been successfully reported out of the Judiciary Committee. Speaker Sam Rayburn (D-TX), with the help of President Kennedy and with much angst and trepidation, successfully arranged for the Democratic caucus to increase the membership of the Rules Committee in 1961 so that a majority of its membership favored civil rights legislation.

The committee system was further weakened by the Legislative Reorganization Act of 1970, which curbed the power of committee chairs and shifted much of the legislative policymaking process to the subcommittees, where younger members—and, as it were, more liberal members—were more powerful. For the first time, subcommittees had named jurisdictions within the full committee and the subcommittee chairs had the authority to hire their own staff and conduct their own hearings. Full committee chairs were losing power not only to their subcommittees, but also to their party leaders. Because of the disjoint between conservative southerners dominating the committee system and northern liberals dominating the Democratic caucus, the latter were less willing to abide by the dictates of the seniority system. Committee chairs began feeling more pressure from their fellow party members. Additionally, House leaders began to reacquire some of the power they had lost during the revolt against Cannon. The creation of the House and Senate Budget Committees in 1975 further reduced the power of chairs over establishing a national agenda, and in the House, the Speaker's increased ability to control the Rules Committee, by appointing both its chair and other committee members, reasserted control over action on the floor, again reducing committee autonomy and undercutting the power of committee chairs.

The committee system changed again in 1995 when the Republicans, under the leadership of the newly elected Speaker, Newt Gingrich (R-GA), took control of the House. The newly empowered Speaker Gingrich exercised more power than any Speaker since Cannon. Because of the mandate that came with the 1994 elections, Gingrich either forced committees to act in accord with the leadership's agenda or went around them by appointing ad hoc task forces, not unlike the committees used during the early congresses. Gingrich was given wide latitude by his conference to name committee chairs, at times ignoring the seniority system to promote loyal allies into important chairmanships over veteran legislators who were more willing to exercise independent judgment. Furthermore, Speaker Gingrich revised the names and jurisdictions of the committees to better suit the Republican agenda. The Education and Labor Committee, for example, became the Education and Workforce Committee. The Speaker's power with respect to committees has not waned under Gingrich's successors.

THE COMMITTEE SYSTEM OF TODAY

Although the committee system has changed since Clay's days, the purpose of the committees has remained constant. Even the ad hoc committees used in the first congresses were composed of members who were to become experts (if they were not already) on a given topic. They were to recommend legislation to their parent chamber, which would usually exercise great deference to the committees' decisions. Those fundamental relationships have not changed for more than two hundred years.

While the duties of committees have not changed, it was only when the committees became institutionalized with stable membership and set jurisdictions that they obtained their most important power: gatekeeping. Upon a bill's referral, that committee has almost complete control whether the chamber ever considers it. This power over the agenda is immensely important and immensely consequential. In the 114th Congress (2013–4), more than 85 percent of Senate bills and 87 percent of House bills died in committee.[2] Only an extraordinary bill that is opposed by the chair or a majority of the committee can ever be acted on by the parent chamber, and then only through a tortured process.

The committees are each given a piece of the entire legislative agenda. One of the first actions when the House convenes after an election is to vote on the committees' *jurisdictions*, which simply outline which committees are assigned which issues. In the Senate, which considers itself a continuously serving body, the jurisdictions remain the same unless the Senate chooses to modify them. As society and technology change, jurisdictional battles can emerge. It is only with great care and after intense debate that Congress changes the jurisdictions of its committees.[3]

Through the established jurisdictions written into both chambers' rules, the committee system mandates a division of labor under which each committee has a particular piece of the legislative agenda to encourage its members to become experts so they help the parent chamber make the best decision. Of course, dividing the entire legislative agenda into committees is not without its downside. If a member and her constituents have a deep interest in legislation affecting a particular industry, they have little influence unless she is a member of the committee that has jurisdiction over the legislation affecting the industry. Even if the legislation reaches the floor, the member has little power. On legislation coming from committees on which she serves, her influence is much greater. Members without expertise in a particular area—which naturally includes most members on most issues—often defer to members who have already studied the issues. As a consequence, they frequently are forced to defer even if they do not want to.

Why, then, do the members continue to accept a system where they can only exercise much power on a select few issues? After all, every two years each member gets to vote on new rules to govern their chamber's operations (at least in the House). Why do they not eliminate committees altogether or weaken their power? The answer is simple: too much legislation is introduced for Congress not to divide up the responsibility of evaluating options and narrowing the final decision. Furthermore, on balance, the committee system helps members achieve their goals by giving them disproportionate power over the issues of importance to their constituents.

The committee system helps members achieve not only Mayhew's proximate goal of reelection, but also Fenno's three goals: reelection, good policy, and influence. In fact, it was in a book about committees where Fenno developed the argument for these goals. The committee system increases the chances of members' reelections as a result of their ability to support federal projects in their districts or to support policies important to their constituents; it enables them to shape policies reflective of their own political philosophy (e.g., reduced federal regulation, lower taxes, more support for the disadvantaged), which is frequently attuned by their constituents' preferences; and it helps them gain influence among their congressional colleagues by virtue of becoming acknowledged experts.

Because Congress today considers so much legislation, each committee may be assigned the task of evaluating hundreds of legislative proposals. In addition, committees tend to be large (in the House, with 435 members, some standing committees may have more than 50 members). With many bills to consider in a limited amount of time and with each committee member serving on other committees as well, there is simply too much work for the development of the kinds of organizational expertise that committees were designed to foster. And with so many men and women sitting at the table, waiting for a chance to speak, debate is often awkward and compromise is difficult to reach. Committees, therefore, divide themselves yet again into smaller subcommittees, each with a smaller membership and narrower jurisdiction. The House Appropriations Committee, for example, has 51 committee members and twelve subcommittees, none with more than 16 members. In contrast, the Senate Committee on Energy and Natural Resources has 22 committee members and is divided into four subcommittees.

The House and Senate divide their respective workloads through these standing committees, of which the Senate has sixteen and the House has twenty (see Table 7.1 for a list of standing committees and the number of their subcommittees). It is through the standing committees and their subcommittees that the House and Senate conduct most of their legislative business. Based on the functions that they perform, standing committees are classified into several groups, which we describe below.

Authorizing Committees

Committees have two basic functions: to legislate and to conduct oversight. When legislators determine that it is necessary to create new laws and new federal agencies to protect workers' safety or to ensure that workplaces and public facilities are accessible to people with disabilities, they use authorizing committees to study these issues, to develop new policies, and to craft legislation. Authorizing committees are responsible for authorizing these new programs or agencies. When forging the compromises necessary to enact new laws, Congress frequently passes broad dictates without the legislative details and minutiae required to carry them out. In these instances, the executive branch, which is charged with executing the laws, is responsible for determining how the new law should be implemented. The disjoint between writing the laws in Congress and implementing the laws in the executive branch gives rise to the second function: oversight. The authorizing committees conduct hearings and investigations to determine how well federal agencies are implementing the laws and gaining from them information for needed new laws. When the space program runs into problems or when questions are raised about military procurement costs, committees need to exercise their oversight responsibility. They call expert witnesses to testify and summon agency officials to defend their decisions. This process sometimes results in new laws, new reporting requirements for agency officials, or, in some cases, cutbacks in the authorized level of funding until their performance is considered to have improved.

Table 7.1 Committees in the House and Senate (and the Number of Subcommittees)

HOUSE OF REPRESENTATIVES STANDING COMMITTEES	SENATE STANDING COMMITTEES
Agriculture (6)	Agriculture, Nutrition, and Forestry (5)
Appropriations (12)	Appropriations (12)
Armed Services (7)	Armed Services (6)
Budget (0)	Banking, Housing, and Urban Affairs (5)
Education and the Workforce (4)	Budget (0)
Energy and Commerce (6)	Commerce, Science, and Transportation (7)
Ethics (0)	Energy and Natural Resources (4)
Financial Services (6)	Environment and Public Works (7)
Foreign Affairs (7)	Finance (6)
Homeland Security (6)	Foreign Relations (7)
House Administration (2)	Health, Education, Labor, and Pensions (3)
Intelligence (3)	Homeland Security and Governmental Affairs (5)
Judiciary (5)	Judiciary (6)
Natural Resources (5)	Rules and Administration (0)
Oversight and Government Reform (7)	Small Business and Entrepreneurship (0)
Rules (2)	Veterans Affairs (0)
Science, Space, and Technology (5)	**SPECIAL AND SELECT COMMITTEES**
Small Business (5)	Indian Affairs
Transportation and Infrastructure (6)	Select Committee on Ethics
Veterans Affairs (4)	Select Committee on Intelligence
Ways and Means (6)	Special Committee on Aging

JOINT COMMITTEES

Joint Economic Committee

Joint Committee on the Library

Joint Committee on Printing

Joint Committee on Taxation

But even after an authorizing committee acts, and even after the House and Senate pass its proposals and the president signs them into law, little tangible change may be felt by the people. That is because much of the legislation passed by Congress requires the spending of federal tax dollars. The executive branch does not have the ability to dip into the federal treasury. Even if it did have greater resources of its own, federal funds usually cannot be spent without congressional approval. Legislation developed by authorizing committees may create new programs or agencies and may even specify an amount to be spent on them, but the authorizing committees cannot provide the money. That is the function of our next type of committee.

The Appropriations Committees

It can be argued that, to a large extent, the ultimate power over federal lawmaking rests not in the White House and not in the authorizing committees of Congress, but in the committees that decide how the national government spends its money. It is the genius of the American system—one that deliberately makes it difficult to impose new laws or taxes—that each proposal must clear numerous hurdles before taking effect. An important step in this deliberate slowing-down process is the division between the authorizing committees, which create programs and agencies, and the two appropriations committees—one in the House and one in the Senate—which decide how much, if any, of the recommended spending is made available to fund the programs. The appropriations committees do not, however, merely wait to get an authorizing committee's spending recommendations, deciding simply to accept, reject, or amend the amount of money to be made available. Instead, their various subcommittees, which roughly parallel the jurisdictions of the authorizing committees, hold their own hearings, conduct their own investigations, and independently determine which federal programs should be continued and at what funding level. For example, the House Homeland Security Committee and its Transportation Security Subcommittee might place a high priority on ensuring the safety of containers as they enter and leave ports in the United States. The Appropriations Subcommittee on Homeland Security, conducting its own separate review of security needs, might place its emphasis on increasing the number of Transportation Security Administration (TSA) officers at airport screening facilities. If the House and Senate approve the appropriations bill that provides more funding for TSA than for port security, what will happen? If the Homeland Security Committee had also authorized the increase in TSA funding, even if the authorizing committee considered it a lower priority, the TSA would get its money. The ports, however, would receive permission (authorization) to go ahead with their projects, but no money with which to do it if the appropriations committee had not yet funded the project. If the TSA increase was not authorized by the Homeland Security Committee, the project would only be appropriated the funds *pending authorization*, ready to be released as soon as the authorizing committee gives its permission for the project to be started.

How, then, do the authorizers keep the appropriators, who are far fewer in number, from dominating the process and rendering the authorizing committees irrelevant? Appropriation bills are generally passed after the authorization bills, and while the appropriations committee may reduce (or eliminate) funding for an agency or program, as a rule, appropriations may not include money beyond authorized levels, nor may they provide funds for programs not included in a previous authorization bill. Nor may members authorize programs in an appropriation bill; the two processes are to be kept separate and members may object through a point of order on the floor if the appropriators overstep their mandates.

As with so much else in Congress, there are rules and there are ways to get around rules. Appropriators are generally cautious about intruding onto authorizers' turf. But it is not uncommon for committee chairs who have failed to win passage of their bills to ask appropriators to include the authorization in the spending bill. In the House, where the Rules Committee determines debate procedures, the rule under which an appropriation is considered may simply prohibit any points of order being raised against the legislation on the grounds that a spending provision has not been previously authorized. It may be helpful to think of authorizing and appropriating committees as being engaged in a formal ballroom dance. While either partner can act independently, the dance only looks good when they dance in harmony.

The Taxing Committees

We have discussed how programs are authorized and funded, but how does the government come to acquire the money to make these appropriations? That is the purpose of the third category of committees. Under the Constitution, all bills to raise revenue (in other words, to levy taxes or impose tariffs that may ultimately increase the cost of a consumer's purchases) must originate in the House of Representatives. Other congressional activities—investigation, oversight, the creation of tax laws, the spending of tax dollars—may be initiated in either the House or the Senate, but the federal government may take money out of the pockets of the citizens only if the House first approves doing so—a protection more necessary when the Constitution was written, since it envisioned a Senate that was appointed by the state legislatures, rather than the popularly elected one we have now.

The revenue committee in the House of Representatives is called the Ways and Means Committee—literally the ways and means by which the Congress comes up with the money to pay for the agencies and departments of the federal government and the programs they administer. As a practical matter, because many large-scale federal programs include provisions for contributions from the beneficiaries (or their employees, on their behalf—Medicare is an example), the Ways and Means Committee also assumes jurisdiction over a number of so-called entitlement programs—programs in which benefits are earned by virtue of one's status, for example, age in receiving social security benefits or income that is below a predesignated level to qualify for Medicaid. In the Senate, the revenue committee with similar jurisdiction to the House's Ways and Means Committee is called the Finance Committee. Although they have different names, they perform similar functions for their respective chambers.

With the government now funded and the programs authorized and appropriated, how is it that Congress sees the big picture to ensure that the money coming in and the money flowing out are roughly in balance? That is the purpose of the fourth category of committees.

The Budget Committees

Prior to the 1970s, Congress took its lead in developing the federal government's budget from the president. After a long-running dispute with president Richard Nixon over who had the authority to spend—or not spend—federal money, Congress passed the Congressional Budget and Impoundment Control Act of 1974, which centered budget making in Congress. The act created the House and Senate Budget Committees as well as the Congressional Budget Office. The committees' primary responsibility is creating one measure every year—the concurrent resolution on the budget. This resolution, which does not require the president's signature, establishes the framework by which the federal government raises and spends money. Not to be confused with the Appropriations Committees, which direct spending, or the Ways and Means and Finance Committees, which primarily raise revenue, the Budget Committees take into account both spending and revenues by establishing limits on how much Congress can spend.

The Budget Committees have oversight over the Congressional Budget Office, which is tasked with supplying economic information to Congress in an unbiased, nonpartisan way. The committees also have jurisdiction over supplemental budget requests, which usually result from unforeseen events in the budget, such as military interventions or natural disasters. The Senate Budget Committee does not place restrictions on its membership, though the House Budget Committees' members are limited. Republicans on the House Budget Committee can only serve four two-year terms in any successive six-term period; Democrats are limited to three two-year terms in any five-term period. The chair and ranking members of the Committee are limited to four two-year terms but can be granted permission by the entire House of Representatives to extend their service on the committee if they desire.

Other Committees

In addition to the authorizing, appropriating, taxing, and budget committees, several other committees play a significant role in the functioning of Congress.

The Rules Committee

In the Senate, members who wish to speak on a bill may do so; they may offer amendments, debate an issue, and even continue to control use of the Senate floor for hours at a time. The House of Representatives, with more than four times as many members as the Senate, maintains much stricter control over debate and amendment procedures. In the House, the Rules Committee acts as a traffic cop. The committee hears arguments from each bill's advocates and opponents and then determines when—and if—a bill proceeds to the House floor, what—if any—amendments may be offered, how long debate may last, what parliamentary objections may be considered, and even which members will control the allotment of time for discussion. The decisions are made and presented to the House as a House Resolution (H.Res.), which is normally called the *rule* that outlines the parameters for debate on that particular bill only. In practice, this rule permits the House, during the debate on that specific bill, to ignore its standing rules, which are cumbersome and frequently dictate actions that neither committee leaders nor party leaders want to follow.

Because the rule may affect the outcome (if certain amendments are precluded from consideration, for example, members may decide to vote for a bill they could not have supported otherwise), major House debates often begin with a struggle over the form the H.Res. takes. Members who wish to offer, support, or prohibit amendments may decide to vote against the rule, which, if it is defeated, is sent back to the Rules Committee along with its accompanying bill. The Rules Committee can then decide to keep the bill or write up a different rule that, again, is put before the full House.

The Rules Committee has become a central player in determining legislative outcomes in the House, and its members are often the first to frame the debates that eventually reach the House floor. In late 1998, for example, when the House of Representatives took up a motion to launch a series of Judiciary Committee hearings to consider the possible impeachment of President Clinton, it was before the Rules Committee that the Judiciary Committee chair, Henry Hyde, and his Democratic counterpart, John Conyers, publicly presented their differing views as to the proper scope of such hearings, and it was the Rules Committee's chairman, Gerald Solomon (R-NY), and his Democratic counterpart, Joseph Moakley (D-MA), who began the debate that was eventually decided by the full House. Because of the importance of the Rules Committee in determining the procedures on the House floor, the majority party usually has twice as many members on the committee as the minority party and Speakers have much freer hands in naming committee members and the chair than they do on almost every other committee.

The Senate also has a Rules Committee, though because of the personal prerogatives that each individual senator has on the floor, it does not serve the same purpose. The Rules Committee in the Senate considers, drafts, and debates new proposed rules for the Senate. It is also responsible for the physical space on the Senate side of the US Capitol. Its jurisdiction is similar to that of the House Administration Committee in the House of Representatives.

The Ethics Committee

Article I, Section 5, of the Constitution makes each chamber the sole judge of the qualifications of its members; the design, debate, implementation, and enforcement of these rules rests in the chambers themselves. Each chamber also retains the exclusive privilege of punishing its members for "disorderly behavior." Furthermore, with a two-thirds vote, the chamber can expel a member; something that the House has done only five times and the Senate has done only fifteen times.

The committee that handles all these inquiries into members' behaviors is the Ethics Committee. The House and Senate committees have several features in common. First, the committees do not reflect party ratios, but are equally divided between Republicans and Democrats. Furthermore, the staffs of these committees are explicitly—and by rule—nonpartisan. Second, because the committees' functions include the roles of investigator, prosecutor, and judge, and because their findings and recommendations may lead to censure or expulsion of members, hearings and deliberations take place behind closed doors to preclude the possibility of damaging persons who may ultimately be found innocent of wrongdoing. Third, because they are called on to sit in judgment—and perhaps to determine the political fate—of their friends and colleagues, members of Congress are highly reluctant to serve on such committees and are often *drafted* by party leaders with promises of short tenure or other favorable committee assignments. Finally, in addition to the investigative function into matters ranging from book royalty arrangements (investigations that led to the resignation of one House Speaker, Jim Wright, and the reprimand of another, Newt Gingrich) to allegations of bribe-taking and sexual misconduct (including House members having sex with teenage pages) to insider trading, the Ethics Committees also serve as advisors to members who seek guidance as to the propriety of accepting gifts, taking expensive personal trips, or including certain kinds of material in their official communications. As with all the other committees, the Ethics Committees make recommendations to their parent chamber. Only the entire House or the entire Senate can discipline a member. Because the jurisdiction and makeup of these committees require bipartisanship, the parent chambers usually follow the committees' recommendations. Because each chamber has exclusive control over its members, ethics decisions reached by one chamber are not subject to the opinion of the other chamber.

Select Committees

Sometimes problems arise that do not fall easily into the standing committees' jurisdictional lines. On occasion, the standing committees try to claim the issue and, after fighting among themselves, one (or more) may convince the chamber that it should investigate the new problem. On other occasions, the chamber instead creates select committees, which exist not in perpetuity, but rather for a limited amount of time, which is usually specified in the legislation that creates them.

Because each chamber retains the power to organize itself as it wants, the House has chosen to include the Intelligence and Ethics Committees as standing committees while the Senate has chosen to classify them as select committees. As an additional piece of evidence for the different paths chosen by the different chambers, the Senate continues to maintain a special committee on aging, which studies and conducts hearings into issues of concern to the elderly. In the l05th Congress (1997–8), the House disbanded its special committees on hunger and aging, concluding that they duplicated the work of other standing House committees.

Joint Committees

While the House and Senate generally function independently of each other, members of the two chambers serve together, albeit in very different circumstances, in two instances.

First, in addition to standing, special, and select committees, the House and Senate have established six joint committees, made up of equal numbers of senators and representatives. The Joint Economic Committee and the Joint Committee on Taxation review, comment on, and occasionally conduct hearings into matters of economic and tax policy, including the decisions of organizations like the Federal Reserve Board ("the Fed"). Two other committees, the Joint Committee on the Library and the Joint Committee on Printing, oversee the House and Senate libraries and the Library of Congress and the printers who prepare official congressional documents ranging from bills and resolutions to the daily publication of the *Congressional Record*, which includes transcripts of all House and Senate proceedings. Two more joint committees were created as part of the Bipartisan Budget Act of 2018: the Joint Select Committee on Budget and Appropriations Process Reform—created in response to difficulties passing appropriation bills on time—and the Joint Select Committee on Solvency of Multiemployer Pension Plans.

THE MAKEUP OF THE COMMITTEES

Because congressional committees are at the center of institutional power, decisions made at the committee level often determine legislative outcomes, so whichever party gains control of the House or Senate has a strong interest in seeing to it that committee decisions reflect the majority party's will. Instead of serving as intermediaries, neutrally evaluating legislative initiatives, the committees often function primarily to advance the majority party's legislative agenda. To accomplish this end, the majority party has more seats on the committee than the minority party, usually in rough proportion to the full membership in the House or Senate. But if a committee is particularly central to the controlling party's legislative agenda, the ratios may be stretched to reduce the possibility of an unwelcomed outcome. For example, in 2018, Republicans, who held 55 percent of the seats in the House, controlled 69 percent of the seats on the Rules Committee. The Republicans still exercised an advantage on the other important committees but not nearly to the extent that they did on Rules. The Republicans had 58 percent of the seats in the Appropriations Committee and 60 percent of the seats in the Ways and Means Committee.

Because of its smaller size, committee ratios in the Senate tend to be less disproportionate. In 2018, Republicans held 51 percent of the seats in the Senate. Most committees were divided so Republicans had one more seat than the Democrats; if the Republicans had given up one seat to the Democrats, the numbers would have been equal and the Republicans would have had no advantage at all as a result of being in the majority. Not only the ratios but also the size of the committees in both chambers are determined through long and tense negotiations between the party leaders at the beginning of each congress, though they can be adjusted if changes in membership alter the party ratios. Such was the case when Doug Jones (D-AL) took his seat in the Senate at the beginning of 2018. The two-seat advantage that the Republicans enjoyed during 2017 shrank to the bare majority they had during 2018.

Committee Leadership

Just as each member has exactly one vote on the floor of the House or Senate, whether she has served one day or ten years, so it is with each member in a committee. But just as the majority party leadership has the ability to control, more or less, proceedings on the chambers' floors, so it is with the committee chairs. The legislative life in committees revolves around their chairs, who are not powerful because they have the most visibility; rather, they have the most visibility because they are powerful. In the insular world of the congressional committee, chairs hold almost all of the most consequential cards. The committee's professional and clerical staff members report to them. When bills are referred to the committee for consideration, the chairs may send them on to a subcommittee or may choose to keep control of the legislation at the full committee level. The chairs may order subcommittees to proceed expeditiously or to simply file the legislation without action. Chairs at the subcommittee level play the same role, subject only to the direction of the full committee chair. As such, the subcommittee chair exercises strict control over handling legislation under its jurisdiction. The chair decides whether bills receive hearings and, if so, when they are held and how many and which witnesses are called. Even if courtesy leads to minority members also being allowed to call witnesses to present a case for the minority view, the chair decides how many witnesses are heard for each side and for how long.

After hearings have been completed, the chair still exercises great powers. At committee and subcommittee markups, the chair comes into the meeting with a *chairman's mark*—a version of the final bill the chair hopes to see emerge. While committee and subcommittee votes are never fully predictable, given the ideological and constituent pulls that influence legislators' decisions, most legislation that advances to the House or Senate floor closely conforms to the chair's wishes. The chair exercises such power through several means. First, because members of the committee staff report to the chair, they are often in a position of having superior information both as to the root problem being addressed and as to the likely outcome of whatever alternatives might be proposed. Second, because the chair determines what bills receive consideration, he or she may simply threaten to kill other legislation championed by uncooperative members, either by pressuring other members to vote against the legislation or by refusing to even schedule hearings or a committee markup. Circumventing the chair's preferences is difficult at best. Third, if the House and Senate ultimately pass different versions of the same bill, both passed bills can be sent to a conference committee, made up of members of the two chambers tasked with reconciling the differences between the two versions. Unless the Speaker or majority leader in the Senate intervenes, the chair has great influence on who serves on the conference committee and thus whether a member is in the room when final decisions are made on bills about which they may care deeply.

The chair's power, however, is not absolute. In addition to chairs being deposed from time to time, the membership of the House can decide to remove a bill from a committee's jurisdiction through a discharge petition, which requires a majority of members to sign. Because of the effort that these maneuvers require, they almost always fail, but they have succeeded often enough that they are a legitimate check on a chair's power.

Chairs also have great power in structuring the subcommittees, though not without some constraints. In both the House and the Senate, for example, committee members have a voice in deciding which of their colleagues chair the committees' subcommittees. In the House, the majority party's committee members may vote on how many subcommittees to establish and the extent of each subcommittee's jurisdiction, while in the Senate, committee chairs generally consult more with members of the committee majority before making such decisions.

During the Textbook Congress era and after, chairs were normally chosen consistent with the seniority system, which places the chair's gavel in the hands of the majority party member with the most seniority on the committee. This system kept infighting within the majority party to a minimum and brought about stability within the committees themselves by not making the position subject to a vote by the membership, which would encourage disharmony and intracommittee factions that could ultimately cause paralysis, an outcome that would reflect poorly on the majority party and the committee. But, the seniority system is a norm—it is not an institutionalized rule. The entire caucus membership of the majority party ultimately has the power to determine who will chair the committees at the beginning of each new congress.

Members have been willing to buck the seniority system when they have felt it necessary. Even when the seniority system was more firmly entrenched both parties violated it on occasion. When Democrats on the House Armed Services Committee became concerned that the committee's elderly chairman, Melvin Price of Illinois, could no longer function effectively, a small group organized a coup that resulted in the election of a younger and more dynamic chair, Les Aspin (D-WI), who later became President Clinton's secretary of defense. Likewise, Republicans skipped over Phil Crane (R-IL) when they named Bill Thomas (R-CA), a younger and more energetic member, the chair of the Ways and Means Committee in 2001.

As the power of party leadership has grown, the seniority violations for the naming of committee chairs have also grown. The more recent violations were more likely due to simple policy disagreements between the most senior members and the rest of their parties. In 2008, the Democratic Caucus voted to replace House Energy and Commerce Committee chairman John Dingell (D-MI) with Pelosi ally Henry Waxman (D-CA). Dingell had been the senior Democrat on that committee for three decades, but Waxman was seen as more willing to work with Democratic president-elect Barack Obama on energy legislation. In 2005, Republicans replaced Chris Smith (R-NJ) as chair of the Veterans Affairs Committee because he had different spending priorities than the rest of his party and his party leadership.

The seniority system rule has become even less sacrosanct as more violations have occurred. Chairs, who during the Textbook Congress had almost complete control over their committees, now exercise less control with less job security. While Republicans have led the charge in violating the seniority system, Democrats have increasingly followed suit. When Newt Gingrich and the Republicans took over the House in the 104th Congress, five committees experienced new leadership, and three of those committees (Appropriations, Energy and Commerce, and Judiciary) were chaired by members who did not have the most seniority on

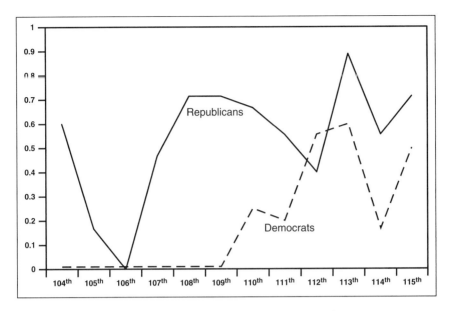

Figure 7.2   The Percentage of Seniority Violations in the Naming of House Committee Chairs, 104th to 115th Congresses (1995–2018).

the committee. It would take the Republicans another four congresses to reach such a high percentage of seniority violations, but since then, they have eclipsed it in more congresses than they have not. It took the Democrats longer to frequently violate the seniority norm, but in three of the last four congresses at least 50 percent of the new chairs did not have the most seniority on the committee.

Just as they were using more discretion in the naming of committee chairs, the party leaders also implemented limits for the number of terms a member could serve as chair. In 1995, the Republicans set the term limit at three congresses (six years). Such term limits increased the number of opportunities party leaders have to select chairs. While the parties maintained the ability to depose chairs at any time they pleased, most chairs continued their service until they reached their term limit. Chairs could only serve longer than three terms if the party conference gave them a waiver, something that has occurred only sparingly. When the Democrats retook the House in the 2006 elections, they kept the Republican committee chair term limits in place for their own chairs, though they repealed the term limit after the 2008 election.

The *ranking member*, the minority party's counterpart to the chair, is typically the most senior member on the committee of the minority party. As with chairs, the ranking members are also determined by the party membership. Although ranking members do not exercise nearly the power that a chair does, the fights over filling a ranking member vacancy can be contentious because ranking members can be thought of as chairs in waiting. Should the minority party become the majority, the ranking member is the odds-on favorite to become the new committee chair.

When the Republicans came back in power in 2011, they not only reinstituted the term limit on committee chairs, but also decided to count the years of service as ranking member as part of that six-year window, which meant that some members who became ranking members in 2007 would only be able to exercise the powers of the chair for two years before reaching their limit.

Committee Assignments

Because of the critical role that committees play in the legislative process, party leaders labor over deciding which members will serve on which committees. Competition for committee assignments is fierce. Some committees are both powerful and prestigious. Members of those committees have influence over substantive policy issues and they are perceived by journalists and even their constituents as important members of the House or Senate. If an issue is of particular importance in a state or congressional district—protecting a military base, for example, or protecting wheat subsidies—winning a seat on the committee with jurisdiction over those matters can be crucial to the members' reelection. By serving on other committees, members can develop relationships with the moneyed interests that can donate campaign contributions or interest groups that can help provide campaign volunteers for subsequent reelection efforts.

Sometimes members mount aggressive campaigns to win seats on committees that address their personal concerns: Robert Smith (R-NH), for example, had dedicated much of his congressional career to prisoner of war/missing in action issues—an attempt to account for American servicemen who were captured or declared missing in action in the Vietnam War. Smith made several attempts to win appointment to the House Armed Services Committee but, for a variety of reasons, was unsuccessful each time. Ultimately, he ran for the Senate, won, and then secured a seat on the Senate Armed Services Committee.

The members who serve on the committees that are charged with making committee assignments weigh many factors. The first factor is the special expertise a member may have. Consideration is usually given to members with special qualifications. If possible, a physician will be assigned to a committee with jurisdiction over healthcare issues, a physicist may end up on a committee charged with dealing with science issues, or a lawyer will serve on the Judiciary Committee.

The second factor is advancing the party's agenda. One can never be certain, of course; Republicans, who supported deregulation of natural gas in the 1970s, placed a Pennsylvania freshman, Marc Lincoln Marks, on the Interstate and

Foreign Commerce Committee, which had jurisdiction over that issue. Marks was chosen because Pennsylvania Republicans, who represented one of the largest delegations on the Republican side of the aisle, argued that the state was entitled to a representative on the committee. Marks voted against deregulation and the issue failed narrowly. Democrats generally opposed Ronald Reagan's support for rebels who opposed the Sandinista government in Nicaragua, but when the House voted on a package of military aid to the rebels, the chair of the Committee on Foreign Affairs (Dante Fascell of Florida), the chair of the Defense Subcommittee of the Appropriations Committee (John Murtha of Pennsylvania), and the chair of the Rules Committee (Claude Pepper of Florida) voted with Reagan and the Republicans. Using committee assignments to predetermine policy outcomes is an inexact science at best.

The third factor is the concern of reelection. We have already seen that both parties go to great lengths to ensure continuation of whatever party advantage they might have or to increase their chances of gaining that advantage. Both parties consider it important, therefore, not to lose the seats they already control. If a seat on a particular committee is seen as vital to a member's ability to get reelected, that need will weigh heavily on the appointment decision.

Another factor that the party leaders consider is regional representation. A New England senator or representative who seeks an appointment to a committee can make a stronger argument if no other New Englanders of his or her party currently sit on the committee. The last factor that we list here is racial or gender balance. Until senators Cory Booker (D-NJ) and Kamala Harris (D-CA) were named to the Senate Judiciary Committee in 2018, no African American Democrat had served on that committee since senator Carol Moseley Braun (D-IL) lost her reelection bid in 1998.

Because of the mix of factors involved, political scientist Kenneth Shepsle of Harvard coined the phrase "the giant jigsaw puzzle" to describe the committee appointment process. Even though the appointing committees may take many factors into account, it becomes the job of the seeker to make the information known. In the House in particular, with 435 members, of which each party usually has around 200 members, many of the more senior legislators have only cursory knowledge of a colleague's interests, concerns, or district. A representative from one of the eastern states, for example, knowing something of the West, may assume that a representative from central Oklahoma will have a special interest in a committee that has jurisdiction over Indian reservations and federal parklands. Yet the congressional district including Oklahoma City is almost completely urban. For this reason, members who seek good initial committee assignments, or who seek, after a term or two, to move to a better or more suitable committee, must often wage aggressive informational campaigns including phone calls, personal visits, letters, and even tweets and Facebook messages from influential outsiders to those senior members who make the ultimate committee assignment decisions. One must be careful though: a member who is generally supportive of legislation favorable to the banking industry may ask friends or lobbyists who work in that industry to call influential party leaders on his or her behalf, but this strategy that may backfire; those whose responsibility it is to make the selections may resent outside pressure and may even resent campaigns that are too aggressive. Some members have suggested that it is easier to win election to Congress than to win the committee seat one wants, and that is sometimes the case.

Who, then, makes these decisions? The parties and the chambers implement different procedures for filling their available committee positions, but the general approach is similar. Committees are placed into categories according to their importance and the most important members from both parties in both chambers review the applications, interview the members, and then make the committee assignment decisions. The decisions, then, are subject to the approval of the entire party membership.

The House Republican Committee on Committees is made up of members who acquire their positions in a number of different ways. Some join by virtue of being in the elected party leadership, which includes the Speaker, the party leader, the whip, the chair and vice chair of the Republican Conference, the chair and former chair of the campaign committee, the chair of the policy committee, and the secretary of the Republican Conference. Another path to the committee is through serving in other institutional capacities, which include the chief deputy whip and the chairs of the Appropriations, Budget, Energy and Commerce, Financial Services, Rules, and Ways and Means Committees (the committee chairs share one seat given temporarily to the chair who has the most direct connection to the committee seat being decided). Finally, the committee includes nineteen regional representatives as well as two members from the sophomore class and two members from the freshman class, all of whom are elected by the respective subgroups of the conference. As a sign of the importance and contention of making committee assignments, the House Freedom Caucus, a subset of the most conservative Republicans, demanded changes to the selection process prior to endorsing Paul Ryan's ascendency to the speakership.

The committee assignments for the House Democrats are made through its Steering and Policy Committee, which is dominated by its leaders. The entire party leadership, elected by the caucus, serves on the committee, including the leader (who names twenty-four other members of the committee), the assistant leader, and the whip (both of whom name nine other committee members). The committee also includes twelve members who are all elected from particular regions as well as the ranking member (or chair, if they are in the majority) of the Appropriations, Budget, Energy and Commerce, Rules, and Ways and Means Committees

Fewer paths exist to serving on the assignment committees in the Senate. The Senate Democratic Steering Committee is made up of seventeen members appointed by the Senate Democratic leader. The committee considers several criteria when making their decisions, including regional diversity, seniority, and policy expertise. The Senate Republican Committee on Committees, in contrast, is smaller (usually around nine members) because the Republican Conference has adopted a more formulaic criterion for filling committee vacancies that relies almost exclusively on seniority. Because both committees are composed of decisions made by the party leaders and subject to a vote of the entire party, the members are usually attuned to the needs of the leadership and party.

So important are the committee assignments perceived to be that many members actively seek to become members of the appointing committees. When newly elected Republican members gather to select their "class" officers, some members campaign for the class presidency. The more astute often seek election, instead, as the class representative to the committee on committees, where they may not only advance their own committee preferences, but also win the gratitude of their new colleagues by effectively championing classmates' preferences.

Winning a cherished committee assignment often takes time. The number of seats is not infinite, and since returning members almost always retain the seats they held in the previous congress, openings on prized committees are sometimes rare. Sought-after seats are likely to become available only when a party gains a substantial number of seats, when one party takes control from the other party (in which cases, new majority-to-minority ratios may create openings), or when many incumbents lose or die. In some years, there may be no openings for new members of the Ways and Means Committee in the House or the Finance Committee in the Senate. Thus, the internal campaigns continue. After each election, several House and Senate members who had previously been appointed to less desirable committees attempt to move up, transferring to committees that are more powerful, more prestigious, or more helpful in terms of constituent interests. And the cycle of lobbying and informing begins all over again. The cost of transferring up is that the member loses all seniority on his or her previous committee. Although the committee may be more prestigious, the years of waiting to become chair, or even subcommittee chair, grow much longer.

Staff

Like members' personal offices, the committees have many staffers assisting the members. Unlike members' offices, few of these staffers deal directly with constituents. The staff can largely be broken down into two broad categories—support staff to help the committee with its logistic functioning and the expert staff that advise members on the various policy alternatives. Some of these committee staffers are the most powerful people on Capitol Hill. In a 2015 list developed by *Roll Call*, the newspaper of Capitol Hill, ten of the "Fabulous 50" staffers on Capitol Hill worked for committees—most of the other staffers on the list worked directly for the party leaders.[4]

Committee staff sizes vary greatly depending on the importance and breadth of the committee. While the House Appropriations Committee had 158 staff positions in 2015, the Budget Committee had only 36.[5] Likewise, in the Senate, the Indian Affairs committee had only 14 staff positions, but the Finance Committee had 26.[6] Without regard to the size or the importance of the committee, the majority party usually hires about two-thirds of the staff for the committee and the minority party hires the remaining third.

RANKING THE COMMITTEES

Categorizing the committees by function makes sense when describing the committee system in total, but a categorization based on power, prestige, or importance is another helpful way to understand how the committees operate inside the Capitol. The two chambers use different names and include different committees in their chambers' hierarchies. The House of Representatives has three categories: exclusive, nonexclusive, and exempt. For many years, only three committees were included in the exclusive category: Appropriations, Rules, and Ways and Means. When the Republicans became a majority after the 1994 election, they added Energy and Commerce to the list; ten years later, they added Financial Services. These committees, because they have such broad jurisdictions and because they perform such fundamental governmental functions, typically dominate the schedules for their members at least while they are in Washington, DC. As such, service on one of these committees severely restricts the members' abilities to serve on one of the other committees.[7]

The nonexclusive committees include almost all other committees. These committees usually have more specific policy jurisdictions, which frequently can make them more important to members' constituencies. For this reason, sometimes these committees are called *constituency* committees. They include, for example, Armed Services, Agriculture, and Transportation. Members usually serve on at least a couple of these committees. The House has two exempt committees (the Ethics Committee and Select Intelligence), which means serving on these committees is usually not taken into consideration when members seek assignment to other committees.

The Senate uses similar categories, though they are labeled Super A, A, B, and C. The makeup of the committees in these categories is similar to, but not the same as, that in the House. The Super A committees are Armed Services, Finance, Appropriations, and Foreign Relations. Republican senators cannot serve on more than one of these committees, and Democratic senators cannot serve on more than one of the first three. Other A committees include the rest of the big authorizing committees, such as Judiciary (which also considers all judicial nominations), Select Intelligence, and Energy and Natural Resources. The B committees, which have smaller portfolios, include Budget, Rules and Administration, Small Business and Entrepreneurship, Veterans Affairs, Special Committee on Aging, and the Joint Economic Committee. The C committees include Ethics, Indian Affairs, and ad hoc committees that the Senate chooses to establish from time to time.

The differences between the House's exclusive and the Senate's Super A committees are explained by three critical differences between the chambers. First, because each senator has the power to disrupt the Senate's schedule by objecting to a unanimous consent agreement, the Rules Committee in the Senate is only a B committee, which is of a similar ranking to its functional equivalent in the House (the House Administration Committee). Second, because the Senate has the power to ratify treaties, the Foreign Relations Committee has a heightened status in the Senate. Finally, because most senators fashion themselves legitimate presidential contenders, they opt for service on Armed Services—the closest thing to being commander in chief for a legislator—and Foreign Relations—to mirror the president's role of negotiating with foreign leaders. Because the Senate has fewer than one-fourth as many members as the House and the same number of issues to consider (perhaps more), senators necessarily must serve on more committees than their colleagues on the other side of the Capitol—most serve on four or five committees.

Most members of Congress like to boast to their constituents about their prized (and, thus, influential) committee assignments. Even those that are regarded as relatively minor can be of vital importance to a member's constituency and, thus, to the members themselves. The House Committee on Merchant Marine and Fisheries, before it was disbanded and its jurisdictions were reassigned, was considered among the least influential and least important committees in the Congress, yet it was vital to the specific economic interests of many seacoast states. Subcommittees with jurisdiction over soybean production, wetlands preservation, or military base construction may be crucial to the economic vitality of many states and communities. A member of Congress who wins a seat on the Natural Resources Committee or the Livestock, Dairy, and Poultry Sub-committee of the Agriculture Committee, may, in fact, be well placed to defend the interests of constituents, with the political benefit that naturally accrues from such a position. The "giant jigsaw" moniker describing the committee assignment process comes clearly into focus when trying to balance all these regional interests with prestige on the Hill and then filling only the vacancies created by members who retire or lose reelection.

THE COMMITTEES AT WORK

Because their jurisdictions, memberships, and histories differ, each committee functions a bit differently. Nonetheless, the work that happens in the various committees is similar enough that we can sketch the broad contours of how committees operate. They play a critical role not only during the committee stages of the legislative process, but also when bills formally leave their jurisdiction on their way to becoming a law—or not. Furthermore, many committees also have the responsibility of conducting oversight on the various departments and programs of the federal government long after the bills have been written and made into laws.

In Committee

Because so much of the work of Congress takes place at the committee level, one might logically expect members of the House and Senate to be eager participants in committee work. Perhaps that would be the case if they had fewer bills to consider, fewer constituent demands, and fewer committees demanding their attention. It is not uncommon for hearings to take place with only two or three members present and rotating in and out as their prescribed roles play out, although all members (and the rest of us) eventually have access to the transcripts. How, then, do members decide which hearings to attend, and when?

One scholar, Richard Hall of the University of Michigan, concluded that members carefully consider their options and then chose the one that makes the most sense: if, on the one hand, the legislation being considered is important to their constituency or of great personal interest, members likely participate in the bill's consideration; if, on the other hand, the members have no leadership position (the chair or ranking member, for example) that requires their presence, and if they have little interest in the bill under consideration or if it will have little effect on their constituents, it makes sense to spend their time elsewhere (often at another committee meeting taking place simultaneously or meeting with groups of visiting constituents). They often spend their time elsewhere, even as their

committees are meeting. Because members of Congress have stronger ideological commitments than the average nonpolitical citizen, controversial issues—issues that clearly divide liberals from conservatives or that can be characterized as probusiness or prolabor, for example—may induce a larger turnout of committee members because they may perceive the stakes as higher and the outcome of the vote more important.

One other consideration is that members of the minority party often have little incentive to take part in committee meetings unless important ideological, partisan, or constituency-related issues are to be considered. Because less public attention is paid to participation in committee hearings and even to committee votes, members often feel free to support the party position without fear of getting in trouble with the people back home. They thus help their own party advance its agenda, even if they may ultimately have to vote differently after the legislation reaches the House or Senate floor. If the vote is going to fall largely along partisan lines, minority members can be almost certain of losing. Members of the minority party may thus decide not to bother attending committee sessions in which their participation may make little difference.

It should be noted, however, that the rules of neither the House nor the Senate preclude minority members from playing an active role in committee proceedings. To a large extent, the role of minority members, including the ranking member, is determined by the nature of the personal relationship between the chair and her or his minority counterpart. Some chairs and ranking members work collegially. As the Congress grappled with the Russian influence in the 2016 elections, the Intelligence Committees in the respective chambers took two different paths. Consistent with the partisan contentiousness that pervaded the inquiry, House chair Devin Nunes (R-CA) conducted what his critics decried as a superficial investigation that was aborted rather abruptly. Ranking

member Adam Schiff (D-CA) and the Democrats retorted by releasing their own report. On the Senate side, chair Richard Burr (R-NC) and ranking member Mark Warner (D-VA) were praised by their colleagues for conducting a bipartisan investigation.

Although the chairs have substantial power over the proceedings in committee, their legislative opponents frequently try to amend the bill while it is in committee. Sometimes these fights within committee are a preview of future floor fights, but because of the restrictions on floor debate, the deliberations within committee can provide the opponents with a more thorough airing of their concerns. Committee debate can get intense, but the chair usually gets her way. In those instances where the legislation is changed in committee in a way that the chair does not like, she still maintains the power to simply block it from going forward.

To the Floor

When bills reach the floor of the House or Senate, most members who vote on them are relatively uninformed about the questions involved, unless they have been the subject of unusual controversy and discussion in the press or have drawn the attention of constituents. Because committees were established to help members divide up their work and develop expertise in narrower areas of legislation, non–committee members tend to defer to those members of their party who participated in the hearings and markup discussions and who may have a greater sense of the issues at stake. While this *signaling* (Member A watching to see how Member B votes) is helpful, it is not the only way in which a committee member may help a non-committee member make up his or her mind. Each bill reported to the House or Senate floor is accompanied by a committee report that outlines the provisions of the legislation, the arguments for it, and the dissenting or additional views of members who wish to bring other considerations to the attention of their colleagues.

When a bill is debated on the floor of the House, the people managing the time for both sides are typically the committee leaders. Because most bills making it this far in the process receive a full review in committee, committee leaders are usually resistant to amendments made by members on the floor, especially when those members do not serve on the committee. Nonetheless, the floor retains the power to amend the bills as it sees fit. The floor managers are usually the last people to speak before an important vote.

Even after floor consideration, the committee leaders retain power so long as a conference committee is used to resolve the differences between the House- and Senate-passed bills. The committee leaders are usually named to the conference committees whose responsibility it is to develop a compromise bill that can pass both chambers. So, even if the committee leaders do not get their way on the chambers' floors, they have one last chance to force their preferences on their respective chambers. Because conference committee reports are not subject to amendment, the conferees need only be certain that their compromise can get a majority of both chambers' conferees and a majority of the parent chamber's votes.

Once Congress is done legislating, the role of the important committee members is not over. If the president decides to sign the bill into law and have a big White House signing ceremony, the committee leaders will typically be the people with big smiles on their face behind the president. During the signing, the president typically uses several pens and then hands them out to the important committee members and party leaders as a gesture of appreciation for shepherding the bill to final passage.

Oversight

While some committees' work is dominated by the legislation that is being developed, committees also importantly conduct oversight. Both chambers have a committee that is tasked with being the primary committee of oversight—the House's Oversight and Government Reform Committee and the Senate's Homeland Security and Government Affairs Committee. When the "Fast and Furious" program, which gave guns to Mexicans involved in the drug wars so that they could be traced, became linked to the murder of Brian Terry, a US Border Patrol agent, the oversight committees had multiple hearings investigating the origins and operation of the program. Additionally, any of the other authorizing committees also investigate government inefficiencies or malfeasances. For example, if air traffic controllers, under the control of the Federal Aviation Administration, compromised public safety, the Transportation Committees, rather than the oversight committees, would hold hearings into the lapses at the Federal Aviation Administration.

Conducting oversight frequently serves multiple purposes. In addition to rooting out corruption and government inefficiency, committees will frequently try to score political points, especially in the House of Representatives. When the House majority is of the opposing party to the president, twice as many investigations occur as when they are of the same party. These investigations tend to last longer and result in more pages of released hearings.[8]

The problem for those who advocate for a strong Congress is not that oversight intensifies when the chamber majority is different from the president, it is that oversight weakens when the chamber majority is of the same party as the president. Such a scenario presents a perilous proposition for a party that enjoys the White House and a majority in Congress. Turning a blind eye to executive branch malfeasance risks not only the proper functioning of the system, but also the long-term prospects for the majority party to maintain its majority status. Congressional oversight can lead to important midcourse problems that, if not corrected, blow up into full-scale scandals, which can lead to losses for the majority party.

As early as 2004, the veterans' community made elected officials aware of the deplorable conditions at Walter Reed Army Medical Center in Washington, DC. Rather than engage in the kind of oversight that would rectify the problem, the Republican-led committees chose against holding hearings that might embarrass the Republican president (George W. Bush) or the Republican secretary of defense (Donald Rumsfeld). In February 2007, the *Washington Post*, in a two-article expose, transformed the issue into a national scandal that led to multiple high-ranking resignations. All the worse for Republicans, it was the new Democratic majorities in the House and Senate that could trumpet their concern for American's veterans in Democrat-led hearings.

As party polarization has increased and as passing legislation has become more difficult, committees are investing less time and energy in producing legislation. The same conditions, especially when combined with divided government, have led to committees conducting disproportionately more oversight hearings. From the 1950s to the 1970s, congressional committees held between five hundred and one thousand oversight hearings in comparison to one thousand to two thousand hearings on legislation (SEE FIGURE 7.3). By the early 2000s, the

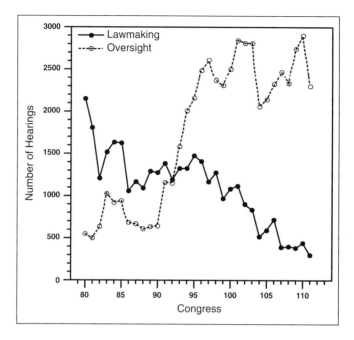

Figure 7.3 Number of Lawmaking versus Oversight Hearings in Congress.
Source: Bryan D. Jones, Sean M. Theriault, and Michelle Whyman, *The Great Broadening* (Chicago: University of Chicago Press, 2019).

number of legislative referral hearings dropped to fewer than five hundred, while the number of oversight hearings exploded to more than two thousand.

CONCLUSION

Throughout the legislative process, the committees, as the center of early congressional action, serve not just as a funnel but also as a magnet: the center of debate and place where powerful forces converge. Much of members' lives on Capitol Hill are seen through the lenses of the committees on which they serve. Good committee assignments align members with their constituents and showcase their power over an area of law or policy important to their constituents' lives, helping members secure reelection.

Because of the crucial role that the committees play in the legislative process, one political scientist, Woodrow Wilson (who would later become president), argued, "It is not far from the truth to say that Congress in session is Congress on public exhibition, whilst Congress in its committee rooms is Congress at work." While the power of committees has waxed and waned and while committee chairs exercise their powers differently, Wilson's observation is as true today as it was when he made it more than one hundred years ago.

=== COMMENTARY ===

The Politician's Take on the Committees

Members of Congress are driven by two primary considerations in seeking committee assignments. One is personal interest, which can be based on preference, ideology, expertise, or experience (I gravitated toward those committees that dealt with foreign policy and constitutional questions); another is constituent interest (I represented an urban constituency that included manufacturing, a considerable white-collar professional community, and a major military base, but agriculture and energy production were essential ingredients of the state's economic well-being). But the committee one lands on may have nothing to do with either factor: party leaders may deny appointment to a committee of great personal interest for fear that you may not faithfully follow the party line on important issues or, conversely, because they can best ensure your reelection by overruling your preferences and placing you in a position to champion local interests.

In either case, as a representative, you understand that it is only by embracing the assignment and mastering its details that you can rise to relevance in Congress. All members of Congress can give good speeches, all are good at making friends, all are pretty smart; as a result, the only way to make an impression on colleagues is by becoming a reliable go-to source for information and analysis. For this reason, members of Congress come to think of themselves largely in terms of the committee assignments they hold. After failing to win a seat on either the Foreign Affairs or the Judiciary Committee (the ones that held most interest to me), I eventually was able to move to both the Appropriations and the Budget Committees, and it was within the context of those committees that I framed my congressional career. Most members of Congress do the same thing.

From a member's standpoint, committees *are* the Congress. One may sit in a committee meeting, listening to expert testimony or debating legislative proposals for hours at a time; time on the House floor, however, is sporadic, generally short bursts of time for the casting of votes, many times relying on staff briefings for guidance on issues about which you may know very little (most votes are that way for most members; the headline-grabbing big debates are vital but occupy relatively little of the time most members of Congress spend at their jobs).

=== COMMENTARY ===

The Professor's Take on the Committees

No area of congressional research is more fertile for an important study than the role that committees play in the legislative process. The contemporary research on committees has its roots in the Textbook Congress. The rise of the party leadership power and the decline of the autonomous power of committee chairs fundamentally reshape how committees operate vis-à-vis the party leadership. Speaker Sam Rayburn had to cajole, plead, and beg committee chairs to report legislation. Speaker Paul Ryan, even though he was very much a product of the committee system, had much more power to get the committees to operate consistently with the goals of the majority party.

If the definition of operational power is getting someone to do something that he or she would not otherwise do, it is fair to ask how much power committees exercise today. Do committee chairs ever get the majority party leaders or the entire chamber to do something that they otherwise would not do? What about the reverse? Do party leaders ever do something that they would not do as a consequence of committee power? These fundamental questions must be reexamined by congressional scholars. The growing divergence between the parties and the growth of majority party leadership have greatly dissipated the power that committees exercised in the Textbook Congress. If that is true, what roles do the committees play in today's legislative process?

CHAPTER 8

Political Parties

M any large organizations, whether in government or in the private sector, are both collective in nature (their members tend to think of themselves as, and act as, part of a group) and hierarchical (a clear chain of command with an understanding that those persons lower in rank follow the lead of higher-ranked persons). A second, somewhat less common, model of organization is frequently associated with persons engaged in creative work. This model tends to feature a more loosely organized individualism, with each member of the organization largely setting his or her own course. The Congress is a hybrid, a group of highly individualistic members working within a tightly structured framework. It is a framework in which institutional cohesion is maintained by the unique combination of a relatively loose and relatively weak form of internal management (directed by teams of democratically elected leaders) and the pull of strong external influences (the two major American political parties, each in the active pursuit of partisan advantage).

Each representative and senator comes to office with a distinctly personal political philosophy; in many cases he or she has been elected largely on the basis of specific positions and promises, either about individual legislative issues or about a general approach to government. In addition, as we have seen, each member of Congress represents a specific and distinct constituency. The states and districts they represent differ economically: some are relatively affluent; others contain large numbers of low-income workers and welfare recipients; some produce wheat, rice, or corn while others import those products; some contain military installations, others do not. They also differ politically: some districts are quite liberal in their voting patterns while others tend to be very conservative; in some, organized labor is a potent political force, while others have few union members. Whether a member of Congress functions primarily as a *delegate* or as a *trustee*, representatives and senators are distinctly individualistic. Whether it is

principle and ideology that determines how legislators vote or a sense of obligation to represent constituent concerns, the natural inclination of legislators is to
view their responsibilities through a highly personal lens and therefore to be generally resistant to direction from above or to being overly influenced by others
whose political beliefs or constituencies are very different (as they all are).

While representation can be an individualistic enterprise, legislating cannot.
A loosely organized and nonhierarchical legislature makes either passing legislation or blocking it exceedingly difficult. The desire to achieve one's policy goals
creates a need for leadership and a need for a structure that enables members to
build coalitions with others whose views may be sufficiently similar to allow a
legislative victory. Without some means of organizing members around common
interests, each legislator would either have to have the legendary oratorical skills
of former House Speaker Henry Clay or risk losing legislative battles repeatedly
in committee and on the House or Senate floor.

Because there are 435 representatives and 100 senators, each with his or her
own political agenda, it is necessary to create a structure that avoids legislative
traffic jams. Someone must decide which bills will be considered by the various
committees, when hearings will be scheduled, and which bills will reach the
House or Senate floor and in what order. And because each member's ultimate
goal is either to move legislation through the process—whether it is to create a
new program or to cut an old one or to block the passage of legislation—people
must be found who will step forward and manage the legislative battles. The
result is a need for hierarchy, leadership, and collective action in a body made up
of highly individualistic members.

In Congress, many informal and unofficial organizations are based on region
(a Sunbelt caucus, for example), economic commonalities (steel, coal, cotton, oil),
or shared policy interests (healthcare, technology, immigration). Other organizations are formed primarily for social and information-sharing purposes; their
members take time away from their offices to sit together and share news about
their committees, their families, or political happenings in their home states.
Groups of members have even formed for prayer or to share religious experiences.
The two common denominators that link these organizations are their bipartisan
nature and the coming together around a relatively narrow central purpose.

When it comes to votes on specific issues, members of those informal
interest-related organizations are often able to work together across party lines:
what matters in such cases is where a member stands on tobacco price supports,
for example, or on wetlands preservation. But a great many of the decisions that
must be made in Congress transcend narrow regional or single-issue concerns.
Someone must decide who sits on which committees, whether the House or
Senate votes on a constitutional amendment to prohibit the desecration of the

American flag, and whether members of the Congressional Hispanic Caucus will be permitted to offer amendments to the immigration reform bill. Since someone must be in charge, since there must be a structure to govern hearings and votes and committee assignments and meeting times and recess schedules, how should those leaders be chosen?

This is where political parties come into play. The writers of the US Constitution did not envision them, and some of the most prominent of the Founding Fathers, most notably George Washington and James Madison, warned of the divisive factionalism that would result if parties were formed. But, perhaps inevitably, given the different political opinions that arise out of region, profession, or ideology, parties did come into being, and they did create useful markers for identifying political soul mates and adversaries. And, in the end, Madison was instrumental in the development of a political party. Today, for the most part, those men and women who register or run for office as Republicans, on the one hand, or as Democrats, on the other hand, tend to hold somewhat—and sometimes substantially—different views of government's role in society.

Although there are a great many shadings of opinion and some members of Congress may be closer ideologically to the leadership of the other party, in recent years Democrats have tended to favor a somewhat greater level of federal activism and Republicans have been more reluctant to use the federal government as a problem solver. On many issues, therefore, even without the adoption of an official party line, most Republicans come down on one side of an issue and most Democrats on another side: natural ideological divisions, which increasingly divide the parties, exist among the political activists who serve in Congress. Since the late 1990s, both parties have become much more homogeneous and thus more separated from each other. While few conservative Democrats and liberal Republicans remain in Congress, in the 1980s they constituted a sizable portion of their respective congressional parties. Even then, when ideological overlap existed, the parties fundamentally organized Congress. On the House and Senate floors and in congressional committees and subcommittees, members are divided not by state or region or alphabet or seniority, but with Republicans sitting on one side (the right, when standing at the back of the chamber or committee room facing the front) and the Democrats on the other side.

While parties may seem like a crucial part of the legislative process—and they are—we must be mindful that parties, much like committees, were created by members to suit their needs.[1] When members' needs change, so, too, does the way they structure the parties and the powers they give party leaders. When the Democrats and Republicans are internally unified and when the two parties have different policy preferences, we can expect party leadership to be strong.[2] But, if the parties are internally divided or if they have difficulty even developing cohesive party platforms, we can expect members to keep the powers of party leaders relatively weak. When John Boehner relinquished the Speakership in the face of strong opposition within his own conference in 2015, his opponents forced his successor, Paul Ryan, to give up significant parts of the power portfolio Boehner had enjoyed before they would support him. Key among these losses of power was a smaller role in determining members' committee assignments. As we discuss political parties in this chapter, a key guiding principle that members have complete and total control over how they structure the political parties to suit their purposes helps illuminate the role that the parties have had in the legislative process over time.

In this chapter, we examine political parties and how leadership is exercised through the party structures within the Congress. Furthermore, we explore the role that party leaders play in influencing how individual members vote on the many legislative issues that come before them. In the first section, we provide a brief historical overview of the role of parties over time. Second, we describe the current structure of party leadership in Congress. Finally, we describe the resources that party leaders have at their disposal to try to keep their party members in line. Sometimes the leader's authority is reminiscent of the old story of the man standing at a bar having a drink, when a large crowd races by outside. "I have to leave," he tells the bartender: "I'm their leader; I have to go get in front of them." It is a feeling many a House and Senate leader has known.

HISTORY OF POLITICAL PARTIES IN CONGRESS

The Constitution never mentions political parties. In fact, inasmuch as the framers thought about them, they were viewed, at best, skeptically. The framers were wary of any group that successfully accumulated power, fearing it would be used to infringe on the liberty of individuals or other, less powerful groups. Madison never used the words *political parties* in Federalist 10; rather, he envisioned factions based on common economic interests, likely to band together when those interests were at stake but not bound to each other otherwise. In a sense, though, political parties are consistent with Madison's ideas of *factions*. Instead of being an instrument of democracy in Madison's eyes, they were to be viewed as impediments to democracy.

President George Washington, in his farewell address, admonished "in the most solemn manner against the baneful effects of the spirit of party." His worry was that a political party's sole purpose for existing is to maintain political power. The pursuit of this power and the desire to keep it once it is obtained, warned Washington, can ruin "public liberty." Washington was not warning his contemporaries of some future harm; the rise of parties, in their then-limited form, had begun during his own administration, led by Hamilton in the administration and Madison, Washington's once compatriot against the evils of parties, outside in opposing the administration. As his impending retirement was becoming more certain, the political rivalries that he was able to keep at bay simply through the power of his personality began rising to the surface with greater frequency as the impending vacuum created by his leaving the stage became more real. By the 1796 presidential election, early political parties had clearly formed: Thomas Jefferson and James Madison and their backers, who came to be known as the Democratic-Republicans, on one side and John Adams, Alexander Hamilton, and the Federalists on the other. Although the latter won that election to succeed Washington, the former ultimately triumphed. Jefferson won the rematch against Adams in 1800. In the next three congressional election cycles, the Federalists did not win more than 30 percent of the seats in either chamber.

Jefferson's Democratic-Republican Party dominated the presidency and Congress for the next twenty years, including the Era of Good Feelings, so named because party rivalry was almost nonexistent. James Monroe minimized the role of political parties during the eight years of his presidency, but by the end of it, personal rivalries and regional differences became too great for the nascent political system to keep them in check.

The disputed 1824 presidential election propelled the reemergence of parties back into American politics. Although the House awarded the presidency to him, John Quincy Adams's faction of the party enjoyed an advantage of fewer than five seats in the House and was a minority party by about the same margin in the Senate. By 1828, Andrew Jackson, now running as a Democrat, had vanquished the Adams forces, which rallied around the National Republican label, brought about the competitive two-party electoral system that more or less continues even today.

Even as the parties were taking form, the Congress was still dominated primarily by individuals. Clay's role in the development of the committee system ensured his prominence in the House and later when he was appointed to the Senate. Throughout much of the pre–Civil War period, the Senate dominated not only the House, but also the presidency. As the House of Representatives suffered through battles even to get itself organized and as the executive branch suffered through a series of weak presidents, the Senate time and again forestalled armed conflict between the states by resolving—at least temporarily—the various crises surrounding slavery. The Senate was the main stage for the development and enactment of the Missouri Compromise (1820), the Compromise of 1850, and the Kansas–Nebraska Act (1854). Its heroes— Henry Clay, John C. Calhoun, Daniel Webster, Sam Houston, and Stephen A. Douglas—continue even today to be models of revered American statesmen.

The rising regional tension coincided with the death of one party—the Whigs—and the rise of the Republican Party, which held the levers of power in not only the executive branch, but also the legislative branch until the end of the nineteenth century, when the Democrats, once again, became competitive nationally (SEE FIGURE 8.1, which depicts party strength in the House and Senate since Reconstruction). As the competition between the parties heated up, so did the partisan tensions within Congress. The Democrats and Republicans were as divided at the turn of the twentieth century as they were at the turn of the twenty-first century.

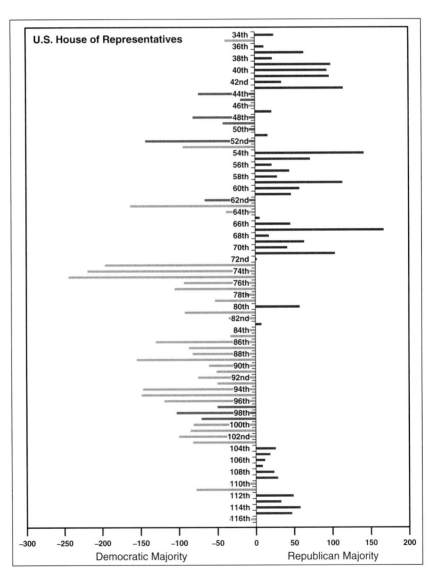

Figure 8.1a Composition of the House by Party, 1855–2021.

Such intense partisan conflict provided the conditions for strong party leaders. In the Senate, Nelson Aldrich (R-RI) used his perch as the chairman of the Finance Committee to lead his party not only on policy grounds, but also organizationally. In time, the role he filled developed into what became the Senate majority leader position, though it did not assume this title for nearly twenty years.

As Aldrich began exercising more power in the Senate, so too did his Republican colleague, Thomas Brackett Reed (R-ME), in the House. Although Reed

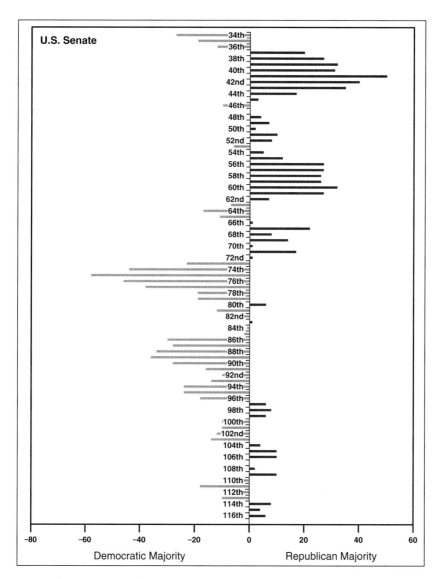

Figure 8.1b Composition of the Senate by Party, 1855–2021.

only served six years as Speaker, the power he accumulated was so great that he began to be called "Czar Reed" by his critics. Most important for the development of party leadership in the House, Reed cracked down on the ability of the minority party to stall the legislation they opposed.

As Reed exited the chamber, Joe Cannon (R-IL) built on the powers that Reed exercised to accumulate even more power. By simultaneously serving as Rules Committee chairman and Speaker, Cannon exerted more power in the legislative process than anyone up to that point in history—and, perhaps, ever since. He appointed members to their committees and named the chairs; furthermore, he scripted the rules governing debate and then carried out their implementation on the House floor. Finally, tensions within the Republican Party broke the iron fist with which he ruled the House when progressive Republicans revolted and sided with Democrats on a key procedural vote. As party competition waned with the rise of the Republican Party in the 1920s, the leaders' accumulation of centralized power also waned.

With the economic collapse and the onset of the Great Depression, the Democrats, under the leadership of Franklin Roosevelt, dominated both the executive and the legislative branches of the national government. Because the Democratic Party was split almost equally between a northern liberal wing and a southern conservative wing, party leadership on policy grounds became more difficult even while it continued on organizational matters. Speaker Sam Rayburn, who served with not only Roosevelt, but also Truman, Eisenhower, and Kennedy, maintained power by devolving most of the policy decisions to the committee chairs even while keeping the Democrats together as an organizational majority. While the two regional factions could not agree on policy grounds, they could agree that they wanted to be committee chairs and in the majority party; the alternative would be a chamber ruled by their Republican opponents.

During the Textbook Congress, sufficient balance was achieved between the parties, committees, and individual members to collaborate in the legislative process. Party leaders did not exercise as much explicit power as they had either fifty years before or fifty years after. The committees and their chairs dominated the legislative process.

As outlined in Chapter 6, the disintegration of the Textbook Congress had a variety of causes and consequences. What is exceedingly clear from this breakdown is that the committee chairs lost power to party leaders, which began the cycle that has led to today's domination of the legislative process by the political parties.

The breakdown of the Textbook Congress coincided with the increased level of party competition in Congress. Ronald Reagan's election as president in 1980 reenergized the Republicans in Congress. For the first time since the 1950s, Republicans wielded committee gavels in the Senate. Republicans in the House, though still a minority, enjoyed policy successes when enough conservative Democrats representing districts overwhelmingly won by Reagan sided with them on a host of issues including military spending, budget issues, and tax cuts. Then just a second-term member, Newt Gingrich (R-GA) began persuading his Republican colleagues that the way the Republicans should operate in the House was not to "go along to get along," but rather to directly confront and ridicule the Democratic majority's use of power. This strategy ultimately paid off in their triumphant victory in the 1994 elections.

POLITICAL PARTIES
IN THE CONTEMPORARY CONGRESS

The tension between the parties' dual goals of offering solutions to public policy problems and comprising the chamber's majority was so great that it prevented the Democratic majority from pursuing an explicit party strategy on many issues for much of the Textbook Congress era. As the situation changed, however, the incentives for developing a party strategy inside Congress grew. It is to those circumstances that we now turn.

Unified Constituencies
As the United States was recovering from the Great Depression and World War II, the Democrats were forging an electoral coalition, which would come to be known as the New Deal Coalition, that included southerners, union members, Catholics, African Americans, and big-city residents. In helping to bring about the 1932 realigning election, this coalition became the dominant electoral paradigm that delivered to Democrats both the White House and Congress for much of the next fifty years. Even as the New Deal Coalition began breaking down in presidential contests, it kept the congressional Democrats in power. As civil rights started getting a full airing on the national stage, the internal tensions began to mount between northern and southern Democrats.

As Lyndon Johnson was winning the presidential election in 1964, Democrats captured more seats in the House (295) and Senate (68) than they would in any congress since. As a consequence of their greater than two-to-one ratio in both chambers, the Democrats represented a wide diversity of constituencies. In fact, Johnson's Republican opponent Barry Goldwater received a higher percentage of the two-party vote in states represented by Democrats in the Senate than in states represented by Republicans. Furthermore, Goldwater did less than

1 percentage point better in Republican representatives' districts than he did nationwide and approximately 4 percentage points worse in Democratic representatives' districts.

The 1966 House elections provided even more puzzling results for the partisanship of the constituencies than the 1964 elections. The Democrats lost forty-seven seats, but those losses primarily came in the north, where Goldwater was trounced; the party remained dominant in the south, where Goldwater had performed better. The partisan difference between the Democratic and Republican representatives' districts became even smaller.

To systematically measure the underlying partisanship of members' districts and senators' states, we calculate the Republican presidential vote advantage in districts represented by Republican members and Democratic members. This statistic, which is sometimes called the *normalized vote*, measures the difference between the Republican presidential candidate's two-party vote in the district and the candidate's nationwide percentage. For example, 2016 Republican presidential candidate Donald Trump received 54.7 percent of the two-party vote in Texas but only 48.9 percent of the vote nationwide, making Texas's Republican presidential vote advantage 5.8 percentage points.

In the 1960s, Democrats represented districts where, on average, the Republican presidential candidate did about 5 percentage points worse than they did nationwide (SEE FIGURE 8.2). Republicans, on the other hand, represented districts where they did about 5 percentage points better. Within thirty years, both numbers would double. After the 2018 elections, Republicans represented districts that were almost 29 percentage points more Republican than the districts represented by Democrats.

In the two congresses after the Senate passed the Civil Rights Act of 1964, Democratic senators came from more Republican states than did Republican senators. Only since the 1990s has the difference between the senators' constituencies varied in a meaningful way. Following the 2018 elections, the Senate Democrats' states are 16 percent less Republican than the Senate Republicans' states.

The growing gap between the two major party constituencies not only tells an electoral story, but also can provide clues to an institutional story. If the constituencies that Democrats represent are increasingly distinct from the constituencies that Republicans represent, the difficult conundrum of members choosing to vote with their constituents or with their party becomes increasingly rare. If members' partisan identification and constituencies' partisan leanings point in the same direction, they will reinforce each other and result in a chamber that is increasingly divided by party. Under such a scenario, the leadership conundrum of a regional party split such as that faced by Speaker Rayburn in the 1950s vanishes.

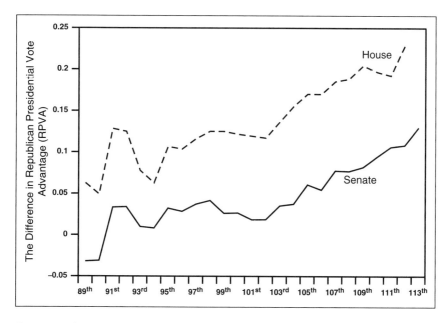

Figure 8.2 The Partisan Difference Between Democratic and Republican Constituencies, 89th–113th Congresses (1965–2014).

Intense Party Competition

As the Democratic and Republican constituencies become increasingly distinct, the margins between the number of Democratic and Republican members in both chambers became smaller. In the 1964 election, the Democrats had 130 more seats in the House and 30 more seats in the Senate than did the Republicans. While these margins are particularly large, they are similar to the margins that the Democrats enjoyed as late as the 1970s.

Except for two Congresses—the 80th (1947–8) and 83rd (1953–4)—the Democrats were a majority in the House and Senate from 1933 until 1980. With the Democrats safely in the majority representing an ideologically diverse set of constituencies, Republicans understood that they could most influence policy-making in Congress by constructively engaging the majority. Because Democrats had so many conservative members and because the Republicans had so many moderate-to-liberal members, Republicans frequently found ideological counterparts in the majority party to help work their will. So long as the Republicans did not mind not being chairs of the committees, policymaking in Congress did not regularly trigger a partisan war.

Republicans achieved majority party status at different times in the different chambers. Heading into the 1980 election, most pundits thought the presidential election between the incumbent, Jimmy Carter, and his Republican challenger, Ronald Reagan, would be exceedingly close. No one thought that the Republicans had a chance of becoming a majority party in either the House or the Senate. From the 89th to the 96th Congresses (1965–80), the Democrats, on average, held a twenty-seat margin over the Republicans in the Senate. When Americans awoke on the day after the 1980 election, Reagan's landslide not only delivered him forty-four states in the Electoral College but also delivered to the Republicans twelve seats in the Senate, which was enough to give them a six-seat majority. They maintained that Senate majority until many of those 1980 surprise victors lost in their 1986 reelection bids.

Prior to 1994, the Democrats' lock on the House had been as great as it was on the Senate before the 1980 election. From the 89th to the 103rd Congress (1965–94), the Democrats held an average of 263 House seats—a margin of 91 seats. Only a handful of people in the United States thought that the Republicans could win a House majority in 1994 and most of them worked for the House minority whip, Newt Gingrich (R-GA). Gingrich's national strategy—codified into the Contract with America—paid off as the Democrats went from an 82-seat majority margin to a minority with the Republicans holding a 26-seat advantage in what became known as the Republican tsunami of 1994.

Since the Republicans became competitive in each chamber, the majority size has been almost two-thirds smaller in both chambers. In the twenty congresses since the Republicans became a majority in the Senate in 1981, the majority has held, on average, about 54 seats. In the thirteen congresses since the Republicans became a majority in the House in 1995, the majority has held an average of 234 seats, resulting in a 33-seat majority. With a few exceptions (only 2008 and 2014), the future majority party in both chambers of Congress is in doubt on the day of the election.

While the American electoral landscape that is competitive may be shrinking over time, the stakes have drastically risen for the districts and states that remain in play on Election Day. This phenomenon has consequences not only for electoral politics, but also for how Congress operates internally. The race for majority party status has frequently eclipsed the desire for Congress to solve real problems. The legislative process and the chamber floors have increasingly become arenas for electoral politics. Congress's already bad approval numbers getting worse is only one consequence of this transformation in the legislative process.

Polarized Parties

Since the party competition has intensified, each succeeding election brings about the most polarized Congress yet. By analyzing roll-call votes on the floor of the House and the Senate, we can measure how polarized the parties have become. An algorithm analyzes all nonunanimous votes simultaneously and places the two members who vote most dissimilarly on opposite sides and then orders all other members between the two based on how much they agree with one or the other of the two poles. These scores, which are called DW-NOMINATE, range from -1 (most liberal) to 1 (most conservative).[3]

The congresses after the 1964 election and into the 1970s were some of the least polarized in modern history. The mean House Democratic DW-NOMINATE scores during these congresses, which is depicted as the black line in the middle of the dark gray bars of FIGURE 8.3, was about 0.5 away from the mean Republican DW-NOMINATE scores, which are depicted as the black line in the middle of the light gray bars. The dark gray bars show one standard deviation on either side of the mean for the Democrats (Republicans). Beginning in the mid-1970s, the parties' means started to separate. The partisan divergence was only slightly less pronounced in the Senate (SEE FIGURE 8.4).

By the 113th Congress (2013–4), the divergence between the parties had more than doubled in the House, to 1.10, and had nearly doubled, to 0.93, in the Senate. Not only have the means separated, but also the parties have become much more internally cohesive. The infusion of Tea Party members in the 112th Congress and the big Blue Dog Democrat losses in 2010 and 2014 exacerbated the divide between the parties.

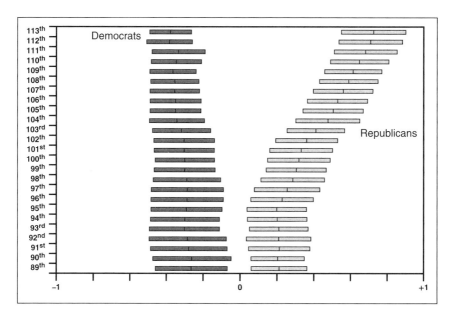

Figure 8.3 Ideology by Party in the US House, 89–113th Congresses (1965–2014).

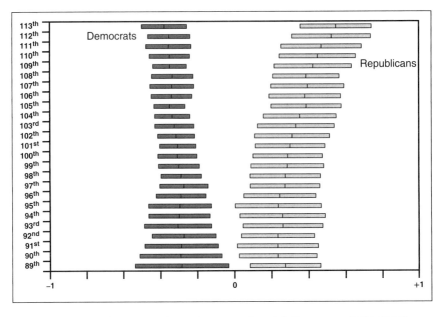

Figure 8.4 Ideology by party in the US Senate, 89th–113th Congresses (1965–2014).

The processes of increasingly divided constituencies, increasingly close seat margins separating the parties in each chamber, and growing polarization feed on themselves in a positive feedback loop. As margins shrink, parties have increasingly relied on only the votes from their side of the aisle, which in turn propels polarization. As the parties became more internally consistent, the divide between their constituencies grows.

THE STRUCTURE OF LEADERSHIP

The current state of the politics practiced in Congress has made party leaders increasingly important—sometimes so important that the individualistic nature of the institution is all but forgotten. In both the House and the Senate, leadership is exercised both formally and informally. Like any major company or organization, the Congress has a need for rules and for people who occupy recognized positions of authority. It is not necessarily true that those members who hold the official positions of authority are always the ones who are steering the congressional ship, but those men and women who are elected by their peers to the formal leadership ranks are most often the people who determine how the Congress operates and how well—or not—it does its job.

Because the leadership positions carry with them such great influence over legislative outcomes and because the leaders are also the most visible representatives of the Congress, members of both the House and the Senate often have a mental checklist of those qualities they look for in deciding which candidates for leadership they support. Among them are managerial competence (often demonstrated while serving in lower party leadership positions or leadership positions on committees), responsiveness (good leaders are good listeners), persuasiveness (given the partisan nature of the Congress, members look for leaders who are good communicators and who can articulate the party's collective point of view), forcefulness in confronting the opposition, innovativeness, and, ideological compatibility. Not all members who rise to positions of high leadership in the House or Senate have all of these qualities (few people do), but most have some and perhaps several of them, because in Congress, where national policies and priorities are set, where the legislative stakes are high in almost every debate and almost every day, the decision as to which of their colleagues are entrusted with power and authority is, in many ways, one of the most critical decisions members make.

The Speaker of the House of Representatives

From a constitutional standpoint, the Speaker of the House of Representatives is the preeminent leader of the Congress. Should the presidency and vice presidency be simultaneously vacant as a result of death or retirement, the Speaker is next in line, ahead of any senator or any cabinet member. Furthermore, the Speakership is the only important position that is voted on by the entire chamber. In modern times, the majority party makes its decision among its members, but the vote for Speaker is still customarily the second vote that a newly constituted House takes in early January of every odd year (the year after an election). The last time that a Speaker was not elected on first ballot was 1923, when it took the House nine ballots to finally reelect Frederick Gillett (R-MA).

The Speaker exercises her power in both formal and informal ways. Formally, the most important power the Speaker has is as the presiding officer of the House, which means that she is responsible for recognizing members who wish to speak on the House floor. In her role as presiding officer, the Speaker also rules on all points of order, though the rulings can be overruled by a vote of the entire membership. In today's House, the Speaker usually does not sit as presiding officer except during important legislative or symbolic events. The Speaker can designate any member of the House to preside in her absence, though normally the Speaker names someone from the majority party for that duty. By convention, the Speaker only votes when her vote would be decisive or on legislatively or symbolically important matters.

The Speaker also exercises the greatest control over committee assignments. She controls the most seats on the party committees that make the committee assignments. The Speaker, with the consent of her party, names all the majority party members to the Rules Committee. Furthermore, the Speaker appoints all the members of the select and conference committees. The Speaker is also responsible for overseeing all of the officers of the House, including the clerk, the sergeant at arms, and the chaplain.

Because representatives cannot filibuster, the Speaker, as the head of the majority party, also has substantial informal power. The Speaker, especially in modern times, is first and foremost the legislative leader of the majority party. When the House and the White House are controlled by opposing parties, the Speaker is usually responsible for bargaining and negotiating with the president.

On an organizational chart, the Speaker of the House appears to be above the partisan fray: both Republicans and Democrats have their own elected party leaders and it is the majority leader of the House who is ostensibly charged with directing that chamber's day-to-day activities and leading the fight for his party's legislative agenda. Different Speakers will emphasize their legislative and partisan roles differently. Newt Gingrich, upon becoming Speaker in 1995, argued that his institutional role was third to his role as, first, the leader of a movement, and second, the leader of the Republicans in the House. Although Speaker Paul Ryan placed more emphasis on his institutional role than Gingrich, even he professed that maintaining a Republican majority in the House was his most important duty. This dual hat complicated legislative negotiations with the president.

Majority Leader of the Senate

While the Speaker of the House of Representatives is technically the preeminent member of the entire Congress, outranking any other member not only of the House, but also of the Senate, he may not, in fact, always be the most prominent member of the Congress. The Senate is the constitutional equal of the House and while it has no office comparable to that of the Speaker, the Senate majority leader rivals, and may often surpass, the Speaker both in political power and in public visibility. Officially, the majority leader is only the third-ranking leader in the Senate, after the vice president of the United States, who is also the President of the Senate (meaning the presiding officer), and the President Pro Tempore of the Senate, who is typically the longest-serving senator of the majority party. The vice president usually takes no active role in Senate activities and can vote only to break a tie. In the vice president's absence, the President Pro Tem assumes the presiding officer duties. In real terms, the majority leader is *the* leader of the Senate; he (or, in time, she) sets the agenda and controls the schedule, just as the Speaker does in the House, though the nature of the institution requires him to consult with the minority leader in a way that the Speaker does not.

Because there are only one hundred senators, because the Senate is incorrectly (as Mickey attests) but widely thought by many to be an upper chamber of Congress, because only the Senate deals with some high-visibility issues such as the ratification of treaties and the confirmation of presidential appointments, and because most senators represent larger constituencies than most House members, most members of the Senate are generally better known—and thus arguably more influential—than most of their colleagues in the House. The office of Senate majority leader has

therefore become, at times, the de facto power center of the legislative branch of government, and it is not at all uncommon for the Senate's majority leader to be better known nationally than the Speaker of the House. A classic example is that of Lyndon Johnson of Texas, who, before being elected John F. Kennedy's vice president, was the Senate's majority leader and probably the best-known member of Congress.

Almost the only real formal power that the Senate's majority leader has over all other senators is the right of first recognition. That means that if another senator seeks the floor at the same time as the majority leader, the majority leader is always recognized first. When neither the majority nor the minority leader seeks recognition, the presiding officer can recognize any senator among those seeking recognition at the same time. This right of first recognition only came into existence after the majority leader's position became formalized in the 1920s. Because the Senate is a more permissive chamber, the right of first recognition is the biggest weapon the majority leader has to regain control over the legislative process in the Senate. This power is best utilized in consultation and agreement with the minority leader.

Majority Leader in the House

Because the Speaker of the House is nonpartisan only on organizational diagrams and not in reality, the majority leader in the House, unlike the Senate majority leader, is actually number two in his party's leadership hierarchy. Nonetheless, it is a position from which a member can wield substantial power. Speakers vary in the amount of attention they pay to the detail of the House schedule and the operation of House committees. In a sense, the Speaker functions as the chief executive officer of the House and the majority leader as the chief operating officer, keeping tabs on the progress of legislation, making sure the House operates smoothly, and running the day-to-day legislative activities.

The office of majority leader can be a stepping-stone to the Speakership (Tip O'Neill, Jim Wright, and Tom Foley all moved up from majority leader to Speaker in due course), but there are no guarantees. When John Boehner announced his decision to leave the Speakership in 2015, majority leader Kevin McCarthy became the odds-on favorite to win the position. Instead, other members of the Republican conference rose to challenge him and, in the end, he took himself out of the race and the members turned to Paul Ryan, who was then chair of the Ways and Means Committee. Ryan had also been the party's vice presidential nominee in 2012, but he had never held an elected leadership position.

The Minority Leaders

In both the House and the Senate, members of the minority party elect their own leaders, who serve as the chief spokespeople for the minority's legislative agenda. There is an important distinction, however, between the American legislative system and the parliamentary systems that have been adopted in many other countries, in which a member of parliament (the leader of the majority party) serves as prime minister and the minority party serves as the opposition, with little influence or power. In a parliamentary system, the prime minister and his or her deputies become, in effect, the government, and the parliamentary majority can generally be counted on to support the prime minister's policies. In fact, when it fails to do so, the ensuing crisis may result in a vote to determine whether the prime minister still has the confidence of the parliament and, if not, new legislative elections are usually scheduled. It is a far different matter in the United States, where, by contrast, the president and his cabinet do not form the government, but merely head one of the government's three equal branches; where the majority in Congress may be fairly consistently at odds with the president; and where the legislative minority may be far from powerless. In fact, the Constitution explicitly prohibits any person from serving simultaneously in the legislative and executive branches of government.

While the minority in each chamber of Congress is relatively powerless in setting the legislative schedule and determining the rules of debate, the minority leader can gain substantial power if his party holds the presidency, in which case the minority needs only the ability to marshal one-third of the votes in either of the two chambers to sustain a presidential veto. The minority leader also gains great bargaining leverage if the size of the majority's margin is so small that the inevitable few defections from party solidarity on any major issue may put the final outcome in doubt.

The Whips

The next highest rank in the leadership structure, after the majority leader and minority leader, is a position that emphasizes the party-driven nature of Congress. The floor leader's deputy in both chambers and both parties is known as the *whip*, a term derived from the British Parliament's chief whip and one that accurately describes the position's duties. Because much of what happens in Congress comes down to a conflict between Democrats and Republicans, with most of one party lined up against most of the other, and because the members of both the House and Senate are individualists answerable to no single boss and driven largely by their own ideologies and constituencies, the leaders of each party are in a constant struggle to learn which of their own members are going to stand with them on an issue, which are going to oppose them, and which are undecided and subject to persuasion. It is the job of the whip to check on party members, determine how each member is planning to vote on an issue, learn what concerns are preventing a member from going along with the majority, and develop a strategy for convincing undecided members to come aboard. The whip's job is to deliver a victory for his or her party. He or she keeps a running head count, lets the party's leaders know how many votes they are likely to receive, and persuades the undecideds to support the party position (that is, he *whips* the members into line). The whip may call on another member of Congress—a personal friend of the undecided member, perhaps, or one who shares a common interest—to urge the reluctant member to fall into line. Or the whip may call on the president or a member of the president's cabinet. Whatever tactic he uses, it is the job of the whip to ensure that each member of his party's congressional membership votes for the party position on every major issue. Because the party's leaders want to ensure the reelection of as many party members as possible, if the vote is not winnable or the issue is not of great importance, the whip may even suggest to some members that they vote against the party position to remain consistent with their own expressed views or with their constituents' preferences (a frequent occurrence when the parties' ranks were more philosophically diverse than they are today); on conflicts of great visibility and importance, however, the whips will try to provide as many votes as possible for the party position.

Regardless, the whip is more than a vote counter and persuader. He is also generally the party's primary legislative strategist and often serves as a leading spokesman for the party. House Republican whip Steve Scalise had always been popular with his Republican colleagues, but his media presence—and power—greatly increased after he was shot while practicing with the Republican team for the annual congressional baseball game in 2017. In the other chamber and in the opposite party, Dick Durbin was his party's face in high-stakes debates such as immigration reform. Because of their influence and visibility, the whip often becomes one of the party's chief fundraisers as well, regularly ranking among the members with the most campaign contributions to their colleagues.

The job of the whip—counter, persuader, and strategist—is more than one person can handle alone. As a result, both Democrats and Republicans, especially in the House, have developed large whip organizations that include deputy whips, regional whips, and assistant whips, with responsibilities for a grouping of states (e.g., the Plains states) or a particular class (freshman). Scalise's small whip's office in the lobby just outside the House chambers is often overflowing with his assistants and members of the president's legislative liaison team. In many ways, the whip organizations, especially in the House, are often the most dynamic centers of congressional activity.

Conference or Caucus Chairs

Next in rank for Republicans are the leaders who chair the broad organizations of all of a party's members: the Senate and House Republican Conference chairs. Each Republican is a member of the conference, regardless of ideology, region, or interest. The same is true of Democrats, who call their organizations *caucuses*. The caucus chair is not the next-ranking Democrat in either the House or the Senate, because the assistant Democratic leader is the next in line after the whip. (In the Senate, Chuck Schumer is both Democratic leader and caucus chair.) The chairs of the Republican Conference or the Democratic Caucus sit with the party leadership and chair meetings in which important policy questions are put to the party membership as a whole.

In terms of the internal tensions within the congressional parties themselves, the caucuses and conferences are the eye of the storm: it is here, with all the party's members assembled, that leadership battles are fought and committee chairs and ranking minority members are ratified. When Texas Senator John Tower, President George H. W. Bush's choice for secretary of defense, was turned down for the job by his Senate colleagues, Bush turned to the House Republican whip, Dick Cheney, of Wyoming. Cheney's departure led to a fierce battle for the newly open whip position, pitting veteran Congressman Ed Madigan (R-IL), Republican Leader Michel's choice, against the brash newcomer, Newt Gingrich. Michel, Hastert, and DeLay all supported Madigan, but other Republicans, eager for a leader who would more aggressively fight for their right to be full participants in floor debates (closed rules dictated by the Democratic majority had effectively cut them out of the process), supported Gingrich. Gingrich narrowly won in a vote held in the spacious Eisenhower room at the nearby Capitol Hill Club. Had party leaders had the authority to choose Cheney's replacement, the deeply partisan divide in Congress that followed Gingrich's ascent might have turned out very differently. It is here that the ability of the entire conference to choose the party's direction comes into full focus. It is, in fact, in these party gatherings that members battle among themselves over strategy and policy positions (as happened years later when hardline conservatives repeatedly blocked legislative initiatives by Speaker Boehner until he stepped down in frustration). If the Congress is, among other things, an arena for battle, it is here, where members of the same party gather together, that some of the fiercest battles are fought.

In addition, the conference and caucus chairs, like other party leaders, have more mundane duties to perform than presiding over internal party conflicts: it is their responsibility, for example, to keep their colleagues up to date on the movement of legislation through the House and Senate, including information about upcoming votes. In addition, they may be assigned to perform clerical tasks such as organizing the resumes of prospective staff members. Leaders may, in fact, spend more time serving than leading.

Other Elected Party Leaders

From here, the elected positions for party leadership vary by both party and chamber. The next most important position for Republicans in both the House and the Senate is called the policy committee chair. While the conference chairs are responsible for running the logistics of the party, the policy chairs are responsible for heading up the development of policy. In the Senate and the House, the Republicans also elect a conference vice chair, who ranks behind the policy chair in the hierarchy of elected leadership positions.

Other Leadership Positions

Other positions, though not elected, also play important roles for both parties in both chambers. Fundraising, candidate recruitment, and all candidate support activities for incumbent members of Congress and for challengers to incumbents of the opposite party fall within the purviews of the Democratic and Republican campaign committees in the House and Senate. Those committees are chaired and governed by members of the House or Senate, who operate with their own staffs, hold their own fundraising events, make their own decisions as to which candidates to support and to what extent, and are answerable only to the Republicans or Democrats who sit in the House and Senate. These committees provide a full range of political support to their party's candidates for the House and Senate: money, voter opinion surveys, fundraising and organizational advice, well-known guest speakers for campaign events—all the accouterments of a modern political campaign.

The House and Senate campaign committees of the two parties are independent of each other: the campaign committees of House and Senate Democrats, for example, may occasionally confer informally, but for the most part each committee concerns itself solely with the task of retaining—or attaining—a majority in its own chamber of Congress. Sometimes the two committees actively oppose one another when the Senate committee tries to entice a House member to leave her seat to run for the Senate. When Senator Jeff Flake's (R-AZ) opened up upon his retirement, both parties experienced this tension as National Republican Senatorial Committee chair Cory Gardner (R-CO) tried to convince Martha McSally to enter the race to fill his vacancy as National Republican Congressional Committee chair Steve Stivers (R-OH) tried to convince her to run for reelection to her House seat. On the Democratic side, Democratic Senatorial

Campaign Committee chair Chris Van Hollen (D-MD) battled Democratic Congressional Campaign Committee chair Ben Ray Luján (D-NM) over the potential candidacy of Kyrsten Sinema (D-AZ). Both women opted for the Senate race, leaving open two competitive House seats. In the end, Sinema won the Senate seat and Democrats won both House seats that were left open by their Senate candidacies.

While the campaign committees are separate from each other, they are not separate from the party leadership within the two chambers of Congress. With polls telling them which issues are most popular—or most unpopular—with voters, and with an understanding of which opposition incumbents are vulnerable on which issues, the representatives and senators who chair the campaign committees may be counted on to advise their colleagues in the party's congressional leadership as to which strategies might be most helpful, not only in creating issues that will help reelect their own members, but also in defeating members of the opposing party. Thus, bill amendments may be proposed for the single purpose of forcing a vulnerable member of the opposition party to cast a vote that will be unpopular with the voters back home. For example, in 2010, Senator Tom Coburn (R-OK), during the Affordable Care Act debate, offered an amendment that would prohibit convicted sex offenders from using their health insurance to purchase Viagra. Of course, every Democrat agreed with the spirit of the amendment—in fact, the existing wording of the bill would forbid such an action—but most Democrats had to vote against the amendment because if even a word of the underlying bill was changed, it would have resulted in a much more complex legislative procedure that would have undermined the bill's passage. It is precisely for this reason that Coburn offered the amendment. If members could always be counted on to vote for their own electoral advantage, such a strategy could not succeed; but since members try to balance their needs with the needs of their party, these coordinated activities between party leaders and the party's campaign leaders often play a role in determining what happens on the House or Senate floor.

While the campaign committees of the two parties' congressional membership may thus have influence over election outcomes through their support of candidates and over some actions on the House or Senate floors, they also have less power than is sometimes believed. Compared to parliamentary systems, the American political parties are relatively weak because individuals in most states and congressional districts select themselves to be candidates. On occasion, the parties will declare a candidate to be preferred, but localities, especially in the Republican Party more recently, may view these candidates skeptically. In only the rarest of exceptions will party committees withhold their endorsement of incumbent members of Congress.

Finally, a number of other official leadership positions, the description of which has varied over time and according to the individual preferences of each party, help coordinate activities within the parties. The Democratic Caucus and the Republican Conference, for example, each have, in addition to a chairman, a vice chairman and secretary, each of whom sits with the party's leadership. Chairs of research groups, policy committees, and even the senior members of the most important congressional committees may sit as elected or ex officio members of the party leadership. Party leaders adjust the positions and their job descriptions as their needs change. As an example, when Newt Gingrich became Speaker after the 1994 elections, he created the new position of chairman of the Republican leadership, filling the job with his chosen appointee: himself.

Leadership Staff

In all these functions—providing information to colleagues, shaping policy positions, lining up votes, acting as party spokesmen—the members who hold these positions find their legislative careers increasingly tied to their leadership responsibilities. To help them with these tasks, they assemble specialized leadership staffs. Unlike the people who assist in a member's office or staff of the various congressional committees, members of these leadership staffs work on projects that go well beyond local or regional concerns and well beyond the boundaries of a single issue. Members of a Speaker's staff, a minority leader's staff, or the staffs of the policy committee chairmen deal with the whole broad range of legislative and, increasingly, electoral concerns. Further, instead of being solely researchers or analysts, assessing the pros and cons of legislative proposals, their focus, under some chairmen, may include strategy and tactics as well, not merely deciding how individual members should vote on an issue but to ensure victory for the entire party on a wide range of issues.

The infrastructure to support leadership positions has grown much faster than the infrastructure that supports member or committee staff. This increase reflects the increasing importance of party leadership relative to committees and members (SEE FIGURE 8.5).

Winning a Leadership Position

Party leaders in Congress do not have as much power as the leaders in some other legislative systems, but given their enhanced media visibility, their roles as party spokesmen, their ability to speak directly with the president, and their control of the flow of legislative information, they hold positions that elevate them above their House and Senate colleagues. As a result, and partly because

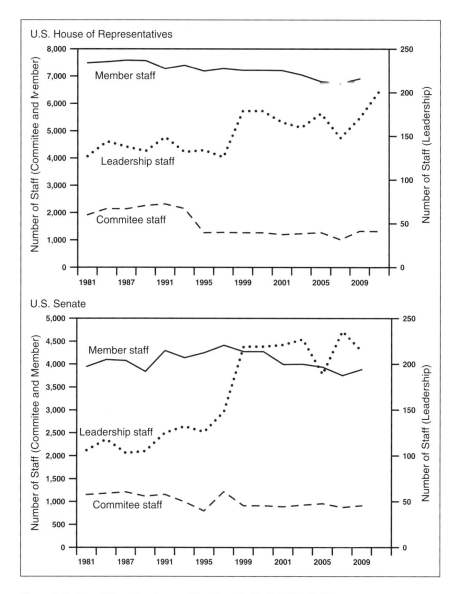

Figure 8.5 Committee, Member, and Leadership Staff, 1979–2011.
Source: *Vital Statistics on Congress*, https://www.brookings.edu/wp-content/uploads/2016/06/Vital-Statistics-Chapter-5-Congressional-Staff-and-Operating-Expenses_UPDATE.pdf, accessed August 26, 2016.

the kinds of people who run for public office may tend to be more ambitious than their fellow citizens, competition for congressional leadership positions can be intense and fierce. Candidates for leadership positions are not hesitant to offer support for a potential supporter's favorite legislation, to try to favorably

influence committee appointments, to promise greater or more efficient services, or to favorably contrast their own personalities or policy positions with
those of an opponent—all of which are traditional means of campaigning for
any office, from elementary school classroom president to President of the
United States. The fact that the parties have become more internally homogeneous only makes the contests more personal and less issue based, as does the
small size of the electorate (almost never more than 250 of a leadership candidate's fellow party members in the House or an even smaller cohort, only as big
as 60 to 65, in the Senate). Individual friendships and regional ties are also
important factors in lining up support.

Making the competition more intense than ever is the tendency of leadership
candidates to set up fundraising mechanisms that allow them to contribute
money to their colleagues' reelection campaigns and to provide campaign funds
to candidates who may join the Congress after the next elections (leadership positions are filled at the beginning of a congress and newly elected members may
play a decisive role in determining who wins or loses).

Furthermore, success in obtaining a leadership position rarely gets its start
when a vacancy is announced. Rather, members who fashion themselves future
leaders are engaging in networking, fundraising, and politicking long before a
member of the leadership decides to step down. As soon as a vacancy is announced—
or even rumored—those waiting to obtain a leadership position put their teams to
work in hopes of showing an insurmountable amount of strength and support so
as to ward off other potential candidates for the position. This behind-the-scenes
organization sometimes averts a potentially damaging intraparty fight. Harry
Reid's impending retirement in 2016 as the Democratic majority leader had been
rumored for several months. Despite Dick Durbin being next in line, Chuck
Schumer, who had been responsible for recruiting and helping many of his Democratic colleagues when he was chair of the Democratic Senatorial Campaign
Committee, quickly locked up sufficient support that Durbin did not even attempt
to become leader.

THE RESOURCES OF PARTY LEADERS

A sense of solidarity, or common purpose, encourages members to be responsive
to the urgings of party leaders. Leaders, even those of the minority party, have in
their arsenals a plentiful supply of both carrots and sticks and are generally willing
to use them to marshal support for the party's positions. On any given vote in the
House or Senate, members of both political parties, either because of their own
views on an issue or because of the perceived preferences of their constituencies,

may not be inclined to support the position taken by their party's leaders or by the majority of their party colleagues. Yet those members may be sufficient in number to determine whether the party's position prevails or is defeated. This is where party leaders can play a crucial role.

Committee Assignments

Beginning with Speaker Henry Clay, party leaders have manipulated committee assignments to facilitate electoral and political goals. When Bob Michel was the leader of a Republican minority in the House, he illustrated the importance members attach to their committee assignments by giving each Republican member a T-shirt with the slogan, "Future Committee Chairman." And if Republicans had taken control of the House in the next election, he would have been in a good position to make that promise come true for those he favored: as we described in Chapter 7, party leaders have a great deal of authority over the committee assignment process. Leaders can use committee assignments to reward certain members or punish less loyal members. When the surge of new House Democrats elevated the party to the majority, then-Speaker Nancy Pelosi (D-CA) called them her "majority makers," giving them prime committee assignments and legislative responsibilities, to the frustration of some more senior Democrats who had been toiling in the minority, some for as many as twelve years. In late 2012, Speaker Boehner and the Republican Steering Committee removed representatives Justin Amash (R-MI) and Tim Huelskamp (R-KS) from the Budget Committee and representative David Schweikert (R-AZ) from the Financial Services Committee after reviewing "all appropriate information" for their intransigence in voting against party policies.[4] This is a risky business: pushed too far; these decisions can easily cause other members to conclude that the same thing could happen to them if they should ever find it necessary to break from the leadership on an important issue. In a small body in which leaders serve at the will of their presumed followers, power is usually best wielded with a light touch.

Party leaders also may use their authority to bypass the seniority system and appoint (or have elected) committee chairs more closely aligned with their goals. After gaining control of the House in the 1994 elections, the Republican conference adopted a party rule that weakened seniority as a criterion for naming committee chairs. The powers of party leadership grow when seniority loses power in the naming of committee leadership positions to ideological purity, fundraising prowess, or basic teamsmanship. Parties and party leaders can advance their collective interests through the placement of committee chairs, not just the assignment of rank-and-file members to particular committees.

The Power of Party Leaders during Floor Debates

Although the insurgent progressive Republicans in the early 1900s thwarted Speaker Cannon's almost absolute power over the legislative process in the House, the majority party leadership retains a great deal of discretion with regard to what happens and how it happens on the House floor through their appointment power to the Rules Committee. Furthermore, as a sign of strength to their constituents back home, a member who has good relationships with the party leadership can manage a bill on the House floor or can even get the leadership to act on a piece of legislation that might be vital to local concerns, but of not much significance to the rest of the country.

On the flip side, party leaders can punish members by minimizing their role in the legislative process either on legislation important to the country or on favored local bills. In the House in particular, where time to speak on a bill or amendment is controlled by the party's designated *floor manager*, members who are out of favor may find that there is simply no time available for them. As time on the floor has become increasingly scarce, this power of party leaders has grown.

Power in the Senate is more decentralized, and Senate party leaders are traditionally thought to have less control over floor outcomes than their House counterparts. The Senate majority leader, in consultation with the minority leader, has the burden of developing unanimous consent agreements, which act as the Senate's counterpart to House Rules. As the Senate floor has become less manageable, unanimous consent agreements have increasingly become intricate agreements between the leaders, specifying even the minutest procedures for establishing the parameters of floor debate.

As the floor organizers for their parties, the leaders have also taken the primary responsibility for organizing and quashing filibusters. Not only have the numbers of cloture petitions filed increased, but also the majority leader has taken an increasingly dominant role in organizing the opposition to filibusters. When Mike Mansfield was nearing the end of his reign as majority leader in the early 1970s, he filed between one-fifth and one-third of the cloture petitions (see Table 8.1). In the 111th Congress (2009–10), the last for which we have data, Harry Reid filed 95.6 percent of them.

Conference Committees and Negotiations between Chambers

If the House and Senate pass different versions of the same bill, party leaders in each chamber typically appoint members to a joint conference committee to reconcile those differences and provide a single piece of legislation to be voted on (subject to chamber approval of a motion to appoint conferees). The only restriction on these appointments is that a majority of conference committee

Table 8.1 Percentage of Cloture Petitions Filed by Senate Majority Leaders

CONGRESS	MAJORITY LEADER	PERCENTAGE OF PETITIONS FILED
92nd	Mike Mansfield, D-MT	21.7
93rd	Mike Mansfield, D-MT	38.6
94th	Mike Mansfield, D-MT	23.1
95th	Robert C. Byrd, D-WV	87.0
96th	Robert C. Byrd, D-WV	86.7
97th	Howard H. Baker, Jr., R-TN	54.8
98th	Howard H. Baker, Jr., R-TN	70.7
99th	Robert Dole, R-KS	61.0
100th	Robert C. Byrd, D-WV	90.7
101st	George J. Mitchell, D-ME	73.7
102nd	George J. Mitchell, D-ME	78.3
103rd	George J. Mitchell, D-ME	67.5
104th	Robert Dole, R-Kan./Trent Lott, R-MS	65.9
105th	Trent Lott, R-MS	52.2
106th	Trent Lott, R-MS	83.1
107th	Trent Lott, R-MS/Thomas A. Daschle, D-SD	40.8
108th	William H. Frist, R-TN	71.0
109th	William H. Frist, R-TN	73.5
110th	Harry M. Reid, D-NV	88.4
111th	Harry M. Reid, D-NV	95.6

Source: Lewallen and Theriault (2012).

members must generally support the bill under consideration and, as such, most members appointed to conference committees also sit on the original committee of referral. Committee members can thus use the deference afforded their position and influence over the conference process to shape final legislative outcomes. This power to shape the legislation at the final stage is often more important than a committee's ability to provide the initial legislative proposal considered on the floor. As such, committees act strategically in reporting legislation and offering floor amendments, but conferees are also often advocates for their respective chamber's desired policy over their own personal preferences. Furthermore, majority party leaders can use the fact that conference reports are not subject to amendment to achieve outcomes that favor the party instead of a particular committee.

Party leaders also are taking a more direct role in avoiding conference committees altogether by negotiation between the leaders of each chamber. The number of public laws that were subject to conference committee negotiations dropped steadily from 13 percent in the 103rd Congress to 5 percent in the 109th Congress. Instead, one chamber simply adopts the other's version of a bill or a bill is amended by each chamber in turn until a final agreement is reached. This development has decreased the committees' abilities to shape the final legislation. Engaging in this ping-pong strategy puts the majority party leaders firmly in control of negotiations, whereas conference committees privileged committee chairs.

Fundraising

Party leaders are assuming a larger role in raising money for congressional campaigns. As individuals they tend to be prolific fundraisers, but because they tend to be electorally safe, their fundraising prowess is usually on behalf of their more vulnerable colleagues. Increasingly, leadership political action committees have been used to distribute money throughout their caucus (see Table 8.2).

Party leaders also often have institutional prerogatives that allow them to recruit and help elect new members, work to reelect incumbents, and achieve other electoral goals. The chairs of the Democratic Congressional Campaign Committee

Table 8.2 The Importance of Party Leadership in Fundraising in 2016 Elections

HOUSE OF REPRESENTATIVES					
REPUBLICANS		RANK IN HOUSE	DEMOCRATS		RANK IN HOUSE
Speaker	Paul Ryan $1,326,238	2	Minority leader	Nancy Pelosi $506,000	13
Majority leader	Kevin McCarthy $2,086,513	1	Minority whip	Steny Hoyer $1,019,499	3
Majority whip	Steve Scalise $942,485	4	Assistant minority leader	James Clyburn $657,500	6

SENATE					
REPUBLICANS		RANK IN SENATE	DEMOCRATS		RANK IN SENATE
Minority leader	Mitch McConnell $378,500	2	Majority leader	Harry Reid $201,500	28
Minority whip	John Cornyn $155,000	62	Majority whip	Dick Durbin $242,500	14

Source: http://www.opensecrets.org/pacs/industry.php?txt=Q03&cycle=2016

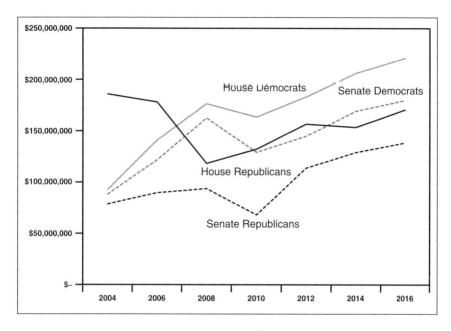

Figure 8.6   Spending by Congressional Campaign Committees, 2004–2016.

and Democratic Senatorial Campaign Committee serve as members of the party leadership and are directly appointed by the highest-ranking party leader in their respective chambers. The National Republican Congressional Committee and the National Republican Senatorial Committee chairs are elected by the chamber's party membership, with significant input from party leadership. These committees raise a substantial amount of money that can then be targeted to close and important races (SEE FIGURE 8.6). The leaders have great discretion in deciding on which races they should invest precious campaign resources.

Heading these committees also serves as a stepping-stone for those who hope to ascend to more powerful positions within their caucus. Both Mitch McConnell (R-KY) and Bill Frist (R-TN) served as National Republican Senatorial Committee chair before being elected to the party's chamber leadership; Senate Democrats created a special leadership position for Chuck Schumer (D-NY) once his term as Democratic Senatorial Campaign Committee chair expired, and he was eventually made their party leader.

CONCLUSION

Leaders not only set priorities, determine committee assignments, or appoint members to task forces, but also do the organizing, the strategizing, and the persuading to try to shape the outcome of legislative debate. They sometimes do so by the book, acting very much in accord with the simple outlines in brochures and videos about how a bill becomes a law, and they sometimes do so by threatening, rewarding, or even manipulating the clock. The legislation they are considering determines the very nature of the society in which we live—how high our taxes are, what level of services the government provides, how well we can defend the nation against its enemies, whether to support or oppose foreign governments or the rebel movements that would overthrow them. For all the criticism aimed at Congress, the fact is that most members of both parties believe very strongly in the principles that compelled them to run for office and that led to their elections. They believe that the welfare of the nation and its citizens is at stake in many of the issues on which members are required to vote.

The two major political parties often differ sincerely and strongly on many of these issues; the work of Congress is to choose between, or find compromise between, these profoundly different visions for America. In its essence, therefore, the work of Congress is a struggle between opposing political parties and their opposing ideologies. And the men and women who play the biggest role in shaping the outcomes of those debates are those who have been elected by their peers and colleagues to serve as America's congressional leaders.

COMMENTARY

The Politician's Take on Political Parties

Political parties and congressional leadership: in a real sense, these are the engines of the American legislative system. The question then becomes, Does this system—this dominance by political parties, this sometimes-weak, sometimes-strong system of leadership—work well? Does it provide Americans with the kind of "virtuous" Congress they might hope for?

America now finds itself with a large federal government, which provides many programs and benefits to which citizens have become accustomed—Social Security, Medicare, occupational safety and health regulations—all of which receive strong public support and, at the same time, increased unease over the cost and scope of the government that created and funds those programs. Conservatives, once a small and ineffectual force in American politics, have become politically powerful. The battle over the national direction has been rejoined, and to a large extent, the Congress is the battleground where the war is fought.

There are two results of this reshaping of the political debate. The first is a greater gulf between Republicans and Democrats on most major issues. Advocates of proactive government need forceful champions and a structure that allows them to effectively battle for the protection of the programs they believe a virtuous government requires. Advocates of a more restrained government also need forceful champions and structures that will allow them to bring about the changes they believe are urgently needed. That structure, those champions, may be found in the dividing of the Congress into competing camps—political parties—by means of which the debate can be joined and alternative views considered.

The second result is an outgrowth of the first; because the stakes are now so high and the differences so great, the passions of true believers have been unleashed. Congressional battles are intense and common ground is harder to find. Politics is, indeed, war by other means, and often it appears that both sides have adopted a take-no-prisoners attitude toward the opposition. Thus, citizens find themselves spectators to a rash of charges and countercharges and what they often see as partisan name-calling and bickering. Because the parties are generally evenly divided within the Congress, and because the Congress is often controlled by one party and the White House by the other, it sometimes seems as though there is not only much conflict, but also little to show for it: the so-called gridlock that prevents Democrats and Republicans alike from making much progress toward their goals.

Just as political parties may serve a uniting purpose, they also serve a divisive purpose. With a system that places all power in the hands of the party with a congressional majority, even if it is a majority of only a few seats, both Democrats and Republicans have a vested interest in demonizing members of the opposition and in shaping legislative battles to gain an advantage in the forthcoming elections. And since members of the House of Representatives must stand for reelection every two years, there is always an election, and a potential opponent, just around the corner.

A former deputy Republican whip in the House of Representatives, Robert Walker of Pennsylvania, told my political leadership class at Harvard that because the majority party holds all the power in Congress, including determining what legislation is considered, the primary focus of the minority party is, by necessity, on becoming a majority. And there is no way for a minority to become a majority other than by bringing about the defeat of the members of the majority. Conversely, members of the majority are committed to hold their power, which requires defeating members of the minority before they can increase their numbers and seize control. The seeking of partisan advantage often becomes the driving force behind the actions of both parties. The battle for advantage thus displaces thoughtful and dispassionate consideration of alternatives.

There are many disadvantages to a congressional system based on party membership: because the majority party so thoroughly dominates the legislative process, particularly in the House, partisan battles are inevitable; increasing the power of the parties, and party leaders, to enforce cohesion among their members would likely lead to constituents finding themselves represented by legislators whose principal loyalty might be to a political party and its leaders, rather than to the needs or preferences of the men and women who elected them.

=== COMMENTARY ===

The Professor's Take on Political Parties

It is dangerous to ask political scientists who study Congress what they think about political parties. It was this question that drove the American Political Science Association, a professional association of political scientists, to develop a committee of political scientists to study the problems of the political parties in the middle of the twentieth century.

In their 1950 report, which was titled "Toward a More Responsible Two-Party System," they warned that "it is dangerous to drift without a party system that helps the nation to set a general course of policy for the government as a whole." They had observed the Textbook Congress and complained that the parties were not democratic, responsible, or effective. They thought the parties needed to be more internally consistent and that their leaders need to have more power to cajole recalcitrant party members to follow the party script.

What the political scientists wanted, they got, though it did take more than forty years before the parties would accumulate enough power to ensure that voters had a clear choice in casting their votes during elections. The presence of strong parties has not been the panacea that the 1950 political scientists thought it would be. Today's political scientists are more likely to decry parties for being too strong and for not allowing their members to enter the ideological middle ground where problem solving can take place with members of the other party.

Before politicians start adopting some of the prescriptions to weaken political parties, we should at least outline the advantages of strong parties. Our ancestors from the 1950s can point us in the right direction. First and foremost, strong political parties ensure that the political system has accountability. So long as both parties had ideological wings, it was difficult for the voters to hold one party responsible for the economic problems or foreign entanglements in which we found ourselves. Strong parties present the voters with two different views, something that the voters in the 1950s did not enjoy to nearly the same extent. Perhaps because of the strong parties, more and more congressional elections are considered "wave" elections (including three in the last twelve years in comparison to just two in the thirty years before that).

Most of the problems associated with strong parties today have their roots not in the strong parties, but in the ambivalence and fickleness of the American voter. In 2002 and 2004, the American voters wanted a government that would cut taxes and an American military force with a big footprint abroad. In 2006 and 2008, the American voters wanted almost the opposite—they wanted a government that kept a close eye on the abuses of corporations that had wreaked havoc on the American economy and they wanted an end to American entanglements abroad. In 2010, the American voters switched sides again and wanted a check on the power of Obama and the Democrats as they tried to implement exactly what they said they would had they won the 2008 election. They did, and they were punished for doing so. In 2012, the American voters reinforced their fervent belief that they wanted a strong Democratic president who would continue to implement his progressive policy prescriptions and a Republican House that would try to thwart him at every turn. And 2014 was a replay of 2010. We are still trying to figure out the lessons from the 2016 elections, which saw the Republicans win the White House with a lower popular vote total than the Democrats and lose seats in Congress. And, in 2018, it seemed as though the Americans once again switched sides in the Democratic wave that swept that nation.

At the end of the day, I guess the old saying is still true: we get the public officials we deserve. And it is only because of strong political parties that this is so.

CHAPTER 9

External Influences
on the Legislative Process

Despite the first sentence of Article I of the US Constitution, which stipulates that "all legislative Powers herein granted shall be vested in a Congress of the United States," leaders in Congress frequently defer to the president when it comes to writing legislation. Prior to beginning a debate on immigration in February 2018, Senate majority leader Mitch McConnell (R-KY) waited for the president to make the first move: "I'm looking for something that President Trump supports. And he's not yet indicated what measure he's willing to sign."[1] This grant of legislative authority to the president is not unique either for the immigration debate or even to President Trump. As the president's prominence relative to the Congress has grown, his (and someday her) voice in the legislative process has grown.

The president is not the only person outside Congress who plays an important role in the legislative process. So, too, do the bureaucracy, courts, interest groups, and the media. Not only do they all influence the legislative process, but also, stemming from the checks and balances created within the Constitution, Congress plays a role in their internal workings. This chapter describes, in turn, the reciprocal relationships that Congress has with each of these external influences.

THE PRESIDENT

The most important outside actor in the legislative process, the president, may at times be even more important than most members of Congress. Presidential dominance, however, in the legislative realm has not been a constant. Power between the Congress and the president has been, is, and most certainly will be a constant tug of war. George Washington famously stormed out of the Senate after senators chose to deliberate in committee on a treaty that Washington had come to the Senate to discuss in person. During the Civil War, Abraham Lincoln decided that the South's rebellion necessitated immediate suspension of habeas corpus. When Congress took too long to act, Lincoln suspended it by executive order, even though most experts agree it required an act of Congress since the suspension clause falls within the congressional section of the Constitution (Article I). During the Great Depression and World War II, Franklin Roosevelt radically transformed the relationship between Americans and their government and with it the relationship between the president and Congress.

Jimmy Carter, in contrast, had much more difficulty implementing his policy ideas into law despite having huge majorities in both the House and the Senate. Even within presidential terms, congressional–presidential relationships experience both great highs and devastating lows. Together, the Democrats in Congress and a Republican president created the Environmental Protection Agency and codified consumer safety into law before congressional hearings on impeachment compelled Richard Nixon to resign the presidency in 1974. Before Clinton faced impeachment, a Republican Congress and a Democratic president advanced free trade, reformed welfare, and balanced the budget.

The Legislator in Chief

Even at their weakest, presidents still exercise a great deal of power in the legislative process. The president's role as legislator in chief is certainly less well known than his role as commander in chief, yet it is his role in the legislative process that he exercises most often. The president performs the final act in the legislative process: if the president signs a bill passed by Congress, the bill becomes law. Signing the bill is not the president's only possible action. If the president does not sign it within ten days (excluding Sundays) of its transmission from Congress to the White House, the bill automatically becomes law so long as Congress is still in session. If Congress transmits the bill to the president and adjourns prior to the end of the ten-day period and the president fails to sign it, the bill dies. This action—or inaction—is called a *pocket veto*.

Normally, when the president vetoes legislation, he does so by returning the unsigned bill to the chamber from which it originated with a description of his objections. Although it is called a *veto*, the president does not tick a box labeled "veto" or, as popularized by Schoolhouse Rock's "Bill on Capitol Hill," stamp the word *veto* across the bill.

To the layperson observing congressional–presidential relations, a veto could be interpreted as a sign of strength. Most political scientists, however, view it as a sign of weakness. Effective presidents work with Congress during the legislative process to ensure that the bill that is ultimately passed is one that he can sign. Little evidence can be gleaned from the list of presidents and the frequency with which they vetoed bills (see Table 9.1). Franklin Roosevelt has the most vetoes and Grover Cleveland has the second most. James K. Polk, usually at the bottom of the list ranking the presidents, and Abraham Lincoln, usually at the top of the list, both used the veto only twice.

Powerful presidents earn the legislator in chief label by being involved in the legislative process at every stage. They use their prestige and visibility to put an issue

Table 9.1 Presidents and Their Vetoes

CONGRESS	PRESIDENT	REGULAR VETOES	POCKET VETOES	TOTAL VETOES	VETOES OVERRIDDEN
1st–4th	George Washington	2	0	2	0
5th–6th	John Adams	0	0	0	0
7th–10th	Thomas Jefferson	0	0	0	0
11th–14th	James Madison	5	2	7	0
15th–18th	James Monroe	1	0	1	0
19th–20th	John Quincy Adams	0	0	0	0
21st–24th	Andrew Jackson	5	7	12	0
25th–26th	Martin Van Buren	0	1	1	0
27th	William Henry Harrison	0	0	0	0
27th–28th	John Tyler	6	4	10	1
29th–30th	James K. Polk	2	1	3	0
31st	Zachary Taylor	0	0	0	0
31st–32nd	Millard Fillmore	0	0	0	0
33rd–34th	Franklin Pierce	9	0	9	5
35th–36th	James Buchanan	4	3	7	0
37th–39th	Abraham Lincoln	2	5	7	0
39th–40th	Andrew Johnson	21	8	29	15
41st–44th	Ulysses S. Grant	45	48	93	4
45th–46th	Rutherford B. Hayes	12	1	13	1
47th	James A. Garfield	0	0	0	0
47th–48th	Chester A. Arthur	4	8	12	1
49th–50th	Grover Cleveland	304	110	414	2
51st–52nd	Benjamin Harrison	19	25	44	1
53rd–54th	Grover Cleveland	42	128	170	5
55th–57th	William McKinley	6	36	42	0
57th–60th	Theodore Roosevelt	42	40	82	1
61st–62nd	William H. Taft	30	9	39	1
63rd–66th	Woodrow Wilson	33	11	44	6
67th	Warren G. Harding	5	1	6	0
68th–70th	Calvin Coolidge	20	30	50	4
71st–72nd	Herbert C. Hoover	21	16	37	3
73rd–79th	Franklin D. Roosevelt	372	263	635	9
79th–82nd	Harry S. Truman	180	70	250	12
83rd–86th	Dwight D. Eisenhower	73	108	181	2
87th–88th	John F. Kennedy	12	9	21	0
88th–90th	Lyndon B. Johnson	16	14	30	0
91st–93rd	Richard M. Nixon	26	17	43	7
93rd–94th	Gerald R. Ford	48	18	66	12
95th–96th	James Earl Carter	13	18	31	2
97th–100th	Ronald Reagan	39	39	78	9

(Continued)

Table 9.1 (*continued*)

CONGRESS	PRESIDENT	REGULAR VETOES	POCKET VETOES	TOTAL VETOES	VETOES OVERRIDDEN
101st–102nd	George H. W. Bush	29	15	44	1
103rd–106th	William J. Clinton	36	1	37	2
107th–110th	George W. Bush	12	0	12	4
111th–114th	Barack H. Obama	12	0	12	1
Total		**1,508**	**1,066**	**2,574**	**111**

Source: http://history.house.gov/Institution/Presidential-Vetoes/Presidential-Vetoes/.

on the agenda. His advisors, both inside the White House and in the bureaucracy, assist in the development of legislation on the issue. They give speeches and encourage the people to contact their members of Congress to ensure the bill gets sufficient support inside Congress to pass. Finally, when the bill is presented to the president, he calls the important legislative leaders as well as important players outside Congress to observe his signing of the bill into law. Frequently, the president gives important legislative leaders or outside political actors the pens he uses to sign his name to legislation as a symbolic way of acknowledging their roles in creating the new law.

Even beyond his official signature, the president directs the bureaucracy on how it should implement the newly created law. Presidents frequently do this when they sign the bill into law through a *signing statement*, which can simply be a message of congratulations to the legislation's sponsor or a much more consequential message. Although he opposed it as legislation, President Bush signed the Detainee Treatment Act of 2005 into law. He included in his signing statement a declaration that his constitutional authority "to supervise the unitary executive branch and as Commander in Chief" could not be limited by the new law and thus he would interpret certain provisions of the law to be unconstitutional and thus void.[2] In giving the new law his imprimatur, he simultaneously undercut its implementation. These signing statements can be considered part of the legislative history of a bill—pieces of information that courts and agencies might use when they try to figure out the meaning of a law, such as committee reports describing a bill or legislators' remarks in floor debate expressing their understanding of the bill's effects. Unlike some other forms of legislative history that courts consider more reliable, signing statements are used exceedingly rarely by courts in construing a statute, and most legal scholars find them of dubious value at best in interpreting a law.

The Commander in Chief
Although the Constitution clearly states that only the Congress has the authority to declare war, presidents have ample power in conducting the war through their role as commander in chief. As with their role as legislator in chief, the individual

power exercised by the president is contingent on his relationship with Congress and the conditions that precipitate military action.

In 1941, after Japan attacked Pearl Harbor, President Roosevelt appeared before Congress to declare that as of the time of the strike, "a state of war" had existed. Nine years later, President Truman sent troops to fight in Korea without Congress formally declaring war. A little more than a decade after that, first President Kennedy and then President Johnson sent American soldiers into battle in Vietnam. President Nixon did the same thing. President Reagan sent American troops into Panama and Grenada. When Saddam Hussein invaded Kuwait in 1993, President George H. W. Bush sent troops to the Persian Gulf. President Clinton sent troops to Somalia and the Balkan Peninsula. President George W. Bush waged military campaigns in both Iraq and Afghanistan. President Obama sent troops to Libya in a multicountry effort to enforce a United Nations Security Council resolution and to Iraq and Syria to retard the Islamic State's advance in the region, a campaign that President Trump continued.

Most presidents view defending the nation from outside attack as their most important fundamental responsibility to the American public. Once the imminent threat has subsided, Congress has the responsibility to weigh in on the military action. And yet, on none of those occasions after World War II described above did the president seek, or did the Congress enact, a declaration of war. In a few of the instances, the Congress authorized the president to use force. For example, without declaring war, Congress nonetheless authorized President Bush to use force to expel Iraqi troops from Kuwait in 1991. Ten years later, his son, President George W. Bush, was given broad authority to conduct the war on terror.

Sometimes Congress signals its view of presidential military action less formally than supporting or opposing a declaration of war. During the 1960s and early 1970s, Congress increased the flow of both troops and money to support the American efforts in Vietnam. In the 1980s, Congress prohibited the use of US troops in El Salvador or Nicaragua. In the 2000s, the Congress attached conditions for continued troop presence in Afghanistan or Iraq. Nonetheless, for nearly three-quarters of a century, the Congress to a large extent has been willing to delegate de facto war-making authority to the president and his subordinates in the Pentagon.

This delegation has not been without contention. The War Powers Act, which authorizes the Congress to step in and withdraw support from a military action after it has begun, is one example. It has been opposed both by supporters of a strong presidency (who argue that it interferes with authority implicit in the president's constitutional designation as commander in chief of the armed forces) and by defenders of congressional prerogatives (who claim that it allows presidents to present them with a fait accompli, in which the only options are either to accede to the White House or to pull the plug on American troops already in combat). To its advocates, the War

Powers Act is predicated on the fact that Congress can neither know as much as the president (for whom the entire Pentagon works) or act as swiftly in an emergency.

Throughout its history, Congress has attempted to rewrite the War Powers Act and to insist on a greater congressional voice in approving military undertakings. More often than not, these attempts fail even before they get off the ground. The presidents' superior information, ability to act unilaterally, and inaugural oath to "preserve, protect, and defend the Constitution" have drained much of the force behind Congress's prerogative to declare war.

Party Leader

Institutional loyalty has increasingly been sacrificed on the altar of party politics and, with it, congressional powers in relation to the president. For much of congressional history, representatives and senators considered themselves, first and foremost, members of Congress, their authority spelled out in the first article of the Constitution. The president has increasingly become not only the chief spokesperson for the executive branch, but also the chief spokesperson for his fellow partisans in the legislative branch. While support for presidential initiatives can never be assumed as a matter of course, presidents have at least two distinct powers to line up congressional votes. First, members of the same political party as the president perceive his popularity as having a distinct impact on their own electability and the chances of their party winning or retaining a congressional majority. If a Republican president succeeds, his partisans in Congress are more likely to win elections. If the Republican president fails, so too may his party in the next congressional election. The link between presidents' public approval ratings and their fellow partisans' electoral results has become increasingly close. Even when the link was more distant, presidents were quick to take advantage of this perception, often warning that their very credibility was dependent on the outcome of an important congressional decision. The inference is clear: if the president's credibility suffers, his entire party is politically damaged.

As a consequence of the president's growing role as chief party spokesperson, the president's publicly stated positions have increasingly divided the parties in Congress. At the end of the Johnson presidency, House Democrats were about 10 percent more supportive of his positions than House Republicans (SEE FIGURE 9.1). In the Senate, the distinction was almost zero. With each president since, the gap between the parties in Congress has grown. In the first year of Obama's presidency, the difference was 64 points in the House and 42 points in the Senate. Eight years later, in Trump's first year, the difference grew to 76 points in the House and 59 points in the Senate.

When the battle lines are so deeply drawn—when a Democratic representative simply will not support a Republican president's initiative and Republicans will turn a deaf ear to a Democrat in the White House—the president can rely on an additional power. Because of the media focus on the White House, the President of the United

States has a clear advantage in appealing to the public, which in turn may be used to pressure individual members of Congress. Political scientist Sam Kernell calls this strategy "going public." On some issues members of Congress have no choice but to recognize the executive branch's monopoly on information. In foreign policy and defense matters, for example, even though presidential preeminence is disputable, the expertise drawn from hundreds of US embassies and consulates, from intelligence agencies, and from trained military leaders makes it difficult for members of Congress, with their limited resources, to challenge presidential recommendations.

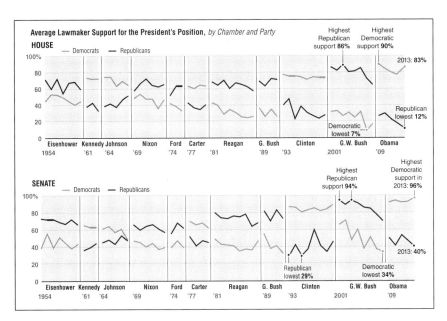

Figure 9.1 Presidential Support Scores by Chamber and Party, 1953–2013.
SOURCE: *Congressional Quarterly Almanac.*

Because of this important partisan dynamic between presidents and members of Congress, perhaps the most important characteristic to assess the standing of the president as an outside influence on the legislative process is whether the United States is operating under *divided government* or *unified government*. Divided government is when the opposite party of the president has a majority in at least one chamber in Congress. With power in just this one chamber, the president's opponents in Congress can bring his agenda to a screeching halt.

Issues arise that divide Congress from the president not based on ideological or political grounds, but simply because of political actors' institutional prerogatives. The War Powers Act is, perhaps, the best example. Issues of bureaucratic structure, presidential autonomy over commissions, and agency budgets are other examples. As members have become less loyal to their institutional prerogatives and as party polarization has grown, fewer members of the president's party are willing to stand up to him to protect congressional prerogatives. In eras of unified government, when the president's party controls a majority in both chambers, Congress has less vigorously conducted oversight on the bureaucracy, given less scrutiny to legislative proposals coming from the White House, and had less desire to investigate potential executive branch malfeasance. In a system that requires ambition to counteract ambition, congressional leaders of the president's party who too quickly acquiesce to the president do so at great peril to the functioning of American democracy. In these highly contentious times when party competition in Congress is fierce, the president's role as party leader in chief has become increasingly important.

Unilateral Actor

Two of the longest chapters of this textbook involve a description of the legislative process and how it has changed. Such process and procedures are required when 435 people have a vote in one chamber and 100 different people have a vote in the other chamber and both chambers must agree. The executive branch, in contrast, has only one ultimate decision maker who is directly accountable to the American people. His strategic position atop the executive branch hierarchy gives the president additional leverage over Congress in several important ways.

First, as head of the executive branch, which is compelled by the Constitution to execute the laws of the United States, the president can issue executive orders. Ostensibly, these orders have their roots within the Constitution or are in areas for which Congress has directly delegated the president authority, but in practice the president can order just about anything so long as it is not against existing law. These orders, like laws, are still subject to judicial review. Furthermore, Congress can create law to overturn executive orders. Nonetheless, perhaps the biggest weakness to executive orders is that any future president can change the mandates of the order as easily as it was handed down in the first place.

Despite executive orders' ephemeral quality, several have been incredibly important. When Abraham Lincoln issued the Emancipation Proclamation, he did so as an executive order; so, too, when Harry S. Truman desegregated the military in 1954. Franklin Roosevelt established the Works Progress Administration (1935), Jimmy Carter created the Federal Emergency Management Agency (1979), and George W. Bush created the Office of Homeland Security (2001), all by executive order. Perhaps the low point of executive orders was when Franklin Roosevelt created internment camps for Japanese Americans, who were then perceived to be a threat to national security, during World War II (1942).

Most executive orders involve more mundane topics, such as when Dwight David Eisenhower established the Good Conduct medal in 1953, when George H. W. Bush closed the government for half a day on Christmas Eve (1990), or when Barack Obama attempted to reduce improper payments made by the federal government (2009). When the action is even more mundane, the president issues a *memorandum* rather than an *executive order*. Both are functionally the same, with the only difference being the higher visibility of executive actions, which are printed and numbered in *The Federal Register*. The more generic term for these announcements is *executive actions*.

A second unilateral action that a president takes is his submission of a budget to Congress. While it is reluctant to surrender the final word on important matters of public policy, the Congress has shown a willingness to delegate some of its power to others when doing so would improve the result. What more logical place to turn than to the executive branch, with its huge array of information gatherers and policy experts? Under the Constitution, the Congress retains the power to set national spending levels and determine tax rates. It also has the right to decide national priorities and to allocate tax monies accordingly. It alone can create debt. Unless the president forces the Congress to reconsider its decisions by using his veto power or manages to persuade the public to demand certain actions from its representatives, the ball is entirely in the Congress's court when it comes to creating programs, funding them, and raising the money to pay for them. All of this together—determining income, determining how much money to spend and what to spend it on—is the essence of establishing a federal budget. For this, the Congress does not need a president. Yet ever since the Harding administration in the 1920s, it has been the White House, using the executive branch's Office of Management and Budget and its precursor, the Bureau of the Budget, that has put together the first drafts of a national budget, setting out in detail how much money should be spent for each activity of the federal government. That is because the Congress recognized that the president, with control over every federal department and agency, and with hundreds of thousands of executive branch employees, was far better equipped than the Congress to determine how much would be needed to carry out the government's already-approved health, education, welfare, transportation, housing, child-care, crime-fighting, immigration control, diplomatic, and military programs. It was Congress that gave the president the assignment to develop an initial budget.

While Congress maintains the right to accept, reject, or modify the president's budget, the act of moving first in the budget process can give the president great power. Instead of Congress relying on its own experts and preferences to determine an allocation to a program or agency, it usually starts with the president's number, and members of Congress argue for increases or decreases from the focal point that the president supplies. On other occasions, the president's budget is dead on arrival when it arrives on Capitol Hill. The extent to which the budget is a guide for the development of the actual budget is left entirely in Congress's hands.

When President Trump released his Fiscal Year 2019 budget, interest groups worried that some of their favorite programs would face significantly smaller budgets. As Congress, with Republican majorities in both chambers, worked through the budget process, it agreed to some of the levels proposed by the president but drastically changed some of the others (SEE FIGURE 9.2 for a few examples). While the president retains the right to propose a budget, Congress has free reign to act however it sees fit, subject only to a presidential veto.

In the end, the Congress has found that it operates best in tandem with, not separate from, the other branch of government at the far end of Pennsylvania Avenue. Woodrow Wilson, even before he became president, was critical of the practical effects of the constitutional separation of powers: "The trouble with the theory," he said, "is that government is not a machine, but a living thing. . . . No living thing can have its organs offset against each other and live. On the contrary, its life is dependent upon their quick cooperation. . . . Government is a body of men . . . with a common task and purpose. Their cooperation is indispensable, their warfare fatal."[3] The question that remains is how much it can delegate, in the name of efficiency, and yet retain final control over the laws and actions that will affect the people whose representatives they are. At what point does delegation of one's responsibilities become *nonfeasance*, the nonperformance of duty?

Congressional Powers over the President

While it is true that the president plays an important role in the legislative process, Congress, in turn, plays an important role in how the president carries out his powers. Unlike with the bureaucracy, which we discuss below, the president has a great deal of discretion for how the White House staff is organized. Congress does not have the ability to restrict who advises the president and how that advice is given. On several occasions, the president has chosen his White House staff because he knew that the Senate would never confirm the individuals for cabinet-level positions. Susan Rice, who was President Obama's national security advisor, and Steve Bannon, who was President Trump's chief strategist, are just one example from each of the last two presidential administrations. Congress does retain the ability to investigate potential malfeasance even within the White House staff.

Congress sets the president's salary, though the Constitution forbids it from lowering the salary over the course of a presidential term. And, as with every

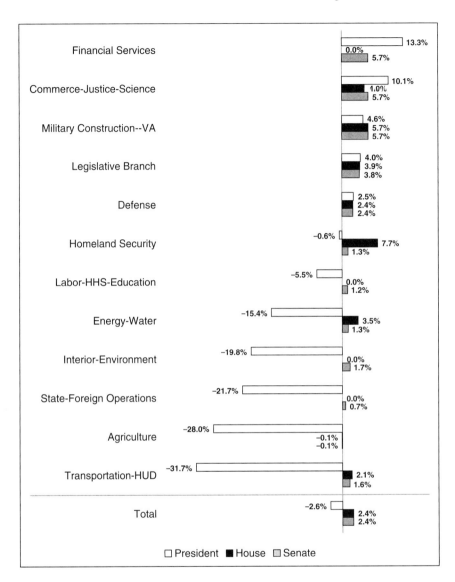

Figure 9.2 FY2019 Funding Proposed by President Trump (*white bars*), and Approved by the House (*black*) and Senate (*gray*).

other penny that the federal government spends, Congress determines the level of funding that the president and his staff receive.

The biggest check the Congress has on the president is its ability to impeach and to remove him from office. The House of Representatives is given the task of developing the articles of impeachment, in essence, the case for the president's removal. If an article receives the support of a House majority, the Senate tries the impeachment, with the only outcome either removal from office or acquittal. The Congress cannot punish the president except by removing him from office, which requires the support of two-thirds of the Senate. During the trial in the Senate, the House serves as the prosecution and the Chief Justice of the US Supreme Court presides. Only two presidents have been impeached. In 1868, Andrew Johnson was impeached, but was saved from being removed from office by a single vote. In 1998, Bill Clinton was impeached, but the Senate did not even have a majority in favor of his removal, let alone the required two-thirds. Impeachment proceedings compelled Richard Nixon to resign in 1974 in lieu of almost certain conviction.

THE BUREAUCRACY

The bureaucracy plays an important role at the beginning and at the end of the legislative process. Its role at the end has been well studied. Its role at the beginning has largely gone unnoticed. Contrary to what political scientists study, the press reports, and elected officials perceive, voting on the floor of the House and Senate is not the only part of the policymaking process. A stylized version of the policy process is depicted in Figure 9.2. While much attention is focused on the region of the policy process that is shaded in Figure 9.2, the parts before and after are also crucial. It is in these unshaded regions where the bureaucracy is especially active.

The bureaucracy is essential in helping Congress define problems. While 535 members of Congress are setting the national minimum wage, approving new weapons systems, and prioritizing space initiatives, thousands of employees of the executive branch are not only carrying out what Congress mandates in legislation but also monitoring the implementation of these directives. Bureaucrats who work in the executive branch, whether for the Social Security Administration, the Pentagon, or the Food and Drug Administration, are the government officials who first learn when the cogs of the huge federal government machinery break down. Bureaucrats, who constantly monitor the implementation and effectiveness of federal policy, are thus responsible for providing an early warning system to members of Congress. Like the police who constantly monitor neighborhoods to ensure that crimes are not being committed, the bureaucracy constantly monitors the implementation of laws. By the bureaucracy's alerting Congress of governmental breakdowns, members have the opportunity to respond by passing new legislation or trying to influence bureaucrats to implement existing law in a new way. In this sense, members of Congress act as firefighters, who respond only after a fire alarm has sounded. So long as there are no fires, the members go about their regular business of approving budgets, reauthorizing programs, and evaluating presidential nominees. If the police do not stop crimes, neighborhoods suffer. If bureaucrats do not constantly monitor the governmental machinery, the United States suffers. When firefighters ignore a fire, it usually grows even more intense—so, too, a government problem when Congress turns a blind eye.

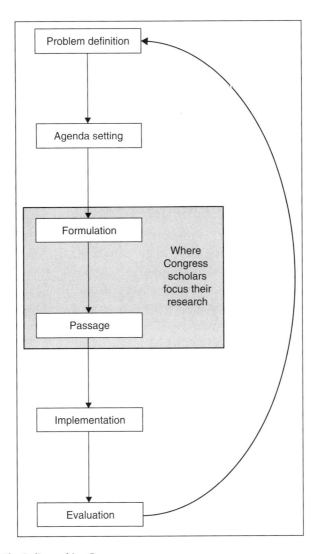

Figure 9.3 The Policymaking Process.
Source: Shafran and Theriault (2013).

Bureaucracies are warehouses of an incredible amount of information. As Congress tries to establish priorities in transportation programs, who better to consult than the secretary of transportation and the 56,173 employees of the department who spend all day, every day focused on making it more efficient and safer for Americans to get from one location to the next, whether it be the morning commute to work or the much-anticipated summer vacation to the beach?[4] When Congress reauthorizes the Department of Defense, who better for them to consult with than the 23,000 employees at the Pentagon, which is tasked with keeping Americans safe?[5] As such, the bureaucracy has a tremendous informational advantage, which Congress relies on to solve problems.

At the end of the process, Congress once again defers to the bureaucracy because it is the bureaucracy that must implement and execute the laws. While the administration of the laws falls within the president's prerogatives, the Congress could choose to be very detailed in establishing program goals, eligibility criteria, and other factors that essentially reduce the discretion of the executive branch to a bare minimum. Instead, it is customary for the Congress to write laws that describe programs, set out goals, and leave the fleshing out of the details to the various federal departments. The words "such regulations as the Secretary may devise" accompany so much legislation that the president's appointees may play as big a role as Congress in determining what, in fact, the laws are and who benefits, or suffers, as a result. As the scope of government has increased and members of Congress have found themselves forced to deal with more and more issues, it is more likely that Congress delegates those decisions to the agencies rather than writing the most specific details into the law.

Under the Administrative Procedures Act, passed by Congress in 1946, executive branch agencies are also largely immune from challenge in imposing penalties for violations of agency-created regulations. Administrative law judges, who are technically executive branch officials rather than Article III judges, can revoke licenses to fly airplanes or operate businesses with little recourse for the citizen. Before a punished citizen can take the case to court, he or she must first exhaust all administrative remedies (that is, he or she must appeal, step by step, one rung at a time, all the way up the ladder of the federal hierarchy). In many cases, it is easier to simply give up than to continue to fight such a long and expensive legal battle. Administrative law judges may render judgment without allowing an accused party to confront the witnesses making the accusations. They may render judgment, in fact, without even reading the material submitted by the accused. Administrative agencies—the subcompartments of the executive branch of government—exercise almost unchecked power in overseeing the implementation of the regulations they have imposed under the authority of federal law. They can do so because the Congress has given them the power to do so.

What should one wonder about such delegation? On the one hand, the government has grown larger, events move more quickly, and the nation's population has grown far beyond anything envisioned by the nation's founders. It is impossible for the Congress, with its relatively small staff and small budget and its cumbersome decision-making process, to know enough, or to move quickly enough, to do all that it was originally intended to do.

On the other hand, Congress may be seriously failing to do its duty. The authors of the Constitution clearly intended that no American would be sent to die in war unless the people's representatives deemed such a sacrifice necessary.

The Congress was given the power to determine how much the country would spend and on what and how much money should be taken from each taxpayer's pocket. The people were to live under the laws imposed on them by their own representatives. And yet, through delegation, the Congress has surrendered to other executive branch officials the responsibilities that had been placed at its feet. Nonetheless, because of the bureaucracy's overwhelming informational advantage, Congress has continued to permit the bureaucracy wide latitude to implement the laws that it helped to draft at the beginning of the process.

Because Congress retains a tremendous amount of power over bureaucrats, they are always mindful of the preferences of it. Congress has the sole responsibility to determine the structure and funding of the bureaucracy. Furthermore, the Senate has the power to confirm—or not—the president's nominations to fill the cabinet and subcabinet officials within the departments and agencies. In addition, Congress can also impeach the appointees. As with the impeachment of the president, the House is responsible for passing articles of impeachment and the Senate tries the impeachment (though the chief justice does not preside). Two-thirds of the senators voting are required for removal from office. The degree to which Congress involves itself in bureaucratic actions is very much dependent on the relationship between Congress and the president and his appointees.

THE COURTS

Article III—the judicial branch—is even shorter than Article II (and both in combination only have 60 percent as many words as Article I). The vague mandates of the Constitution have given Congress the ability to speak where the Constitution was silent. Congress establishes the structure of the federal court system. It determines how much judges and their staffs are paid. The Senate has the power to either confirm or reject the president's nominees for federal judges and, as with the president and cabinet officials, can remove them from office through impeachment proceedings. At times, Congress has even weighed in on which cases the court system could hear—an action that courts view skeptically. The courts have far fewer powers over Congress and, yet, the one that they do have at times is more powerful than all the checks the Congress has on them: the courts can declare laws unconstitutional.

This power, which the Supreme Court claimed in the 1803 case *Marbury v. Madison*, was not explicitly granted in the Constitution but is now generally accepted by the other branches of government and by the public. The Congress can pass new legislation that essentially renders the Court's finding moot (in some cases) or can initiate a constitutional amendment (as can the states), but both avenues are very difficult to pursue successfully. Constitutional amendments require two-thirds approval in both chambers and then ratification by three-fourths of the states.[6]

By virtue of their decisions, judges can not only stop the enforcement of bills, but also instigate new legislation by pushing Congress to act. Despite media coverage suggesting it, the Supreme Court did not strike down the Voting Rights Act of 1965 in its 2013 *Shelby County v. Holder* case. It did not even strike down the preclearance provision, which required approval from the attorney general or a federal court before any voting changes could be made in certain states, mainly in the South. The Supreme Court simply said that Congress needed to establish a new criterion, responsive to current needs, by which states and localities would become subject to the preclearance provision. The primary way for the states and localities to be subject to Department of Justice preclearance was if Congress enacted a new law.

Sometimes, Congress responds to court decisions even when the courts do not explicitly invite it to do so. A day after the *Shelby v. Holder* decision, the Supreme Court struck down the 1996 Defense of Marriage Act. Although most of the decision's opponents regarded the decision as the final word, Representative Tim Huelskamp (R-KS) speculated that Congress would need to pass and the states ratify a constitutional amendment banning gay marriage, something that has not yet happened and is unlikely to occur.

At other times, court decisions hinder legislation rather than propelling it. In the 102nd, 103rd, and 104th Congresses (1991–6), members of Congress introduced eighty-five different bills, attracting 626 cosponsors, to limit the number of years that they, themselves, could serve in Congress. In 1995, the Supreme Court declared that congressional term limits were unconstitutional because they added an additional requirement to serving in Congress beyond the age, citizenship, and residency requirements spelled out in the Constitution. Term limit proponents now had to get two-thirds of the members to vote against their own congressional livelihood to get the ball rolling. Then, three-quarters of the states would have to approve it for members' terms to be limited. These barriers proved to be too high to pass legislation; in fact, the barrier was sufficiently high that members barely introduced any term limit bills. Even after George W. Bush became president in 2001, with Republican majorities in both chambers of Congress, only two such bills, which garnered no cosponsors, were introduced in the 107th Congress (2001–2).

Judges, too, must mediate the relationship between Congress and the president, and sometimes even the relationship between the Congress, the president, and the Court itself, as it did in *Marbury v. Madison*. For example, in *NLRB v. Noel Canning* (2014), the Supreme Court decided that it was Congress itself that determined when it was in recess—and thus when the president can make temporary recess appointments without a confirmation vote. The Court decided, in *INS v. Chadha* (1983), that legislative vetoes of presidential action—at least as they were written then—were unconstitutional because they reversed the roles the Constitution established for the executive branch and Congress.

Judges play one more crucial role in the legislative process: frequently they must determine the meaning behind the words of legislation enacted into law. Even though the executive branch is charged with implementing and enforcing the legislation, its decisions can be subject to review by the courts. These decisions sometimes affect only the particular parties to a case; at other times they affect the actual implementation of the law. When the courts decide in a way that Congress disapproves, members must pass new legislation to clarify its initial language. All of this is to suggest that Congress may face obstacles erected by officials in both the other branches in getting its preferred policies implemented. It is exceedingly difficult for Congress to imagine all the different scenarios and contingencies so that it could write an exhaustive list of directives to fit every conceivable future course of action. Because of these limitations, bureaucratic implementation and court interpretation will be a constant part of the checks and balances between the branches of the federal government.

Because of the increasingly important role that judges play in the implementation and direction of public policy in the United States, the politics of judicial nominations has become increasingly fraught. Only twenty years ago, most appointees faced minimum opposition as typified by the confirmation votes of the liberal justice Ruth Bader Ginsberg (in 1993), who only had three votes against her nomination, and Stephen Breyer (in 1994), who had nine (see Table 9.2). Two earlier conservative justices—Antonin Scalia (in 1986) and Anthony Kennedy (in 1987)—did not get a single "no" vote. Since 2000, though, no justice has had fewer than 20 votes against his or her nomination.

These nomination fights had gotten so contentious that the party leaders in Congress have changed the rules. In 2013, Harry Reid (D-NV) changed the procedures so that nominations to both executive branch positions and courts below the Supreme Court were not subject to filibusters, thus requiring only a simple majority. Reid argued at the time that such a change was required to thwart the Republican efforts to stall newly reelected Obama's nominations.

Table 9.2 Supreme Court Justices and Their Confirmation Votes

YEAR	JUSTICE	YES	NO
1991	Clarence Thomas	52	48
1993	Ruth Bader Ginsburg	96	3
1994	Stephen Breyer	87	9
2005	John Roberts	78	22
2006	Samuel Alito	58	42
2009	Sonia Sotomayor	68	31
2010	Elena Kagan	63	37
2017	Neil Gorsuch	54	45
2018	Brett Kavanaugh	50	48

When sufficient Democratic opposition to the naming of Neil Gorsuch to the Supreme Court in 2017 prevented the Republicans from invoking cloture on his nomination, majority leader Mitch McConnell (R-KY) and Senate Republicans extended the Reid-initiated rule to Supreme Court nominations. In both cases, the votes were mostly along party lines: almost all Democrats voted in favor of Reid's use of the nuclear option, opposed by all Republicans; all Republicans voted in favor of McConnell's rule change four years later, opposed by all Democrats. The filibuster, at least for the time being, still applies to normal legislation, but it can be removed just as easily if a majority of senators wished to do so.

INTEREST GROUPS

When Congress attempted to crack down on abuses within the financial industry, members of Congress were besieged by representatives of large banks, small banks, credit unions, insurance companies, and savings and loan institutions. When Medicare changes are discussed, other groups descend on Capitol Hill: representatives of hospitals, nursing homes, rehabilitation centers, and senior citizens' groups. When changes in environmental laws are considered, House and Senate offices may be filled with advocates from the Sierra Club, the Wildlife Federation, the Audubon Society, independent oil producers, ranchers, farmers, timber companies, and land developers. These interests are better organized into groups so that they can coordinate their activities rather than as individuals petitioning their government.

Interest Groups as an Extension of the Members' Offices

The influx of special interests has led some congressional observers to refer to Washington's legislative corridors as Gucci Gulch, a reference to the omnipresent high-priced lobbyists who attempt to persuade members of Congress to support positions favored by their organizations or industries. Interest groups wield their influence in three ways.

First, interest groups tie their preferences to the interests of a member's home state or district. Thus, spokesmen for the oil industry or for the farming or ranching communities may attempt to show how proposed legislation may harm, or help, the local economy. Lobbyists for small banks may attempt to show that permitting branch banking or allowing insurance companies to offer traditional banking services will draw venture capital out of the local community, making it harder for prospective merchants to open new hardware or clothing stores.

Second, interest groups provide members with expertise. House members, with fewer than twenty staff assistants, including receptionists, information technology specialists, in-district caseworkers, and legislative assistants, cannot hope to master the important economic and social ramifications of the scores of complicated bills they must deal with in every session of Congress. Even senators,

with their larger staffs, cannot hope to keep up with the mass of detail involved in every major piece of legislation. Enter the lobbyist: with the expert resources of entire industries, or large staffs assigned to a single issue area, lobbyists are able to provide legislators with much more information than would otherwise be available to them. Because much of lobbyists' influence depends on their credibility, members can generally count on them to be truthful. A well-known saying in Washington captures this sentiment—Question: "What do you call a lobbyist who lies to you?" Answer: "A former lobbyist." Because lobbyists use all the information they have at their disposal, they can help congressional staffers analyze issues. Members appreciate getting information from sources outside the executive branch when making policy. By helping members understand the impact of an issue on constituents, they may gain a distinct edge as they write and vote on legislation.

Third, special interests gain influence by becoming part of a legislator's reelection team. Critics have suggested that this is buying influence, suggesting that members of Congress voted a certain way because the supporters of that position contributed to their reelection campaigns. This presupposes that either (a) legislators have no views of their own or (b) they are corrupt. Yet studies have shown that legislators do, in fact, have very strongly held views on most major issues. And despite the existence of rather stringent federal laws and congressional ethics standards, few legislators have ever been found to have "sold" their votes.

What happens is subtler: For much of the year, legislators are busily immersed in the day-to-day activity of a fast-moving job. To raise campaign funds, they must not only solicit contributions themselves but also rely on other people. They hire fundraising consultants and they put together finance committees. The consultants and committees get together to sell tickets to breakfasts, dinners, and receptions. The members meet with their finance committees and see familiar faces: people who are supportive and friendly. They arrive at the fundraising event and again see those familiar faces. The lobbyists begin to take on the hue of allies, people who share the legislator's interests and concerns. They move from an outer circle of paid influencers to an inner circle of friends. They play on human nature: people are more inclined to listen to the concerns of their friends than to strangers. It is not the money—the campaign contribution—that influences the decisions, but the ritual of rubbing shoulders at cocktail parties, the building of personal relationships. Almost all research in political science shows the absence of a relationship between receiving money and voting a particular way. When political scientists find a connection between the two, it is almost always that special interests give to members who have a demonstrated record of supporting their causes; in essence, money follows votes, not the other way around.

Interest Groups and Watchdogs over the Bureaucracy

Interest groups play an important role in the legislative process beyond their specific connection to members. Much like the bureaucracy, the interest group community is constantly monitoring the implementation and execution of the laws. Members need not pay attention to every little mandate that the bureaucracy operationalizes because interest groups inform members when they think the bureaucracy is straying too far from Congress's intended purpose.

This crucial role played by interest groups can only be carried out because almost all legitimate interests have an interest group working on their behalf. More than four thousand groups have registered to lobby Congress. As an example, many groups are registered to lobby Congress on behalf of animal rights (see Table 9.3 for a list of these interest groups).

Because these animal rights interest groups are constantly monitoring every decision that the bureaucracy makes in carrying out the laws that Congress

Table 9.3 Animal Rights and Welfare Interest Groups

American Humane Association
American Society for the Prevention of Cruelty to Animals
Animal Legal Defense Fund
Animal Protection Institute
Farm Animal Reform Movement
Friends of Animals
Fund for Animals
Humane Society of the United States
In Defense of Animals
National Audubon Society
National Wildlife Federation
People for the Ethical Treatment of Animals
World Wildlife Fund

Source: http://www.smallwhitefilter.com/animals.html

passes, Congress does not need to invest much time and energy in a constant surveillance of the bureaucracy. And, because interest groups exist on the other side of the animal rights debate, such as groups organized to assist scientists, pharmaceutical companies, or developers, if the bureaucracy makes a decision that benefits animal rights groups, these other groups inform other members of Congress in hopes of obtaining legislative remedies.

THE MEDIA

The final actor that we discuss in this chapter is the media. The media play an important part in how members of Congress do their job. While the relationships between Congress and other outside actors inevitably change over time, perhaps no other change has been as profound as that with the media. Most of that change has come about not because of changes within Congress, but because of changes in the media.

Thirty years ago, most members had a dedicated staff member, usually called the press secretary, who would handle all press requests. Most members had a clear hierarchy for dealing with these requests. For most members, requests from the district were always fulfilled first, even before the national news media. Satisfying the needs of the local newspaper or the local television channel was paramount. A negative story—or not capitalizing on a good story—in the local media could reverberate in a way that national stories probably would not. Granted, few members were getting regular requests from the *New York Times* unless they were committee chairs or party leaders.

No longer is the news business consolidated into newspapers and television news shows. From blogs to reddit and Twitter to Facebook, the landscape of a member's media world has grown from a pixel to a screen in less than a generation, which has presented members with both new challenges and huge advantages. The problem is that members, by virtue of their being in Congress, have demonstrated at least enough ability in handling the media to win an election. Members like stability and continuity. These media changes have upset the entire dynamic of representation. Members who are quick to adapt to new technological advances are likely to pad their incumbency advantage. Members who do not adapt run the risk of being defeated by an upstart who utilizes the new media landscape to reach potential voters. A well-timed and executed Facebook message can be more effective than knocking on three hundred doors and having ten-minute conversations with those few constituents who are at home and who answer the door.

The new landscape of the media also presents members with an opportunity. No longer does the member need the local news to pick up a story for constituents to learn about their legislative accomplishments. Even while constituencies are becoming more complicated and diverse, members have much more immediate and direct access to potential voters. While the landscape has radically changed,

the importance of the local media remains paramount. Most studies show that the local news is still the primary source of political information for constituents (and voters). The environment in which the press secretary operates continuously changes—more so than probably any other position on a member's staff. Despite all the new avenues to reach constituents and potential voters, members must not ignore conventional local reporters who can still provide the members with the biggest stage from which they can get attention.

Just as the bureaucracy and interest groups constantly monitor how the laws are being executed, so, too, do the media. Although Congress has a system in place to ward off potential scandals, sometimes that system breaks down. When it does, the media are more than willing to fill the void. Investigative reporters have been responsible for some of the biggest political news stories. For example, the Department of Veterans Affairs and veterans' rights groups were unable to get President Bush and the Congress to respond to the deteriorating conditions facing veterans at the Walter Reed Army Medical Center. It was not until 2007, when the *Washington Post* did an exposé documenting the dilapidated infrastructure and chaotic bureaucratic snafus, that the public got involved. Within months, three high-ranking army officers resigned or were forced out. Although they were slow to act prior to the *Post*'s exposé, the Bush administration and Congress tripped over themselves to get in front of the scandal by holding hearings and issuing reports.

The media constantly monitor not only the implementation and execution of the laws, but also the members' personal and professional behavior. Catching members with their pants down—sometimes literally—is part of what a pervasive and investigative media does. Few have learned the lesson as thoroughly as Representative Vance McAllister (R-LA), who won a surprising special election on November 16, 2013. Less than five months later, his local newspaper, the *Ouachita Citizen*, posted online a surveillance video from his district office of him kissing a woman who was not his wife. Eight months later, he finished fourth in the primary election, receiving less than 12 percent of the total vote. In 2017 and 2018, Senator

Al Franken (D-MN) and Representatives John Conyers (D-MI), Ruben Kihuen (D-NV), Blake Farenthold (R-TX), Trent Franks (R-AZ), Pat Meehan (R-PA), and Tim Murphy (R-PA) were all caught up in the #MeToo movement, with women accusing each one of sexual harassment, leading them to resign before the end of their terms, except for Kihuen, who finished out his term before retiring.

CONCLUSION

Even if most of the lawmaking powers of government were given to the Congress, it has little authority on its own. Just as presidents cannot write laws, neither can the Congress implement laws or force the president to implement them. At almost every stage of the lawmaking process, presidents, members of his executive branch, and the Congress must ultimately work together.

Members of Congress have the most direct link to the people; they meet with their constituents almost every day and on almost every issue to be decided by government. Presidents are selected not by small segments of the national population, but by the people as a whole. Members have the direct interests of the people—their constituents—most clearly in mind. Presidents have access to more information and more, if not better, expert analysis through the bureaucracy. The Constitution deliberately created a tension, a jealousy, a rivalry between these two branches of government, the better to protect against concentrations of power that might endanger liberty. But while the president and members of Congress are, and are intended to be, competitors for power, they are nonetheless part of the same government, serving the same people. If competition is good, so is cooperation.

The sign on president Harry Truman's desk made it clear who ultimately was responsible for the decisions of the executive branch of government: "The buck stops here," it said. In the same way, the buck stops at the front steps of the Capitol when it comes to setting national policy. Because they command great visibility and have a national constituency, presidents have a significant amount of influence over congressional decisions. But in the end, it is the Congress that decides. And it is the Congress that must answer to the public for its decisions. It is obvious, however, even to the most ardent defender of congressional privilege, that some responsibilities, for one reason or another, are harder for Congress to handle. In such instances, the Congress may decide to delegate part of its job to someone else. As a result, members of Congress are only one set of actors in setting national policy. Other officials outside the legislative branch play important roles in setting the legislative agenda, writing legislation, and implementing it once passed on Capitol Hill. Congress, though, largely defines the relationship it has with the other branches and the structure it has put in place goes a long way to ensuring their compliance with congressional preferences.

Other actors beyond those established by the Constitution also play an important role in the lawmaking process. Interest groups and the media serve as watchdogs for the people, policy conduits between legislators and their constituents, and reflections and generators of public opinion. The tension created among these internal and external actors makes a system dependent on an uninformed and uninterested public function, admittedly not always perfectly.

COMMENTARY

The Politician's Take on External Influences

For a member of Congress, *external influences* are simply a necessary—and welcome—part of the job. When Edmund Burke cautioned that a legislator was to exercise judgment rather than simply act as a rubber stamp for the views of constituents, his caveat presupposed that the legislator's personal views would have been shaped not just by internal musings and personal experience but also by knowledge gleaned from a variety of sources. In today's world, with members of Congress called on to make decisions on often-complicated questions about internet access, healthcare research, expensive weapons systems, and many other issues that extend far beyond the personal expertise of any of the men or women serving in the House or Senate, it would be foolhardy not to tap into the many sources of information available.

Of those external sources, Burke aside, the single most important—not decisive but nonetheless influential—is the preference of one's constituents. They may be uninformed—even misinformed—but the essence of the American form of self-government is that each citizen has his or her own representative at the table where the decisions are made; that is why the Constitution mandates that all senators and representatives be an actual inhabitant of the state from which they are elected, so they are familiar with the interests and preferences of their constituents. To a member of Congress, therefore, the number one external influence is not really external at all—it is the extended congressional district "family" of which one is a member and whose other members one wishes to please, not just for reelection concerns (although that is a part of the influence constituents wield) but also because you are constitutionally obligated to be their voice and, when you believe they are right, their champion.

Many members of Congress, unfortunately, do not sufficiently understand their constitutional role and tend to defer too much to the executive branch on important matters, such as foreign policy and defense issues. Whether to go to war, which side to support in overseas conflicts and what support to provide, what treaties to enter, who may represent the United States in foreign capitals, who should be entrusted with the responsibilities of a general or admiral, what weapons systems to build—these are all congressional decisions. And yet, while members of Congress should do more to live up to their obligations in these areas, one cannot dismiss the much greater information and expertise in the executive branch. Failure to draw on that expertise and to lend it great weight in congressional deliberations would be foolish. Congress ultimately must be the decider, but members are not likely to know enough about transportation concerns, infrastructure maintenance, medical research, or any of the other areas in which the executive branch specializes. When it comes to external influences to which Congress must pay close attention, none is more important than the departments and agencies under the direction of the executive branch.

Finally, a word about interest groups: As a member of Congress entrusted with the power to tax and regulate, to mandate and to seduce with incentives, one holds an awesome ability to affect the lives of the men and women engaged in almost every line of work and activity. The Constitution is predicated on the need to protect the citizen against harm flowing from governmental error or mischief. That is why the very first amendment spells out the citizen's right to petition the government for redress and why the courts have long upheld lobbying as an essential ingredient of a self-governing democracy. A member of Congress needs information as to how his or her actions affect an industry, an association, a citizen. Once that information is obtained and potentially negative effects are weighed against potential benefits, representatives and senators are in a better position to act accordingly. Special interests—advocates for corporations, labor unions, farmers, universities, children, senior citizens, towns and cities, teachers, and firemen—all feed into the congressional need for that most basic governing tool of all: information.

Yes, there are many external influences and some of them are not always helpful, but generally speaking, members of Congress do not tolerate external sources of information; they depend on them (I know I did) and the national welfare depends on a wise use of the information those sources provide.

COMMENTARY

The Professor's Take on External Influences

Although the system in which Congress operates can be efficient, productive, and, of course, self-serving, it can also lull members of Congress into complacency. The system only works when members of Congress recognize that they are, first, members of Congress and only second members of a political party. The danger comes when members of Congress cede too much power to the executive branch. The system the framers put in place counts on the ambition of the president counteracting the ambition of members of Congress and vice versa.

Too frequently, the president's partisans in Congress are too willing to go along with presidential action—or inaction—as the case may be. The Walter Reed scandal is just one example of when members decided that protecting the president was more important than investigating the executive branch for possible malfeasance.

When the president's party has a majority in Congress, members are less likely to investigate the executive branch and their investigations are less comprehensive. This strategy works so long as the executive branch is perfectly performing its duty. If malfeasance arises, though, and if Congress turns a blind eye, the media perform an important corrective in the situation. Media exposés are usually much more damaging to a party than congressional investigations.

Although it may be counterintuitive, the Congress works best when its members are loyal to congressional prerogatives even before their own parties' prerogatives. A congressional investigation that results in a one-day story (or, more likely, no story at all) is better than an exposé that feeds the battered minority party's claim of political corruption. Frequently, it is better not only for politics, but also for the people who are hurt by executive branch malfeasance.

CHAPTER 10

The Congress of the Future

For years, the inner workings of the federal government, especially Congress, have looked much the same. Whether one is writing about the roles played by the elected congressional leadership or the rank-and-file senators and representatives who make up the Republican conference and the Democratic caucus, the committee structures, the election process, the various subgroups that make up congressional constituencies, or the ins and outs of how a bill becomes a law, not much changed from World War II through the end of the Cold War. In contrast, the past twenty to thirty years have seen some fundamental changes in how Congress works—or does not.

The Congress of the United States, like almost every other governmental structure in America, is built on a partisan model. Except for a few independents (who nonetheless caucus with an established party cohort), members of Congress are elected as either Republicans or Democrats, and with the exception of three instances (which we get to in a moment), they win their place on the general election ballot only after being designated as the official standard-bearer of a political party. Whichever partisan group holds a majority elects the legislative leaders (majority leader in the Senate, Speaker in the House of Representatives), and those leaders exercise great control over the flow of legislation, with few exceptions determining which proposals can be considered for possible adoption. Committees are key focal points in the legislative process and committee membership is determined by party leaders. To a large extent, which partisan club you belong to and whether it is in the majority determine not only how much influence you have as a member of Congress but also whether your ideas are taken seriously. It is not exactly a zero-sum game—where your team wins only if the other team loses—but it is close.

307

Signs indicate that the future may be somewhat different. Partisanship and polarization are not the same. In a diverse nation of more than three hundred million people, one in which citizens get to choose who makes the laws, there is always, and inevitably, disagreements about the right course for government to take. And in a constitutional democracy, those diverse viewpoints engender vigorous conflict. That is not a failing; it is the strength of a democracy. Partisanship, however, is not based solely on one's political opinions. While some commonly held views bind Republicans together and others bind Democrats, partisanship adds another dimension: tribal loyalty that elevates defeat of the other team to a goal unto itself, one that makes compromise and the development of bipartisan proposals almost impossible. In such a case, one can predict with a reasonable degree of certainty that if a Democrat is president, almost every Democrat in Congress supports the president's proposals and almost every Republican in Congress opposes them. And if a Republican is president, the roles are reversed; the partisan cohesion remains firmly fixed. Sometimes even the language members use to defend their positions is reversed simply because of who sits in the Oval Office. The American system of constitutional government presupposes that it is difficult to change law and that prolonged deliberation and debate are necessary protections against too-hasty responses to popular but unwise public opinion. But to function as a government with specific and important responsibilities, there must ultimately be a means to come together in compromises that partisanship makes nearly impossible.

This awareness is beginning to take hold among important segments of the American public. Although the numbers are constantly changing, roughly 40 percent of the electorate now self-identifies not as Republican or Democratic but as independent. It is true that even independents tend to lean in the direction of one party or the other, but it is also true that unlike hardline partisans, they are open to persuasion and resistant to overtly partisan appeals. In addition, numerous groups of reform activists have begun to come together specifically to combat the effects of the extreme partisanship that has overtaken the political process. One group, No Labels, claims tens of thousands of supporters and has brought together dozens of members of Congress of both parties to discuss possible joint sponsorships of legislation. In one month near the end of 2014, 90 pro-democracy reformers gathered at a three-day meeting in Baltimore, two dozen more met at a conference near Dulles Airport in suburban Washington, DC, and another two dozen came together at a meeting at the Esalen conference center in Big Sur, California. An organization called Independents Rising has convened well-attended meetings across the country. In a nation the size of the United States, these occurrences fall short of being a mass movement, but there are signs that discussions about the partisanship problem are drawing serious attention in political circles and on college campuses across the country.

In 2006, Washington (the state) responded to partisanship concerns by changing state laws to take congressional redistricting decisions out of the hands of partisan state legislators. Following in the footsteps of Louisiana, Washington (the state) ended the system of allowing party primaries to control access to the general election ballot, choosing instead to allow all registered voters to choose among all eligible candidates. In 2010, California did the same thing. There is not yet sufficient evidence to know where such changes increased voter turnout or moved those congressional delegations to the left or the right, but it does mean that those states are represented in Congress by senators and representatives who must concern themselves with the preferences of all the voters in their states or districts, not just the party activists who previously held considerable power over one's prospects for reelection. Because election laws are state specific and changes occur only one state at a time, it is notable that similar proposals have been introduced in other states as well. Whether others follow in the footsteps of California, Washington, and Louisiana—three states that together account for nearly 16 percent of the House of Representatives—or follow the eight states (Arizona, California, Hawaii, Idaho, Iowa, Montana, New Jersey, and Washington) that have turned redistricting over to nonpartisan commissions, there is a distinct possibility that the hold of party cohesion will be diminished in the years ahead and legislators will become more independent of party leaders and more attuned to the wishes of the broader general electorate in their communities.

As this movement toward independence among the electorate grows, it is also more likely that members of the two parties will grow more resistant to either top-down direction from their elected leaders or bottom-up direction from the other members of their respective conferences or caucuses. It is impossible to predict whether those changes will lead to a more activist and liberal government or one that is more restrained and conservative, but in either case it will be more democratic (that is, it will more closely represent the wishes of voters).

From time to time, control over the legislative process has moved upward (highly centralized control by the elected leadership, as was the case during the reign of House Speakers like Joe Cannon and Newt Gingrich) or downward (in 1974, newly elected young liberal Democrats broke the hold of previously powerful committee chairmen and gave the party's rank-and-file members the final say over the appointment of committee chairs). In each case, individual members, supposedly elected to represent the views of their specific constituencies, were pressured from above or below to serve the goals of the political party of which they were members. Reform in the new age of independence, should it develop, would finally take Congress in the direction of true representativeness, a change that might also alter the internal dynamics of the legislative branch and the ways in which proposed laws are considered and voted on.

The authors of this book have only two sources to rely on—scholarship and experience. We cannot foretell with any certainty in which direction the modern reform movements will take us. It is quite possible, however, that thirty years from now, the story we tell in this textbook will, again, look different.

APPENDIX

Modeling the Legislative Process

A s we have shown in this textbook, understanding the Congress and its legislative process can be exceedingly difficult. When describing the process, politicians and journalists are wary of getting too far "in the weeds." Getting in the weeds has two potential problems. First, it requires a tremendous amount of knowledge. While the broad contours of a bill on Capitol Hill are as familiar as the old Schoolhouse Rock song, understanding the nuances, permutations, and rules that can be used to either propel or interrupt the normal process requires a great deal of information and a complex demand of applying that information to all sorts of conditions that may or may not fit with existing precedent. Sometimes it even seems that members of Congress make up, reinterpret, or ignore the rules to fit the situation.

The second problem is that getting in the weeds can be boring. Nothing will make a person's eyes glaze over more quickly than an explanation of arcane legislative procedure. Nonetheless, as Ezra Klein notes, "The weeds are important, as any gardener can tell you. If you don't know what's going on in the weeds, you don't know what's going on in the garden."[1] Regrettably, the weeds are our business. To understand Congress, one must know the weeds in all their complexity. The main part of this textbook is the weeds.

Must not only political scientists know the weeds, but also legislators (at least good ones!), journalists, and historians. At different times, all these professionals need to be in the business of the weeds. At times, they revel in the weeds, which, subsequently, can make them boring guests at dinner parties. Though all are in the weeds business, the individual groups focus on different aspects. Legislators are responsible for the action. They draft, compromise, persuade, cajole, amend, vote, negotiate, defeat, and pass legislation. Journalists are primarily responsible for describing the action. Historians are primarily responsible for putting the action into a historical perspective. Sometimes these perspectives are consistent with a broader historical narrative that the historian offers; other times the episode serves as the exception that proves the narrative's rule.

Political scientists must not only describe as a journalist and contextualize as a historian, but also tease out a systematic understanding of the action so that it can be utilized in making predictions. By virtue of their social scientific training and their abilities to apply past lessons to current contexts, political scientists have the additional burden of predicting future actions. The primary duties that we have offered for these groups of professionals are too regimented. Certainly, journalists place into context and predict just as historians describe and tease out systematic explanations. Nonetheless, political scientists bear the responsibility of making predictions because if they do not leverage this comparative advantage, they offer little to the other groups and become irrelevant in developing an understanding of Congress.

Political scientists use models to aid in their duty of prediction. Models provide political scientists with pathways out of the weeds by highlighting which weeds are important and which can be ignored. These models, then, become the means by which political scientists make predictions. In this chapter we discuss several models of the legislative process that political scientists use to make predictions. Before discussing the models, we first discuss the criteria for evaluating models.

CRITERIA FOR EVALUATING MODELS

Between 1998 and 2013, the Bowl Championship Series (BCS) selected which college football teams would play for the national championship as well as the other prestigious college bowl games. Rather than using a blue-ribbon panel of experts to decide which teams would play for the national championship (as is done now), the BCS relied on computer selections and the national polls, which were combined in a complex formula that produced a ranking. The two teams at the top of the ranking were awarded an invitation to play for the national championship. The BCS used three different polls that relied on three different sets of people (coaches in the Coaches Poll; a selection of former coaches, players, administrators, and current and former media in the Harris Poll; sports writers and broadcasters in the AP Poll). Furthermore, it relied on six computer rankings. Each of these nine components used a methodology to derive the number that it contributed to the BCS average. Some of these components considered the historical legacy of the football program; others explicitly ignored it. Some value score differential in games; other explicitly ignored it. Some gave extra weight to the conference the team played in, the opponents it faces, and its most recent games. All these characteristics were legitimate criteria for determining who ought to play in the national championship game.

If only two teams who both play in competitive conferences are undefeated, the BCS need not go through the difficulty of figuring out who should play. It is obvious that the two undefeated teams would play against each other to determine the national championship. If, however, there were more than two undefeated teams, if there was only one (or none), or if one of the two undefeated teams did not play a rigorous schedule, the task of determining who should play becomes much more difficult. Hence, the BCS's nine separate components each emphasize different characteristics to summarize a football team's worthiness of competing for a national championship.

So it is with models that can be used to understand the legislative process. If all the models yield the same prediction, it is easy for a political scientist to make a prediction—and make it she does, with a great deal of confidence. If, however, the models yield different predictions, the researcher is forced to evaluate the models to choose her prediction. Different researchers prize different characteristics. We outline five characteristics that researchers could utilize in evaluating the models used to generate predictions.[2]

Clarity of Assumptions, Processes, and Outcomes

Some football fans prefer the polls to the computer rankings because the polls allow for the intangible characteristics that cannot be accounted for in statistics. The fans can never be certain that the poll respondents care about the same intangibles, but they like the human dimensions for which the computer rankings simply cannot account. When the poll respondents vote, the fans are not sure whether they are responding to the big win a team enjoyed over the weekend, the fact that they are leading a conference that had a successful weekend, or the fact that their coach just went public with a disease that he is battling. How the poll respondents vote is a black box to the fans. Sometimes it can even be a black box to the respondent making the decision. A gut feeling is no more revealing to football fans than it is to the respondents participating in the poll.

Other fans prefer computer rankings because they are explicit and cannot be swayed by the intangibles that should, in their minds, have no place in determining what constitutes a great football team. These computer-ranking fans like the automatic and nonbiased results that come with the rankings. They like the transparency. The data needed to generate the computer rankings can be peeled back even if the precise algorithm is never revealed. In other words, the underlying assumptions and processes of the computer rankings are much more explicit than the human calculations that go into the polls' results.

Whereas some researchers value knowing how the internal mechanisms of the models work, other researchers are less concerned with the black box of prediction. The nature of the game for the BCS components is that they yield an explicit and clear outcome. The components awarded an explicitly clear number attached to a team that is aggregated in a very particular way to result in a ranking of that team among all the top football programs. Such clarity in model predictions is not guaranteed. Some models may yield a specific outcome; other models may simply predict more of something, or less. Researchers who prize precision choose the specific and clear prediction; other researchers are less concerned that a model does not yield a specific outcome.

Simplicity

Simple models are frequently described as more "elegant" than complex models. In the language of research, when the models are all else equal, a simple model is preferred. In other words, if models are equal on every other dimension, a model that incorporates only a couple of weeds is better than one that includes almost all of the weeds. Why would a researcher go to the trouble of learning and incorporating all the extra weeds if it does not result in a better prediction?

Consider for a moment two stock market analysts. The first analyst makes buy-or-sell recommendations based on the employment rate, the company's profit, and the company's outstanding loans. The second analyst incorporates everything under the sun in the model, taking into consideration not only the same data as the first analyst, but also the weather forecast, the existence of the hurricane season, and expected rainfall. If both models are otherwise equal in growing their clients' portfolios, why go through the additional work of building weather into the model? So it is with researchers wanting to make a prediction about a legislative outcome.

Surprise Value

Good models provide analytic heft. If researchers can quickly make a prediction without using a model, then the model is not doing much analytic work. If a model yields predictions that are otherwise obvious, the researcher can save time by simply making the obvious prediction without utilizing the model. In this sense, models should have some surprise value. That is, the model should yield a prediction that is not obvious. Again, all else being equal, a model is preferred if it yields nonobvious predictions. An obvious prediction may indicate that the researcher did not need to use the model at all.

Generalizability

Researchers generally prefer models that are more general compared to models that can be used in only specific situations. In a congressional context this can have two interpretations. At a more local level, a model that can be used for healthcare reform, campaign finance reform, and trade sanctions is preferred to a model that can only yield accurate predictions in one policy area. Again, this criterion has a bit of the all-else-equal flavor. If a policy-specific model makes more accurate predictions, the researcher likely sacrifices generalizability for accuracy.

At a more global level, generalizability could also imply that models that work for many different legislatures or other decision-making bodies are preferred to Congress-specific models. Because Congress is a unique institution, congressional researchers do not place much importance on this interpretation. A researcher who studies how groups make decisions may prefer a more general model, but only if all else is equal.

Accuracy

If a model continuously provides surprising predictions, but those predictions are always wrong, the model suffers from inaccuracy. In the world of prediction making, no single criterion is more important than accuracy, which means that the model's prediction is borne out. Most of the other criteria have the flavor of all else equal, but not this criterion. If a model is more accurate, it is better. Among the five criteria, accuracy is paramount. If a model is not accurate at some base level, it should be rejected even if it is transparent, simple, surprising, and generalizable. In this sense, accuracy can be thought of as a football team's win–loss record. If the team has fewer wins than losses at the end of the season, it need not be anxious about which prestigious bowl it will play in even if it had a tough schedule, played in a difficult conference, and has a quarterback battling a neurological disease.

Beyond accuracy, the other criteria can trade off against one another. One researcher may prefer explicit models, while another may place more emphasis on surprising predictions. These models must be viewed holistically in that they inevitably make tradeoffs in one criterion for another.

LAWMAKING MODELS

Now that we have outlined the criteria that political scientists could utilize in selecting a lawmaking model, in this section we outline several models. Some of these models were developed explicitly to characterize the legislative process, whereas other models emerged for more general purposes and were only subsequently adapted to suit the legislative process. Some models could describe other political processes and some even could provide insight into more mundane decisions that groups must make every day. No one model best fits all five criteria. As such, the models a researcher utilizes depend on the tradeoffs she makes among the criteria. Explicitly stating a hierarchy among the various criteria goes a long way in making the researcher transparent to her audience.

The Median Voter

The first of the five models we discuss is the median voter model. This model predicts that Congress chooses the policy that is most preferred by the median voter, which is defined as the legislator who has as many legislators to her ideological right as to her left. The model, which is derived from the median voter theorem, rests on three fundamental assumptions. First, the members in a legislature can be accurately placed along a one-dimensional ideological continuum. At various times in congressional history this assumption has been less true than at other times. In the 1950s, most Democrats in Congress favored more government intervention to furnish citizens with their basic needs, though the party was split on questions of race. Southern Democrats thought that racial issues should be handled at the state level and most northern Democrats thought that the national government needed to guarantee basic civil rights throughout the United States. The Republican Party was also split, but less so than the Democrats. During this era, it was harder to fit all the legislators onto a one-dimensional ideological scale that worked for all issues. More recently as polarization has grown, most public policy issues have collapsed into one dimension. The second assumption is that the members' preferences are single peaked, which means that the farther an alternative is from the member's most preferred policy, the less the member likes it. The third assumption is that members' actions are based on their sincere preferences, which dictate that they choose the best option at every stage of the legislative process without regard for the consequences of those actions on downstream decisions. At times, a decision maker might end up with a better outcome if she votes strategically rather than sincerely. Strategic preferences take into account how the actions of one stage affect the options of later stages.

The following example illustrates the mechanics of the median voter model. Suppose that a corporation has a five-member board that makes all its business decisions. The board, which is composed of Jennifer, Juliet, Elizabeth, Marcus, and Emily, must first decide how much to pay its workers, who for simplicity's sake all make the same wage. Jennifer prefers a worker's wage of fifteen dollars per hour. Juliet prefers eighteen dollars, Elizabeth prefers twenty-five dollars, Marcus prefers twelve dollars, and Emily prefers thirty dollars. The board could use a variety of methods to determine the wage. It could take the average of the five members' most preferred wage, it could draw one of the wages from a hat, or four of the members could defer to the most powerful fifth member. If, however, they opted to decide by majority rule, a researcher would align the five most preferred options along a one-dimensional continuum (SEE FIGURE A.1).

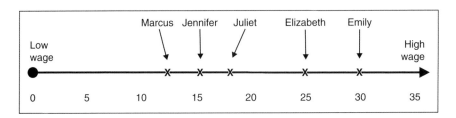

Figure A.1 The Median Voter Model.

So long as the majority rules and the members of the board have single-peaked preferences, a decision can be reached—usually without too much difficulty. If, however, the assumptions are violated, the model unravels. For example, Jennifer prefers fifteen dollars per hour, but likes twenty-five dollars per hour more than twenty dollars per hour because the higher wage would guarantee an educated workforce, so her preferences are not single peaked. Trying to determine how Jennifer would vote adds great complexity to the model. Luckily for researchers, rational decision makers generally have single-peaked preferences. Because Juliet has two fellow board members who want a lower wage and two who want a higher wage, she is the median voter on the board. No matter where they begin, so long as each board member can make a recommendation and put that option up for a vote, the board always converges to Juliet's preferred wage of eighteen dollars.

It is similar with Congress. If the entire House was made up of five members, the one in the middle would set policy. It does not matter whether the two more conservative members have very close views to the median voter and the two liberal members are near the endpoint on the left or whether all five members are somewhere in the middle. The decision whether to vote with the two liberal members or the two conservative members always falls to the member in the middle.

The median voter model is simple and its assumptions, processes, and predictions are exceedingly clear. It incorporates only the most basic features about Congress, which makes it generalizable, not only across issues but also across decision-making bodies. As such, we can think of the median voter model as barely getting in the weeds. This does not mean that it is not a good model, just that it accentuates parsimony above nuance. Nonetheless, if it makes accurate predictions, it can still be the researcher's most preferred model.

Pivotal Politics Model

Stanford Political Scientist Keith Krehbiel relied on some of the mechanics of the median voter model in developing a more complicated model that built in some key congressional features.[3] Before developing his model, Krehbiel outlined two empirical regularities that any lawmaking model needed to satisfy. First, Krehbiel argued that the model must show that most legislation fails to pass, but, on occasion, some does pass. While congressional productivity has decreased recently, even in the highly productive congresses, few pieces of legislation become law.

Second, Krehbiel maintained that any lawmaking model needed to show how legislation, when it does pass, has more than a bare majority supporting it. In looking at legislation that Congress passes, he noticed that most of the final passage votes were rather lopsided. Neither of these empirical regularities can be explained by the median voter model. When the median voter changes, so, too, do the policies to the new median voter's ideal points—not just some policies, but all of them. Furthermore, the new policies would typically pass with a bare majority.

Krehbiel accounts for these empirical regularities by building two key congressional features into his model. First, the only way that a president's veto can be overridden is if two-thirds of both chambers vote to do so. The president's veto is sustained if even one-third plus one member in either chamber—just 34 senators or 146 House members—vote against the override attempt.

Second, invoking cloture requires the votes of sixty senators. The more majoritarian nature of the House of Representatives precludes a minority of its members—even a motivated and determined minority—from impeding the majority's will. Because of the higher barrier to passing legislation in the Senate, Krehbiel does not include the House in his model. Although he could include the House, it would make the model more complex without necessarily yielding more accurate predictions. Furthermore, because it takes more votes to override a veto than it does to invoke cloture, we need not consider the scenario of the president's party members filibustering a bill. In reality they could, but the party opposite the president would not be concerned simply with invoking cloture: its primary concern would be overriding the president's veto. As such, the sixty-seventh senator who supports the policy is ultimately more important than the sixtieth. Achieving the support of the latter only postpones the policy's ultimate defeat by presidential veto and the inability to garner enough votes to override his veto.

Consider the interplay of these additional features in the corporate board example we used to illuminate the median voter model. Suppose that the company now has a chief executive officer (CEO), whose decisions can only be overridden by a unanimous board. Furthermore, they have decided to adopt a filibuster provision in the board that requires the vote of four board members to stop one fellow board member from filibustering a proposal. For the purposes of this example, suppose that the CEO prefers a low hourly wage. All five board members would have to vote to override his veto. If a group on the board wanted to raise the minimum wage, the hardest person for them to convince to go along with this proposal is Marcus, who prefers a low wage like the president does. Because his vote is crucial for the board to raise the wage, Marcus is considered the *veto pivot*—the board member whose vote is critical in determining whether a veto override attempt passes or fails.

The board could be confronted with members trying to filibuster wage proposals that either increase it or decrease it. If board members were trying to increase the wage, Jennifer's vote would become critical for invoking cloture. If she voted to invoke cloture, cloture would be invoked. If she voted against it, the filibuster would succeed in killing the proposal. Jennifer's preferred wage is fifteen dollars. Because Marcus's preferred wage is lower than Jennifer's, we do not have to take into consideration Jennifer's preferences in this example. If the board cannot satisfy Jennifer, they certainly cannot satisfy Marcus, whose vote is crucial for overriding the CEO's preference for a low wage.

Consistent with the CEO's preferences, the board may try to reduce the wages of their workers to reduce the overall costs. If the board were entertaining such a proposal, Elizabeth's vote would be crucial. Like Jennifer, if Elizabeth votes to invoke cloture, it is invoked. If she votes against cloture, the filibuster kills the proposal. In this scenario, the median voter does not play an important role except as one of a collectivity that can either invoke cloture or override a veto. The median voter's support is necessary for either of these actions, but it alone is not sufficient for them.

The region between Marcus and Elizabeth is sticky. That is, no proposal for an existing wage between twelve and twenty-five dollars could succeed. If the board tried to increase the wage, Marcus (and the CEO) would object, and they have the power to defeat the proposal. If the board tried to decrease the wage, they would have to please Elizabeth. So, if the existing wage were twelve or twenty-five dollars, it could not be changed because a powerful person—or *pivot*, in Krehbiel's language—could not be made better off; likewise with any existing wage between twelve and twenty-five dollars.

Suppose that an extremely worker-friendly board had been in place last year. Because costs were so much greater than revenue, the CEO was run out of office. The board and the new CEO must lower the wage to become profitable. With a board consisting of Marcus, Jennifer, Juliet, Elizabeth, and Emily and a CEO who prefers a low wage, what would happen if the prevailing wage were twenty-two dollars? Elizabeth would object to lowering the wage and the proposal would fail. So, too, with any wage between twelve and twenty-five dollars. Because this region precludes any policy movement, it is referred to in Krehbiel's pivotal politics model as the *gridlock zone* (SEE FIGURE A.2). No status quo points in this zone

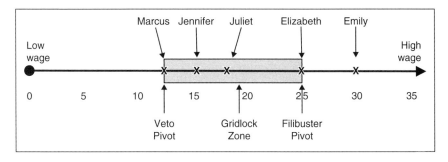

Figure A.2 The Pivotal Politics Model.

are ripe for alteration. Now suppose the prevailing wage was thirty dollars. Although it is Emily's preferred wage, she alone cannot stop it from being lowered. She needs Elizabeth's help to keep her filibuster going. As such, the wage could be lowered to Elizabeth's preferred wage of twenty-five dollars, but not lower. If such a policy change were to occur, the vote would be four (Marcus, Jennifer, Juliet, and Elizabeth) to one (Emily).

In this scenario, gridlock is common (for any existing wage between twelve and twenty-five dollars), but not constant (for any existing wage lower than twelve dollars or higher than twenty-five dollars). Furthermore, when changes are made, the vote for the change is more than minimum-winning sized. In this case, the vote is four to one or five to zero instead of the minimum-winning size of three to two. The scenario satisfies the two empirical regularities that Krehbiel observed about Congress.

The pivotal politics model is sensitive to who the president is (because that determines which side has the more veto pivot, which is more difficult to overcome than the filibuster pivot) and who the senators are (because they determine where the filibuster pivot is on the side opposite the president). While the pivotal politics model has assumptions, processes, and predictions that are as clear as those of the median voter model, it is much less simple and much less generalizable. Can you imagine any decision-making group incorporating a filibuster into its processes other than the US Senate? For the loss of generalizability and simplicity to be worth it, the benefit in surprise value and accuracy must be greater. It is the researcher's burden to make these tradeoffs in deciding which model to employ.

The pivotal politics model is transparent, but demands a great deal of information for its mechanics to work. Not only must the preferences of the decision makers collapse to one dimension, but also they must be single peaked. These assumptions only scratch the surface. All of the decision makers must know what their ideal point is and they must reveal it through the series of votes. Furthermore, they must express themselves sincerely. Beyond that, the alternatives must be completely spelled out and well understood. They also must fit on the one-dimensional continuum.

Incrementalism

The pivotal politics model falls in a long line of economic-based models that Charles Lindblom referred to as *rational comprehensive*. It was this general class of models to which Lindblom was reacting as he developed the theory of incrementalism in the 1950s.[4] The rational comprehensive models placed exceedingly high burdens on the decision makers to define their goals, study all the alternatives, and pick the alternative that best matches the goals. From an academic perspective, the model made a great deal of sense. Lindblom argued that it was too heroic in its demands for it to be of much practical use. He thought it required too much time and too much information to be an accurate representation of the decision-making process.

In his model, which he introduced in an article subtitled "The Science of Muddling Through," Lindblom used some of the concepts from the rational comprehensive model, but relaxed its rigorous demands. For example, rather than examining all possible policy alternatives, decision makers are more likely to search for alternatives that are in close proximity to the current policy. And, rather than selecting the best alternative policy, decision makers are more likely to *satisfice*, that is, to select a policy alternative that is good enough. If the new adopted policy works, the decision makers may choose to make another alteration in the same direction. If the policy does not work as expected, they will likely go in another direction. After many incremental changes, the resulting policy may be quite far away from the initial policy, but the change is not made all at one time. Rather, it is made through several minor adjustments that may aggregate into a much different policy.

Now, let us return to our example of the board of directors that must determine a wage. If the prevailing wage is eighteen dollars and the board decides that competition requires them to increase their wages to maintain their knowledgeable workforce, they could decide to first increase the wage to nineteen dollars. After monitoring the number of employees who leave the company under the new wage and the number and work habits of new employees, they could decide to increase the wage again to twenty dollars and then, after six months, increase it again to twenty-one dollars. After a few years, their workers' wage may be twenty-five dollars, but they have increased it several times rather than all at once.

Incrementalism is not as consistent as the pivotal politics model at satisfying Krehbiel's empirical regularities. The logic of it could comport with them, but they do not naturally fall out from the model. In part, this disjuncture is caused by the fact that Lindblom was not trying to specifically model the legislative process in Congress; rather, he was trying to model the larger policymaking process, in which Congress plays an instrumental role. Incrementalism, then, is more generalizable than the pivotal politics model, even while it is not as transparent. Again, the researcher must decide which of these criteria matters more and how much to sacrifice one to receive a benefit from another.

Streams Analysis
Political scientist John Kingdon, like Lindblom, thought that the prevailing economically natured models were too demanding on the inputs of the decision makers and did not appropriately reflect the inherent politics in the legislative process.[5] To more explicitly model the legislative process, Kingdon adapted the

garbage can models of public policy, which indicated that the decision making was more haphazard than most scholars wanted to suggest. His model conceived of three streams that flowed continuously and contemporaneously; that is, all three were always flowing.

The first stream in the streams model is filled with several problems that must be addressed, everything from crime to budget deficits to sexual harassment in the military to rogue dictators threatening American interests seven thousand miles away. These problems continue to flow. Sometimes a problem is fixed and leaves the stream, and other times new problems arise and enter the stream.

The second stream, which flows independently of problems, contains policies. They operate at a more general level. Increasing taxes, reducing government red tape, strengthening the military, centralizing government decision making, and expanding the social safety net are all examples of policies that run through the policy stream. These policies represent the broad philosophical arguments that can be brought to bear on many problems. Some may be potential solutions to certain problems but irrelevant to others. For example, reducing taxes to spur the problem of stagnant economic growth may make sense, but reducing taxes to deal with a tyrannical dictator seven thousand miles away does not.

The final stream is composed of the politics of the day. These politics can include the ideological distribution of congressional members or the management style of the president. Other politics can be shorter term, like the latest news of the unemployment rate or the results of a highly contested special election. The components of the politics stream are more fleeting than the components of the other streams. While the problems and policies that can be adapted to fix them have more permanence, the politics of the day can switch as quickly as the news cycle; some components of this stream can last longer such as broad economic conditions.

These streams, as they are continuously, simultaneously, and independently flowing, sometimes align such that the right problem matches up with the right policy and the right political situation. When they do align, a *policy window* opens. Sometimes these policy windows result in new policies, but other times they do not. If, however, a window does not exist, policy change is exceedingly difficult.

The streams model includes one added feature that makes it more proactive. Kingdon argues that *political entrepreneurs* play a critical role in the policymaking process. These entrepreneurs can try to create policy windows where they might not otherwise exist and can open them earlier or keep them from closing as quickly. They are still subject to the whims of the flowing streams, but entrepreneurs can try to manipulate those streams so that they align or stay aligned long enough for a new policy to be adopted. Entrepreneurs, who can be inside actors (such as Paul Ryan or John McCain), outside agitators (such as Ralph Nader or Steve Bannon), or even nonpoliticians (such as the Marjory Stoneman Douglas High School students or Joe the plumber), can change the politics by getting a critical report issued, framing their preferred policy as a solution to a scandal, or providing a focusing event for the media to cover. They can also draw connections where they may not obviously exist between problems and policies. In other words, entrepreneurs give direction and purpose to a model that would otherwise be too robotic to be of much use to researchers.

Applying the streams model to our board of directors who must determine their employees' wages is not straightforward. Much like legislators, they are held hostage to the problems, policies, and politics that revolve around their decisions. In a way, each of them could be an entrepreneur if they change a wage consistent with their preferences by manipulating how and which problems, policies, and politics are flowing through the streams.

The streams model is not particularly transparent in either processes or predictions. When the streams align, policy change may happen, but it is not clear how that happens or what it is that happens. Nonetheless, it is helpful in thinking about how gridlock is common, but not constant. The streams model provides language that is helpful in understanding why legislation does not pass: it could be that the politics were not right or that the problems and the policies did not match. In this regard, the model would yield results consistent with Krehbiel's empirical regularities that policy change happens only occasionally, and when it does, those who enact it are larger than minimum-winning size.

Punctuated Equilibrium

The last model we discuss is based on punctuated equilibrium. Like incrementalism, this model argues that most of the changes in policymaking are minor, but unlike incrementalism, it argues that on occasion—much less frequently than the minor changes—large policy changes happen. This model has its roots in evolutionary biology, where Niles Eldredge and Stephen Jay Gould argued that species, such as the land snail, did not evolve continuously over time, but rather stayed much the same most of the time and then quickly adapted as they confronted a new environment that required more drastic change. As such, the punctuated equilibrium model, unlike pivotal politics, was not designed with Congress in mind, let alone the public policymaking process.

Much as with Gould's land snail, political scientists Frank Baumgartner and Bryan Jones, in examining budgets, found many small changes and then, infrequently, big, dramatic changes.[6] The small changes come about as a consequence of minor perturbations in the government subsystem, which is composed of a congressional committee (or subcommittee), the corresponding bureaucratic officials responsible for implementing and executing the law, and the relevant special interest groups. Because of their institutional cultures, their vested interests, their own analytic shortcomings, and the larger environment in which they operate, most policy is "sticky." On occasion, as with Gould's land snail, policy must adapt to much greater outside forces that do not normally operate within the specialized subsystem. Scandals within the subsystem or events that create media firestorms force the subsystem to react and quickly adapt. During these unusual times, the way an issue is defined or portrayed undergoes change, as does the venue that ultimately makes the change. Once the outside forces stop infiltrating the subsystem, the subsystem actors use the new major policy change as that which anchors the small changes they make in fleshing out the new equilibrium in which they operate.

Consider again the wages of the worker. The subsystem in this case would be the board of directors, the CEO, and the workers. As the three actors use new information to update the workers' wages, we would expect a series of minor adjustments to take account of the various factors that influence the wages. Suppose that a much bigger outside force enters their cozy subsystem. A major recession, a new competitor coming to town, or a major scandal within the subsystem would influence the larger environment sufficiently that a major change in the workers' wages may be warranted and may come into existence. Following the big change in wages, the subsystem would use that as the starting point for their constant negotiations rather than the wage before the environment radically changed.

If we think of minor changes as basic gridlock, the punctuated equilibrium model satisfies Krehbiel's two empirical regularities: new policies (major policy changes in the model) happen infrequently, and when they do, they enjoy more than minimum-winning support. Like the streams model, the punctuated equilibrium model is not particularly transparent with respect to predictions, though its logic can be compelling. Furthermore, given that it has its roots in evolutionary biology, its generalizability may be its greatest comparative advantage relative to the four other models discussed in this chapter. Again, the researcher must decide what criterion is most important and how much it can be sacrificed to ascertain benefits in the other criteria.

CONCLUSION

Studying Congress from a political science perspective requires a skill that other researchers do not possess or emphasize. It is hard for political scientists to know more history than historians or to get access to more inside interviews than journalists. Political scientists bring a systematic understanding to the study of

Congress. At their best, political scientists are able to make predictions about future events based on their analysis of previous events.

To engage in the tricky task of prediction, political scientists who study Congress can rely on the various policymaking models described in this appendix. None of the models should be considered the best in all situations. It depends on the leverage the researcher wants to utilize and what the researcher wants the model to yield. The power of these models and the entire enterprise of political science grow when our models yield accurate outcomes that are consistent with the events as they are played out.

COMMENTARY

The Politician's Take on Modeling

In his corresponding commentary, my partner in this endeavor describes the light bulbs that go off in his students' heads when they are given the opportunity to see how political scientists predict what is likely to occur in the making of legislative decisions. I am glad he adds that the modeling procedures he and other scientists use do not offer a complete picture. So let me chime in as we wind up this enjoyable collaboration by suggesting that those of us who were members of a party leadership and deeply engaged in dozens of policy challenges simultaneously would have gladly given an arm or a leg to be able to get even a close approximation of the levels of predictability these models suggest.

Here is why the reality is so messy. There are not merely 435 members of the House of Representatives and 100 senators, with clear preferences, but thousands of members of Congress (because each of us has several competing selves within us). As a member of Congress I had a policy preference on each issue, but it was sometimes firmly held and sometimes only a very slight preference; I might have seen an opportunity to lend support to a committee chair to whom a bill was important and who had the power to advance or derail legislation that was more important to me; I might have just heard from a press assistant that one of the larger newspapers in my congressional district had just endorsed a particular course of action, or perhaps a staff member in the district had called to report that a group of community leaders had dropped by the office to urge me to adopt one position or another. Perhaps I was only infrequently engaged in transportation questions, inclined to follow the lead of others who were more familiar with those issues, but nonetheless voted for more stringent requirements that train crossings be equipped with modern crossing gates, going further than committee leaders wanted to go because my father had died when his car was struck by a train at a nongated crossing. It is easy to predict that an apple that breaks free from the branch holding it to a tree will move downward; it is much harder to have such accuracy when dealing with humans. These models—even the best of them—cannot read motivation; they can only provide a rendering of past actions that can help

(Continued)

researchers guess what is likely to come next; those predictions may be accurate if enough is known about why a member of Congress voted a certain way, but otherwise, it is a leap.

In *Young Frankenstein*, Madeline Kahn, alone with the now dapper and suave Frankenstein's monster, belts out a great refrain: "Ah, sweet mystery of life." That's politics: humans being humans, it's a mystery. And it's fun.

COMMENTARY

The Professor's Take on Modeling

Within the study of Congress, it is in the modeling of the legislative process that I think political scientists can best illustrate to our students that we are worthy of the second half of our name: *scientists*. Most of the other material in this book lives up to the first half of our name: *political*. It is the modeling of the process that yields predictions that best differentiate us from our academic cousins of history and journalism. They make predictions based on the word of political insiders or patterns from the past that repeat themselves. Both are worthy enterprises. We make predictions by trying to systematize what can seem to be a chaotic process.

In my eighteen years of teaching Congress classes, I have seen more light bulbs go off for my students during my modeling lectures than I have for any other topic. Taking 435 members of the House, 100 senators, a president, and a complex legislative process that has been through more than two hundred years of history can render students paralyzed with information—especially if we also consider all the contingencies that Mickey suggests we must take into account. The beauty of modeling the legislative process is that it strips the clutter from the working parts—the weeds from the produce, if you will. While different political scientists and politicians may quibble about what is clutter and what is working parts without isolating the most important features, however determined, paralyzed they would remain.

While I applaud political scientists for modeling the legislative process, we must recognize that what we have modeled is only part of the lawmaking process. Too frequently, congressional scholars equate the two processes. Figure 9.2 shows that what takes place on the floors of the House and Senate is only one small—though admittedly important—step from idea to the implementation of the law. The models of the legislative process provide us with a good start in systematizing what takes place within Congress; we must take more seriously the parts of the public policy process before and after congressional decision making.

Notes

Chapter 2

1. Simms (2007, 175)
2. Jane Mansbridge (2003), a scholar at Harvard, has suggested several variants and even uses different terms to classify the theories presented previously.
3. In 1790, Virginia's population included 292,627 slaves; Each only counted as three-fifths of a person for congressional representation.
4. Survey results from Sniderman and Theriault (2004). See also Gamson and Modigliani, 1987, 1989; Nelson and Kinder, 1996; Zaller, 1992.
5. Justin McCarthy, "U.S. Approval of Congress Improves, but Still Low at 18%," Gallup, August 18, 2016, http://www.gallup.com/poll/194684/approval-congress-improves-low .aspx?g_source=CONGRESS&g_medium=topic&g_campaign=tiles.
6. Justin McCarthy, "Confidence in U.S. Branches of Government Remains Law," Gallup, June 15, 2015, http://www.gallup.com/poll/183605/confidence-branches-government-remains-low.aspx.
7. See Mathew McCubbins and Thomas Schwartz (1984).
8. See Douglas Arnold (1992).

Chapter 3

1. Several former Speakers stayed in the House after their tenure as Speaker ended. Dennis Hastert (R-IL), whose party lost the majority in 2006, assumed a back bench in the Republican Conference until he finally resigned his seat at the end of 2007. When Nancy Pelosi lost the Speaker's gavel to the Republican majority in 2011, she resumed her position as minority leader.
2. Public Policy Polling, "Obama trails Republicans in WV by 14 to 21 points," Press Release, October 7, 2011, https://www.publicpolicypolling.com/wp-content/uploads/2017/09/ PPP_Release_WV_1007.pdf, accessed September 21, 2018.
3. Data from Jacobson (2013, 68–69).
4. Data from the Citizens Research Foundation (*Congressional Quarterly Almanac* 1971, 85).
5. Quoted in *Congressional Quarterly Almanac* 1973, 751.
6. See Gierzynski (2000) for a thorough analysis of how the *Buckley* decision affected campaign financing.

7. These five advantages are reworked from Hedrick Smith's (1988) "Four Pillars of the Incumbency Advantage."
8. All turnout data are self-reported to the Census Bureau (https://www.census.gov/data/tables/time-series/demo/voting-and-registration/p20-580.html; accessed April 26, 2018).

Chapter 4

1. Quoted in Ed O'Keefe, March 28, 2014, "Michigan Rep. Mike Rogers Retiring from Congress to Host a National Radio Show," *The Washington Post*, https://www.washingtonpost.com/politics/michigan-rep-mike-rogers-retiring-from-congress-to-host-a-national-radio-show/2014/03/28/345800ea-b688-11e3-a7c6-70cf2db17781_story.html, accessed August 4, 2016.
2. Quoted in Catalina Camia, May 23, 2013, "GOP Rep. Jo Bonner to Resign from Congress," *USA Today*, http://www.usatoday.com/story/news/2013/05/23/jo-bonner-congress-resign-alabama/2355573/, accessed August 4, 2016.
3. *Annals of Congress*, 8 June 1789, p. 457.
4. These data come from "Life in Congress: The Member Perspective," released by the Congressional Management Foundation and the Society for Human Resources Management in 2013, http://www.congressfoundation.org/storage/documents/CMF_Pubs/life-in-congress-the-member-perspective.pdf, accessed June 6, 2013.
5. For more on George Miller's place, see http://www.nytimes.com/2007/01/18/garden/18roomies.html.
6. Alduncin et al. (2015).
7. Poole (2007).

Chapter 5

1. http://thehill.com/blogs/floor-action/house/265740-speaker-ryan-closes-iran-vote-early-to-enforce-tardiness, accessed December 2, 2017.
2. http://www.newsweek.com/gop-health-care-bill-repeal-and-replace-70-failed-attempts-643832, accessed April 27, 2018.
3. For more information, see *CRS Report for Congress (98-706): Bills and Resolutions: Examples of How Each Kind Is Used*, by Richard S. Beth.
4. Shepsle (1989).
5. Sinclair (2000).
6. 101 Cong. Rec. S2984 (May 9, 1989).
7. 101 Cong. Rec. H1690 (May 9, 1989).
8. Quoted on page 2 of the press release from the White House, July 26, 1990.

Chapter 6

1. 106 Cong. Rec. H4 (January 6, 1999).
2. As quoted in Jared Allen, February 5, 2009, "Pelosi Tells Dems Regular Order Will Return," *The Hill*, http://thehill.com/homenews/news/18122-pelosi-tells-dems-regular-order-will-return, accessed January 24, 2014.
3. Quoted in John Feehery, October 1, 2010, "Regular Order," *The Hill*, http://thehill.com/blogs/pundits-blog/lawmaker-news/122159-regular-order#ixzz2rKs25f2I, accessed January 24, 2014.

4. Quoted in Gabrielle Levy, October 29, 2015, "Speaker Ryan Pledges Return to Regular Order," *U.S. News and World Report*, http://www.usnews.com/news/articles/2015/10/29/paul-ryan-pledges-return-to-regular-order, accessed August 10, 2016.
5. This analogy is borrowed from Barbara Sinclair (2011).

Chapter 7

1. See Gamm and Shepsle (1989) for an excellent review of how the standing committee system came into existence in the House and Senate.
2. Data from Legislative Explorer. Access the website for a remarkable visualization of the amount of legislation that ends up in committee and never leaves, http://legex.org/index.html, accessed July 19, 2016.
3. Professor David King (1997) has chronicled these attempts to defend or expand committee jurisdictions. He appropriately labels these contests *turf wars*. In fighting to retain—or gain—control over important legislative initiatives, the chairs (who are always members of the majority party) compete for the support of party leaders. In those rare instances in which jurisdictional battles are decided in a vote of the full House or Senate, the chairs engage the entire membership in the contest for power. These battles are more than mere personality contests: different committees with different members may also have very different voting tendencies. Which committee first considers a proposal may make a real difference in the ultimate legislative outcome.
4. See http://media.cq.com/media/fab50/?ref=rc for a full list, accessed July 25, 2016.
5. Data from Inside Gov, http://congressional-committees.insidegov.com, accessed January 18, 2018.
6. Data from Inside Gov, http://www.insidegov.com, accessed January 18, 2018.
7. Except that Ways and Means and Appropriations get to name five members from each to serve on the Budget Committee. The Rules Committee gets to name one member to the Budget Committee.
8. See Parker and Dull (2009) and Kriner and Schickler (2016).

Chapter 8

1. Aldrich (1995) develops this argument in his classic book, *Why Parties? The Origins and Transformation of Political Parties in America.*
2. Rohde (1991) and Aldrich and Rohde (2001) developed this idea, which they called *conditional party government.*
3. Poole and Rosenthal (1997) generate these data so that they are comparable across congresses within party systems. More care should be used in comparing these scores across chambers.
4. Quoted in Kate Nocera, "Boehner: Scorecard Not Behind Committee Purge," *Politico*, December 11, 2012, http://www.politico.com/blogs/on-congress/2012/12/boehner-denies-scorecard-used-in-committee-purge-151706.html, accessed February 28, 2014.

Chapter 9

1. As quoted in Jacob Pramuk, "Mitch McConnell: Senate Needs to Figure out Where Trump Stands on Immigration Bill Before It Can Pass One," *CNBC*, January 17, 2018, https://www.cnbc.com/2018/01/17/senate-will-take-up-immigration-daca-bill-that-trump-supports-mitch-mcconnell-says.html, accessed February 23, 2018.

2. George W. Bush, "Statement on Signing the Department of Defense, Emergency Supplemental Appropriations to Address Hurricanes in the Gulf of Mexico, and Pandemic Influenza Act, 2006," The White House, December 30, 2005, www.presidency.ucsb.edu/ws/index.php?pid=65259, accessed September 16, 2018.
3. Wilson (1908), 56–57.
4. As reported by the Department of Transportation, https://www.transportation.gov/sites/dot.gov/files/docs/DOT_BH2017_508%5B2%5D.pdf, accessed February 24, 2018.
5. As reported by the Department of Defense, https://pentagontours.osd.mil/Tours/facts.jsp, accessed February 24, 2018.
6. Approval by Congress and then the states is not the only way that the Constitution can be amended. The other way—though not yet used—is for two-thirds of the states to call for a constitutional convention.

Appendix
1. Ezra Klein, "The Substance of Things," The American Prospect, August 11, 2010, http://prospect.org/article/substance-things-0, accessed June 3, 2014.
2. These five criteria are loosely based on Kuhn (1962).
3. See Krehbiel (1998) for more about this model.
4. See Lindblom (1959) for more information about the model.
5. See Kingdon (1995) for more about this model.
6. See Baumgartner and Jones (1993) for more about this model.

Credits

Chapter 1

p. 2: Fred Schilling/U.S. House of Representatives; p. 6: ©Ron Sachs/CNP/ZUMA Wire/ Alamy Live News; p. 9: ©Jay Mallin/ZUMA Press; p. 11: U.S. Senate Historical Office; p. 12: U.S. Congress; US NETWORK via AP, Pool; The White House from Washington, DC; House of Representatives photographic studio; United States Congress; Bob Brown/Richmond Times-Dispatch via AP; p. 22: U.S. Department of State.

Chapter 2

p. 40: Angela Hart/The Sacramento Bee via AP; p. 45: Rock Valley College; p. 48: Joaquín Castro via Twitter; p. 53: AP Photo/Charlie Neibergall; AP Photo/Mark Foley; p. 55 Gage Skidmore; p. 56 Congressman Vern Buchanan via fans.vote; p. 58: AP Photo/Rick Bowmer.

Chapter 3

p. 70: Doug Jones for Senate Committee; p. 73: Transylvania University; p. 75: United States Congress; p. 80: Tom Williams via Getty Images; p. 83: United Sates Congress; p. 84: Thomas Good/NLN; p. 94: U.S. Senate Historical Office; p. 95: United States Senate.

Chapter 4

p. 108: Office of Senator Kamala Harris; p. 110: AP Photo/Bill Allen; p. 113: Office of Nancy Pelosi.

Chapter 5

p. 140: C-SPAN, July 27, 2017; p. 164: Hepburn Rate Bill by Clifford K. Berryman, May 15, 1906. U.S. Senate Collection, Center for Legislative Archives.

Chapter 6

p. 168: Alex Wong/Getty Images; p. 170: Ron Sachs/CNP; ©Pete Marovich/ZUMAPRESS. com; ©Oliver Contreras/ZUMA Wire/Alamy Live News; p. 174: U.S. Congress; Mark Kauffman/The LIFE Picture Collection/Getty Images; p. 186: John M. Butler and Alfred Long, c1855 via United States Library of Congress's Prints and Photographs division.

Chapter 7
p. 210: DoD Photo by U.S. Army Sgt. James K. McCann via Alamy Stock Photo; p. 237: Alex Edelman/CNP/MediaPunch Inc/Alamy Stock Photo; p. 238: AP Photo/J. Scott Applewhite; p. 239: NASA/Bill Ingalls.

Chapter 8
p. 244: Chris Kleponis/CNP/dpa/Alamy Live News; p. 259: Ron Sachs/CNP; p. 261: United States Senate.

Chapter 9
p. 280: Official White House Photo by Joyce N. Boghosian; p. 287: Alex Edelman/Consolidated New Photos; p. 299: Karl Sonnenberg via Shutterstock; p. 302: Leon Roberts via DVID.

Chapter 10
p. 306: Architect of the Capitol.

References

Aldrich, John Herbert. *Why Parties? The Origin and Transformation of Political Parties in America*. Chicago: University of Chicago Press, 1995.

Aldrich, John H., and David W. Rohde. "The Logic of Conditional Party Government: Revisiting the Electoral Connection." In *Congress Reconsidered*, 7th ed., edited by Lawrence C. Dodd and Bruce I. Oppenheimer. Washington, DC: CQ Press, 2001.

Alduncin, Alexander, Sean Q. Kelly, David C. W. Parker, and Sean M. Theriault. "Foreign Junkets or Learning to Legislate? Generational Changes in the International Travel Patterns of House Members, 1977–2012." *The Forum* 12, no. 3 (2014): 563–77.

Arnold, R. Douglas. *The Logic of Congressional Action*. New Haven, CT: Yale University Press, 1992.

Baumgartner, Frank R., and Bryan D. Jones. *Agendas and Instability in American Politics*. Chicago: University of Chicago Press, 2009.

Cox, Gary, and Eric Magar. "How Much Is Majority Status in the U.S. Congress Worth?" *American Political Science Review* 93, no. 2 (1999): 299–309.

Gamm, Gerald, and Kenneth Shepsle. "Emergence of Legislative Institutions: Standing Committees in the House and Senate, 1810–1825." *Legislative Studies Quarterly* 14, no. 1 (1989): 39–66.

Gamson, William A., and Andre Modigliani. "Media Discourse and Public Opinion on Nuclear Power: A Constructionist Approach." *American Journal of Sociology* 95, no. 1 (1989): 1–37.

Gierzynski, Anthony. *Money Rules: Financing Elections in America*. Boulder, CO: Westview Press, 2000.

Jacobson, Gary. C. "How the Economy and Partisanship Shaped the 2012 Presidential and Congressional Elections." *Political Science Quarterly* 128 (2013): 1–38.

King, David C. *Turf Wars: How Congressional Committees Claim Jurisdiction*. Chicago: University of Chicago Press, 1997.

Kingdon, John W. *Agendas, Alternatives, and Public Policies*. New York: Longman, 1995.

Krehbiel, Keith. *Pivotal Politics: A Theory of U.S. Lawmaking*. Chicago: University of Chicago Press, 1998.

Kriner, Douglas L., and Eric Schickler. *Investigating the President: Congressional Checks on Presidential Power*. Princeton, NJ: Princeton University Press, 2016.

Kuhn, Thomas S. *The Structure of Scientific Revolutions*. Chicago: University of Chicago Press, 1962.

Lewallen, Jonathan, and Sean M. Theriault. "Congressional Parties and the Policy Process." In *The Parties Respond: Changes in American Parties and Campaigns*, 5th ed., edited by Mark D. Brewer and L. Sandy Maisel. Boulder, CO: Westview Press, 2012.

Lindblom, Charles E. "The Science of Muddling Through." *Public Administration Review* 19: 79–88.

Mansbridge, Jane. "Rethinking Representation." *The American Political Science Review* 97, no. 4 (2003): 515–28.

Mayhew, David R. *Congress: The Electoral Connection*. New Haven, CT: Yale University Press, 1974.

McCubbins, Mathew D., and Thomas Schwartz. "Congressional Oversight Overlooked: Police Patrols versus Fire Alarms." *American Journal of Political Science* 28, no. 1 (1984): 165–79.

Nelson, Thomas E., and Donald R. Kinder. "Issue Frames and Group-Centrism in American Public Opinion." *The Journal of Politics* 58, no. 4 (1996): 1055–78.

Parker, David C., and Matthew Dull. "Divided We Quarrel: The Politics of Congressional Investigations, 1947–2004." *Legislative Studies Quarterly* 34, no. 3 (2009): 319–45.

Poole, Keith T. "Changing Minds? Not in Congress!" *Public Choice* 131 (2007): 435–51.

Poole, Keith T., and Howard Rosenthal. *Congress: A Political–Economic History of Roll Call Voting*. New York: Oxford University Press, 1997.

Rohde, David W. *Parties and Leaders in the Postreform House*. Chicago: University of Chicago Press, 1991.

Shepsle, Kenneth A. "Studying Institutions: Some Lessons from the Rational Choice Approach." *Journal of Theoretical Politics* 1, no. 2 (1989): 131–47.

Sinclair, Barbara. "Hostile Partners: The President, Congress, and Lawmaking in the Partisan 1990s." In *Polarized Politics*, edited by J. R. Bond and R. Fleisher, 144–45. Washington, DC: CQ Press, 2000.

Sinclair, Barbara. *Unorthodox Lawmaking: New Legislative Processes in the U.S. Congress*. Thousand Oaks, CA: Sage, 2011.

Sniderman, Paul M., and Sean M. Theriault. "The Structure of Political Argument and the Logic of Issue Framing." In *Studies in Public Opinion: Attitudes, Nonattitudes, Measurement Error, and Change*, edited by Willem E. Saris and Paul M. Sniderman, 133–64. Princeton, NJ: Princeton University Press.

Wilson, Woodrow. *Constitutional Government in the United States*. New York: Columbia University Press, 1908.

Zaller, John. *The Nature and Origins of Mass Opinion*. Cambridge: Cambridge University Press, 1992.

Index

Note: Page references followed by a "*t*" indicate table; "*f*" indicate figure.